TOM CULLEN
OF BALTIMORE

" . . . and as much as necessary."
—page 393

Tom Cullen at the Church Home Hospital,
Baltimore

TOM CULLEN
OF BALTIMORE

BY

JUDITH ROBINSON

GEOFFREY CUMBERLEGE
OXFORD UNIVERSITY PRESS
London   Toronto   New York
1949

✓

Oxford University Press, Amen House, Toronto
LONDON, EDINBURGH, GLASGOW, NEW YORK, MELBOURNE,
WELLINGTON, BOMBAY, CALCUTTA, MADRAS, CAPE TOWN
Geoffrey Cumberlege, Publisher to the University

1669

43
___
119

Printed in Canada

TO KATE

PREFACE

Maccabees II: 15: 38.
J.R.

Toronto, Canada,
March 26, 1949.

* And if I have done well and as is fitting the story, it is that which I
desired: but if slenderly and meanly, it is that which I could attain unto.
Maccabees II: 15: 38.

CONTENTS

. . . resuming in the green room.

ix

ILLUSTRATIONS

TOM CULLEN
OF BALTIMORE

. . . resuming in the green room.

DR. CULLEN's operative clinic in Fourth Year Gynecology adjourned to the green room. The young men jostled and joked in the glass-walled gallery behind the operating theatre, waiting their turn to hang surgical gowns on pegs and drop caps and masks in the basket set for them. But all were in place in the chairs along the walls when the round man in white came to sit behind the lecturer's table.

The lecturer's table in the gynecological department lecture room at Johns Hopkins hospital is an old-fashioned short operating table with a cracked glass top. It was made for the use of Dr. Howard Kelly when he came to the new hospital as its gynecologist in 1889, four years before the medical school opened. The walls of the lecture room are lined with pictures, The long wall has portraits in oils: the first, Thomas Corner's portrait of Professor T. S. Cullen, head of the department when the gynecological floor was added to the Woman's Clinic.

The other walls are hung with photographs, some brown with age, some as fresh as last year's diplomas: the likenesses of successive senior residents in gynecology from the beginning at Hopkins. All of them — *or just about all* — bear the stamp of the man at the old fashioned table: teacher to them and to their fellows since the first class graduated from Johns Hopkins Medical School in 1897. Still the teacher, he sat down to discuss with the graduating class of '47 the operation they had watched.

The chin was a degree less challenging than the chin pictured in the portrait, the mouth under the white moustache smiled more tolerantly, but the eyes were no less

3

bright and the curve of the nose no less arresting than when the artist noted them on canvas. It was the same man and, having completed an operative clinic, he went on to the next thing in his accustomed way:

"All right, Mr. Brown, in just a minute you can tell us what we did . . ."

(I don't teach 'em. I never have. I just try to show them what there is to learn. It's all anybody can do.)

Sitting behind the books piled on the scratched table-top, forearms bare, small thin hands clasping upper arms or moving in quick, curved gestures from the elbow, black eyebrows, red face and white chin-whisker set against a blackboard for contrast, battered sneakers neatly crossed on the bronze table-foot, the man fitted the room like a part of it; easy and accustomed as the big study table, the sag-cushioned lounge, the cool air from the open gallery door.

Here he had sat to show what there is to learn to 20 Medical School graduating classes. Here he had brought his habits of unbashful humility and unquenchable interest from old B-operating room where, under God and Kelly, he had laboured to perfect and impart them for thirty years before that. This was his place. These were his men and the sons of his men.

He read the roll, stopping now and then at a name. " . . . Any relation to the Marine who graduated with the class of '20? . . . His son? Please give my very best regards to your father when you see him . . . Novak? I'm glad to see you here, boy. Your father is a friend of mine and I taught your uncle gynecology twenty years ago. . . . Robinette? Your father still practising in Missouri? I remember when he graduated and started out there. Give my best regards to the family — by-the-way, how many are there in the family? . . . Too bad there aren't more. Your father's a good man; we need a lot like him. Now, Mr. Brown . . ."

An unhappy Mr. Brown stood, giving wrong answers with dreadful facility, smothering right ones in hoarse uncertainty. Remote behind his table, mild-voiced and questioning, Professor Cullen sat out Mr. Brown's disaster. Only the right eyebrow lifted higher and the blue eyes beamed brighter interest as the answers grew more wild. At last, appraisal warmed to kindliness and the inquisition ended.

"That's a mean question, Mr. Brown," the inquisitor said. "Never mind about it. Sit down and I'll tell you how I became interested in finding an answer."

Then to the young men before him, the old man spoke, unfolding the riches of his remembrance; of things learned and how they were learned, of men long dead whose lives had widened knowledge, of the work they had done and why; of how, doing it, they had served their generation.

Stopping here to explain a pathological procedure — *you want always to be as explicit as you can*—turning aside there to point an emphasis with a story — *that's not a bad one about the mole on the colonel's shoulder; it should help 'em remember that moles can make trouble* — the professor emeritus talked to the graduating class. He talked and, for the moment, the moment in his memory came alive from the past. This is what it was to be young at Johnny Hopkins when it was young. This is as they were, the giants of those days, who are no more than ghosts now to the young men who walk the corridors they walked in the hospital whose fame they made.

When he had ended, his class crowded around to get his name in the books he had given them, and a boy from China — "China? My sister Rose lived there long ago" — climbed on the big table to snap a candid camera shot. Fifty years ago taking a photograph was a more difficult business. That faded group, for example, on the wall to the left of the lecturer; that was the reward of effort.

5

They are all young in the faded picture, and they look with awful confidence straight ahead. They stand, immutably poised, about a metal-footed table draped in white; the same table the class of 1947 crowds around, waiting a word with the old man sitting behind it. Beneath each figure in the pictured group a name is printed: *Dr. Kelly* — out in front, his boy's face wearing its long moustache like an imperfect disguise. *Miss Beckwith* — in nurses' white at the foot of the table, young, intense, under rein. *Max Broedel . . . Dr. Elizabeth Hurdon* and, between them, behind the table *Dr. T. S. Cullen . . .*

The Hopkins Resident in Gynecology in 1896 was slim, thin-faced, beak-nosed, black-haired, with a jaw all stubborn angles, a wide and friendly mouth and eyes as dark as caves under their dark bushes of brow . . . The last book was autographed, the last hand clasped. The man in white got up from behind his table and turned to look again at the picture out of the past.

"I'm glad," he said presently, "to have lived when I've lived. There won't be another time like it in ten generations. It's been a lot of fun and" — the tuft of chin-whisker stuck out defiantly — "and I'm still having it."

6

PART I

CANADIAN PREPARATION

I

BRIDGEWATER CHOIR SINGS HANDEL

ON THE FOURTH SUNDAY in November in the year 1868 the choir of the marble church in the village of Bridgewater, Ont., in the new Dominion of Canada surprised their minister with an anthem he had not heard them practising.

"Unto us a child is born!" they sang, "Unto us a son is given!"

The chin whiskered young man in the high pulpit stopped trying not to smile. The smile spread along the pews. The choir sang louder. The sound of Mr. Handel's triumphant chorus made its way through windows closed against the November cold into the front bedroom of the parsonage next door. The minister's wife, lying in the big bed with her son's head on her arm, smiled too.

The boy was christened Thomas Stephen; Thomas for his father and for his mother's father, Rev. Thomas Greene of the Bible Christian connexion, Stephen for his Grandfather Cullen in Flesherton. He was a comfortable baby, rosy and round with a smudge of down on top of his bald head and eyes of a deep, astonishing blue. "Tom," his mother always said, "has a violet blue eye." The younger children made a family joke of it; "Tom has a violent blue eye, hasn't he, Mother?" Mary Cullen would shake her head, refusing to be parted by their teasing from the phrase that held the lovely memory of her first baby's first clear regard.

9

"Tom," she continued to say, "has a violet blue eye."

Bridgewater was Rev. Thomas Cullen's first charge. He had been appointed in 1866 when he was new from the Methodist divinity college in Cobourg and had brought his bride with him to the square parsonage beside the new marble church Hon. Billa Flint of Belleville had built to serve the spiritual needs of fellow-Wesleyans in his village.

Like its founder, Bridgewater was a product of the nineteenth century. Like its founder, it is dead. Not even a name is left. When the country around was timbered off and the mills closed a hopeful postmaster promoted a roofing factory and renamed the place Actinolite after the roofing. But the change brought no luck. The big fire came next and took everything, including the roof and spire of the marble church. Only the parsonage and the village hall, the school and a couple of other buildings were saved. They and the re-roofed church and a general store and a gas pump are almost all there is now. In Billa Flint's day it was different. Then Bridgewater was bigger than Tweed; it was the biggest and busiest town north of Belleville.

In spring, when the run was on, the place was alive with loggers and logs filled the Scoutamata River all the way from the lake above Flinton to the Moira and on down to the log gates at Belleville; more than thirty miles of white pine running solid from bank to bank. Four big timber companies floated logs down the Scoutamata in those days but Billa Flint owned the biggest part of them. He had the timber rights for miles back and he bought up the town site at the falls and named the town — it used to be called Hell Gate, and Troy — and started an axe factory and the mills and a tannery and the Bridgewater marble quarry. That was how the church came to be built of marble; the only marble Methodist church in Ontario.

Sunday services are held in the evening only in Actinolite. The United Church minister comes up from Tweed and the service is in the Sunday school room at the back of the marble church. It would hardly be worth while to open the church itself for so few people. Closed, it looks a sad little place. Time and weather and the fire have taken the shine off it. The marble no longer catches the light as it did when it was new. Long after she left Bridgewater, Mary Cullen remembered how white it was then and how it sparkled on sunny days. She used to hold her baby up to the parsonage window just to see it that first winter.

At five months the education of Rev. Thomas Cullen's firstborn was already under way. He had been spanked for disobedience by a stern young father. Echoes of the chastening may be caught in a joint letter addressed to Mr. and Mrs. Cullen, Bridgewater, and postmarked at Fullarton, Upper Canada, May 8, 1869:

"My dear Children: Yours came yesterday and we were grateful to learn that you were all three so well and that sonny is doing well but you will have to watch him and keep him in his place. We shall be much pleased to see you in the will of the Lord. I think when you get a buggy made it would be well to have its body long enough to fit a little seat in the front at your feet. You might have it made so as to put it in or take it off as you please. I would not have it made too heavy but of good material, if I could. As to raising a colt from your mare it depends much on where you have to go; if you have to ride or drive much you will find it somewhat in the way, unless you were to let them run awhile after foaling. Perhaps you would not like to part with your beast but I think you should not have one that is very high life as you have not steady work for a horse for you may endanger your own safety and that of your little family.

"I do not like a covered buggy myself not because it costs more only but we are more confined if anything should happen and cannot see so well when danger is near; neither will it run so easily. So I advise but after all use your own judgement. I hope and pray that you may be appointed to a station that is suitable for you and that the Most High approves of and all will be right. You will find it somewhat strange to leave the friends after being with them so long but Mary has had a lifetime of changes and I hope all the better prepared for it. But don't stay packing all night as we did at Peterboro for you might let the boy fall out of your arms should you take a nap by the way *as then* . . .

"Dear Thos. & Mary, Your father has left a little for me to say but it is almost night and if it is a little crooked I rely on you to excuse it as I do not feel very well either. I think that Pa has begun very early to bring the dear baby to subjection but I suppose not too soon if he is capable of understanding what the correction is for. The sooner their will is broak the better. I long to see you all in the will of Providence. We shall be glad if your next appointment is nearer but I have learned to say O Lord Thy will be done may we ever be resigned. If you could get the Observer for the 5th inst. you will see something of your father's travels for a fortnight or nearly so and also our little surprise party which might be interesting to you. We shall be expecting to hear from you again before Conference all being well. We trust that you, with us, will have our appointments agreeable to the divine will, so prays your affectionate father and mother T.&M. Greene.

"Kiss the dear child for us all. It is late, goodnight. M.G."

Two letters more, the last to go from the parsonage in Fullarton to the parsonage in Bridgewater, complete the picture of the life into which the eldest child of Rev. Thomas Cullen was born; the life of the Methodist circuit and its itinerant preachers in nineteenth century British North America. The Wesleyan ministry of the time and place was a family calling. On lines laid down anew each year at Conference, in conduct faithfully surveyed at Quarterly Meetings, in service devoutly fitted to the needs of changing and growing societies, Canadian Methodism, its ministers and its ministers'

Mary Cullen remembered how it sparkled on sunny days.

Marble Church and old Wesleyan parsonage in Bridgewater, Ontario, where Thomas Stephen Cullen was born
November 20, 1868

wives were shaping a mould for a people not easily mould-
ed. Where the work was best done the impress has
remained. Even through the overlay of forgetful years
the old design can be traced here and there all across
Canada, showing as a pattern on dulled metal will show
when the light is right.

In young Tommy Cullen's first year, the pattern was
plain. However difficult to fill in, it was perfectly plain
to all concerned. Rev. Thomas Greene wrote from Bow-
manville, Ont., to his daughter and son-in-law. The Bible
Christian Conference was over and he was on his way
home:

" . . . We are appointed to Mitchell again. I received
a letter from Mother yesterday stating that, should you
be stationed further off, she would very much like you
to come and see us before you go, at least for Mary and
baby to do so. We have had a good conference. Please
drop us a line at once and let us know where you are
going &c. Hope you are all well. Kiss the pet for us. The
Lord be with, bless and make you a blessing. So prays
your affectionate father. Thos Greene."

Mary Greene wrote ten days later, June 21, 1869; as
pathetic a letter as weariness and disappointment could
wring from a valiant spirit. She was not to see her daughter and her grandson after all:

"Dear Thos & Mary, Yours came to hand on the 17th
inst and I felt sorry and glad, glad to get the dear child's
likeness and to know that you & he were well but sorry
that Thos was porely and that you could not come to
see us before you left Bridgewater. I should have urged
you to come but I thought that as you would leave and
would be busy it would be useless but we found by Thos.
previous letter that you had thoughts of coming. I felt a
hope that you might be nearer to us on your new station
but it looks rather more difficult as the water rolls between but I am sure that it will never sever our affection

13

from you. Perhaps Thos will say if I tell you I wept when I found you could not come, The assertion is true, once a man & twice a child. Well so it is and I hope that you may never have such a feeling but then I know that circumstances sometimes alter the case & it would incur some extra expense but I think it would not have all devolved on you, nevertheless I hope it is all right, we are shortsighted. We feel satisfied that Thos will do all he can for your comfort and I am sure that you have a sweet child which I trust if spared will be a comfort to you both. Precious boy I would like to give him a few kisses do it for me. I look at him or his picture every day since we had it except yesterday, Sabbath, and still hope when convenient to see you all.

"If spared you are soon about to leave old friends for new ones. You will now know something of the trial of parting with them which pang I have many times felt but still if you go armed with the grace & love of God in your hearts you will soon feel a love for the people and they for you, while you have an eye to please God He will soon rise you up friends. . . . I am glad we have not the bussel of moving this year for I believe I never was more unprepared to do so than now. I believe I have passed through more affliction this past year than in any other of my life yet when I look back I see my mercies have been many and God's favour great. We still hope to be strengthened by your prayers and be assured we do not forget you and trust the Lord will bless you and render you a blessing. Your father is now gone to Logan to a Sabbath School tea meeting. . . . Please write as soon as possible after you get settled with all particulars. Send us a good long letter. I hope M will not allways have so much to do that she cannot find time to write. We thank Thos for doing it when M cannot but we like a little from both. Maggie sends a kiss for baby and love to Uncle T and Aunt M. Father's love with mine to both & a kiss for little Tommy. Your affect. mother Mary Greene.

"P.S. I hope this will reach you in good time before you leave."

Tom Cullen recalls his mother's father dimly as a quaint old man with a fringe of whiskers, a merry eye, a soft voice and a smile that drew a child to him. His grandmother he remembers better, for she came on a long visit after his grandfather died. He remembers her as grave and tall, wearing starched muslin caps that tied under the chin and seemed as much a part of her as her serenity. Every Sunday evening while she stayed her grandson used to read one of the eloquent Dr. Thomas Talmage's sermons aloud to her, then scrape an apple for her to eat. Nothing in the gentle bearing of either of his grandparents as he remembers them would lead a boy to regard them as dramatic or adventurous figures. Yet if ever there were figures of drama and adventure these were.

Their story is in a journal their grandson treasures, the journal of Thomas Greene begun on the night of his conversion at Boscastle in Cornwall in the year 1827. Continued through the years of his service as a Bible Christian preacher in his native duchy and southern England, the record was resumed and concluded when the old man, his ministry of love all but fulfilled, was living in retirement near his last Canadian charge. Two sentences, covering with completeness a decision reached in 1844, give the tone of all:

"At this time," Thomas Greene wrote, "missionaries were needed in Canada and I was asked to go to this sphere of toil. After duly weighing the matter and conferring with God and my wife, consent was given to go."

At Helston in Cornwall on the coach road to Wadebridge, when he was twenty-one and still a sinner "yielding to the influence of bell-ringers, dancing-parties, wrestling matches and the wine-cup," Thomas Greene had first begun to long for peace with God. He had been at Helston six years then. When his time with the farmer who employed him ended he went, still seeking peace, to St. Austell to work in the china clay pits. He was a tall, comely and powerful young Cornishman, the child of devout Wesleyans and with the book learning most poor farmers' sons lacked. "Feeling within the desire to become a scholar" he had spent more evenings over books than at dancing-parties, "but his mind was in a state of unrest. He wanted to find rest he knew not how."

Not having found it after two years in the clay pits he determined to find change at least. So he left St. Austell for Devonport "to enlist as a soldier in the Queen's Guard." The Queen's Guard was not at Devonport when he got there. It had marched away, but there were ships of the Royal Navy in harbour; Thomas Greene decided that he would sail to foreign parts. He went on board a man-of-war and told one of the crew he wanted to enlist in the ship's company. The seaman went below to look for an officer, but there was no recruit on deck when they returned. Providence had taken charge of him. It is written in his journal that while he waited "a little gentleman officer" drew near and asked Thomas Greene why he had left home. What had he done?

"I have done nothing criminal. I can show my face at home any time," said Thomas Greene. The small gentleman advised him warmly to go home then, and show it. "I am here," he said, "and must remain but I would rather beg bones from door to door." Thereupon he hailed the boatman who had brought the would-be sailor to the ship, hustled the young man overside into the boat and sent him back to shore. Thomas Greene returned to Cornwall, hired out in the neighbourhood of Boscastle and resumed his bell-ringing, dancing and wrestling, but with an "occasional attendance at Methodist meetings."

First sign of active grace the unregenerate bell-ringer noted in himself was an offer to a fellow-worker who was seeking conversion to do Sunday chores for him while he attended the means of grace at a Bible Christian meeting. The next was an offer to fight another of the farmer's men who had mocked the seeker and "disturbed him in his closet devotions." Thereafter the question "Shall I ever be saved?" pressed more and more heavily and many a time weeping in solitude he resolved to be better "but again would join wicked companions in the belfry." The rest his young heart sought came at last at a preaching at Tregoodwell in the new year of 1827.

"I believe I slept little for the night but rejoiced with a joy unspeakable. I was filled with love." Thomas Greene wrote it in his journal the morning after his conversion, and began his new life. Less than two years later he was noting his acceptance as an itinerant preacher of the Bible Christian society "to serve on the Mevagissey circuit."

The Bible Christians were an offshoot of Methodism which, taking root among the Cornish miners and fishermen in the early nineteenth century, spread across England, to America and as far as China before the century ended. They differed from Wesleyans in no doctrine but in a happy indifference to doctrine. Their strength was in a single-minded acceptance of the teaching of their master, a cheerful determination to keep the words of Jesus as guide in all they did. The Mevagissey circuit of the connexion included a class meeting at St. Just-in-Roseland. The leader of the class was Mary Nicholls, daughter of a man of property, niece of the rector of the parish of St. Just.

The year was 1828. Methodists were still the outcasts of the Established Church of England, the Cornish Bible Christians the most disregarded of Methodists. A niece of the rector of the Parish of St. Just needed a strong will as well as a strong faith to withdraw from the church of her family's respectable allegiance and worship with her father's labourers. Mary Nicholls had both and with them

17

she had steadfastness. For nine years, from the time of her conversion at sixteen, she had gone on quietly ignoring the proprieties of her time and station to attend, then to lead, the cottage class-meetings of a despised and simple sect of Cornish countrypeople. When a blue-eyed young giant, born of those people and possessed of an heroic simplicity of purpose, came to hold preachings in her meeting Mary Nicholls knew that she loved him and thereafter while she lived did not depart from the certainty.

It was to be eight years before they married. The groom was thirty-five, the bride thirty-three when evidence that his daughter knew her own mind triumphed at last over the opposition of an Anglican and a man of property. In October of 1836 Mary Nicholls, spinster, of the parish of St. Just (Roseland) was united in matrimony to Thomas Greene, an itinerant Methodist preacher. Her uncle, the rector of the parish, married them in the church of St. Just.

When Mary Nicholls Greene was nearly eighty she dictated to a grand-daughter some memories of St. Just class-meeting:

"At those times the Methodists allowed some of their females to preach and one woman was the means of conversion of one of my father's workmen. Being converted under her preaching he became concerned about his wife then bed-ridden. The Bible Christians being preaching about two miles from there he invited them to come over and preach in his house. The design was answered, his wife was converted. Being previously dumb for nine years her heart and tongue were again set at liberty so she spoke clearly of what God had done for her soul and exemplified outwardly what was wrought by God's spirit in her heart. Margery's conversion caused a great stir in the neighbourhood and started the cry of many a great sinner to be saved. By which means a small church was established to God's glory and God poured out his spirit

18

and many became the people of God who were not a people and were thus raised up to call Him blessed. Believing it to be the will of God I united with those people and did what I could to promote its interest where I met a large class for several years who would not consent to be separated till I was married and left the neighbourhood. The year before I left England a great revival took place in the little church where many were brought to a saving knowledge of the truth as it is in Jesus, which has many times since encouraged me in trying to fill that important station, that of a minister's wife. . . . Since filling that station I discover much of my defects and shortcomings but the Lord has proved his loving-kindness. . . . Praying breath cannot be lost. We cannot pray in vain."

Tom Cullen knew nothing of Thomas Greene's journal until long after he was grown, but its stories coloured his boyhood. When he and his mother were doing the washing together in the dark of winter Monday mornings, when he was helping her with the preserving or the candle making, or when he was blacking the family boots for Sunday in front of the kitchen stove on Saturday night, he would ask for the stories he liked best and Mary Cullen would tell them.

There were stories of the Scilly Isles and the island wreckers and pirates who knew no law and had no faith, and of his grandfather, strong in the Lord and "six feet in his stocking feet," going among them unafraid to preach obedience to the law of love. There were stories of hairbreadth escapes from among the rocks and currents of the Cornish coasts and from the enmity of wicked men. There were stories of the preachings in the chalk pit outside Brixham in the year when Bible Christians of that port dared not accept the shelter of any roof lest poor tenants who offered it be turned out of doors by their landlords. There were stories of the long voyage to Canada from Padstow in Cornwall when the story-teller was a little girl of three. Mary Cullen could just remember her mother's happiness when it was done, and the river passage too, and they all came safe to shore on a bright October morning at Cobourg on Lake Ontario.

There were stories of the early days in Upper Canada's new settlements, of long winter drives through blizzards and drifts to preachings and of summer camp meetings in the bush and the people of God coming singing among the dark trees by the light of cedar bark torches. There was a story of a spring moving to a new charge across the ice of Lake Scugog and of how the ice cracked and the water came up around the sleigh and Rev. Thomas Greene and his wife drove on with their children across the breaking ice and did not turn back. And a story that was like a picture; of the little girl who was his mother helping her mother pack the saddlebags in the early morning and of her father mounted and ready to ride his circuit, sitting straight and tall in the saddle while the chickens that were his pets fluttered around, flying up to perch on his horse's neck and be stroked goodbye.

The Cullen side of the family saga young Tommy got as he grew older from his father and from his Aunt Eliza. Aunt Eliza was his father's youngest sister. She came to stay at the parsonage in Demorestville on the Bay of Quinte after Mary Cullen's second baby was born and thereafter, until she married, as family emergencies would occur Aunt Eliza would arrive. She and her nephew were friends from the beginning. In the chastening processes of education she solaced the wilful Tommy with a love only less understanding than his mother's, and she could tell stories about Flesherton, about his father when he was young, and about Stephen Cullen his grandfather.

Stephen Cullen had come out from Ireland with his family in 1848. Thomas, the eldest of his five children was a boy of twelve then and Eliza a year old. Sarah Keys

"Praying breath cannot be lost . . . "
—page 19

Rev. Thomas Greene of the Bible Christian connexion
and his wife Mary Nicholls Greene, as their grandson
remembers them

Cullen, his wife, died in Toronto of typhus — ship fever they called it — a few days after they landed. Her eldest son's first memories of Canada were of her death and of walking with his father and brother behind the hearse that carried her body to a grave in this strange land.

The family stayed two years near Toronto while Stephen Cullen made himself used to loneliness and learned the ways of pioneer farming. He was a resolute man, Scottish by inheritance, red-whiskered, land hungry. In Ireland he had been a tenant farmer; he had come to Canada to own land. He bought it in the western Ontario bush and went with his five children to make a farm of it. He had neither horses nor oxen. His tools were axe and spade and mattock, scythe and flail. His helpers were his sons, fourteen and thirteen years old. Of the other three children the eldest was a little girl of seven. His was the first family in the new settlement. With his sons he felled the trees for his log house, planted wheat among the stumps, cut it as it ripened, flailed and bagged it and, carrying the sacks, walked the miles of bush road to the nearest mill.

The settlement grew and took a name; Flesherton. Presently there was a store, a smithy, a school. Stephen Cullen and his sons cleared more land, bought a plough and oxen, cows, horses. The children went to school when they could but the nearest church was more than twenty miles away. At home, in County Fermanagh, the Cullens had been members of the Church of Ireland. All the children had been christened in the parish church of Ederny. But there was no provision for an Anglican ministry to the new Georgian Bay settlements in Upper Canada; only the Methodist circuit rider came. Before a second crop was harvested on the Cullen farm he came riding through the bush. Stephen Cullen took his family to the Methodist meetings. When the Wesleyans built their church near Flesherton he joined it, walked four miles to its services

21

every Sunday and became a class leader. When his eldest son set his heart on being a Wesleyan preacher and not a farmer he gave him his blessing. He had not much else to give.

Alone, the boy set himself to prepare for the life he had chosen. He built a log cabin in the woods and studied there. His father was still clearing land for crop. All day Thomas worked with his brothers in the summer fallow cutting and burning brush and pulling stumps. After supper he would take his candle to his cabin and work at his books till the light burned away. The Flesherton schoolmaster helped. He was employed to teach the children of the settlement, but he gathered a handful of older boys eager for learning and taught them in winter evenings, and when they could be spared from the fields and slashings.

It was slow, for money had to be found for the books and saved against the time when an aspirant to the ministry should be ready for his divinity course at Victoria College in Cobourg. Thomas Cullen was twenty-six before he got to college but his resolve had never weakened. The one serious threat to his plans to be a preacher was an encounter, long known in local legend as the Battle of the Boyne, which nearly ended them and him together.

Young Tommy Cullen could not often get his father to tell him the story of that battle but when he could he was a happy boy. It was the best story of all. It began with the building of the Flesherton sawmill. As was the custom, a work gang was brought to the settlement to build the new mill; twenty-two French Canadian lumberjacks; young, strong, hard-drinking and spoiling for trouble. They found it when the suckers began to run in the creek on Stephen Cullen's farm. Suckers are not private property and, as Johnston Cullen explained to his nephew more than sixty years later, the milljacks could have taken all they needed if they hadn't wanted to take all. All was too much for Stephen Cullen and his sons. The invaders rigged a big willow basket to put in the water where the banks narrowed to a little waterfall. Every sucker that ran in Cullen's Creek, they boasted, was going into that basket. The Cullens got word of the boast and started for the creek with William Rutledge and his son George from the next farm. The two eldest Cullen boys were men grown; Thomas handy and quick on his feet, William as strong as a young ox. Johnston, the youngest, was fifteen and counted himself a good man in a fight too. They started for the waterfall, through the bush. When they got within a stone's throw, the stone was thrown. A rock half the size of a man's head hurtled from the creek bank. Thomas Cullen dodged and the rock hit George Rutledge, crushing in three ribs. The fight proceeded without him, the invaders advancing in a body across the creek. Stephen Cullen, his neighbour and his sons grasped their sticks and went into the thick of the gang. The adversary who nearly finished Thomas's career was armed with an axe. He swung it but as it came down Thomas stepped back. The blade grazed him from head to foot and drove deep into the ground. Before the axeman could recover Thomas rushed in and toppled him, axe and all, backwards into the creek. William meantime had met an enemy with a flintlock, who put the gun to his chest and pulled the trigger. But the flintlock misfired and William laid out that enemy and two others while his father and William Rutledge cracked heads as they came on them, and Johnston the boy belaboured an oversized but fuddled foeman. The swift boldness of the attack broke the invaders' nerve. Leaving axes, guns and demijohns of whiskey with their fish basket by the creekside they turned and ran. The victors got back to the clearing in time to meet a breathless messenger from the settlement who came pounding down the

23

bush road calling "For God's sake don't go near the creek!" The Frenchies, he panted, were heading there mad drunk, promising to kill every damned Orangeman they found.

Though not a member of the Orange Order, Rev. Thomas Cullen confessed long afterwards to his son Thomas Stephen, that he had enjoyed, while it lasted, his part in the encounter long remembered in Flesherton as the Battle of the Boyne. But he did not permit prowess in a fight to deflect his aim or weaken his sense of vocation. Even a first experience of preacher's pay could not do that.

The apprentice divine was offered, during his first year in Cobourg, a temporary charge not far from his home on Lake Huron. He was to supply the Wesleyan pulpit in the village of Kincardine for a year and receive $200 in payment. He accepted the offer for he needed the money as much as he needed the experience. Of the promised payment $178 is still unpaid, but the student preacher did not take his venture's financial failure too much to heart. His heart was otherwise occupied at the time. When he went back from Kincardine to Cobourg to finish his studies on borrowed money he had met and proposed marriage to the woman he loved. She was Mary Greene, daughter of the Bible Christian minister at Clinton. She was teaching school near Goderich. She loved Thomas Cullen and would marry him. The year that had brought him only $22 in cash had confirmed him in his vocation and ensured his happiness.

For a wedding present Stephen Cullen gave his eldest son Fan, a driving mare bred on the farm at Flesherton. When young Tommy Cullen had reached an age to enjoy a burst of speed Fan was still the fastest driver on the Bay of Quinte circuit. A little high life, perhaps, for a preacher, but Rev. Thomas Cullen liked a good horse.

2

OYSTERS FROM B-A-L-T-I-M-O-R-E

MEMORY BEGAN at Demorestville. A child who knew he was Tommy watched Aunt Eliza pack snow around the baby's head. The poor baby was sick his mother told him. He unlatched a picket gate and escaped from home with his bib on, to run on a resounding wooden walk after his father who had gone away and left him. He was taken on his first fishing trip to a place called Big Bay, riding behind Fan. His interest in catching fish was not then what it was to become for he remembers no fish, only a little toy boat his father found washed up on the shore and let him keep as his dearest thing.

The child still had the boat when Demorestville and the picket gate and the wooden sidewalk were gone and he was Tommy Cullen living with his mother and father and his little sister Minnie in the parsonage opposite the stone church at Sydney. At Sydney times and places and people began to fit together to make patterns for memory. He was nearly four and the baby was big enough to play with.

Sydney parsonage was a pleasant place for children; a comfortable square house of pale red brick with wide windows and a big garden. It was not built in a village street but alone on a hilltop with the prosperous farms of Rev. Thomas Cullen's new parishioners spread out below.

Canada has nothing more beautiful in its quiet kind than the country that sweeps down and away from the front doorstep of the Wesleyan parsonage on the Fourth Concession of Sydney, back of Belleville. A wide well-watered valley, it lies among sheltering heights as it might be the delectable country engraved in an old Pilgrim's Progress. It has river-meadows and woodlots and sloping pastures, wide-roofed barns and gabled houses in green lawns, farm lanes shaded by maple trees, elm tops marking the curve of hidden creeks and a long straight road running downhill from home and up again beyond the farthest pasture to woods and the edge of the sky. Tommy Cullen, discovering the world so pleasingly arranged before his eyes took a liking to it. He was a fat and friendly little boy and the neighbours were kind. Sydney laid the foundation of a conviction that has served him long and well; that the unknown when you come to know it is as likely as not to be pleasant.

The Fourth Concession church in Sydney was a fine solid one built of rubblestone laid in narrow courses. It stood in a big graveyard facing the parsonage across a country road. Beside it on the edge of the hill was the driving shed where the horses and rigs of the congregation stood hitched in long rows on Sundays and on class-meeting nights and for funerals. The church wood was piled in the driving shed. It was tamarack. The preacher's boy, Tommy Cullen discovered, had rights in the gum. It was a valuable monopoly. As every boy then knew, tamarack is the best gum there is. To have tamarack gum in lump to share with a friend, to be able to invite a visiting parishioner's child to come to the church shed and hunt for tamarack gum; these were advantages more than balancing the drawbacks of clerical eminence.

The drawbacks were chiefly in the way of neatness of person and speech and promptness in obedience. They began to be felt at Sydney. It was required in a preacher's boy that he have clean hands and a washed face at times when dirt on his contemporaries went unregarded. It

26

was further required, even before he was old enough to go to school, that he avoid slovenliness in speaking. It was above all required that he observe without wasting time the rules laid down for his guidance. Any requirements he forgot were impressed on him. Rev. Thomas Cullen was not neglecting his firstborn's education:

"There are some advantages in being the eldest and some disadvantages. It has always seemed to me that the experimentation in the rearing of children fell to the eldest child and he was the one who received most of the punishment. By the time the eldest has been duly handled the proper routine for the oncoming children is established. I surely had plenty of whippings and punishment but being a boy and full of devilment I certainly deserved plenty. . . ."

Mary Cullen's corrections, more gentle, were not less memorable for that. It was she who began early to see to it that Tommy should speak the King's English with proper respect for consonants. Her lessons combined with her son's powers of observation to produce occasional embarrassments. One, dissolved in good country laughter, checked forever any trend to priggishness in a five-year-old Tommy.

The preacher's son had been asked to stay to dinner with his playmate, Sam Lloyd, who lived at the first farm down the hill. There was pumpkin pie. After pie, Tommy Cullen expanded. He had made an interesting discovery. He wished to share it with his friends. "You farmers," he said, "say taters. We preachers say potatoes. You farmers say punkin. We preachers say pumpkin."

Forty years after, Tom Cullen came back to Sydney and found the story still being told on him at Sam Lloyd's farmhouse table.

In Sydney two babies were born, the second a baby brother who died. The baby's death, or the solemn pro-

27

cessions that came to the graveyard across the road, or
the men from Belleville marble works arriving at intervals to fix tombstones; an enthralling thing to watch; one
or all set Tommy to playing funeral. He conducted obse-
quies in winter under the dining room table, in summer
in the side garden among his mother's dahlias, where the
graves were dug and the headstones erected for Minnie's
broken dolls. Minnie, round-eyed and impressed, made a
suitably earnest mourner and, with luck, Tommy wore
white bands.

By the custom of the time the minister at a child's
burial wore white bands on his shoulders and around his
hat. White bands, when they could be annexed from the
father's clerical wardrobe, added much to the enjoyment
of the funerals the son conducted. But an attempt to bring
more realism to the drama by harnessing the cat for a
hearse horse was to fail, permanently discouraging a taste
for tragedy. The officiating clergyman used his mitten
strings to harness the cat. They were new Christmas mittens, a double pair; inside ones of wool for warmth, outside ones of leather for style; and they had double strings.
Before the harness was secure someone opened the parsonage door and the cat left, taking mittens and strings
with her into a snowbank and coming back alone. With
the spring thaw they were found, but in a state of ruin.
Their owner's interest in funerals was not the same
again.

There were other interests enough; butternuts stored
in the loft of Vermilyeas' driving shed down the road;
the cow that rose up and ran with him when he tried to
sit on it at Sam Lloyd's uncle's, the egg hunts in haymows,
the bent-pin fishing in valley creeks; the weddings and
christenings and socials of a sociable community; flowers
in Mary Cullen's garden, growing so tall under the windows that before summer was half gone the shutters would

. . . set his heart on being a Wesleyan preacher.
—page 22

Rev. Thomas Cullen, eldest son of Stephen Cullen of
Flesherton, the year of his ordination, 1866

not close; the snow caves he and Minnie made in winter when the drifts on their hilltop had frozen hard; the surprise party.

Tommy Cullen saw the surprise party coming late in a winter afternoon. He had been visiting up the line and had caught a ride home on a farm sleigh. Near the parsonage gate he saw it a mile away moving down into the valley; a line of teams and sleighs and horses and cutters black and small in the distance but coming nearer. It looked like a funeral but the expert knew it was too late in the afternoon for funerals. He dropped off the sleigh at the gate and ran in to find his mother and forgot about the sleighs until suddenly they were there in the yard. Sleighs filled the yard and the church shed, sleighs were hitched to fenceposts up and down the road and still they came. All the people from the three churches on Sydney circuit were there to make a surprise party for their preacher and his wife:

They brought all sorts of good things to eat and presents of silver and linen for Mother and said the nicest things about Father and Mother. We had a big pantry, but when they all left after supper it was full of eatables; we were eating party provisions for fully six weeks. The linen lasted years, the silver Mother used as long as she lived. Every time I came home and saw it it carried me back to the Fourth Concession parsonage and the surprise party. I have always had a warm spot in my heart for Sydney and its people. Even as a little fellow it made me happy that they were so fond of Father and Mother.

Memories of Sydney are like that; clearer than other memories and more shining. There was a little room upstairs that Mary Cullen trimmed with maple leaves. She stripped the walls herself, covered them with cotton stretched tight, fixed coloured maple leaves to the cotton and varnished over all so the leaves stayed there, brighter

29

almost than when Tommy helped her gather them, to delight her young son's heart with their beauty.

There was Abe Finckle and the sound of him praying in the little Front-of-Sydney church on the bay shore. The Front-of-Sydney church was the third on Rev. Thomas Cullen's circuit and Abe Finckle was its class leader:

I can see him now, a big man with a head of grey curly hair bald on top. He was the loudest prayer on the circuit. He prayed so loud that on summer evenings when the church windows were open people could hear him praying clean across the bay, a mile away in Prince Edward County. I loved to go to service in the bay front church to hear Abe Finckle pray and once in a while Father would take me. . . .

There were the first oysters Tommy Cullen ever ate. His father brought the tin home from Belleville for a special treat for his mother the winter he was six. It was a flat oblong tin lettered B A L T I M O R E . Tommy had an oyster out of it, and another. On consideration, he found he liked oysters. He had another. He liked oysters very much, and oysters came from a place called Baltimore. . . .

The picture taken in 1874 is a cabinet group. It shows Blanche, the baby, in her mother's arms, Minnie, sashed and ringletted, at her father's knee. Thomas Stephen Cullen stands in the middle. He wears a handsome costume distinguished by velvet bands descending slantwise across his stomach. The velvet was brown, as he remembers, and he spilled steak and gravy on it when it was new.

That summer after Conference the Cullens moved to Belleville. Rev. Thomas Cullen's new charge was there. It had no parsonage and they lived in small rented houses for the three years of their stay. Three babies were born in Belleville and one died. The children all had whooping cough and chickenpox. The careful savings of their life together were lost. Yet Mary Cullen contrived to make her children's memories of those years happy ones.

She was aided greatly, insofar as her eldest was concerned, by the Bay of Quinte. Belleville is on the Bay of Quinte and its summer life still centres on the long lovely reach of sheltered water. Seventy years ago its whole existence depended on the bay. The town was then a port of consequence in Canada's grain and lumber trade with New York State, a fishing centre from which twenty tons of skinned catfish alone were shipped weekly to American markets, a trading point where the farmers of a rich community came to buy the manufactured luxuries brought back across Lake Ontario from "the States." Into the middle of this new amphibious life, eager as a young gull, Tommy Cullen followed a nose already beginning to be notable.

In summer the Moira River below Belleville dam was little more than a trickle over its stones, but in spring it ran bank full and above the sluiceways it was packed with logs. In spring Belleville boys haunted the river waiting to see the sluices opened and the logs sent down. Their heroes were the lumberjacks who broke the jams, jumping from log to log across the shifting mass to find and loosen the key log, leaping clear at the last moment or riding the log down perilously erect in the swift turmoil where a slip meant certain death:

In spring all of us boys wanted to grow up and be lumber jackies. We took a fiendish delight in running across the river on the logs that had come down. The large ones held us well, but on the small ones we had to step lively or they would sink with us. A mis-step and we could have drowned. Naturally we said nothing at home about these escapades or about our summer sailing excursions.

Rev. Thomas Cullen's son usually joined the sailing excursions when his father had gone out of town. An old punt was the craft in which the sailors voyaged out from Belleville harbour into the bay; six or eight of them all under ten and all with an equal ignorance of sailing and swimming:

We none of us had permission to go because none of us asked for it, knowing very well it would be refused. Why we were not drowned I shall never know. But it was a lot of fun. So was the fishing. We used to fish off the wharf, just where the Moira empties into the Bay. We caught catfish and anything else that would bite. I loved fishing already.

As compared with the punt, steamboat excursions on the bay were tame. But there was an exception; an evening excursion as far as Big Bay and back on a Twenty-fourth of May, the Queen's Birthday holiday. Rev. Thomas Cullen and his wife went and took all the children and so did nearly everybody else in town. A whole flotilla of steamers and little tugs left Belleville wharf that evening and steamed away past Mississauga Point where the Sunday school picnics went and on down to Big Bay:

I remember we got there just after dusk and the tugs got busy at once. They moved into the still water in front of the steamboats and from their sterns dropped Roman candles and all sorts of other fireworks just lighted. Each was fixed to a thick board on which it floated. In a moment or two the whole bay seemed lighted up; fiery fountains, pinwheels, rockets and every sort of firework going off together and all reflected in the water. It made a wonderful spectacle, the most beautiful fireworks I have ever seen. We children were almost beside ourselves.

As Tom Cullen remembers them, only Hon. Billa Flint's evening garden parties with Chinese lanterns could approach the Big Bay fireworks for enchantment. Hon. Billa, long vague in family myth as the patron saint of Bridgewater, had materialized in light waistcoats and a good deal of whisker with the move to Belleville. He lived in a big house up the hill from the post office. His grounds were the showpiece of the town and his evening garden parties had more Chinese lanterns than a boy could count.

For a garden party hundreds of Chinese lanterns decorated Hon. Billa Flint's grounds. Men hung them all afternoon in long strings from tree to tree, above the white iron urns of geranium and wandering Jew, the round beds of begonias and cannas and the raked gravel walks. With dark the men came again to loosen an end and let down each string and light the lanterns one by one. Tommy Cullen whose father knew Senator Flint was permitted to stand close and watch.

When all were lighted and the strings fastened up again, there the paper lanterns hung while the party lasted, swaying among the leaves overhead, exotic as oysters and dripping desirable gobs of wax if they drooped askew. Rev. Thomas Cullen's eldest, blessed with permission to stay up late, walked beneath them drunk with garden party lemonade and Chinese lanterns in a summer night. But he did not forget to collect some gobs of wax.

Aunt Eliza came to stay while her brother Thomas and his wife went to the Philadelphia Centennial Exposition. The children were happy with their visitor. The travellers came home impressed with seventy solid acres of commercial exhibits in memory of the Declaration of Independence. But there was a painful aftermath. Tommy lost the pictures of the Centennial his father had ordered. He was nearly eight, quite old enough to go alone for the mail, but he dropped the packet from Philadelphia on his way home from the post office. Going back to pick it up he could not find it anywhere. He postponed telling his father the bad news:

33

That evening Father said it was strange the pictures had not come. I told him then I had lost them. I remember being sent out to look for them and how I trudged the streets long after midnight knowing I could not find them and unwilling to go home.

Mary Cullen, who remembered the night's discipline even more vividly than her son, said of it many years later that she thought Tommy would never come back and she would not have blamed him if he had not. It was as near to criticism of her husband's educational methods as she ever permitted herself to come. The waiting seems to have shaken the disciplinarian too, for Tommy's ultimate punishment was not heavy:

Father gave me the option of paying for the pictures out of my own money or sawing eighty sticks of wood. I thought a moment and said I would saw the wood. Looking back, I think my judgment was good. In the first place I was bankrupt. In the second place I would have had to saw the wood anyway.

By the time Thomas Stephen Cullen was eight years old his future had been mapped. He was to be a lawyer. To that end five hundred dollars had been saved, Mary Cullen alone knew how, out of a Wesleyan preacher's stipend. The sum was to have been devoted to the prospective lawyer's college education but before he was nine it was all lost. An investment made on the advice of a trusted friend turned out disastrously, not through the friend's fault but through a less trustable nephew's. The money was nonetheless gone, and with it Thomas Stephen's chances of subsidized learning.

The loss did not weigh too heavily on its young victim. He had already made the interesting discovery that money can be earned. During his first winter in Belleville, he shovelled a neighbour's walk and was paid for it: five cents cash. Having thus early lost his amateur standing

34

he went further and with all the other little boys in the street became a collector of rags, bones, bottles and old iron, all of which he sold for copper money to a local dealer in such wares. He had also a private income:

I got five coppers every Saturday afternoon from Father and as soon as I got it I would walk down to Front street nearly a mile away and hire a velocipede for an hour. It was a great thing to go peddling around the street on the three-wheeled cycle and the owner of the store was generous. If by chance I kept it a little more than an hour he did not penalize me. I looked forward to Saturday afternoons.

The private income was regarded by its possessor as unearned. He did not associate it in his mind with the circumstance that about the time he started getting it his father taught him to saw wood.

Taught to saw wood, Tommy was encouraged to practise the art. Before he was eleven his duties included sawing all the household wood both for cooking and heating:

Ten cords of beech and maple a year; four-foot sticks, two cuts to a stick; takes a lot of sawing. Father started me when I was six with a saw of my own and the small sticks. He kept the saw sharp for me and showed me how to grease it with a piece of fresh pork rind when it heated and started to lock in the cut. From the beginning I had so many sticks to cut each day. I could cut as many ahead as I felt like, but I must not get behind. I can remember clearly times when I did. One was in Colborne after we moved there. Father had been away all day. He came back after midnight, looked at my wood and found I had not sawed it. I got up and sawed my wood. I was pushing ten then.

Long before Colborne the young woodcutter had made his second discovery about money. Money, he found, could be used for greater ends than buying rides on a velocipede. Money would buy a boy free time to do what he wanted to do. He opened negotiations with his sister Minnie who, being still a child, valued money because it bought candy. For one cent Minnie would saw a medium-small stick of cordwood in three. For three cents paid to Minnie half an hour's freedom from woodsawing could be purchased. The hired girl's suitors were also useful. There were two of them, both brakemen on the Grand Trunk Railway, both big men with strong arms. Either one could be persuaded to show his skill with a bucksaw to an admiring audience. Tommy Cullen and his ally the hired girl did not fail in admiration and a lot of the biggest sticks got sawed that way. With increasing years the technique was perfected and extended, much in the manner of another Tom. At twelve, the woodpile was no longer a problem:

I would come right home from school and start sawing and pretty soon four or five of the fellows would come along and ask me to go skating or fishing or swimming according to the season and I would say I had to saw my wood first. So they would offer to help and we would all take turns at it, sawing against each other to see who could finish two cuts in a stick fastest and they would get so interested that pretty soon it would be supper time. Or else Mother would come out with cake and raspberry vinegar for us. We all loved Mother's raspberry vinegar. In an afternoon like that I could get enough wood sawed ahead to set me free after school for two or three days.

Freedom, Tommy Cullen learned in Belleville very soon after he learned to saw wood, was what he needed to lay hold upon. Freedom earned, planned or purchased, was the supremest good to a boy with things to try. And wherever he turned were things to try.

He tried stealing apples and was caught and let off with a warning. He tried hooking rides on the back of the

. . . teaching school near Goderich
—page 24

Mary Greene, daughter of Rev. Thomas Greene, the year
before her marriage to Rev. Thomas Cullen

expressman's waggon and very nearly ended all experiments squeezed flat against the edge of the station platform. He tried smoking in the shed at the back of the yard:

The shed was stored with lumber that belonged to our landlord and we boys would frequently repair to it for meditation. It was there we decided to learn to smoke and started on umbrella ribs. In those days umbrellas had cane ribs. We got an old umbrella, cut out a rib, divided it in pieces and lighted up. It burned all right but so did our tongues. We gave up umbrella ribs and tried again. After several tries we settled on cedar bark from the fence posts, nicely ground between the ball of one hand and the palm of the other and smoked in pipes made of acorn shells with stems of elder pith. After we got over feeling wicked it was pretty tiresome so we stopped. Later I tried half a cigar behind our barn at Brighton but it didn't appeal to me much so I smoked no more till I was twenty-six.

The third baby born in Belleville was a brother. The eldest of the Cullen children was nine at the time and he remembers the day well for it nearly cost him his Queen's Birthday fireworks:

An early stir in our house and the arrival of the doctor convinced me it was the wise thing to absent myself. I went down to the Burrells' who were kindness itself to all of us children. Mr. Burrell had an axe factory where it was my delight to spend hours. I had a fine day and towards evening Father came along. He had been looking for me everywhere he said, and he would have to punish me for leaving home without permission. I could have no fireworks on May 24th, the Queen's birthday. This was serious, everybody had fireworks on the Queen's birthday, but the news that I had a baby brother softened the blow a good deal.

Father, who was very happy and proud of the baby, relented later. "Boy," he said, "you can have your fireworks on the twenty-third," and I did.

Seven weeks after the baby, the inevitable moving came. Mary Cullen who had moved four times in nine years prepared with cheerful equanimity to move again, packing the household goods, the bedding, the clothing, the preserves, the pickles, the china and the children. Tommy helped his mother. He liked it when she needed his help:

The life of a Methodist minister's wife was hard but Mother took the hardships in her stride. No amount of work could daunt her. She would do it and still have time to help Father, to entertain the scores of friends who came and always stayed to meals and to enjoy things with us children. My memory is that wherever we moved it was fun and Mother was always in the middle of the fun. I have never known anyone like her.

3

FISHING AND AN ACCOUNT BOOK

THE MOVE THAT summer of 1878 was to Colborne, a village set back from the lake. The landlocked interlude lives in memory chiefly for a creek where chub could be caught right in the school yard, for a bigger creek with a swimming hole conveniently accessible by way of a loosened board in the school fence, for dooflickers, mixed pickles and the blue of swallows' wings:

The most birds I ever saw in one place at one time were swallows on the telegraph wires along the Kingston Road from Colborne. I can still shut my eyes and see them and the flash of purple as they rose and flew for their holes in the sand banks. Thousands there must have been.

The dooflickers were made by Mr. Leake the Colborne baker, on Saturday mornings. They were buns made of long thin strips of dough rolled around and around on themselves and painted, before they went into Mr. Leake's brick oven, with egg-white to make them shiny. A messenger sent from the parsonage for Saturday's bread learned to time his visit to the dooflickers:

When Mr. Leake approached the oven with a long pole flattened at one end like a spatula I would be right behind him. As he opened the door to shift the pans of bread I could catch a glimpse of the dooflickers cooking to a fine golden brown. When a pan of them came out I was allowed to take one. I would pick it up, turn it on

39

its side, make a small slit with my pocket knife and then, taking care that the knife cut the crust only at the point of entrance, gouge a hole in the centre. I then squeezed the bun at right angles to the hole made by the knife-blade, went to the golden syrup barrel, turned the spigot and let the syrup run in until the dooflicker was brim full. Then I ate it and it was good.

The pickles were company pickles bought at the store and as such to be carefully distinguished from family pickles made at home. There were two large bottles of them; Crosse and Blackwell's Mixed; bought by Mary Cullen and put away on the high cellar shelf against the expected arrival of unexpected company. The cellar door opened close to the woodshed. With winter approaching Tommy Cullen found he had to spend a good deal of time in the woodshed sawing wood, and pickles, especially company pickles, were what he liked only less than doo-flickers.

In less than a week from their purchase company pickles were needed, but when Mary Cullen went down cellar to get a bottle, both bottles were gone. The punishment fitted to that particular crime has been long ago forgotten and, whatever it was, the pickles were worth it. So the offender thought at the time and has continued to think; there was nothing like a stolen pickle, particularly a pickled onion, for the tedium of sawing wood.

They were a year in Colborne. Mary Cullen had expected to stay three, as in other charges where they had been stationed. In all three churches of the circuit her husband's gift for rousing congregational interest had been effective. Wicklow and Salem parishioners had joined Colborne church in asking the Conference stationing committee to send their minister back. But a call came from Brighton a few miles down the Kingston Road. The committee put it to the minister concerned: They had him down for Colborne; he could return there if he wish-

ed at the same stipend; $1,000 a year. Brighton needed
and had asked for him to help build up a rundown
church; but Brighton could pay its minister only $800
a year. With the approval of his wife, Rev. Thomas Cullen
accepted the call to Brighton:

I was only ten at the time but I remember Father
and Mother talking it over and the decision made a great
impression on me. It showed me that Father was infinitely
more interested in the lives of people than in making
money, and helped me realize what wonderful stuff
Mother was.

Entries in an old green account book are headed in
Rev. Thomas Cullen's abrupt hand: "Household Expenses Since Coming to Brighton July 2nd 1879" . . .
There were five young Cullens and the eldest was ten.
All five were well grown, healthy, hungry and hard on
their boots. Even with milk at four cents a quart and
eggs at eleven cents a dozen, beef at ten cents a pound,
apples at $1.75 for two barrels and oatmeal at $2.40 a
hundredweight, the cost of feeding them mounted; to say
nothing of boots. And there was more to it than food and
clothing. Among the evident essentials listed in the green
account book; "elastic and buttons .28; tweed $1.00;
mending tea kettle and teapot .20; boots for Ernie .80;
10 cords hardwood (dry) $24.00"; are essentials of other
sorts:
"New York Christian Advocate $1.53; paper collars
.18; Second Book for Minnie .25; Missionary Society (for
family) $10.00; croquet set $1.35; music lessons for Tommy $10.00; Social .85; Chambers Encyclopaedia $20.00;
fishing tackle .12; 2 lamp chimneys .10; Mrs. Potter weav-
ing 25½ yds. carpet $2.15 . . .":

We could never have come near to making $800 a
year do if Father and Mother had not been fine econ-

omists. We got flour and apples by the barrel, beef by the quarter and whole pigs in winter. The meat was hung up in the woodshed where it froze solid and had to be cut with a saw. The apple barrels, and about a waggon-load of potatoes were stored in the cellar each winter with crocks of eggs and firkins of butter and bowls of the head-cheese Mother made from the pigs' heads — the most delicious headcheese you ever tasted — and carrots and cabbages and turnips and parsnips and onions by the bag. I never forget the cellar of the Brighton parsonage.

It was dug only under half the house but the founda-tion was high so there was room under the other half to store potatoes and other vegetables on the ground. That is where I would sit hunched up sprouting potatoes in spring; having got there by navigating the cellar in a washtub. Mother and Father used to dread the spring rains in Brighton for the cellar always flooded a couple of feet deep. But I welcomed them; it meant another chance to use the tub for a boat. It was no end of fun punting around the cellar in it. To the swing shelf for bread and butter, over to the corner where the eggs were kept on top of an empty wooden butter firkin; to the preserve shelf for a jar of preserves; back across to the side where the vegetables were stored; Mother would stand on the cellar stairs above flood level and I would push my tub around collecting what she needed and bringing it to her. I can remember only one disaster. I paddled too fast to the egg corner and the waves of my tub upset the firkin and all the eggs dumped out of their basket into the water. But that was fun too; trying to fish them out. Except fishing there was no spring sport I liked better than sailing around the cellar in our Saturday night tub collecting the provisions for Mother.

Except fishing. At Brighton the fisherman was back beside the lake again and fishing was good in Presqu' Ile Bay. The taste which had survived in Colborne on chub caught in the schoolyard creek grew strong in Brighton and became a passion. Saturdays in spring, fish-ing for small-mouth bass and perch from one of the old docks in Brighton harbour, Tommy Cullen had as good luck as he has ever had anywhere although, with no reel to play them, the big ones often got away. Brighton had all sorts of fishing and Rev. Thomas Cullen and his son between them sampled most of the sorts. They spent evenings trolling for swamp bass and pike and summer mornings, fishing from the old warehouse half a mile out in the bay, watching a three or four pound bass come up to rub his nose against the worm, waggle his tail and swim away a dozen times before he bit. They went, for the junior fisherman, on inland expeditions to spear suckers. When the spring run was on the creeks and little streams were so full of them that they rustled in the water with the same noise as dry leaves in a windstorm; spearing suckers was a lot of fun. It also helped a boy get his hand in for jacklight fishing; to go jacklight fishing was every boy's ambition.

Tommy Cullen's father let him go one night with Eli Pringle, an old hand at it. They went out after supper across Presqu'Ile Bay towards the lighthouse, taking the jacklight and spears and plenty of pine knots in Eli's flatbottom boat. When they had got more than half way to the light Eli stopped rowing and rigged up the jack. It was a round basket of iron strapping fixed on an L-shaped iron bar in such a way that when the foot of the L was fitted in sockets in the bow of the punt the basket sat upright at the far end about four feet ahead of the boat and less than two feet above the water. Eli filled the basket half full of knots, lighted them and dropped the bar into its sockets. The knots flared up in a long bright streamer of flame and Tommy Cullen crouched beside Eli Pringle in the bow of the punt to watch the dark water through the shifting patterns of brightness the jacklight made for the first sign of fish:

Pretty soon you could begin to see them coming from all directions and we started using our spears. They had

43

four or five prongs and a two or three foot handle. You
had to be quick and to allow for the deflection in the
water and I missed every time at first, but after while
I did better. Eli seldom missed and he got the eels too.
Every now and again he would point to a faint trail of
cloudiness in the water near the bottom. That meant an
eel down there in the mud. Eli would strike and Mr. Eel
would come up wriggling. A couple of them were five feet
long.

We had 117 bass and sunfish and seven eels before we
stopped fishing about midnight. Eli made for the bar
and lit a fire and we camped all night. A high wind had
come up and I lay there too cold and excited to sleep
until daybreak. Then Eli wakened. The wind was blow-
ing a gale by then so we had to leave the flatbottom boat
on the bar and come home in a little duckboat, skirting
the shore. I remember coming into the house as proud as
a peacock to tell of our night's luck. Needless to say Eli
had speared nearly all the fish I was boasting about. Jacklight fishing was certainly good fun but it's just as well
for the fish it was outlawed.

Brighton had trout fishing too. On a gusty day still
present in memory Tommy Cullen made the catch of a
lifetime in a trout pond back of Brighton:

It was a small shallow pond not more than a hundred
feet long by sixty wide but it held about a hundred of the
most beautiful trout you ever saw, many of them twelve to
eighteen inches long. I fished that pond again and again,
tempting the trout with the freshest worms, the finest
line, the longest pole and all the patience a twelve-year-
old had. It was no use. The trout knew too much for me.
I waited a while and when a day of squally weather came
went back to try again.

Gust after gust was sweeping across the little pond
when I got there, making the surface all choppy. I
dropped in a worm and bang! — pulled out a beautiful
speckled trout almost fourteen inches long. I rebaited
and in a moment had his mate. That was enough. I
clutched those two fish and ran all the way home with
them. I couldn't wait any longer to show them to Father.

Early in the second Brighton year — "pint whiskey .25; Notice of birth in the Ensign .50; Postage .5; Postage .25; paid Mrs. Peterson for 2 wks nursing $6.00; Baby's boots .90" — Rose Nicholls Cullen was born. Rev. Thomas Cullen's record of household expenses had shown a cash deficit on the first year of $51.98. To fill the gap he arranged to sell Bibles and hymn books on commission. His wife devised new economies. She made soap; soft for washing, hard for family; leaching the winter's hardwood ashes with Tommy's help into a lye pot, saving rough scraps and trimmings of fat beef and mutton for soap fat, boiling it with the lye in an old kettle; so much boiling for soft soap, so much longer for hard. She bought a candle mould and taught Tommy how to thread it with wicks, how to ladle the hot tallow in, how to dip it in hot water and pull out the candles by their wicks after time enough to let them set. She had the sewing woman in — "making Tommy's suit of three pieces $1.25; making pinafores .20; making pants .25." She preserved — "30 qts strawberries $1.92; Pail of Black Currants .60; 1 Pail cherries .50; Pail Black Cherries .60; Berries (rasp) 6 qts .30." She did, again with Tommy's help, the washing for her family:

As I look back it is perfectly clear that Mother did the work of three people. Yet she was always bright as a dollar and looked after us children to perfection, teaching us how to do things and to take our part happily in the family routine. Over a long time it was impossible to get any hired help for love or money. Mother and I would get up at a quarter to four Monday mornings, I would light the fire and put on big boilers full of water while she was getting breakfast; sliced cold tongue or some of her headcheese, coleslaw or ketchup and bread and butter; then we would do the washing. Week after week for months at a time it was done and on the line before I left for school at a quarter to nine. I just began to know

45

Mother in those Monday mornings. I would not have missed them for a lot.

Don't think all our time was work. We had plenty of fun at home, playing games, popping corn, listening to the talk when visitors came, having Father and Mother tell us stories. Father was a wonderful story-teller, we children liked nothing better than to get him started.

Fun was always stirring someplace. In winter there was skating on the bay and sleighriding on the hills behind the town and holiday sleighing parties to tea meetings in the back concessions. In spring there was sugar making. Children fortunate enough to be asked to a sugar making came home at dusk down the road from the sugar bush full of maple sap and maple taffy and sunlight, the smell of maple smoke in their hair, the uneaten remnant of a day's taffy-making piled for safe carriage on a broad maple chip and patty cakes of maple sugar bulging their pockets.

In summer it was berry picking. Wild strawberries grew thick in the fields outside Brighton but Tommy Cullen liked picking wild raspberries best:

Did you never take wild raspberries and two or three beech leaves and make a sandwich and eat it? . . . I have walked two miles down the road to Oscar Lawson's the night before we were going picking, slept with him in his father's haymow and got up at daybreak to start out so we could be first in the berry patch. Awkie and I would each have a package of breakfast, a ten quart pail and a quart pail with a handle. Monday morning was usually the best picking because nobody went picking Sunday. We would walk anywhere from one mile to three, depending on what patch had the best crop, and start in. The large pails we would put in the shade but in a conspicuous spot, the small pails we fastened to our belts by their handles. Then we began picking.

The best way was to hold the bush with one hand and pick with the other. Where the berries were good and

46

thick I have picked three quarts in a space not ten feet square. The temptation was to leave a good patch before it was picked clean for another that looked thicker. You run into the same temptation all your life but I learned in Brighton you fill the pail quicker if you stick to your own raspberry patch.

We never wanted to stop picking till we had our big pails full to overflowing and no matter how far we had to walk we never took a ride home. It makes no difference how carefully you carry them, raspberries are sure to sink some, but after a two or three mile ride jolting over a rough road a full pail would be a third empty. We were so anxious to make a good impression at home we would rather walk any distance than risk having our berries shaken down. In one summer in Brighton, I remember, I picked seventy-five quarts of wild raspberries. Some we ate fresh, some we preserved and the rest Mother made into her raspberry vinegar.

Under date of June 28, 1881, Rev. Thomas Cullen's household expense book shows an odd entry. It is set down between "13 milk tickets .50" and "Handbook of Methodism, nett . $5.00":

"Fishing fine $5.50."

His son and fellow fisherman remembers about that fine:

It was Saturday, April 30, and another minister, a friend of Father's who was to preach for him at the Sunday morning service, was staying with us. Like Father he was an ardent fisherman and Father and he had planned an expedition. Several miles back in the country was a famous trout pond and the owner had asked Father to come with his guest for a day's fishing. The trout season opened May first, but that was Sunday and Father was going to be busy Monday and far into the week. To my delight it was decided to go Saturday and to let me come along.

It was a lovely day and an hour's drive. Our host had asked us to dinner and afterwards he and one of his sons fished with us all afternoon. The pond was one he had made on his own farm by damming up the end of what had been a swamp fed by very active springs. The water was icy and when the owner had stocked it with brook trout he had left it unfished for several years. So we had ideal sport and a good catch. Father was the expert of the party. I spent a good deal of my time snagging my hook in roots and old logs, but we all enjoyed ourselves. Towards evening we hitched up and drove home happy and tired. I didn't always remember the sermon texts but I can tell you the one Father's friend preached from that Sunday morning: "Cast the net on the right side of the ship."

Some weeks later Father and his guest, their host and his son all received summonses for fishing out of season. I was the only one of the fishing party overlooked. All four appeared, pleaded guilty and were fined a dollar and costs. In time we learned how our offence had been discovered. Our host had another son who had just bought a new top buggy for a hundred dollars. In those days in Canada the informer reporting a breach of a game law got half the fine and fines were sometimes as much as fifty dollars and costs. Half of four fifty-dollar fines would have just paid for the new buggy. I have often smiled to think that all the young man got for his trouble in this case was two dollars.

Naturally the joke was kept up on Father for a long time. The weekly papers had a lot of fun with him and his minister friend, especially over that text. But it did Father no harm with the Brighton people.

Rev. Thomas Cullen and his Brighton parishioners understood each other. Their choice of a minister had been proved by that time. Church and Sunday school attendance were both growing. The preacher came to see them in their homes and his wife made them welcome in the parsonage. The preacher's children, handsome, healthy, well-mannered and well-scrubbed decorated the preacher's pew every Sunday. The sermons he preached were direct and forceful, little concerned with church dogma, much with the relationship of man to man;

always spiced with a good story. If a local issue rose between right and wrong as Rev. Thomas Cullen saw them the Wesleyan congregation of Brighton could depend upon hearing it discussed from the pulpit plainly. The parishioners liked that, liked it that the preacher could tell the sin from the sinner and keep a friendly weekday greeting for sheep whose blackness it was a Sabbath duty to denounce.

So, meeting him of a late afternoon, striding up the back road, fishpole on shoulder, or seeing him start off towards the bay with his boy Tommy for an evening's trolling, they would call to the preacher to cast his net on the right side of the ship and like him all the better. . . .

When Rev. Thomas Cullen and his wife Mary closed the green account book on three years of household expenses since coming to Brighton they were well content. Their joint venture of faith had been justified. They were leaving the church that had called them built up even beyond its people's hope. The sale of Bibles and hymn books on commission had more than sufficed to cover the gap between an $800 yearly salary and the necessities of a family of eight; there were three hundred dollars of savings in the Hastings Loan. Moreover, the good work done in Brighton had not gone unnoticed. A call had come to the workman from Old Richmond Street Church in Toronto.

4

NEWSPAPER ROUTE TO MEDICINE

THE MIXED TRAIN from Brighton got to Toronto towards evening. It was crawling along the waterfront to the Union station with eager young Cullens at all available windows when a tall thin man with a big moustache stepped into the car and began a friendship that was to last for life.

I can see George Blackwell yet as he boarded the train that evening, and hear him. He had a fine North of Ireland voice and a twinkle in his eye. He welcomed Father and Mother for the members of Richmond Street Church and we children were his friends at once. We had reason to be for he was one of the kindest men I have ever known and one of the best. Mrs. Blackwell was just as kind. They lived in a flat over the Bank of Toronto where Mr. Blackwell worked as a bank messenger and it was soon one of my regular places of call.

Saturday forenoons were the times. As regularly as clockwork Tommy Cullen would arrive in Mrs. Blackwell's kitchen for a visit. He would have a junior Cullen or two in tow as a rule and Mrs. Blackwell would have a coconut cake to cut and George Blackwell a good story to tell. At the Blackwells' and at Mrs. Burns' house next door to the parsonage in George Street Tommy Cullen was as much at home in a month as though he had known them always. Like the Blackwells', the Burns family's friendship was to be enduring and to include all Cullens. Its immediate effect was that Tommy Cullen was added to the number of the Burns boys for pie-eating and other essential purposes and had friends to show him how to get fishing again without losing too much time.

George Street ended below the parsonage only a block or two away from Toronto Bay, and across the bay not fifteen minutes by Captain McSherry's ferry was the island. A series of low sandbars grown thick with willows, alive with wild birds and intersected by lagoons, Toronto Island was a paradise for the little city's boys. East of the main island was Wiman's, and north of Wiman's was Ashbridge's bay with the Don flowing into it. In and around Ashbridge's bay and Wiman's island a boy could find fishing, to say nothing of boating and bathing. There was a floating island in Ashbridge's that shifted about with changing winds and currents. Tommy Cullen got some fair fishing close to the edge of its matted reeds and water-weeds before he had been long in Toronto.

But the island could not command the newcomer's undivided affection. The fishing was not that good and he had much to do.

Toronto had hardly more than a hundred thousand people when the Cullen family came to live there. The eldest son, having grown to be thirteen in villages, rightly assumed that his new place of residence was not different in essentials, only in size. He set about making friends with it:

I had far more time to myself, for the parsonage in George Street had a coal furnace. The only wood I had to cut was for the kitchen stove. The ashes had to be sifted of course but that was only once a week in winter. Saturday mornings were generally my own. I could go visiting or exploring or card collecting. All the Toronto stores had business cards and all the boys collected them and the local merchants vied with each other to get out the prettiest. One of them outdid everybody by giving away red dinner pails. I collected one of those too. It was a lot of fun.

51

Living in the city could not help being a lot of fun. There were more things to find out about, more people to get to know, more places to explore and, the new citizen discovered with interest, more ways of earning money. For one, there was the Exhibition.

Toronto's annual exhibition — "The Ex." to succeeding generations of Toronto children — was already an institution in the 'eighties. Their father and mother had been to it; the young Cullens were eager to go to it too. To get pay for going to it was fortune beyond a child's highest hope; yet it was Tommy's the first year. One of his father's new parishioners needed a boy to help in his refreshment stand at the big fair and Tommy was hired.

When he had made three or four hundred sandwiches and a barrel of lemonade to start the day, the junior helper was free if things were slack at the stall to go around the Exhibition and look at it. He wasted none of his freedom. He could go in and out unchallenged and uncharged whenever he felt like it; and he was paid to be there. For being there and having fun and doing not much more than fourteen hours' work in any day, he was paid.

He was lucky enough to be employed at the same refreshment stand making sandwiches and lemonade for two Exhibitions. He still remembers the recipe for Exhibition lemonade. "Take six lemons and a barrel of water" it begins. The third Exhibition after he came to the city he had a job with more pay but less fun taking tickets at the main entrance. As some compensation for the loss of fun he wore an official badge and had a title; Assistant Superintendent of Admission. But whether with fun or glory Exhibition jobs had one drawback in common; they were transitory like the Exhibition. Tommy Cullen wanted all-year employment in which to invest free time.

Tom was always there when morning service started.
—page 54

Old Richmond Street Church, Toronto, from an illumi-
nated address presented to its pastor in 1885

For his first months in Toronto the graduate of Brighton public school attended Dufferin School entrance class. He started at Jarvis Collegiate in September of 1883. The same fall he got a newspaper route by negotiation with Harold Parsons, another minister's son, who was giving it up. From that time until he graduated M.B. in 1890 he went on delivering papers:

For a year or two after I started Father and Mother threatened time and again to make me give it up but I was so insistent they let me go on. The feeling of independence that comes with being able to make one's own way had gotten hold of me and I could not bear to think of losing it. Besides I knew how difficult it was with a family the size of ours to make ends meet and I saw no reason for not helping when I could. And I was having fun.

The newspaper route was continued on condition that if either his health or his lessons showed signs of suffering from it Tommy would have to give it up. The second half of the condition made a student of him.

Waking up was his difficulty. Every weekday morning he must be awake by half-past three to reach the mailing room of the Mail by four. At first his mother wakened him but that would not do. He devised other means. Art McKay whose father had a dry-goods store down Queen Street had a morning Mail route too. He was older and had been at it longer and was used to waking up:

Art undertook to wake me if I overslept. We arranged that I should go to bed with a long piece of string tied to my arm and hanging out the window far enough down for Art to reach it. He would come past our house on his way to the Mail office and if the string was still hanging out give it a good pull. This worked well until the neighbourhood boys got wind of it and took to pulling my string on their way home from parties around midnight. So we had to give up the string and make another arrangement.

We agreed on the saloon at the corner of Queen and George as a checking point. If I wakened in time to get there first I was to go on, leaving a small stick leaned up against the saloon front. If the stick was not there when he came Art was to walk up the street as far as our house and whistle.

Fortunately, alarm clocks were introduced in Canada before Art McKay grew tired of whistling. Tommy Cullen bought himself one and found his difficulty overcome. Or almost:

When I had had the clock long enough to be used to it I had one bad lapse. I wakened one morning at seven, three hours and a half late, and discovered to my dismay that I had the alarm clock clutched between my hands under the blankets. After that I borrowed a tin dishpan from Mother, set the clock in it each night well out of reach of the bed and had no further trouble. Few people could ignore the racket made by that combination.

With time, waking grew less difficult for the waker and Tom Cullen's habit of early rising was established. He came to like being up early even on dark winter mornings after a snowstorm:

There was something about it, once you were up and out. The streets were so quiet and unmarked. Mine would often be the first footprints for blocks and blocks. In summer it was a pleasure. The most delightful time of a summer day is from four to five in the morning.

Sunday mornings were for sleeping and Mary Cullen saw to it that the sleep was undisturbed. But Tom was always there with the other children when morning service started in Old Richmond Street Church:

I missed part of Father's sermon quite often but I don't think he guessed it. I had refined and perfected my system of church sleeping. I would sleep sitting bolt upright so that if by chance my head should bob a little it was always forward. When that happened I would not jerk it up but let it drop a little lower, keep it down for a moment and then raise it very slowly as if from deep meditation. That way I caught up quite a bit of lost sleep the three years we were at Old Richmond Street. But I didn't skip any of the services. I liked going.

Old Richmond Street Church suited Tommy Cullen. He liked it from the moment he saw it. It had been built in 1827 by builders who remembered from youth the solid classic tradition in which they had been trained at home, before Regency set in. It looked what it was; a plain country-bred Upper-Canadian heir of eighteenth century England.

Tommy Cullen liked everything about it; the low-pitched roof, the wide pillared porch, the box pews with their doors, the rows of round-topped windows, the scroll on the wall behind the pulpit platform. "Worship the Lord in the Beauty of Holiness" the scroll read. In the opinion of the young newcomer to the preacher's pew, this was it.

Upstairs and down, gallery to basement, he explored Richmond Street Church to its remotest corner. He learned to pump the organ, the first pipe organ he had ever seen; and to light the church gaseliers, the first he had ever lighted. He learned where the gas meters were in the basement and how they turned off and on. He was thus enabled comparatively early in Rev. Thomas Cullen's Toronto pastorate to do his father a good turn.

Holiness of a type less beautiful than that which Old Richmond Street Church itself embodied for Tommy Cullen was rife among a small group of its congregation. Weekly class meetings had become "holiness meetings" prolonged by apostles of holiness far beyond reasonable class meeting limits, as the preacher's son saw reason:

55

They were nice people but their doctrine made me tired. One Wednesday evening I remember they were holding forth at great length. Father was very broad-minded and patient and he let them talk on and on. At last I slipped out and went and turned off the gas at the meter. I got the wrong meter the first time and somebody rushed in from the mission room to ask what was wrong. Their lights had all gone out he said. I said I was sorry, it was a mistake; and turned that meter on again. The second time I got the right meter and the holiness meeting ended abruptly and about two hundred people came scrambling out in the dark.

On the way home Father said, "Boy, did you do it?" I said "Yes. I knew you were tired." He didn't say a word, just smiled.

The smile marked the beginning of a new relationship between father and son. Tommy was growing up.

The youngest Cullen was born in the parsonage of Old Richmond Street Church and christened Katherine. When memory began for her the process of growing up was almost complete for Tom. To his small sister Tom was a godlike creature who came and went without parental questions asked, carried a little girl when she was tired walking and sometimes let her play with bits of his skeleton. It had been decided by that time that Rev. Thomas Cullen's eldest was not going to be a lawyer.

5

HOWARD KELLY ACQUIRES AN INTERN

REV. THOMAS CULLEN went to call on Dr. Thomas Aiken, professor of surgery in the University of Toronto medical school. Mr. Cullen's eldest son had changed his mind since coming to Toronto. Before approving the change Mr. Cullen wished for expert advice. It was given:

Dr. Aiken said "Does the boy smoke?" Father said "No."

Dr. Aiken said "Does he drink?" Father said no again.

"Lots of room at the top," Dr. Aiken said and as far as I was concerned that ended the interview.

In the fall of 1886, two months before his eighteenth birthday, Tom Cullen entered medical school.

The Cullen family was living then on Shaw street in the west end of the city; a ravine conveniently placed for sleighriding on tea-trays opposite their front door, Wesley Church, Rev. Thomas Cullen's new charge, hardly a block away. Tom had exchanged his old paper route for a handier one and arranged to pick up his papers at five each morning at the police station in Dundas street. He was able to cover the route and be home for breakfast at seven. He continued to go every Saturday morning to the Mail office downtown to stuff papers. It was a profitable job. The boys who worked at it were paid six cents for every pile of supplements four feet high inserted in the Saturday morning Mail as it came off the press.

57

With the two Burns boys and Albert Awde, Tommy Cullen had started his career as a stuffer soon after he got his first route:

We would all go to bed early Friday evening at the Burnses' in the biggest bed I have ever seen. The four of us slept in it crosswise without our feet hanging over. At 2:30 in the morning we would get up, dress, have a snack and leave in time to walk two miles and a half and get to the Mail office. We would stuff until after five and then I would ride out with my papers to the west end, deliver them and be home for breakfast with the family not much later than usual.

After a time the foreman who had charge of the supplements ran away with a girl and didn't come back. Tommy Cullen was given command of the stuffing and thereafter earned a dollar every Saturday morning before six. During the Christmas holidays boys could have all the extra work they wanted at ten cents an hour, wrapping sample copies for the Mail's annual circulation campaign. By working sixteen hours a day for the three or four days between school closing and Christmas it was easy to earn Christmas money.

It was while he was thus coining wealth in the newspaper business that the younger Cullen's income came up for discussion in a meeting of his father's church board:

Father came home from the meeting smiling broadly. One of the trustees had asked, while finances were being discussed, how much I made out of my newspaper route. He said he thought Father's salary was enough for the family and since I was bringing extra money into the house an amount equal to my income should be deducted from Father's. No other member of the board thought much of the idea so it went no further. But for a good many years I got angry whenever I thought of it. As far as I can tell the man had no unkind feeling towards Father or me. He was just naturally mean; the meanest man I have ever known.

58

It wasn't until Ernest grew up and brought home the story of the old lady in prayer meeting that I could laugh about him. The old lady was thanking the Lord for helping her to be long-suffering; "Oh Lord I have tried to lead a good life. I have done the best I could to bear and forbear. I have lived at peace with my neighbours — " She suddenly stopped there. Her feelings had got the better of her — "But that Mrs. Brown damn her soul . . ." I knew just how she felt.

Wealth accumulating, the foreman stuffer and two of his assistants became land speculators. They bought a lot between them in a new subdivision on the edge of town, putting all they had into a down payment. Unluckily, collegiate fees fell due the same week as the payment. For the first time since his twelfth birthday, Tommy Cullen had to ask his father for money:

Mother came to me next morning looking very upset. She said Father had slept badly; he had been worrying about me all night. Not that he objected to giving me the money I needed for my fees but that he wondered how I had been spending the money I had earned. So I had to let go my secret and tell Mother about the lot instead of waiting till we sold it and surprising her as I had planned.

We did sell it very soon, and made a fair profit. The next one I bought by myself. It was at a camp ground and had a big hickory nut tree on it. I doubled my money on that deal. Some time later I bought an acre in an outlying district, sold it after I started medical school and paid my fees with what I made. That was the sum total of my land speculation. I stopped. I had come to the conclusion that a fellow who wanted to make a success of studying medicine couldn't waste time watching the real estate market.

Dr. Lesslie M. Sweetnam was the man responsible for the early closing of the real estate operations. It was his example that made Tom Cullen a doctor.

Coming to the city at the hero-worshipping age of thirteen, the boy had been fortunate in finding a hero who wore well. A tall, ruggedly made young man topped by what his admirer recognized as "a wonderful suit of hair," Lesslie Matthew Sweetnam had great charm and integrity as great. He had graduated from medical school and started practice in Toronto the year before the Cullens moved from Brighton to the parsonage on George Street. He became before many months a family friend as well as physician. To the eyes of the eldest, he appeared as a mixture of Saint Luke and Daniel Boone.

The young doctor, hardly more than a boy himself, shared the boy's delight in doing things and his curiosity about them. He was a fisherman and at home in the woods. He knew the Ontario bush country as Tommy Cullen longed to know it. He had travelled it by canoe with his father when that postal official's duties took him on outpost inspections and he could talk well of his experiences. Beyond these evident advantages was his love for his profession and a passionate interest in the science of medicine as well as its practice. Presently Rev. Thomas Cullen's firstborn discovered that he no longer wanted to be a lawyer. He wanted to be a doctor like Dr. Sweetnam.

Having received good assurance that opportunity was open at the top his father questioned the boy's new direction no further. Out of early stresses a curiously equal relationship had developed. More slowly than his wife but as completely at last Thomas Cullen had come to recognize in his son Thomas a self-governing entity best approached on even ground. On that ground the two got on well, building understanding in mutual respect, a kindred sense of fun, fishing expeditions together and the deep affection for Mary Cullen they shared.

It was a complementary affection. Rev. Thomas Cullen was not designed by nature to be helpful in life's minor details. His son was. He had inherited his mother's gift for applied devotion. It was his happiness, as it was hers, to put his love to work in the most commonplace as in the greatest of services. By the time her last baby was born, many commonplace things needed doing to lighten the burden of Mary Cullen's housekeeping. Tom did them and with them took a share large for his years in the government of six younger Cullens. When he and the other children preserved the strawberries, for example, he was not yet fifteen.

His mother had been sick that spring and his father had taken her away for a rest. The strawberry season came before she returned and the berries were good and cheap. Tom bought two crates of them; one hundred and eight quart baskets. He bought sugar, he assembled sealers and sealer rings. He marshalled his young sisters and brother into the parsonage kitchen, set them to hulling strawberries and kept them at it until every berry was hulled. Meantime he went ahead with his part, boiling jars, cooking and bottling the fruit. When the last jar was filled and sealed he dismissed the work party to bed.

To the younger children, Tom's right thus to turn them into a juvenile canning factory was beyond doubt; even before fourteen his word was with authority. When Tom said they could do something pleasant they did it, never for a moment supposing it necessary to refer the ruling to a higher court. If by chance mother or father should question what they were doing they had only to say "Tom said we could" and it would be all right. Equally, when Tom said to do something less pleasant, like staying in from play to hull strawberries, they did it without question. And, Tom having set it, the task became a game. Working with Tom was nearly always like a game.

Moreover there was the delight still to come with their mother's surprise. From oldest to youngest all their lives together her children liked nothing so much as to sur-

prise Mary Cullen. No youthful indulgence was as much
to be desired as her smiling approval. Her praise was the
best of rewards. To Tom it was something more. He and
his mother were workfellows and had been for years.
Building the fire, filling the boiler, turning the washer
in the dark of Monday mornings before school had been
no hardship for him even when he was small; he was
working with his mother. So with the egg-packing,
the ketchup-making, candle-moulding, leaching ashes and
making soap, cutting and stringing apples to dry; in all
the housekeeping he shared with his mother or did for
her, Tommy Cullen had always enjoyed himself. To be
entirely happy he had only to know she was pleased with
what he had done.

The comfortable every-day certainty of it ended in
the summer of 1888. Rev. Thomas Cullen was transferred
from Toronto to a charge in Sarnia, nearly two hundred
miles west. Bereft of the companionship he had always
known a homesick young medical student went to share
a classmate's room in a boarding house. There melancholy
was prevented from marking him for her own by an unforeseen embarrassment:

The day after the family left for Sarnia the evening
papers came out with large headlines: "Murder Perpe-
trated Near Shaw Street Bridge Part of Remains Found."
Next day there were more headlines: "Mystery Solved
Bones Belong To Medical Student."
The fact was that I had done some dissecting on a leg
in the top of our woodshed. Our landlord, being in a
hurry to relet the house, had thrown the bones out the
same day the family moved, not giving me a chance to
come back and take them away. After the headlines I
didn't know what to do about them, so I decided to do
nothing. I was hoping they would be forgotten but they
weren't. A day or two later they turned up in print again
with my name attached: "Mr. Cullen is requested to call
at the Dundas St. Police Station and remove his bones."

I didn't call. I was too embarrassed. I wanted to keep as far as possible away from those bones. So they and I got into the papers once more: "Mr. Cullen not having called for his bones they were buried yesterday in the back yard of the police station."

As far as I know my bones are still there, buried in the back yard of a police station.

That summer vacation and the next, living in a room and walking Saint John's Ward, the toughest in the city, as an assessor's clerk, Tom Cullen earned the rest of his medical school fees. For living expenses he still counted on his paper deliveries and his earnings as head stuffer at the Mail. He changed his west-end route for one that included the General Hospital on Gerrard Street opposite the medical school. It kept things together during the school year and left more time for study. He had been plucked in physiology at the end of his second year, something that must not happen again. His enemy again was sleep. He could beat it in winter by keeping cold. He took to studying by an open window in an overcoat and ear-muffs. But he was not a Spartan by preference. He dropped in quite often at the Burnses' or the Blackwells', to be fed and made much of and, whenever his funds could be stretched to it, he took the Saturday train for Sarnia.

Ponto, his Newfoundland dog, was always first to give the signal of Tom's coming. When Ponto, ears pricked, started down the street towards the station, running hard, the Cullen family knew who was in town. Once Ponto and Tom between them broke the parlour window in the Sarnia parsonage. Mary Cullen was sitting sewing at the window that day with Ponto asleep beside her. He wakened at the sound only he could hear and went through the glass in a single bounce. That visit started happily as always, but with everybody picking up broken window in the front garden.

In the old Toronto General in the fall of 1888 a third year medical student saw his first operation. It was a leg amputation and it did not rouse in him any latent desire to be a surgeon. He had decided that medicine was his field. The decision was almost too well supported by the results of the third year examinations. They showed Tom Cullen in first place in medicine, leading his friend and classmate Lewellys Barker:

We all knew there was something queer about it. Lew was the most brilliant student I have ever known. He had an encyclopaedic knowledge of every subject in the course and medicine was almost his best subject. Yet there I was first in the list with Lew second. Dr. H. H. Wright, our professor in medicine, had been the examiner. He was a delightful old fellow but odd. I can see him now, walking along Gerrard Street to morning lectures in a pouring rain, coat collar up, hat brim down, dripping wet but scorning the umbrella I had hurried to offer him. "Never use 'em" he said, as though umbrellas were a sign of moral weakness, and walked on.

H.H. was a character and his lectures were first class. We all took care not to miss them. I confess that I occasionally slept through others. With a big breakfast on top of my newspaper route it wasn't easy to keep awake if the lecturer was dull, and there were back benches well out of sight where you could lie flat and have a good sleep. But I had no trouble keeping awake in Dr. Wright's lectures or in making good marks in his subject. Not better than Lew's though; the whole class knew that and so did the faculty.

One of the other professors tackled Dr. Wright about it in a faculty meeting. "Barker knows more medicine than Cullen," he said. The old man agreed with him:

"I know he does but, damn it, I don't want a book. Barker wrote fifty-two pages. Cullen wrote eight."

When we started our final year the secret of my success in medicine was out and we had a great joke on Lew. He outdistanced us all of course in the finals; won the gold medal and the star medal as well. I counted myself lucky to come second with a silver medal.

For half of his final year in medicine Tom Cullen lived with his preceptor, Dr. Lesslie Sweetnam. The title and the custom were survivals from the old days of apprenticeship. For six months before graduation a medical student served a physician in private practice, living in his house, helping him with the preparation of medicines, accompanying him on rounds of calls, learning from his preceptor some of the things books do not teach. Dr. Sweetnam's student moved into the room above the doctor's office late in 1889 and was given a latchkey to the office door.

It was the first Russian influenza winter. The epidemic reported from Siberia the previous October reached Canada in January of 1890. In the weeks that followed the student learned a great deal. Telephones were few then but at all hours of the day and night messengers came and the office bell rang with calls. Dr. Sweetnam took to sleeping on a board when he slept at all, so that he might be more easily roused.

The picture of that time remains in Tom Cullen's memory as a night picture; of sleet and slush and wind, dark houses, faint lights in upper windows and a muffled figure climbing strange stoops to fumble above black doorways. Making late calls with his preceptor the boy could trace the spread of the epidemic by the lighted upper windows. In some streets the sickness was in every house and the problem was to discover the one from which the call had come. One or other would make his way in the dark to a dark door and, taking off his glove, reach above to find and feel the lead numbers nailed to the lintel. If they felt right, the groper would knock on the door. If they felt wrong or if there were none to feel he must try another door.

They did not talk much on those rounds, they were too cold and tired, but their joint silences sufficed to turn a boyish admiration into an enduring regard. Before the epidemic passed its height the student had learned, watching his preceptor, how far beyond exhaustion a man's will can drive his body.

Himself, Tom Cullen came through the experience on his gift for sudden sleep perfected in church under the eye of his father and the congregation. He could sleep at any time in any place, at any opportunity and in any position. The ability has stood him in good stead many times, but never better than during the influenza epidemic of 1890 when, as he remembers, he got so he could sleep on his feet and keep walking.

Later that year he began to learn about surgery. His preceptor's interest in it was keen and his surgical practice growing. The laborious home surgery of a period when none but the poor, the friendless, or the virulently contagious was ever sent to hospital was his field. His student's part was in the preparation. Scrubbing, sterilizing, draping an improvised operating table with carbolic-scented sheets, it took hours to make a bedroom ready for an operation, to assemble the towels and gauzes, the catgut in alcohol, the basins of disinfectants, and to boil the surgeon's instruments on the kitchen stove. When the operation was done, the student's task was to dismantle the operating room and, while Dr. Sweetnam and the nurse were caring for the patient, clear away the trappings of surgery, clean the instruments, boil them once more on the kitchen stove and pack them in their cases. Lesslie Sweetnam was a Lister man; for antisepsis and asepsis both, sub-iodide of bismuth as well as surgical cleanliness. His student did not lack employment:

Dr. Sweetnam used a vast amount of sub-iodide of bismuth, a reddish disinfectant hardly ever seen any more. I have helped him asseble eighty dollars' worth of ingredients at a time and make the powder in a big porcelain bath. All his patients were supplied with vials of it to dust on cuts and scratches and it was remarkable how

66

quickly ugly cuts would heal with its use. I noticed when I became an intern that my preceptor was well ahead of several senior men on the surgical side in his precautions against infection. It was quite a shock to me, coming from my preceptor's training, the first time I saw a well-known surgeon put the knife between his teeth after making an incision, hold it there while he tied off a blood vessel and then take it out and go on with the operation. The older surgeons were finding it hard to take germs seriously and a good many of them didn't try. I was lucky to get my grounding in aseptic techniques under a man as meticulous as Sweetnam.

It was from his preceptor, while he was getting his grounding, that Tom Cullen first heard of Howard A. Kelly. Dr. Sweetnam had already made several visits to Philadelphia to see for himself the work of the young gynecologist whose operative daring was alarming cautious confrères. Each time he had found more to admire in Kelly's surgical innovations and more to like in Kelly. They had interests other than surgery in common. Like Sweetnam, Kelly was a woodsman and an enthusiastic nature-lover. Some time soon, Tom Cullen learned, the two were going to make a canoe trip together to a lake Dr. Sweetnam's father praised as the most beautiful in the northern woods: Ahmic Lake in the Magnetawan country. Dr. Kelly was hoping to find a place there for a summer camp.

Mary Cullen and her youngest daughter came from Sarnia for Tom's graduation. Convocation was in a big tent on the university lawn that year; the university building had burned the winter before. Katherine had a new dress for the great day and she and her mother had taken the train long before daylight; Tom had met them and had found a place for them in the big tent where a little girl could see the procession and the platform. But the waiting was long and the afternoon sun hot on the canvas.

Presently the youngest Cullen fell asleep. The procession of the faculty passed and she did not waken. Tom came, dark-moustached, handsome and eager, in his graduate's gown, to kneel and receive his hood from Sir Daniel Wilson, came again to be given his silver medal. Each time he turned to smile towards them. The little girl slept on.

Mary Cullen did not wake her daughter. She was alone again with Tom; as alone in the crowded tent as on the November morning in the front bedroom of Bridgewater parsonage when she heard the choir singing in the marble church and smiled, holding her son close.

With graduation Dr. Thomas S. Cullen's newspaper deliveries ended. Three weeks after he skimmed his last paper under the door of the staff quarters at the old Toronto General Hospital he entered the same door as one of the interns selected from the class of 1890.

That year was the first in which appointments were by class standing. Of fifty-two applicants for internships the six chosen were the top-ranking graduates in medicine, three from the University of Toronto medical school, three from Trinity. The interns' year began in July. Young Dr. Cullen and young Dr. Barker started together on the medical side and ran into a typhoid epidemic. By fall the hospital was crowded with fever cases. Within four months Tom Cullen, fresh out of medical school, had been put in full charge of 144 typhoid patients:

I learned then to know the peculiar smell of typhoid so thoroughly that I could never forget it. I remember coming on it without warning many years later in a Baltimore hospital and recognizing it at once. The patient was one I had operated on. She was convalescent and almost ready to go home when she developed a temperature the resident staff could not account for. So they sent for me.

68

In Sarnia, nearly two hundred miles west . . .
—page 62

The Cullen family, taken when Tom was on holiday from medical school. Standing, from left: Minnie, Tom, Lillie. Seated: Rev. Thomas Cullen, Ernest, Blanche, Rose, Katherine and Mary Greene Cullen

The first breath in that room took me back to the fever wards in the old Toronto General. I ordered a test made for typhoid. It was taken and proved negative. I visited the patient again, verified my memory and ordered another test. It was negative too. I came again next morning and there was the smell; I couldn't mistake it. I ordered a third test. It was positive. The patient had typhoid all right.

We traced it to some oysters a friend had brought her as a treat. The only other case that developed was one of the interns. She had shared the treat with him. Fortunately they both recovered but while they were sick the resident staff had a chance to learn something about typhoid. It had grown so rare by then that none of the young doctors had ever seen a case — or smelled one.

But I had, when I was twenty-one — day after day and week after week — and again when I was twenty-six. Many disease odours are more offensive in themselves but no other is more characteristic than the smell of typhoid. And none has the same horror for me.

The round of an intern's duties in the old Toronto General took him through medicine, surgery and obstetrics in a year. The work was heavy but still left a little free time to invest:

I taught a class in bandaging that fall and made fifty dollars. At Christmas when I went home I had a little chamois bag made and put ten five-dollar gold pieces in it for a present for Mother. I think it gave her a great deal of pleasure; it gave me a thrill I have never forgotten.

For all the interns of his time duty was lightened by Dr. Charles O'Reilly and the gas bill. Dr. O'Reilly was the hospital superintendent, curly-headed, unpredictable, genial when the gas bill was not troubling, given to sudden descents on the junior staff when it was. Tom Cullen recalls one such descent as typical of many. The interns were eating late supper in their dining room when it came:

All six of us, Lew Barker, Bob Hillary, Eugene McCarty, Charlie McGillivray, Roland Hill, and I were there together. It was after ten and we were not expecting visitors when we heard Dr. O'Reilly coming and knew by his speed it was the gas bill again.

He rushed in calling "Who lives in the sitting-room? The gas jets are on full tilt!" Barker and I stood up and Dr. O'Reilly looked at us as though we had robbed his mother. "My gad!" he said. "And the gas bill was six hundred dollars last quarter!" Without another word he turned and went out.

In less than a minute he was rushing back calling "Who lives in H? The gas jets are on full tilt!" Roland Hill and Bob Hillary stood up. They lived in H. Dr. O'Reilly looked at them as though they had robbed his grandmother. "My gad!" he said. "And the gas bill was twelve hundred dollars last quarter!"

Their service on the medical side being accomplished, the spendthrifts who lived in the sitting-room were transferred to obstetrics and given charge together of the Burnside, the Toronto General's lying-in hospital. There Tom Cullen first heard, from Lewellys Barker, that there was in Baltimore a hospital called Hopkins:

I can remember that day like yesterday. Lew and I had been having a wash-and-dress-the-baby race. When things were not too busy at the Burnside we used to run races to see who could wash and dress a baby faster. Lew usually won. I could never get below eleven minutes. This day when the race was over Barker turned to me and said "I'm going to Hopkins, Tommy."

I said "What's Hopkins, Lew?"

He pulled a Johns Hopkins Hospital Bulletin out of his pocket and showed me the cover. It had the picture of the new hospital, open only about a year then. I studied the picture and looked through the bulletin a bit. Then I said "Shake, Lew. I'm going too." But it wasn't quite as easy as that.

Barker, whose people knew Dr. Osler, the medical chief of the new hospital, had already been in touch with him. Lew's appointment as an intern under Osler came through and he arranged to leave for Baltimore as soon as his year at the General was done. I went to see Dr. Osler who had come up to Toronto but there were no further vacancies in his department. I was still set on going to Hopkins; more and more so the more I heard about it. How I was to get there was the problem, and I could see no answer.

The answer was to come through Tom Cullen's preceptor. In the late spring of '91 Lesslie Sweetnam heard from Howard Kelly about the canoe trip they had planned. Dr. Kelly had left Philadelphia for Baltimore. He was Dr. William Osler's associate in the new Johns Hopkins Hospital, heading its gynecological department. He could take his vacation early and be in Toronto in June to start the Magnetawan trip if Dr. Sweetnam could arrange to go then.

Dr. Sweetnam arranged more than the canoe trip. The Ontario Medical Association was meeting in Toronto in June. Johns Hopkins' young gynecologist was invited to come from Baltimore to speak at the association's meeting. The canoe trip was planned to begin the day after his address was delivered. For the interval, two operations at the General Hospital were scheduled. Dr. Kelly approved the arrangements, consented to operate and brought his assistant, Dr. Hunter Robb, with him from Baltimore.

The interns on operating-room duty at the General the day of the scheduled operations were T. S. Cullen and L. F. Barker. Tom Cullen noticed his preceptor in the group of doctors who came to watch the visiting surgeon at work. The first operation began:

Lew was giving the anaesthetic and I was handling the instruments and Roland Hill had been brought in to help. I turned around to thread a needle and when I turned back found to my amazement that the operator had the abdomen open. Operators in the General often took ten minutes to get that far. After cutting through the skin, fat and fascia they were apt to get lost in the muscles. Kelly and Robb working together used dissecting forceps as I had never seen them used. One man pulling each way, the cleavage between the muscles was seen at once and the opening in the abdomen could be completed without difficulty.

I watched, fascinated, while Kelly went ahead and finished that operation and did the second, working with clock-like precision and at a speed I had not imagined possible. By the time he had finished, the course of my professional life was decided. Up to that afternoon I had intended to be a physician. From that afternoon I knew I had to be a surgeon.

I remember turning as soon as the second operation was completed to Dr. Sweetnam, my preceptor and friend, and saying "That is the man I want to go with. Do you know him? How can I get there?" Sweetnam told me who he was and added "He is stopping with me; come down and take dinner with us."

At ten that night when I started back for the hospital I had been promised a place on the junior staff of Dr. Howard Kelly, gynecologist-in-chief of Johns Hopkins. The gas jets were on full tilt in the sitting-room for a long time after I got in.

The internship under Kelly was not to begin until January. The internship in Toronto ended with the end of June. Tom Cullen wanted a holiday but not a six-month holiday. Since he was going to be a surgeon and gynecologist there were things he needed to know more about; pathology among them. The place to learn it was Johns Hopkins University, in the pathological laboratory directed by William H. Welch; everyone interested in the subject agreed on that. Howard Kelly's prospective intern waited for the end of the canoe trip and another talk. Dr. Kelly advised that Dr. Cullen should come to Baltimore ahead of time and spend three months studying at Hopkins Pathological; he would arrange it with Dr. Welch.

The holiday at home began. The Cullen family had moved again; this time to a country charge in the London Conference. Tom came home to help his mother with the settling and clean the well, to fish a little and loaf a lot, to organize hilarious picnics for the younger children and their playmates, to fill the twelve-year-old Ernest with resolve to be a doctor too, to wind up a waning flirtation with one of his sister Minnie's boarding school friends and to grow a set of correctly professional side-whiskers. He and Mary Cullen made the ketchup together in September before he left for Baltimore.

PART II

HOPKINS BEGINNINGS

I

APPRENTICE PATHOLOGIST

A SLUM CLEARANCE SCHEME has brought the old house down. Model tenements for the use of Baltimore's negro citizens cover the site. But when young Dr. Thomas Cullen finished his internship at Toronto General Hospital and came south to Baltimore, things were different. Fayette Street and Broadway were only beginning to go off then and Mrs. Gill's boarding house at 1640 East Fayette was high class.

The year was 1891. Harrison was still President and the Republicans in office at Washington, but the Sherman Silver Purchase Act had been passed and William Jennings Bryan elected to Congress. The second presidency of Grover Cleveland was just ahead, the Homestead steel strike and the currency panic of '93 less than two years away. In Baltimore, sewers were open, streets cobbled, all the crossings had stepping stones, drug stores sold leeches, soil-carts made their rounds after dark, Ferdinand Latrobe was Mayor, and Rhetter's the best place in town for oyster pot pies.

The War Between the States was no longer fought again at the drop of any hat at any street corner, but life for Baltimoreans had a new complication; the Baltimore and Ohio Railroad had stopped paying dividends in the slump of '87.

In Canada, Premier Macdonald, the great "Sir John A." was dead. Emerging only slightly tarnished from a redistribution scandal, the number one Father of Con-

federation had that year defeated his enemies, the annexa-
tionists, in a general election, and died of apoplexy. With
him had died the new Dominion's first expansive era,
dominated by his vision, his wit and his superb effrontery.
Hard times were ahead for Canada too.

This was the stuff of outer circumstance. The mous-
tached and sidewhiskered professional man who reached
Baltimore Union Station in a Wagner Palace sleeping car
early in the morning of September 22, 1891, did not dwell
on it. He was almost twenty-three. His thoughts were of
greater things. They centred in one word: Hopkins.

A crowd filled the station entrance. Making his way
through it, the newcomer walked into Baltimore to look
for a barber before he looked for breakfast. Observation
in the station had, characteristically, produced decision.
Decision demanded action. None of the young fellows
in the crowd had been wearing sidewhiskers. At the other
end of Jones Falls bridge stood a barber pole. Johns Hopkins' newest recruit crossed the bridge and turned in
beside the pole. Presently he came out without side-
whiskers and went on down Charles Street to find breakfast.

He found none for quite a piece. No sandwich spots
defaced the red brick propriety, the vistas of white stone
steps and polished bell-pulls that were North Charles
Street in 1891. By the corner of Eager Street the hungry
newcomer asked a direction and followed it west to Cathedral and the Albion Hotel.

At half past nine, no longer hungry, riding a bob-tailed
Monument Street horsecar, Thomas Stephen Cullen,
M.B., Toronto, came to Broadway and his first sight of
Johns Hopkins. Set among green lawns, bayed, domed,
many-windowed, the big new hospital that was to be "like
a home to me" for the next half-century and more, met a
boy's expectant eyes with solid assurance. Dr. Cullen
went in at the front door and asked for Dr. Kelly.

Dr. Kelly had gone to Washington for the day. Dr. Kelly's assistant had gone to Washington for the day. Dr. Osler had gone to Washington for the day. Tom Cullen left his valise with Johns Hopkins' doorman and went to Washington for the day:

Nothing I could do. Nobody I could talk to. No use sitting around till night waiting for them all to come back, and I'd never seen Washington.

In the train to Washington somebody called "Tom!" It was Lew Barker. Lew was going to Washington for the day too. He wanted to know where Tom was going to stay in Baltimore. Tom didn't know. "Meet me at the hospital when we get back tonight," Lew said, "I'll take you to the Gills'." That night when they all got back from Washington the promise was fulfilled. Tom Cullen was taken to the Gills'.

Though the new hospital had not then been open two years, the Gills' was already an annex. All the boarders were either associated with, or doing postgraduate work at Hopkins and all were friends. The Gills, as memory recalls them, were wonderful people. They treated their boarders like family and the meals they served were notable. No more than five or six ever lived in the house, but there were always more at dinner, and still more in the evening around the piano in Mrs. Gill's parlour, or sitting late in the side garden when the nights were hot.

The new boarder of 1891 can see it all still, and best of all Mrs. Gill, a large woman with any amount of horse sense. She ran things, while her sister, Mrs. Kemp, saw to the cooking. Mr. Gill was a messenger for Old Town National Bank. He looked after odds and ends around the place, but Mrs. Gill ran things and her horse sense never failed her, even when the other Canadian boarder fell off the wagon.

79

The other Canadian boarder had come down earlier that year to do postgraduate work with Dr. Osler. He was a medical school professor from Halifax, sixty-five, bald as a bat, and a great favourite with the younger men, for he was a witty, lovable fellow. When the word went around that he was off the wagon all the Gills' other boarders would turn out and go the rounds of the saloons until they found him. Then they would bring him home to East Fayette Street and Mrs. Gill would meet the situation with horse sense and black coffee. She was as fond of him as any of the boys were. Nobody could help being fond of him. He was a fine character wherever you found him. Tom Cullen was proud of the other Canadian boarder.

From first to last there were always characters at the Gills'. When Max Broedel landed from Germany in '94 with his music and his curls and his stiff black hat, Tom Cullen brought him straight to the Gills'. Max settled in and took over the musical evenings and stayed year after year, until he married. Max, being there, brought his two associates in medical art and they in turn settled in. The two, Hermann Becker, and August Horn, stayed on, until at last Mrs. Gill's horse sense told her it was time to quit. Her final stand was against the possibility of being invaded through partition walls by neighbours' bed bugs. With high-class determination Mrs. Gill ignored both the possibility and the bedbugs a good deal longer than the roomers were able to. It was Becker who broke her down at last. He stabbed eleven invaders with specimen pins in one night and left them all fixed to his mattress next morning.

The end came soon after. The Gills gave up and moved away, and 1640 East Fayette adjusted itself to its environment. In the fullness of time, slum clearance took it. But that low-class conclusion was still nearly fifty years away when, on young Dr. Barker's recommendation, young Dr. Cullen was added to the fortunate company of those who, working at Hopkins, boarded at the Gills'.

The new boarder started work without loss of time. He had come to work, arriving more than three months before his internship was due to begin, stretching his small means to cover the cost. He came convinced that the chance to study pathology under Welch was worth any effort. He found that it was. Those months in Dr. Welch's laboratory were to make young Tom Cullen a pathologist.

Among the world's rare epochs of beneficent discovery the latter part of the nineteenth century has its place. It has been rated by historians as an equal of that which opened with the discovery of the law of gravity. The rating is based on its revelations of the part played by germ life in nature. Pathology was the key to them; pathology as redefined after Pasteur: "The application of the exact methods of chemical and physical research to the elucidation of the complex problems of disease."

This laborious approach to the art of healing was not well regarded by many of the epoch's senior healers. The search for clues to disease in the tissues and excreta of its victims, using the techniques and submitting to the disciplines of the science laboratory, attracted only eager and questioning minds. The explorers opened new worlds and, outside their ranks, the openings were widely ignored. Among the established and respectable, revelation had a long time-lag.

In Europe when the beneficent epoch reached the 'nineties its prophet, Louis Pasteur, and its crusader, Joseph Lister, were still patiently demonstrating the obvious to the unseeing. Twenty-five years before, Semmelweis, its first martyr, had died heartbroken in a Vienna asylum, his discoveries discounted even by Virchow as speculative. Virchow himself, though his *Cellularpathologie* had supplied the germ-theorists with a solid

81

basis of doctrine, was still struggling to get the doctrine applied to Berlin's sewage. Von Recklinghausen, who had identified the typhoid bacillus early in the 'seventies, had yet to see his discovery used in the practical business of preventing typhoid.

Moreover, some of the germ theorists were going too far. There was, for example, a mad French doctor named Beauperthuy, who, in 1891, published an idea he shared with an equally mad Cuban doctor named Carlos Finlay that yellow fever was a microbe infection carried by mosquitos. Accepted theories of the genesis of the disease he ridiculed in print as "rubbish." This antagonized saner members of his profession. They all knew noxious marsh gases produced yellow fever, just as miasma produced malaria.

Koch, the German, had better luck with an idea about cholera. Appointment to an official commission of inquiry gave him, in 1886, the chance to publish in its report his conclusion that human cholera was caused by the comma bacillus. Besides being official, the report came a sufficient length of years after Pasteur's practical demonstrations that bacilli and chicken cholera were not unconnected. Koch escaped denunciation.

In the pathological institutes of European universities, revelations of the part played in nature by germ life were quietly accumulating. Working with the solid culture media Koch had developed, Klebs and Eberth, Cohnheim, Ludwig, and their fellow-scientists of the new pathology, were amassing and systematizing that factual knowledge of micro-organisms which was to revolutionize the treatment as well as the conception of disease. But in all North America, when the last decade of the nineteenth century began, there was only one pathological research laboratory adequately equipped and organized; the one lately established at Johns Hopkins in Baltimore under the direction of Dr. William Henry Welch.

Among American doctors the new pathology had made its converts, as the fame of German pathological discoveries had spread, by word of mouth. Young men eager to learn were being drawn to Germany from the medical schools of the western world and returning on fire to share and to apply what they had learned.

A Canadian of their number, Dr. John Caven, had come home from working with Von Recklinghausen at Strasbourg and been appointed professor of pathology at Toronto in Tom Cullen's graduating year. "A born teacher and bubbling over with pathology" the youthful professor infected his students with his own enthusiasm. On one at least the effect was lasting. After nearly sixty years, he was to write with undimmed gratitude that he owed to Jack Caven his first clear conception of what pathology could mean to medicine. "I don't suppose I should ever have taken to pathology as I did except for Jack Caven."

Young Dr. Cullen entered the pathological laboratory at Hopkins prepared for any discovery. He looked it. Photographs of the period show a dark-haired youth with a square brow, a square jaw, a prow of a nose, a wide determined mouth, eyes disconcertingly interested and an air of eager confidence that might, at first glance, be mistaken for cockiness.

Some such mistake may account for the marked lack of enthusiasm with which the newcomer was welcomed by Professor Welch's associate, Dr. William T. Councilman. That distinguished pathologist set his stuttering and caustic tongue to the task of deflation, and pursued it with a persistence which, the victim cheerfully acknowledges, did good.

The first check was over an angiomatous tumor, one of a barrel of specimens in the laboratory. It had come in from Dr. Kelly's clinic and Dr. Kelly's prospective intern followed it with Dr. Kelly's request that he, Cullen, be permitted to section, stain and study it. The answer was no: "C-c-c-cullen, you are not s-s-s-s-sufficiently t-t-t-trained."

Taking this rebuff with unbowed head, the confident apprentice was presently allowed to report an autopsy, writing the findings to Dr. Councilman's dictation. The finished report brought new scorn on the reporter:

"C-c-c-cullen, g-g-g-get a c-c-c-copybook and l-l-l-learn to write." Thus for some days, with indifferent success, the senior laboured to instil diffidence. The end of the schooling came suddenly. Cullen again reporting, Dr. Councilman was again performing an autopsy. He turned from consideration of an abnormal liver to question his junior:

"Wh-wh-what's this, Cullen?"

The answer was prompt as ever. "Miliary tuberculosis of the liver," Cullen said.

"T-t-t-tisn't." Dr. Councilman replied. The autopsy continued. In due course the liver was frozen, sectioned, examined under the microscope. The examination revealed an unusual liver condition; miliary tuberculosis. Dr. Councilman put aside the frozen section. "B-b-boys," he said, "L-l-l-let's go over to the ch-ch-church." They went.

"The church" was Hanselman's saloon, across the road from the laboratory. There Hopkins men gathered to eat sandwiches, drink beer and pop, talk shop. No further mention was made of miliary tuberculosis of the liver, but Tom Cullen counted, from that day's visit to the church, his acceptance as a fellow-enquirer by William T. Councilman.

He was fortunate in that, as in the timing of his start in the Pathological. Coming later, he would have missed Councilman altogether. Dr. Welch's brilliant associate left Hopkins early in 1892 to begin his great work as pro-

Dr. Lesslie Matthew Sweetnam

Dr. Henry Mills Hurd

. . . was a Lister man.
—page 66

Dr. Lesslie Matthew Sweetnam, "my preceptor"

"Concerning Maryland beaten biscuits . . ."
—page 89

Dr. Henry Mills Hurd, first Superintendent of Johns Hopkins Hospital fessor of pathology at Harvard Medical School. In those last months of '91, Dr. Welch and he were both working at high pressure, with George H. F. Nuttall and Simon Flexner to complete their team. From the moment of his acceptance by Dr. Councilman the eager novice was given the run of the laboratory and an increasing share of its work:

It was the chance of a lifetime. From September to January, I literally soaked in pathology from that wonderful group of scientists. . . . Life reminds me of swinging on the rings in a gymnasium. You can be the finest athlete in the world but if the ring isn't there when you reach for it, you're out of luck. It wasn't anything to my credit that the ring was there for me.

2

THE ROOM NEXT THE BULGE

SOUTH OF THE BROADWAY ENTRANCE to Johns Hopkins Hospital the car slowed. Tom Cullen said to wait a minute and nodded his head sideways towards an upper window in the soot-grimed main building:

I was in that room next the bulge, and there was a fellow along the corridor who used to drop his boots outside his door every night at ten and come pattering past to his bath every morning at seven and be waiting outside the dining-room doors for them to open at seven-thirty. That was Dr. Osler. Let's go, Jimmy . . .

In the new year of '92 Tom Cullen left the Gills' and the Pathological to begin his internship in gynecology at Johns Hopkins. He left both with regret. The Gills had been good to him. At the Pathological Dr. Welch and George Nuttall were at work, with all the laboratory, verifying findings that were to prove of first importance to pathologists.

The discovery of the gas bacillus — *B. welchii* — was William H. Welch's last and most important major research. He had begun it in October of 1891, only a few weeks after Tom Cullen entered the Pathological. An autopsy on a patient who had died in the Hopkins and whose blood vessels had swelled after death, revealed a rare condition. Punctured, the swollen vessels emitted a gas which would light with a match and burn with a pale blue flame. With Nuttall as his assistant Dr. Welch undertook research into the cause of the flame. Their joint effort discovered the gas-producing bacillus, identified it with a bacillus, until then unidentified, present in certain forms of gangrene, peritonitis and kidney and womb infection, and located its normal habitat as the intestinal tract and the soil. Their success resolved the mystery of a series of problem cases reaching back beyond medical history into myth and magic, and opened a new chapter in medicine: pneumatopathology.

The groundwork had been done at the Pathological under the excited nose of young Tom Cullen, before he had been there three months. It was hard to leave a place where such things were happening. On the other hand his internship would be under Kelly. He would be working in the new B operating room. He would see Dr. Kelly operating every day, and nearly all the laboratory men were in residence. He could keep track of what they were doing at the Pathological. Interested, as always, in what was coming next, Dr. Kelly's new junior intern moved his books and belongings from the Gills' to the hospital residence, settled in the room next the bulge and presently found himself at home.

It did not take long. Since Hopkins had no medical school, its clinical and laboratory staffs were recruited from all over. An Englishman, a Hollander, two Canadians, not counting the punctual fellow along the corridor, and Americans trained in medical schools of the east, south and middle-west made up the residence roll. All were young, all were keen, all were where they wanted to be, doing what they most wanted to do. Friendliness was in the air, and something more than friendliness. Tom Cullen remembers with delight the arguments that started at dawn between two eager scientists in nightshirts, went on all day as opportunity occurred in the intervals of duty and wound up at the dinner table, with reckless disregard of cost, in a wholesale burst of forbidden "shop" and forfeits all around:

Every time we talked shop in the dining room we had to pay a fine of five cents. It went into a fund for jams and pickles and we always had plenty of jams and pickles. You couldn't help talking shop at Johnny Hopkins in those days.

"In those days," as William H. Welch was to write long after they were gone, "everything was small and everyone was interested in what was going on. . . . Those were very happy days." Henry Mills Hurd, the first superintendent of the new hospital, has described their effect on his resident staff men. "They shared," he said, "a general spirit of research . . . a fine esprit de corps; clinicians and laboratory men living together under circumstances of delightful intimacy, each one interested in all that was going on. . . . The tone of Dr. Welch's laboratory set the tone of the whole hospital."

To his staff, the young men whose working lives were ordered by his rule, it might have seemed more accurate to say that the tone of the whole hospital was set by Dr. Hurd. Tall, thin, severely side-whiskered, looking as though born in a prince albert coat, Henry M. Hurd by his very appearance gave respectability to innovation. The orthodox exterior and deceptive mildness masked a lot of revolutionary ideas on hospital management and a deathless determination.

Dr. Hurd had come to Hopkins from Michigan where, as head of the state hospital for the insane at Pontiac, he had made his name as an administrator. He had determined that the new hospital should have a sound progressive direction, a solid scientific reputation and an efficient staff. He set about it, Tom Cullen remembers how, and if he guessed that his residents and interns knew him irreverently and affectionately as "Uncle Hank," he never gave them cause to suspect it:

Concerning Maryland beaten biscuits, it is a well-known fact that the more they are hammered in the making the better they turn out. Dr. Hurd applied that principle to good purpose in his training of men. . . . I have always felt that Hurd should have been included in Sargent's portrait group of the "big four." It should have been five. In his life Dr. Hurd did as much for Johns Hopkins as any of the four and it might easily be shown that he did as much for them as he did for Hopkins.

Welch and Osler and Halsted and Kelly would never have had the reputations they made, except for Hurd. He founded the Hopkins Hospital Bulletin before there was a medical school and he started the Hopkins Reports and edited both for years. The four others recognized in theory that they should record what they were doing and finding out; but it was Hurd who made them do it. He kept after them all the time to write up their experimental work and their interesting cases, their clinical observations and laboratory findings, for the Bulletin first and then for the Reports; never let them rest until they had done it.

And that more than anything else, as they all recognized, was what made Hopkins' name, and theirs. Especially in Europe. Hopkins Bulletins were known in the European clinics before the hospital had been going three years. So, thanks to Hurd, were the names of the big four. Like most men who do things, they got their satisfaction in doing them. It was Hurd who made them write and made them famous.

He drummed the importance of writing into us young fellows, too, in a way we couldn't forget. We all owe any reputation our writings have earned for us to Dr. Hurd.

The young fellows in residence when Tom Cullen came under Henry Hurd's beneficent rule included his seniors in Dr. Kelly's department; Hunter Robb who had come from Philadelphia with Kelly, A. L. Stavely, gynecological resident that year, and W. W. Russell; "a fine fellow who died too young." Lewellys Barker and William Thayer were the medical interns; both serving under Osler and each, in due time, to succeed to Osler's chair of medicine in the Medical School that was still a dream:

Billy Thayer was brilliant, lovable and always broke. Lew had one of the best minds I have ever known. Even as a boy at Toronto Medical School he could absorb information like a sponge, discard the non-essential and organize and present the rest in absolutely masterly fashion. There were others I was fond of; John Hewetson, Parker, August Hoch. And of course there was Frank R. Smith. He was new, too, that year. Dr. Osler had just appointed him his assistant-resident.

Of the laboratory men Tommy Cullen knew already, W. T. Councilman was in residence only briefly. Then he left for Boston. Simon Flexner, who had not been two years at the Pathological but was already on his way to becoming Dr. Welch's chief associate, shared the newcomer's room, and George Nuttall his affection. Nuttall, who came from the middle west, was to have the most unlikely fortune of them all. He was to marry a German countess and become an editor of German scientific journals, to leave Germany and become England's foremost authority on parasitology and a Fellow of the Royal Society and to live his life out with his countess at Cambridge, as Quick Professor of Biology:

George had studied in Europe before he came to the Pathological. He knew a great deal about German laboratory methods and was a first rate man in research. He was very good to me when I was beginning. So was Lotsy, our Hollander; John Paul Lotsy. He had come to the Pathological to work on plant pathology. It was a new idea then that plants could sicken and die of bacterial infection just as animals could, but John Paul had it and was working on it under Welch.

John Paul Lotsy became in time the foremost plant pathologist in Holland, but he was just a young fellow then like the rest of them; a likeable young fellow with a Dutch accent and an idea that possessed him. Another man with an idea, Franklin P. Mall, was to come later from Chicago. He had been the Pathological's first Fellow, had gone west to make a name for himself as Professor of Anatomy at the University of Chicago. When the decision to start the medical school was made he returned to Hopkins to organize the new department of anatomy for Dr. Welch and moved into residence with the staff men:

The first day I found him there we were talking for a long time before I knew he was a professor. We got onto laboratory work, I remember, and he gave me a lot of good tips. You could always get Mall started on laboratory work at any hour of the day and if he hadn't finished by bedtime he would start again next morning. I would go into his room or he would come into ours. Flexner would still be in bed and Mall would lean over the foot and they would talk pathology and anatomy until we nearly missed breakfast.

In the evenings after six o'clock supper most of us got into the habit of going to Frank Smith's room to hear Frank read. He had a beautiful reading voice. It had been trained at a cathedral school in England where Frank was a scholar. He had gone to Cambridge too and taken a classical course there.

Frank was older than the rest of us. He must have been thirty-three or four. His family in England had wanted him to be a clergyman but he had been against it and had come to America instead; to Grand Forks, North Dakota. He stayed there for a while keeping books and then decided to study medicine. He got his degree at the University of Maryland medical school in '91 and Dr. Osler picked him for an assistant resident in medicine. In no time he was a figure in all our lives. We all gravitated to Frank's room when we were free for an hour, as we were after supper.

They were free after supper. So they gathered in Frank Smith's room in the gas-lit winter evening and Frank opened the book — "Tom Sawyer" and "Huckleberry Finn" are the two Tom Cullen remembers best — and began, in his fine English voice, reading the hilarious classics of a new world to the young men embarked on one of its great adventures. After an hour the reader put the book away and they separated to make rounds, or to work a while longer in the laboratory, or to prepare case histories for tomorrow.

William Osler, who knew how to pick men, had made no mistake in choosing his assistant resident. Frank R. Smith, as Tom Cullen remembers, was a friend to all the young fellows. When they came to him for advice they got the best that a gentleman and a scholar with a medical training and a sense of humour could give; and it was very good. Dr. Osler himself found his assistant resident's mastery of English both a joy and a resource, and at least one edition, the first, of Osler's "Principles and Practice of Medicine" was edited by Smith. Following so good an example, Hopkins staff men, senior as well as junior, soon formed the habit of bringing their monographs and books to him before publication and asking him to go over the English:

Frank had a phenomenal command of English. I learned very early to recognize it and, for forty-five years, everything I wrote and published went to him for correction in manuscript. It was remarkable how, by a slight change here and a little alteration there, he could transform a clumsy paper into a respectable one. But his greatest gift was character. In all my life I have never known a man more generous and honourable.

Frank Smith's chief, the fellow along the corridor, did not so quickly command a fellow-Canadian's affection. That mixture of earnestness and wayward impulse, of compassion and impish humour, of boundless enthusiasm for medicine and open skepticism concerning its specific powers had baffled many of Tom Cullen's elders. Osler, the artist, working from choice in the uncertainties of the human spirit, playing his wit on its absurdities and finding his reward in its deep unpredictable responses was too complex a mind to meet direct approaches. Tom Cullen's youth knew no others:

I didn't know Osler well for a long time. The fellows in his service, Lew Barker and Billy Thayer and August Hoch and Frank Smith were devoted to him. My chief, Dr. Kelly, who was closer to him than anyone at Hopkins, had the greatest affection for him. He was always pleasant to us who were juniors in other services, and that was all for quite a while.

Osler was at his best in personal relationships. He had the greatest charm, but he had to feel some sort of temperamental sympathy before he could release it, and his sense of humour was apt to interrupt. I know one Baltimorean who never forgave him a trick he played on her when I was a resident. She was a nurse in training at the time; a probationer taking her duties very hard. Dr. Osler came into her ward one evening just as she finished preparing the evening medicines. He eyed the tray with the glasses and pills set out and ticketed, an impulse hit him and he picked them all up and poured the doses into each other. For years after she gave up nursing and married me that probationer could not hear of Dr. Osler without feeling indignant all over again.

Teasing was incurable in Osler. All his life it got him into scrapes in all sorts of places with all sorts of people. The last one I heard of was in Oxford with the Archbishop of Canterbury. It would have made him more enemies than it did, except that it was never deliberate and he was always surprised and sorry when it offended. If he discovered that a trick or a joke of his had hurt anyone, especially if it had hurt someone defenceless, he would regret it sincerely, but he could never resist the impulse when it took him again.

93

There was a little nurse I remember, who came new to the hospital and had never seen Dr. Osler until she met him in a ward one morning. She was carrying a bowl of broth with a napkin over it and Dr. Osler was with a group of physicians and the usual retinue of nurse and residents and interns. When they met the impulse took him and he stopped, put his finger on the napkin and pushed it down into the broth. Then he got a surprise. The little nurse turned on him, half-crying.

"I don't know who you are," she said, "but I think you're the meanest man I ever saw."

Osler didn't say anything. What could he say? But shortly after he went home that day Mrs. Osler came to the hospital to find the nurse and apologize for her husband. I am perfectly certain that, until the girl flared up, it had never occurred to him that he was joking at the expense of someone who had no defence. It was a blind spot, and those who were fond of him allowed for it.

Kelly could handle Osler in a teasing mood as no one else could; smile affectionately when Dr. Osler started to joke at his expense, and reach over and chuck him under the chin. The joke would end right there. The idea that he could be funny too always surprised Osler; I doubt whether he would have taken it as kindly from anyone but Kelly. There was a remarkable understanding between those two. Each seemed to know as much of the other's thoughts as of his own. I can remember as though it were yesterday one afternoon when I was bicycling down Broadway with Dr. Kelly, and he suddenly started to talk about Dr. Osler.

"Do you know what Osler wants, Tom?" he said. "He wants to go to England and he wants to be knighted. How would you like to come to England with me and practise in Harley Street?"

That was in '94, twelve years before Osler went to England, almost twenty before he got his title. I am sure Osler had not spoken of such a wish then. I doubt if he knew he had it. But Kelly knew; it was one of his intuitions; and he was considering the possibility of pulling up stakes in mid-career and going to England too, if Osler wanted to practise there. That is how deep the friendship went with him.

As I grew older, I came to appreciate the reason for it. Beneath the jokes there was Osler's humanity, a loyalty to his friends that never failed, a delightful personality and, in his professional relationships, absolute honesty and generosity. I have a note from him that I have kept for forty years. It will give you the picture.

Written in 1905, when William Osler was fifty-six and at the height of his Hopkins fame, the note went to a hospital staff man twenty years his junior who, after consultation, had deliberately disregarded his advice on the treatment of a patient:

The patient was very ill and weak when she came to us. Dr. Osler had examined her with me and advised delaying the operation until she was stronger. I felt it should be done before she grew sicker and went ahead with it on my own responsibility. Next morning, when Dr. Osler came in to see her, the patient herself told him the operation was over and she was feeling much better. Osler might easily have been annoyed at having his advice ignored; he was the medical chief as well as the senior consultant. But he wasn't. Like the rest of us, he had plenty of foibles but none of them counted where the good of a patient was concerned. Personal feelings and professional dignity didn't exist for him then. He simply forgot them, as you can see.

The note Tom Cullen kept for forty years reads:
"Dear Cullen: It is very satisfactory to have the thing over. I felt perhaps there was a little risk in her debilitated condition and thought it would be just as well to postpone for the sake of the poor daughter. Of course if there were any signs of obstruction the operation was imperative. She is evidently doing very well.

"Sincerely yours,
"Wm. Osler."

95

3

IN B OPERATING SUITE

REGRETS FOR THE PATHOLOGICAL lingered for a while in
B operating room. Howard Kelly had designed the new
gynecological operating suite to meet his own requirements and equipped it largely at his own expense. B was
a surgeon's dream realized; so thoroughly that thirty-five
years later it was still good. Dr. Kelly's new junior intern
found it ideal to work in; but he did not like his work
so well.

Giving the anaesthetic was a junior intern's operating-
room task in those less specialized days and, for four
months in B, young Dr. Cullen did nothing else:

It got on my nerves considerably. They used a lot of
chloroform then and chloroform is tricky. I began to have
a dream every little while. It was always the same dream;
that I had gone to sleep giving the anaesthetic and my
patient had died. I would waken with a start and be
greatly relieved to find myself in bed in the residence.
Fortunately I didn't lose any patients on the table while
I was on anaesthetics, but it was close more than once.
Three times in ten days I have had to turn a patient up
by the heels and now and then I had to carry one along
for three-quarters of an hour with no wrist pulse. Had I
told Dr. Kelly the condition it would only have worried
him; he was in such a predicament each time that he
could not have stopped. But it got on my nerves. I was
only twenty-three.

96

Surgery was making magnificent gains in the 'nineties but it was still dependent on speed and stamina — the surgeon's speed and the patient's stamina — to a degree unthinkable now. There was no plasma, no blood transfusion or other supporting measure to tide over a bad spot. It was surgery without gloves, moreover, and without the guidance of X-ray. An operator went in barehanded to try to find what he thought was wrong where he thought it likely to be.

To those early gloveless days at Hopkins can be traced the wholesale manner of scrubbing up for an operation that distinguishes Dr. Thomas Cullen's preparation from that of surgeons less ruggedly trained, and tries those among them with spirits easily dampened.

"Scrub up with Tom Cullen?" one such has been heard to protest. "I'd sooner scrub up with a seal!"

When Hopkins opened its new hospital, the advantages of hand-scrubbing were generally allowed though not, perhaps, as exhaustively pursued in all operating rooms as in Halsted's and Kelly's. But Hopkins surgical heads had gone beyond handscrubbing and were sacrificing professional dignity to cleanliness. In their jurisdictions surgeons were required to wear white cotton trousers and shirts under their sterile gowns, and white cotton caps on their heads. In no other hospital had the fad for asepsis been carried so far past propriety. Traditionalists who held the frock coat with sleeves turned back to be the dignified working costume for a senior surgeon were affronted. Even the liberal-minded felt that innovation could be overdone. Hopkins men defended the revolutionary cottons as washable and sanitary, but found occasional complications.

One, for example, on a busy morning when Dr. Kelly got word that a patient on whom he had been asked to operate had been admitted. Between operations he made time to go across from B to the private ward to see the new patient and get some necessary information. Being hurried, he stopped neither to change his suit nor to ask the ward nurse to introduce him, but went directly to the patient's room. He spent a few minutes with her, found her unusually reticent, and left for B and the next operation. Behind him, an indignant lady reached for her bell.

"A nice kind of hospital this is!" she complained to the nurse who answered her summons. "A fine sort of institution! The cook has just been in and asked me some very impertinent questions!"

Youth was another embarrassment. Of the four heads of departments at Johns Hopkins when the new hospital opened in '89, the eldest, Osler, was forty. Welch was thirty-nine. Halsted, in charge of surgery, was thirty-seven and Kelly, the gynecologist-in-chief, was thirty-one and did not look it. In an era when a set of grey whiskers was more essential to success in medicine than a knowledge of the germ theory of disease, the youth of the Hopkins chiefs was a serious initial handicap. It was accentuated by the youth of their staff and by Howard Kelly's continuing failure to look his age. The last made difficulties for Dr. Thomas Cullen when he took up his duties on the wards:

As a junior intern, it was my duty to take histories in the wards and to see patients in the dispensary, as well as to assist in the operating room. I remember particularly well one old lady who came in for an operation. Dr. Kelly was to operate and I was getting her history when he came in, so I introduced them. Dr. Kelly had shaved off his moustache that morning and certainly did not look like a senior surgeon in a great hospital. The old lady stared at him scornfully and then turned, with more scorn, on me.

"You can't fool me, young fellow," she said, "that boy's not Dr. Kelly."

It was another old lady, a relative of one of the hospital staff men, who decided I wasn't old enough for my job. I went over to the private ward to see her when she had settled in, talked for a while, came to the necessary inquiries and found she had her own ideas of how these things should be done.

I asked her a question and she said "I told the nurse that."

I asked a second question and she said "I told the nurse that."

I asked a third question and she said "I told the nurse that."

I asked a fourth question and she said "You are too young."

I explained that this was the third hospital I had been in and she sniffed loudly. "Hmm! You couldn't have stayed long in any of them," she said.

I laughed then and so did she, and we were friends.

Four months on anaesthetics, and Tom Cullen was released from his nightmare and nearing the goal of his desire. He was a surgical assistant now, free to watch Howard Kelly at work, to study his superb technical skill and to help in the application of his new operative procedures. Dr. Kelly at that time was only beginning to develop the technique for removal of myomatous tumors, gradually working out the best methods of doing what had never been done before: the excision of densely adherent pelvic structures. The work wakened in his junior intern an interest that was to endure and increase and to produce, among other things of value, the volume on uterine myomata in which, seventeen years later, Kelly and Cullen collaborated.

With his gynecological work, Dr. Kelly had begun to develop, in the early 'nineties, a new and original approach to the diagnosis and treatment of kidney and bladder diseases. Having discovered a technique for introducing a cystoscope into the bladder, he was able, by its means, to examine the interior for stone, for inflammation or for tumors and to clear up, bit by bit, the obscurity of bladder and kidney conditions that until then, had defied accurate diagnosis.

Many of the techniques Howard Kelly worked out and introduced are the routine of the diagnosticians and surgeons now. Some have been superseded by the X-ray and other more lately discovered helps to diagnosis and treatment. But the things young Tom Cullen watched his chief doing then had been never before attempted. The work in which he had begun to share was unravelling, one after another, problems of disease that had baffled physicians and surgeons down the centuries:

It was like watching a master detective trace from clue to clue a mystery that had seemed insoluble, and being on the spot helping him when he reached the solution. I have never known anything more fascinating in my life.

There was another fascination, too; the fascination an apprentice craftsman finds in the company and the talk of those most practised in his chosen mystery:

Although the medical school did not then exist, the benches in Dr. Kelly's operating room were invariably full. They were occupied not only by Baltimore physicians but by well-known men from all parts of the United States and Canada who had come to see Kelly's work. I have, as a matter of fact, met more of America's leading surgeons in old B Operating Room than in years of travelling around the country.

Those were great days to be a beginner in. We interns under Kelly had the privilege of meeting the top men in our profession right on our own home ground and of hearing them discuss on the spot the new things being attempted and accomplished in front of their eyes and ours. I marvel, looking back, to think what a large share of American progress in medicine came out of old B-suite at the Hopkins while I was there in Kelly's service.

[*Photograph by* ANTHONY MURRAY

"It got on my nerves considerably . . ."
—page 96

Dr. T. S. Cullen, junior intern in Dr. Kelly's service, giving an anaesthetic; B operating room, Johns Hopkins Hospital, 1892

Remember, I began my internship at Hopkins in a different world. Though I had done four years in medicine and a post-graduate year in Toronto General, I had never seen an appendix operation when I came to Baltimore. As a matter of fact, I didn't see one there until I had been in residence nearly two years. I had got my first glimpse of what surgery might be watching Dr. Kelly operating for Dr. Sweetnam during my Toronto internship. But there was virtually no one but Kelly then who entered with any assurance into the human abdomen, and Kelly was supported by a magnificent self-confidence against the doubts of nearly all his seniors except Osler, and of many of his contemporaries.

At that time very many simple muscular tumors were considered inoperable and when a surgeon undertook to remove a womb it was with the greatest trepidation and only in cases where a stout rubber ligature could be temporarily tied around the cervix. When, as happened from time to time, this ligature slipped, the most alarming hemorrhage followed. The systematic controlling of the cardinal vessels to prevent bleeding was new procedure in my Hopkins internship and the bisection of the cervix came later still. Finally, the transverse severance of the cervix as a preliminary step in the operation in exceptionally difficult cases was worked out and, at present, a myomatous uterus that cannot be removed is almost unheard of.

Many American surgeons shared in the work of simplifying pelvic surgery and reducing its risks but I know of no other man either here or abroad who did, or has done, as much to the purpose as Howard Kelly. And in those early days the sureness and swiftness of his work was a revelation as it remained a constant delight to us who worked with him.

It was Howard Kelly's fame as an abdominal surgeon that brought the distinguished visitors to crowd the benches of his clinic. In most hospitals, abdominal operations were still rare and dreaded expedients to be attempted only in desperate cases. At Hopkins, in B operating room, they were being done increasingly and with increasing success. So the older surgeons came to watch Kelly and eager young men to count a chance of interning under him the chance of a lifetime. There, where new techniques were being tried and new operations developed day by day it was a matter of course that all should share in the work. From the first no man of ability was deprived, merely because he was a junior, of opportunity to apply it to the problems that presented themselves in Hopkins' gynecological clinic:

To take one example, we all had a part in working out methods of saving the ovaries wherever possible in operations involving them; and we found more ways of making it possible as our joint stock of knowledge and skill increased. Dr. Kelly never rejected an idea as unimportant because it was an intern's and he never failed, if it proved useful, to give his junior full credit for it. The jealousies you find in some clinics were always absent from Kelly's.

4

IMPROMPTU TO GÖTTINGEN

On March 19, 1893, a Johns Hopkins intern nearing the end of his service, mailed a letter home to Canada. Everything was going well, he had written. The Chief was pleased with his work and had promised him the residency in gynecology Billy Russell had decided not to take. It would start next fall and in the meantime he could scrape along all right. There was plenty to be done in the laboratory and plenty to learn. He owed the bank $4, but he wasn't worrying. George Nuttall and Simon Flexner were off for Europe next week. He had been down to the steamship office with them yesterday to see them buy their tickets. Some day he would want to know how it was done. Not yet, of course, but some day. He thought a man should see things for himself, watch the big pathologists over there at work in their own laboratories. Nuttall was going to Göttingen.

The young man finished his letter and put it in the mail box. After supper he went for a long walk with George Nuttall; along Broadway and over Preston Street under the gas lamps, talking:

Suddenly Nuttall said, "Tommy, why don't you come with us?" The next morning before breakfast I had seen Dr. Kelly. He had lent me $600 and given me six months' leave of absence and I had been down to the steamship office to buy my own ticket for Europe.

Five days later, bucking a March blizzard, the steamer Sparndam — 5000 tons, New York to Rotterdam — passed Sandy Hook outward bound with three wan but determined young scientists aboard.

It was April, all the tulips in Holland were in bloom and a welcome was waiting on the wharf when the three disembarked. The welcomer was John Paul Lotsy's brother who lived in Dordrecht. So, before they saw Rotterdam, they all went to Dordrecht to visit the Lotsys, travelling through a fairytale landscape. The youngest of the party found it:

. . . perfect, a tremendous checkerboard of fields of tulips and jonquils and hyacinths, each field a checker square and nearly every field a different colour.

Holland went on being perfect. The two older of the three travellers were ready for a junket before they settled to the summer's work. To Tom Cullen all was new delight; he could not do or see enough. Writing long after of that time he wrote as though no years had intervened: of the statue of Erasmus in Rotterdam, forever waiting, Bible in hand, to open its pages when it hears the clock strike ten in the old tower across the square; of looking down on roofs and chimneys from the deck of a boat on a Dutch canal; of Leyden with its students and book shops; of the fishing boats at Scheveningen and of the galleries of Amsterdam and the Hague.

George Nuttall, who knew and loved the Dutch masters, made it his business to instruct his companions in their beauties. He found an eager pupil and took him early to the Mauritshuis at the Hague to see the greatest of the great Rembrandts and the one most sure to move a young physician's heart; the master's grave and compassionate *School of Anatomy*. But Nuttall was no one-picture man. He delighted in any number of the old Dutchmen and was eager to share his delight. Together, he and Tom Cullen went the rounds of the galleries again and again

. . . until I could recognize the work of a given painter without seeing a catalogue or a signature. Those weeks in Holland were one of my most happy experiences.

They included one professional interlude; of larger importance than a novice then could guess; a visit to Dr. Treub's cancer clinic in Amsterdam. There the Hopkins trio not only saw the famous Dutch surgeon operate, but met him in his laboratory. There the youngest caught Treub's liking and established the beginning of a friendship that was to be renewed in succeeding visits and strengthened by a correspondence extending over years.

After Amsterdam the three parted, Simon Flexner went on to Prague to work under Chiari. Tommy Cullen went with George Nuttall to Göttingen where Johannes Orth had his laboratory. Between Amsterdam and Göttingen another decision was made; minor but characteristic and, in its effects, enduring; the decision to talk German and to start now. Fellow-travellers in the railway carriage were all German and George Nuttall was soon talking with them; enjoying what bore every visible sign of an interesting discussion. But the talk went wide of an unaccustomed ear and a too-strictly pathological vocabulary. Tom Cullen, as communicative a spirit as ever the Wesleyan itineracy produced, was out of it. He endured isolation for a hundred miles or two, but he was not happy:

There I sat like a bump on a log, saying nothing for hours. Finally I came to the decision that this would not do. I spoke a few words in German, then a few more, and then gradually entered the conversation.

With a carriage full of passengers all enthusiastically helping an enthusiastic beginner to talk German, the train came to Göttingen where Johannes Orth had his laboratory.

Johannes Orth was the great Virchow's chosen disciple, his *Lieblingschüler*. In his laboratory at the Pathological Institute of the University of Göttingen he was doing important and original work in pathology. So the 24-year-old Canadian, a beginner in pathology in a new American hospital still without a medical school, came on an overnight decision to study under Orth. No arrangement was made beforehand. There was no time, and no need in those fortunate days:

I took a letter from Kelly to Orth, and Orth put me to work in his laboratory. That's how it was done then. You chose the man you wanted to work under and went where he was and started to work. The only other man working under Orth at the time I was in Göttingen was Charlie Martin of Montreal, who was later Professor of Medicine and Dean of the Medical School at McGill. We spent a semester in Orth's laboratory together.

George Nuttall fell in love with his German countess — he married her in due time and never came back to Baltimore — so his fellow-voyager did not see a great deal of him that summer. But Professor Orth was good to the two young Canadians, talking of his work to them in his formal way, and of his master's, Virchow's, work, showing them how to work in the German fashion. Tom Cullen got good quarters cheap at Frau Doktor Hummel's, with a nice feather tick instead of sheets and blankets on his bed. The one shadow on those first weeks of eager discovery was cast by John Paul Lotsy back in Baltimore. The kindness of John Paul's family in Dordrecht had made a warm place in his friend's heart, but the warmth was cooled abruptly. A cable came collect to Göttingen for Dr. Thomas Cullen and collecting it cost more than half a week's board. Opened, it read: "What did you do with my specimens?" and was signed "Lotsy."

"And I never had his darned specimens!" Sixty years have not sufficed to calm remembrance in the victim of

Lotsy's cable. But at the time, even that shadow passed quickly. Tom Cullen, friendly as a child and twice as curious, was tasting the student life of Göttingen and liking it. There were Sunday picnics with the ladies on the Hainberg above the town. There were Sunday excursions by invitation, with Professor and Frau Geheimrat Orth in a carriage as far as ten miles. There were German conversations at Frau Doktor Hummel's in the evenings, and other more enchanted evenings, as spring turned to summer, sitting among friends under the lime trees in one of the beer gardens beyond the old ramparts, talking, listening to the singing, joining in the choruses. Belief that all things must work together for good for those who love pathology was easy in Göttingen in the happy year 1893.

Only here and there did things ominous of evil in the first German Reich strike a newcomer's eye. Prince Bismarck came to Göttingen where he had been a student sixty years before. The boy from Canada saw him at the railway station; old and sick, in disgrace with the "crazy ill-bred cub" his master, forgotten by the nation of underlings he had raised to dominance, but with his guard of arrogant cynicism unbroken. He took a Verein cap from the head of one of the students in the small crowd that watched him and demanded to be told why they had changed the badge since he wore it . . . In Göttingen too, early one Saturday morning Tom Cullen saw the *Mensur:*

We went out to where the fighting was to begin and sat around a table for a while, talking to several of the students. Someone called *Auf die Mensur!* and the students with us got up and started fighting other students, slashing at each other's faces with long curved swords. One of the men I had been talking to returned in ten minutes with many wounds, so many that it took 36 stitches to close them. The whole procedure was *Unsinn* — madness.

So the young pathologist from Johns Hopkins thought, and dismissed it from his mind. He had work to do in the laboratory. That was the best of Göttingen; the six long days a week of work in Johannes Orth's laboratory, doing what a disciple had come to do under the master of his choice. In the autopsy and routine laboratory work of the Pathological Institute the two graduate students assisted Professor Orth's two associates. They worked under the Herr Professor himself on the operative material from the neighbouring clinics. It was delivered fresh every morning in shining cans; a dozen to thirty of them like small milk cans. It came by train from nearby centres and by hand from the Göttingen hospitals and it was the task of the Institute's director and of the young men working under him to examine microscopically, analyze and report on it all:

I can see Professor Orth now, sitting on the back of a chair with his feet on the seat, watching while one of his associates dumped the contents of a can on a large tray in front of him. I can see him pointing a long finger at a specimen in the tray and asking one or other of us what it was. I remember the first time he asked me he pointed to a cone-shaped roll of laminated fat and I reached out to pick it up and examine it more closely. I can still hear him saying sternly *Hände weg* — hands off, don't touch it.

That was one of his rules; we must always learn all we could of a specimen from sight before touching it. It was his way of increasing and quickening his students' powers of perception, and it was effective. I pulled my hand back, I remember, and guessed, wrong as it turned out; the cone was a piece of thin omentum from a hernial sac. But my score was better before I left Göttingen. Orth was a great teacher.

It was under Orth in the Pathological Institute that a maturing Tom Cullen first consciously grasped the root fact from which his own greatness as a teacher was to grow:

You can't teach a man anything worth knowing. You can only show him what there is to learn.

Johannes Orth showed it in aloof and abstracted fashion. Only the professor of astronomy, who walked to a morning lecture with one foot in the gutter and arrived a little worried because he had developed a limp, was more famed in Göttingen for absentmindedness:

Orth would often go about his laboratory a whole week in deep contemplation oblivious to what was happening around him and only to be roused by a question or comment that linked with what was in his mind. But on Saturday afternoons he would return to earth and if there was an excursion planned, come up to one or other of us before he left the laboratory, put an arm across his shoulder and say with his shy delightful smile: "We are going to have a picnic tomorrow. Frau Orth and I should be happy to have you come with us."

It always meant a fine time, Tom Cullen remembers, for the young man who was asked. Years later he was to have his chance of repaying Johannes Orth's courtesy to youth in a coin as fine. The old man came to America, early in 1914, to be welcomed as the last of the great pioneers of pathology, the worthy successor to Rudolf Virchow's professorship at Berlin. In Baltimore, the guest of his senior Göttingen student, he was an insatiable inquirer into everything Johns Hopkins was doing in pathology. When Dr. Welch, his host and their fellows had shown him everything, he still wanted to see more. So Tom Cullen took his old teacher to Philadelphia, where the University of Pennsylvania had lately completed a new and lavish pathological laboratory. It was an excursion that promised as well as the picnics of long ago, but it came near to ending badly:

I had planned to go the rounds with Professor Orth in Philadelphia but I had been operating all night the night before and I could not keep awake. So I turned him over to the Philadelphia men, who were only too happy to show him everything they had, and went to the hotel and took a snooze. When I caught up with the party a couple of hours later I could see at once that something had gone wrong. Orth was in the middle of the new laboratory looking pretty glum. I fished to find out what was the matter, and soon I had it. The old man told me in German how he had worked and struggled to get the finest possible laboratory established in Berlin as a memorial to his master, Virchow, and how twelve years after Virchow's death it had only now been achieved and opened and named for him; "and here they have a laboratory finer and better equipped than anything we had dreamed of."

I saw that Orth was grieved less for his own sake than because he felt having his memorial surpassed in this way somehow belittled Virchow. So I said: "Haven't you forgotten one thing, Professor Orth?" He said: "What?" and I said: "The man. It is the man that makes the laboratory, not the laboratory the man." He cheered up at once and in no time was as happy as a clam and demanding to be shown all the Philadelphia laboratory's latest improvements. There is a right way of putting everything, I've found.

The summer of '93 was waning when young Dr. Cullen left Professor Orth's laboratory and the friendliness of Göttingen to continue his pathological journey. He went to Halle and to Dresden and to Leipzig, stopping in each to see what was being done in the laboratories and the men who were doing it. In Leipzig Professor Paul Zweifel had as his associates in the pathological laboratory Karl Menge and Bernhard Krönig, two young scientists with whom the observer from America found it easy to work and to play. They agreed, when he left for Vienna, to meet him in Paris before he went home.

It was vacation time in the University of Vienna medical school, but the professors whose work Tom Cullen wanted to study were daily in their clinics and laboratories and he had letters from Dr. Kelly:

The Hopkins had not been established four years, but it was remarkable how well its work was known already in the Viennese clinics. Dr. Kelly's letters opened all doors for me in the Allgemeine Krankenhaus; Chrobak, Schauta and Braun von Fernwald gave me every facility in their clinics and since there was room, with men away on holiday, I was invited to live in the hospital. I was there three weeks and in that time they had more than three hundred deliveries and twenty-four obstetrical operations. It was the most valuable kind of experience.

With money and time both running out, the guest resident left the great Viennese hospital for Paris, the Charité and his meeting with Menge and Krönig. The crowded weeks in Paris were almost as happy as those with Nuttall and Simon Flexner in Amsterdam. Tom Cullen, grappling with French as resolutely as he had attacked German, had rather less success. But his struggles were a never-failing source of laughter for his companions and himself, and he continued them on holiday excursions to Versailles and Fontainebleau and in evening explorations of quays and bookstalls, restaurants and theatres. Working hours he spent at the Charité, haunting the clinics of Segond and Pozzi to study their operative techniques. There his irrepressible interest made him another friend in Professor Pozzi. The great French gynecologist and the beginner from Hopkins surmounted the language barrier to establish an understanding which expressed itself, on the senior's side, in much kindness and a habit of addressing his junior in English as "young man." The habit, like the friendship, was to be lifelong:

The last time I was with Senator Pozzi was here in Baltimore shortly before he was killed. He stayed with me and saw what we were doing in surgery. He was as brilliant and delightful as ever, and we were still "young man" and "old man" to one another; the terms of affection we had first begun to use in the Charité when I was a boy.

Cherishing a microscope; the best he could buy for himself in Germany with the present Dr. Kelly had sent him for the purpose; Tom Cullen reached London on his way home. He was baffled there by something harder than French to understand; the stupidity of success. The very well-known English surgeon he had come to watch in action was agnostic about germs. Bacteriology, he said, was "all poppycock." He said it in his clinic, operating in a black Prince Albert coat, and getting down to business with no more preparation than unbuttoning and rolling back the cuffs.

It was 1893. The year before, Louis Pasteur had been honoured by the French Republic as the benefactor of his people and Sir Joseph Lister had come to Paris to offer, before the assembled scientists of Europe, the homage of British science to the old French bacteriologist. Tom Cullen in London was hearing one of the most brilliant of English surgeons — "and he *was* brilliant, technically" — telling his students and associates that bacteriology was all poppycock. Holding fast to his microscope, young Dr. Cullen took train for Liverpool and the steamship Paris, westward bound.

5

"TO SERVE WITHOUT COMPENSATION"

WHEN TOM CULLEN got back to Baltimore with his microscope in October of 1893 he was twenty-four years old, $800 in debt, had fifteen cents in his pocket and no job. The Hopkins residency he had been promised was not open. W. W. Russell who had planned to leave the hospital that summer had changed his mind and stayed on as resident:

It was perfectly square. Billy was senior to me and entitled to it and as it turned out it was the luckiest thing that could have happened. I went into the Pathological, was given charge of gynecological pathology and stayed there three years. I didn't get any pay to speak of but I got my board and room and laundry, and experience that was priceless.

It must have looked from outside as though I was in a backwater, but those three years made all the difference. I had a chance to study all the material from Dr. Kelly's clinic and I had Dr. Welch and Simon Flexner as my laboratory seniors. When I came back to surgery I knew my way around the human belly and could recognize things I found there. I remember, years after, Dr. Kelly saying to me that he would give fifty thousand dollars to have had my experience in pathology. I told him I owed him the money then, because he gave me the experience. It was perfectly true. The place was made for me at Kelly's request and I stayed there doing Kelly's work and it was the time of my life.

Let me give you the picture. If I had got the residency in '93 I would have been through in a year and away someplace, starting to practise, creditably I hope, as a surgeon, but I would never have had the chance to do the sort of work that came my way because of those laboratory years. And I doubt whether the pattern of interdependence between surgery and pathology would have been established as clearly; certainly it would not have been established as soon. We were first to do it, training men in gynecology at Hopkins, and it was worth doing. It has saved a lot of lives and prevented a lot of suffering and it helped to check the tendency for a surgeon to become a mere technician. Technical skill in surgery is an important thing but it is not the most important. Pathology teaches a man that, and makes him humble. That is one reason why it is so necessary to make men pathologists before you let them become surgeons.

In his backwater at the Pathological, doing the laboratory work for Dr. Kelly's clinic, young Dr. Cullen stayed gathering experience until the autumn of '96.

The great panic of '93 gathered and broke. The Sherman silver purchase act was repealed. The bottom fell out of prices. Western farmers and eastern manufacturers were ruined together. Trade paralysis and railway strikes tied up transportation from Cincinnati to San Francisco. Rioting spread. President Cleveland ordered Federal troops to Chicago to protect the mails. Demands for redemption in gold of gold certificates nearly bankrupted the Republic. Cleveland appealed to Wall Street for help, J. P. Morgan saved the treasury with a loan of sixty-five million gold dollars, the Democratic party split on it and Congressman William Jennings Bryan led the Silver Democrats in the revolt that elected McKinley President.

It was as interesting as a play to watch from Hopkins pathological laboratory when time permitted. But time did not always permit. The important affairs of life went

114

on inside the laboratory among sections and stains and slides, and they were urgent. What was bad was the way the play, spilling over into life, threatened the important affairs. Hopkins endowments had been invested by the founder in railroad shares. They melted and income waned.

Nevertheless life went on at the Pathological and important affairs kept their importance. Johns Hopkins Medical School registered its first freshman class in the fall of '93 and embarked, with William H. Welch in command, on its revolutionary career as "a place where medicine is not only taught but also studied."

There could not, in all cautious reasoning, have been a worse moment for launching such a venture. It had not thirty thousand a year assured income. It had set its entrance requirements so high that Osler told Welch they were both lucky to be in as professors for they would never have been accepted as students. It was starting in a time of national desperation, and in a place where desperation was deepest, Baltimore's prosperity having been built on trade and its wealth sunk in railways, both bankrupt now. There was no hope of early affluence or promise of swift returns to draw the eager and ambitious to the new medical school. There was only the chance to study medicine.

It proved to be enough. Baltimore, as Tom Cullen remembers it in the panic-ridden middle 'nineties, was "heaven to a young fellow starting medicine." As in heaven, poverty was unimportant. Himself, Dr. Cullen got two hundred dollars in all from Johns Hopkins for three years' work in charge of gynecological pathology. For two of the years he worked without pay or position, but late in '95 he achieved position. A vote of the Hopkins trustees appointed Dr. T. S. Cullen "instructor in gynecology to serve without compensation." More than a year later compensation was added moderately. Another vote of the Hopkins trustees authorized the payment of $200 to Dr. T. S. Cullen, instructor in gynecology; "salary for the academic year 1895-96."

Hopkins' first instructor in gynecology had one other source of professional income: an occasional fee from an outside surgeon for a report on operative material sent to the laboratory. The rule at the Pathological was that any fee for a laboratory examination and report should go to the man who did the work. The fees were welcome when they came but they did not come often enough to count on. Yet Tom Cullen never thought of leaving Hopkins or giving up pathology:

I had made up my mind what to do if I couldn't make ends meet; get a night job as a streetcar conductor. I was not going to quit Baltimore or the laboratory. The work was too interesting. When I began in '93 relatively little had been done in gynecological pathology anywhere. The field was unworked and we were among the first in it. There is nothing better than that. I know how a lumberman feels when he comes on a stand of first-growth timber, or a prospector when he hits the gold-bearing rock. But this was more like placer-mining. We panned everything, picked out the nuggets and added the general run to the records.

No life, Tom Cullen believes, could have been more exciting than his in the backwater. All the tissue from B operating room came to his small laboratory for examination and description and each piece held potential discovery:

Every now and then some rare picture would show under the microscope and we often found things that had never been noted before. Anything out of the usual was carefully studied and all the relevant literature read. If no similar case had been recorded, the complete history of this one would be written up, including the clinical data, the operation performed and the laboratory find-

116

ings, and the full report would be published in the Hopkins Hospital Bulletin.

Those early reports for the Bulletin were the beginning of many fruitful journeys to Washington and the Surgeon General's Library. There, if Hopkins' medical library could not supply his need, Hopkins' new gynecological pathologist went to find, in one of the world's greatest collections of medical works, the references and data he required. There he learned to delight in the tireless and detailed research that was to make his own published works definitive; the "three afternoons a week in the Surgeon General's Library" that was to become a recurring design in the fabric of his life.

In the Pathological young Dr. Cullen worked downstairs in a small room set apart for him. Upstairs, on the second floor back, Dr. Welch had his laboratory. There, in his chief's absence, Schutz the Pathological's *Diener* ruled. Schutz had been there from the beginning. No hands but his prepared material for Dr. Welch, and he laid down laboratory law for Dr. Welch's young assistants. Schutz was a privileged character; even with Dr. Welch he did things his own way in his own time; and he knew a great deal of pathology. It was good for any man to be on the right side of Schutz. He could give valuable pointers to one he approved and show him many useful things about the preparation of material and media.

It was the rule of the laboratory that every man but the chief and his senior associates must prepare the media for his own cultures. They were simple in those days; agar, gelatine, potato. But they took time to prepare, so they were precious. A pathologist of experience guarded his own supply like a jewel-hoard and collected all that the less experienced left unguarded. The disappearance of a fine mess of potato taught Tom Cullen early that, in the matter of media, there was no honour among scientists. He saw to the catch of his locker door and set up as a raider himself; bringing to the new field of effort the craft he had learned among his mother's mixed pickles. One way and another the gynecological laboratory locker was kept well stocked with agar, gelatine and sliced potato for Dr. Cullen's work.

It was increasingly fascinating work, done in the happiest of circumstances. The basic assumption of the Pathological being that every man there was there to study medicine, no fixed rules prescribed how any one must go about it. The atmosphere differed completely from that of the rigidly ordered German laboratories. There were no immovable working hours. There were no set subjects of investigation. There was no assurance that Dr. Welch would feel like lecturing when his students arrived at the time appointed for his lecture. It was quite as possible that, if the afternoon were pleasant and the Baltimore Orioles playing a home game, the Dean of the Medical School might suggest adjourning to the ball park, and lead the way, gathering associates and assistants into the party and leaving the laboratory deserted for the day.

But what was lacking in rule and discipline was more than made up in opportunity and the spirit of generous emulation, plus the certainty that a man with a problem worth weighing could find, on the second floor back, the mind prepared to weigh it. That, Tom Cullen believes, was Popsy Welch's special strength, the ability to humanize his science and to draw out the best in men, not by demanding it but by creating an atmosphere in which nothing but the best was good enough:

You could always go to Popsy for help when you needed it and he would encourage you by asking your opinion first on a subject that he knew infinitely more about himself. But you didn't go to Popsy until you had something worth bringing.

6

YOUNG FELLOW IN HEAVEN

EACH A SELF-PORTRAIT in script, two notes were mailed to Dr. Thomas S. Cullen in September of 1895. They acknowledged receipt of copies of his earliest collection of reprints; papers written for publication in the Johns Hopkins Hospital Reports during his first two years in charge of gynecological pathology:

"Dear Cullen:
"Very glad to have your long lost fasciculus today. 'Tis A.1. & reflects great credit on your industry. Broedel's work is fine. Next? Hurry, 'the night cometh etc.'
"Yours
"Wm. Osler."

"Dear Cullen:
"You are to be congratulated upon the excellent way in which you have written up and discussed these interesting cases. The drawings are works of art and make everything clear. You are taking the right way to build up a scientific reputation. . . .
"W. H. Welch."

Coming from the two senior professors in Johns Hopkins medical school to a laboratory junior working under another chief, the notes reveal more than the characters of the writers. Reading them, it is easy to understand why Baltimore was heaven then to a young fellow starting medicine.

It is as a commonwealth of discoverers that Tom Cullen remembers the Hopkins of those early years; a commonwealth in which the common good was knowledge. Each, in his search for new truth and new approaches to old truth, was helped by all and the achievement of one was the interest of everyone, from dean to bottle-washer. Early volumes of Hospital Reports and Bulletins record in part the achievement of those years. From 1894 on, T. S. Cullen's share in it grew steadily. Behind forbidding titles in old indexes the excitement of discovery waits to be released by memory. Take four of the more forbidding with his name attached:

A Rapid Method of Making Permanent Specimens from Frozen Sections by the use of Formalin. — Johns Hopkins Hospital Bulletin Vol. VI.

Hardening tissue for examination was a slow business when Tom Cullen came to the Pathological. Muller's fluid or alcohol was the first bath. Thereafter, the tissue to be examined had to be immersed for fixed periods in alcohols of varying strength and in celloidin, before it could be blocked, sectioned, stained and mounted for microscopic examination. The process could not be hurried and might take days. Meantime the patient, on whom one operation had been done to obtain the specimen, had to endure with any fortitude available the suspense of waiting to be told whether another was needed. If the pathological report, when it came at last, indicated more surgery there must be another anaesthetic, a second operative shock and a convalescence made more precarious by the uncertainty.

If tissue could only be hardened quickly for immediate examination in cases of suspected cancer, for example, surgical treatment of the majority of them could be completed in one operation, more than half the suspense and fear of surgery could be lifted from the patient and the chance of recovery would be that much better. These things being recognized, the hunt for a quick and practic-

able method of hardening tissue was on in every pathological laboratory. It was Tom Cullen's fortune to find
one in his second year at Hopkins' Pathological, and to be
the first in America to publish his find:

I tested the formalin method I had worked out on
every sort of tissue and in every way I could think of.
Then I went upstairs, showed one of my sections to Dr.
Welch, and told him how I had hardened it and how long
it had taken me. He looked at it and listened. Then he
handed me a piece of some tissue that Schutz was about
to prepare for him.

"Take this and prepare it your way," he said. "If you
make me a satisfactory specimen I will be convinced."

I took the tissue and made a specimen and brought it
back. Popsy looked at it, looked at his watch and said
"Publish it." So I did. I wrote up the method and took
my paper to Dr. Hurd the same night, but it was nearly
too late. Dr. Hurd said he was sorry but the last of the
copy for the next issue of the Bulletin had gone to the
printer and mine would have to wait a month.

I was going away on that, but he called me back and
asked how much space I would need to describe my hardening method. I said half a page and he said to go ahead
and write it then.

"It's written," I said, and gave it to him and it was in
print in the Bulletin two days later.

Naturally, I was happy. There was all the fun of a
race in publishing your discoveries in those days. So many
things were on the verge of discovery, so much original
work was being done and so many ideas were in the air
that you had to get into print fast or somebody would get
there before you. Yet, for your own credit and the credit
of your school and your chief, you dared not go into print
with a discovery until you had checked the accuracy of
your findings in every possible way. You held your breath,
checking and rechecking, and when you were as sure as
you could be you published as quickly as you could.

It was a great thing for a young fellow, to gain recognition by his work and to be first in a race where all
started even, but beyond that was the chance that your

discovery might help another man to his. My method of making permanent specimens, for instance; it was no time at all after I published before other men had improved on it; worked out methods of doing the same thing faster and more effectively and, just as I had used earlier findings in my work, they used mine in theirs.

It is the way with all scientific discovery and half the fun of it; watching what other men build on your beginnings, or making other men's beginnings serve your different ends.

Post-operative Septic Peritonitis — Johns Hopkins Hospital Reports. Vol. IV, 1895.

In its issue of February 1, 1896, the British Medical Journal, reviewing Volume IV of the Johns Hopkins Hospital Reports, discussed with exceptional care an article on post-operative septic peritonitis by Dr. T. S. Cullen. It was, the editor of the journal explained, "a very grave report of a run of ill-luck in an institution where the minutest precautions seem to be conscientiously enforced and observed. Four out of five abdominal sections performed in one week last January were followed by death. The authorities of the hospital and Dr. Cullen are greatly to be commended for this full record of a week's disasters. . . . "

The staff meeting that Saturday morning in January, 1895, had been the saddest in Tom Cullen's remembrance. When the head of the department had reviewed the week's work they all sat and looked at one another, saying nothing. Howard Kelly broke the silence.

"What shall we do?" he said.

Silence again, broken again by Dr. Kelly. Once more he went over a record all present knew too well. Five operations had been performed in B operating room — their operating room — that week. Of the five, four were clean and comparatively simple. One was "dirty," infected before operation. The infected case was making a good recovery. The four clean cases had all developed septic peritonitis after operation and all had died.

There were the dreadful bones of the record. The rest was as comfortless. All operations had been cancelled in B for the week. Every thing in and about the operating room, every member of the operating team, had been tested for possible sources of infection. None had been found. Yet the four autopsies had shown an identical infection; *staphilococcus pyogenes aureus* of a most virulent type. Four persons took part in the autopsies. In spite of every precaution known in those days before rubber gloves, every one had subsequently shown infection of the hand.

One possible source of infection could not be checked; the catgut used in the four operations. A small lot, it had all been used up, so no bacteriological test was possible. Being unusually brittle, it had been sterilized in a juniper oil solution, instead of in pure alcohol. It was the one clue running through all four cases that could not be followed to a conclusion. Without a bacteriological examination the evidence against the catgut must remain circumstantial and unsatisfactory.

The head of Hopkins Department of Gynecology ended his recapitulation and asked again, "What shall we do?"

Another silence. Tom Cullen broke it this time. "Report it," he said. "Report everything. Work up the cases in detail, report them and publish the report."

Such a thing had never been done before by any clinic anyplace, but Kelly said at once, "Very well. You do it."

And that is exactly what I did; made a full report of the four cases and all the circumstances. It was printed in the Johns Hopkins Hospital Reports as I wrote it, and it brought credit to the hospital and Dr. Kelly.

It was the first time in medical history that a hospital had thus made a clean breast of a major surgical disaster before the world and the medical profession, and the effect was what I had hoped. Medical journals not only here but in Britain commented on the courage and honesty of the Hopkins men, and Hopkins' reputation was increased far more by the report of the disaster than it would have been by a report of any number of successful operations.

You can see clearly what manner of man Kelly was. The tragedies were in his department. If there was blame he could not escape it. Yet, once it was suggested, he did not hesitate a moment in his decision to publish.

Adeno-myoma Uteri Diffusum Benignum — Johns Hopkins Hospital Reports, Volume VI, 1896.

At twenty-seven Hopkins' instructor, without compensation, in gynecological pathology found himself differing in print with one of the most famous of German pathologists, von Recklinghausen of Strasbourg.

The point of difference concerned myomatous womb tissue; a subject on which the great German expert had published his findings and was about to publish a book. For pathologists of his day a von Recklinghausen finding had supreme authority. But the enquiring mind in Hopkins gynecological laboratory kept its respect for authority within bounds. Tom Cullen had examined for himself the myomata that came from B operating room. Concerning the origin of certain specimens of adeno-myoma of the uterus — tumors developed as a muscular thickening of the inner wall of the womb — his conclusions were not those of the great von Recklinghausen.

Untroubled by that fact he embodied them in a paper; described the specimens on which he based his findings, and presented the evidence which had convinced him that such tumors were of endometrial origin and did not originate, as von Recklinghausen held, in remains of the Wolffian body. The paper, with T. S. Cullen's signature, was published early in 1896, in Volume VI of the Hopkins' Hospital Reports. Almost at the same time Friedrich von Recklinghausen's book on the same subject was published in Germany. Since their difference

124

was basic, von Recklinghausen's young opponent took it
to the second floor back for an opinion:

Popsy had read von Recklinghausen and he wanted to
pull me out. "You're wrong in your interpretation, Cullen," he told me, "von Recklinghausen says . . ." But I
had brought the evidence with me, sectioned and mounted for examination.

"I don't care a hoot what von Recklinghausen says," I
said, "Look down the barrel of that microscope."

Popsy looked and let me go on. I soon heard from
von Recklinghausen and I answered him and we had a
long and interesting correspondence on our subject. I
sent him large sections of my tumors — the ones I had
described in my paper — and it ended with something
as near an admission of error as an old and famous Herr
Professor could be expected to make; "On all material
points there is no difference between us."

There was a difference, of course, and the real reason
for it was that von Recklinghausen had obtained his
material from autopsies, after the changes due to death
had occurred. I was working on living tissue, or on tissue
so lately removed from living patients as to be the next
thing. So I knew I was right. It is the difference between
trying to find the cause of a fire after the house has burned
down, and getting there while it is still burning. The
earlier you get to a fire, the better your chance of discovering how it began.

Herr Professor von Recklinghausen had his own explanation of the fact that an unknown laboratory instructor had found and corrected him in error. Dr. Cullen had
reached the right conclusion because Dr. Cullen had a
microtrome with which to make serial sections. He explained it to Emil Ries, a young German scientist working
in his laboratory at the time. Years after, Dr. Ries told
the story to Dr. Karl H. Martzloff, one of Tom Cullen's
students, who wrote it down:

"When the great Recklinghausen read Cullen's article
he turned, somewhat chagrined, to Emil Ries and said

'Cullen has proven his point. This merely shows what this young ingenious American *(junger kunstlicher Amerikaner)* has been able to accomplish with the aid of a mechanical device while we still potter around making sections with razor and amyloid liver'."*

Adeno-myoma of the Round Ligament — Johns Hopkins Hospital Bulletin, Volume VII, 1896.

It was, as far as the records show, the first myoma of the type ever diagnosed and removed. It was also the means of sealing the peace between Cullen and von Recklinghausen:

The patient was thirty-seven at the time Dr. Kelly operated and had been conscious of a lump in the right groin for seven years. Latterly, it had grown larger and had caused her severe cutting pain after exertion and at the menstrual period. Operating, Dr. Kelly found an irregular ovoid nodule in the round ligament firmly fixed to the deeper tissues. He removed it. I made the pathological examination. Under the microscope it presented the typical appearance of adenomyoma.

I wrote up the case for the Hopkins Bulletin in a paper illustrated by Max Broedel and sent a copy, with sections of the tumor, to Professor von Recklinghausen in Strasbourg.

The peace-offering was graciously received. The Herr Professor wrote to thank Dr. Cullen and to tell him that he had demonstrated the sections at a medical meeting in Frankfurt. Thereafter, an amicable pathological correspondence passed between Strasbourg and Baltimore as matters of interest arose. It continued for ten years without a meeting, then Tom Cullen took the matter in hand. It was 1906 and he was making his fourth visit to Germany.

I decided that this time I wouldn't miss von Recklinghausen, so I telephoned from Tübingen to Stras-

* Karl H. Martzloff in the Western Journal of Surgery, Obstetrics and Gynecology, Vol. 54, August 1946.

bourg to make an appointment. The Professor set a time and I came by train and had one of the most comical experiences of my life. Though an old man then, von Recklinghausen was still doing original work in pathology and had just published some results of his recent researches in bone infection that were perfectly fascinating. But do you think I could get him talking about them or showing the work going on in his laboratory? Not a bit of it. What he wanted to talk about and show off was an autopsy table his son had sent him from Pittsburg.

We spent nearly all the time I had with him admiring it; just an ordinary American-made autopsy table.

Tom Cullen was never to see Friedrich von Recklinghausen again. Before he returned to Germany the old man was dead. The anticlimax was final.

At twenty-one, a student in a Canadian medical college, he had first heard of the great German pathologist and dreamed of seeing him in his laboratory:

That was when Jack Caven came home from Germany so full of what he had studied under him that he couldn't talk anything but pathology and von Recklinghausen.

At twenty-seven, becoming a pathologist in his own right, his first brush with accepted authority on a pathological point had been with von Recklinghausen. Thereafter, for a decade of maturing experience he had been the famous German's correspondent. With his whole generation he had come to think of von Recklinghausen of Strasbourg as pathology's symbolic figure; the survivor of the age of giants, the man who had worked as a fellow-pioneer with Virchow and Koch and Ehrlich, Klebs and Weigert and Cohnheim.

At thirty-eight, remembering a boy's dream, he had made his pilgrimage to Strasbourg to talk face to face at last with the master pathologist in his own laboratory. And they had spent their brief time together admiring the beauties of a new autopsy table made in Pittsburg, U.S.A.

7

PARTNERSHIP IN SORROW

THE BEGINNING of recognition had been made sweeter for Tom Cullen by the presence of his preceptor. Lesslie Sweetnam was in Baltimore in the autumn of 1895, in part for treatment, in part to see what Kelly and the other Hopkins men were doing. His pleasure in his pupil's progress crowned the happiness of working hours at the Pathological and doubled that of the talks after working hours. Tom had made friends at the hospital and in Max Broedel, the young medical artist Dr. Kelly had brought from Germany, had found the friend of a lifetime. He took a boy's gregarious pleasure in bringing new friends and old together and finding them congenial. There had never been a sunnier October than that across which his life's first tragedy struck.

The shadow of it darkened an unexpected letter from home. His mother wrote that Minnie was ill with a fever and she feared his father was getting it. Her letter was followed, too swiftly, by one from the family doctor that sent Tom Cullen straight to his chief to ask leave of absence. The sickness at home was typhoid. His father was gravely ill, and his eldest sister. His mother needed him.

A line from Howard Kelly followed him home to Canada:

"Dear Cullen: Look out for yourself & *don't drink the native water unboiled* or you'll be down. Of course that is your present duty. Do you need any money, can I help you? I'll *gladly* do it. You can't safely do nursing. Get a nurse."

Not two, but four members of his family were down with typhoid by the time Tom Cullen reached the parsonage in London. A fifth sickened a few days later. Mary Cullen and two young daughters had been the only members of the household to escape the infection. In the nightmare weeks that followed his homecoming, Howard Kelly's young pathologist did more than nursing. By day he washed clothes and dishes and bedding, sterilized and scrubbed and sterilized again, chopped wood, made fires, prepared food, ran messages. By night he took his turn of nursing so that his mother and the nurse might sleep. At odd moments he answered the anxious inquiries that flooded in from friends.

Three weeks after he came home, his sister Lillie died. The nightmare dragged on. Three weeks more and, after a weary, losing fight, his father's life ended. The tragedy of that time, Tom Cullen wrote years later, "burned itself into my marrow." Characteristically he drew strength to meet it from friendships and, even in its presence, remembered them gratefully. Every note of sympathy, each offer of help that came to the shattered family, he acknowledged and carefully preserved for his mother's comfort. There were many of them. Affection had followed Mary Cullen from one charge to another, wherever her husband had served, and her boy Tom had inherited her gift.

The ink is faded and the paper brittle, but the letters that came to mother and son in that dark beginning of winter half a century ago still hold the warmth that filled them then. Howard Kelly wrote again and again, giving advice, encouragement and warning, pressing new offers of help. The other Hopkins heads, the senior staff men in laboratory and hospital, their juniors in the residence, wrote what they could to comfort. Practical, earnest, candid, expressing in half-formal, wholly-unembarrassed phrases a surer faith and simpler loyalties than now are current, the letters wear well. In all is the texture of that serener time, as in these four; three written from Baltimore to Tom Cullen after his father's death, one from Toronto to Mary Cullen:

"Dear Cullen:

"I have just learned (11 p.m.) of the death of your Father. Mrs. Kelly and I have just talked it all over with the deepest sympathy. You stand very near to heaven now with two such dear ones there looking for you and the others they have left behind. I pray that the impression you now have of an earnestness which now fills you and the sense of the infinite importance of a consecrated life may never fade but grow stronger the longer you live as God's servant here taking your father's place as a witness to the truth. Call on me for any help you need. I enclose a check for $100 to help along and will send more as you need it. You must not think of giving up your work here; I will help you out. Think the situation well over when you have settled down a little & then we will talk it over & get things arranged for you.

"Would it not be better to bring the family down here near you? Don't worry, all will be well. Count on me to help right along.

Faithfully your friend,
Howard A. Kelly."

"Dear Tom:

"You are going through one of the hardest trials in life but I believe you are equal to it, hard as it is. Livingood has been taking your class since Hoen finished with them and the other things are going along all right. Broedel is looking after lots of little things for you and feels much sympathy for you.

"We shall all be glad to see you back as soon as you can come.

"Yours sincerely,
"Lewellys F. Barker.

"P.S. Bender in last No. of Central Journal of Pathology speaks enthusiastically of your formalin method and gives a further application of formalin."

"My dear friend:

"I cannot tell you how I felt when I learned Saturday that your dear father died. Everybody in J.H.H. seemed to be shocked with the news for wherever I looked I saw grave faces. All the boys, Becker, family Gills, want me to express their deepest sympathy. That is again all we can give and that is very little indeed, my poor good Tom.

"Tell me what you are going to do and how you intend to direct your little ship in the great ocean of life.

"With true love,
"Yours,
"Max."

"My dear Mrs. Cullen: Try and do not ever murmur as God has given you such Faithful children they will stand by you and be a Comfort as the days and months go by. What a *Son* Tom is.

"Geo. Blackwell."

The early Baltimore spring was near when Tom Cullen came back to his work at the Pathological, his classes and his friends. He was no longer a young disciple of science without responsibilities, but the head of a family. The household he had moved to Toronto and left settled there was dependent on him for its security. Of his sisters, only Blanche was earning her living, as a junior teacher. His brother was a schoolboy. His father's small insurance and the meagre pension of a minister's widow made up the total of the family resources. Three Cullens, the youngest only a child, were still to be prepared for college and financed through it. And he, the eldest, qualified five years ago as a physician, was unprofitably employed in research and had done nothing to establish himself in the lucrative practice of his profession.

Faithful friends had been careful to review these facts with him and with his mother, and to indicate that Tom's duty was plain; he must settle down where the family was known and begin to practice medicine, relieving his mother of anxieties, "carrying his share of the load."

131

Mary Cullen heard the good advice and did not regard it. The concern of those whose confidence in Tom was less sure than her own she recognized as natural and dismissed with untroubled serenity. Tom had his work to do. Tom was going back to Baltimore to do it. That was to be taken for granted as the basis of all planning for the Cullen family. Armoured by her certainty, her son also rejected cautious counsels. From the long struggle made together and the grief of loss their understanding of one another had emerged as a clear trust, flawless and never to be flawed. Each was secure in the other's strength. What Mary Cullen believed her boy Tom could do, he could do. Tom went back to Baltimore. His mother came to the station with him to say goodbye:

When she kissed me she said, "Take care of yourself Tom. If anything were to happen to you I wouldn't want to live." That was the greatest compliment I have ever been paid, and I got it from Mother. I didn't tell her, but I'd made a pact with my sister Rose to take care of her. Rose was in her 'teens and mother's messenger. I had her promise that whenever the bank balance went below a dollar she wouldn't worry Mother about it but write and let me know. We kept the pact until Rose was through college and the need for it was past and Mother never guessed we had one. When I would get the word from Rose, I would scrape around and somehow get enough to send a draft through to Mother's bank or enclose a bill in a letter. In the first years it wasn't always easy, but I got it every time.

Mother would remark in her letters sometimes how nice it was to receive an unexpected present, just when she was "beginning to think funds must be running low"; but she never guessed how it happened and we never told her. She liked feeling independent.

In Baltimore Tom Cullen found his work waiting. His seniors and the fellows in the residence made him welcome and life returned to its good pattern; the long days in his little laboratory at the Pathological, the eager discussions eagerly renewed, the demonstrations to prepare for his students, the teaching that already he did confidently and well. There were friendships to enjoy again, outside Hopkins and in, trips to the hills of Pennsylvania for a weekend at Waynesboro with Barr Snively's family, night voyages down the Bay to Sunday in Cambridge, holiday trips to Tolchester on a pass provided for the staff by a benevolent steamboat owner, German to practice in long sessions with Max Broedel, plans for the future to shape with the advice of Dr. Kelly. The last months of the third year in the backwater went by too fast.

Before they ended, an invitation came from Vanderbilt University in Nashville, Tennessee. Vanderbilt wanted Dr. T. S. Cullen on its staff as Professor of Pathology. His youth found the invitation flattering; not many men were heads of departments and professors at twenty-seven. As a gateway to security it should have been tempting since it offered an assured and honorable position, doing work in which he delighted, to a devotee of pathology with empty pockets and large responsibilities. But the plans shaped with his chief did not include Vanderbilt. He was going to be a surgeon as well as a pathologist, and he was going to work at Hopkins, under Dr. Kelly.

Refusing the flattering invitation from Nashville, Tom Cullen left the Pathological to begin his sixth Hopkins year as resident in gynecology — salary $500 per annum; board, room and laundry found.

8

DR. KELLY'S RESIDENT MAKES UP HIS MIND

It was October of 1896 when Tom Cullen came to take charge of B operating room as resident in gynecology. He had been away from surgery since March of '93, more than three years, and there were doubts among Dr. Kelly's associates concerning the wisdom of the appointment. If Kelly shared them, he gave no sign. He had promised Cullen the residency if he would wait for it. Cullen had waited; he was entitled to the position. It was true that much had been added to the knowledge of operative gynecology while the new resident had been specializing in gynecological pathology; but frequent visits to the operating room had kept him abreast of things there. He would soon find himself.

As it turned out, the new resident had to find himself very soon. Before he had been many days in charge of B-suite his test came:

I had assisted Dr. Kelly in several operations. In one, which he left me to start while he saw another patient, I had got on so far when he came back that he told me to finish it while he watched. That gave me confidence, although I would hardly have chosen to meet an emergency single-handed so soon. But it came, and I had no choice.

Dr. Kelly had operated, removing a womb that contained a large muscle tumor, in his usual masterly manner. He finished the operation and left me to close the abdomen. I did so and was in the dressing room and changed when I remembered that I had left my watch in the scrubbing-up room. The assistant went to get it for me, going by way of the operating room from which the patient had not yet been moved. In passing, he noticed blood on the operating table, stopped to investigate, found the patient was bleeding from below — a rare thing after such an operation — and sent for me.

I threw off my coat, put on a rubber apron, washed up hurriedly and opened the abdomen. Everything was in perfect order. So I opened the neck of the womb and there was the trouble. An artery in a most unusual position was spurting, the blood coming out below. I caught the bleeding vessel, closed the stump of the womb, closed the abdomen. The patient was breathing but had no pulse at the wrist. What a godsend plasma or a transfusion would have been — but we knew nothing then of those life-savers.

The patient was so nearly gone that wherever she was given a hypodermic there was a slough. She was too weak to move back to the ward. For two days we kept her in a room adjoining the operating room, looked after her there and managed to pull her through.

Next day, I remember, Dr. Kelly came over and said, "Tell me about the case, Cullen." I did and he patted my shoulder when I had finished and said, "You will never have a harder case than that Tom. There is nothing you can't do now. Go ahead."

The capability of the new resident in gynecology having been proved Howard Kelly grew to depend on it more and more. He was much occupied that year with his bladder and kidney work and with the preparation of his first book; the two-volume *Operative Gynecology* which was to appear in 1898. His resident was given all the gynecological work he could handle.

Work was waiting. Kelly's department at Hopkins had fallen heir to the troubles of years; the long-accumulating results of neglect and despair. Down the generations it had been assumed that women must endure women's ills with modest fortitude until such time as they became unendurable. The assumption was still prevalent. All too many women came to Kelly for cure when it was already late, even for relief. But in an encouraging and increasing degree the methods of diagnosis and the operations worked out by Kelly and his helpers were making cures possible even in cases complicated by long neglect.

Kelly's staff had to deal, in those days, with very many cases of dense pus tubes, demanding long and tedious operations. They removed, in the course of the day's work, tumors of a size that now would be considered fantastic. They operated on many cases of cancer of the neck of the womb; operations that involved the lower end of the tube running from the kidney to the bladder on each side, and required its most careful isolation. When the cancer was far advanced in such cases the operation was frequently followed by the partial or total collapse of the patient on the table.

The last is a type of case now treated by X-ray without surgery. But they had no X-ray. The knife was their only resource and, in Kelly's hands and the hands trained to use his operative methods, it could do astounding things. So patients came crowding to his clinic for help and the work piled up. Time and again in Tom Cullen's year as resident they operated all day in B and sometimes far into the night; with Dr. Kelly and without him. To make things harder, the department was shorthanded. Cullen had preached pathology too successfully for his own ease:

A conviction I had brought with me from the laboratory was that no man should qualify in surgical gynecology until he had first had a full year in gynecological pathology. Dr. Kelly agreed with the principle and laid it down as a departmental policy for the future. But it was a little hard to get started in practice. Ernest Stokes, who was to be my first assistant in gynecological surgery, had never had his time in our laboratory at the Pathological. He wanted it and I wanted him to have it, and it was perfectly clear that if I would not shoulder the extra work involved in getting the new system started no future resident could be expected to do it. So, though it left me with no man on my operative staff who had been in the department more than a month, Stokes went to the laboratory.

As first assistant in Stokes' place that year Dr. Halsted let us have Dr. Edward Garrett from the general surgery side. He was a peach and a great comfort to me I can tell you, and thanks to him we got the revolution under way. Since that year, no man has been resident in surgical gynecology at Hopkins until he has had his full year of laboratory work in gynecological pathology. We were the trail-breakers there and the remarkable thing is that Kelly, who had not had it himself, was the senior surgeon who first grasped its importance and made the pathological year obligatory in his service. His was then the only department in the only hospital in America that required it.

Nearly all the first-rate schools followed his lead in time and it has been a big thing for surgery in this country. There was a danger that clever surgeons might become mere technicians. I know no better insurance against it than the pathological year.

Personally, I could never forget some of the products of operative skill, unbalanced by pathological training, that I had seen during my service in Hopkins dispensary. They came and came again as patients; women prematurely aged and physically wrecked who had had their ovaries removed in early life by technically good surgeons who had no idea of the damage they were doing. In Kelly's clinic we were loth to remove any ovary, and if it were at all possible to save it, we did so. One of the things it pleases me most to remember of my work as Dr. Kelly's surgical resident was its conservatism. Apart from operations in which I was first assistant to the chief, and apart from very many plastic operations, I did, myself, 128 abdominal operations that year and in all removed only two ovaries.

In old bankbooks headed "Cullen & Path" the expense accounts of Johns Hopkins' first gynecological pathologist may still be read: "Supplies $1.23; typ. $3.25; lab help

$1.34; supplies $3.25;" and so on down the ruled columns. After the residency year began and Stokes took charge at the laboratory entries lapsed for a time and there were no withdrawals. Early in '97 they began again — "Wash. exp. $3.50; Wash. exp. $3.25; Wash. exp. . . Wash. exp. . . " The new resident had the work of B suite under control. He was resuming his visits to the Surgeon General's Library; with an end in view.

A resolve already shaping in the laboratory years had become clearly defined. Tom Cullen was going to write a book and he had chosen his subject. At the Pathological he had seen that someone must prepare to do for gynecological pathology what Dr. Kelly was doing in his book for operative gynecology. Someone must organize and make available to practising physicians the new knowledge of uterine diseases and their manifestations that had been accumulating under the microscopes of the laboratory scientists. He knew, since he had had a hand in it, that no other clinic and laboratory had more carefully preserved and meticulously examined and recorded material for such a work. At the Pathological, even before his paper on myomata brought the difference with von Recklinghausen, he had begun to plan a book on uterine tumors. He put that material aside now. Experience in the operating room had convinced him there was a more urgent need.

Daily in the gynecological clinic Howard Kelly's resident was meeting tragedies produced by want of knowledge of cancer and by inability to recognize its early pathological signs. Daily he was being cheered by the increasing promise of cure that early recognition and removal of cancers could bring. But early recognition depended on knowledge the medical profession as a whole still lacked; knowledge of the pathological symptoms of uterine malignancies, of how to identify cancerous tissue

138

under a microscope. Tom Cullen's decision was made
for him; his first book was going to be on cancer of the
uterus:

I felt it was incumbent on me to help men reach an
early diagnosis in cancer cases, since it was mainly in the
early cases that a permanent cure could be looked for.
I had had the advantage of being closely associated with
both the clinical and laboratory sides. I had access to
the most complete case records that then existed, and
could follow up the cases. I went to my chief. I would
like to bring out a book on cancer of the uterus, I told
him and explained why.

He said at once "Go ahead, Cullen. I will back you,
up to $10,000." So I went ahead, and *Cancer of the
Uterus* was probably the most important book I ever
published.

D'you wonder I was loyal to Kelly? I borrowed just
over six thousand dollars from him to finance that book
on cancer when I hadn't a cent. He'd said anything up
to ten and it cost me just over six and he gave it to me
as I needed it without any assurance that I could ever
repay it. When I paid him back, I remember, I told him
that since the money had been spent for the Department,
I couldn't think of paying him interest. Then I gave him
a cheque for $7,000. You should have seen his face.

That first book, or the big part — organizing the
material for it — was done before breakfast while I was
resident. At 5:30 I would go over to the ward for coffee
and toast in the ward kitchen. Then I would begin, work
through until 8:30, have breakfast and start the day. They
weren't light days.

Dr. Kelly had promised, when Tom Cullen took charge
of B, "a big year's work and all that is possible in practical experience." His promise was thoroughly fulfilled,
yet not without diversions.

Among them "Mr. Anthony Murray, a retired Pittsburg industrialist" appears and reappears, giving the right
touch of ardent amateurism, the authentic period flavour

of art for science's sake. He carries a folding tripod, a black cloth and a large black box. He is a camera enthusiast.

Mr. Anthony Murray tired early of being a Pittsburg industrialist. He had made all the money he wanted. He preferred photography to industry. He was interested in humanitarian experiments. He left Pittsburg for Baltimore, took a house in a tall red-brick row in Eager Street and attached himself firmly to Howard Kelly's department at Johns Hopkins. He was the gynecological clinic's unofficial photographer and a self-appointed godfather to its staff.

When Dr. Kelly's Canadian intern decided on a moment's impulse and a four-dollar overdraft to go to Germany and study pathology, Anthony Murray, all unasked, had promoted the project with a $150 loan "which helped out considerably." When new operations of importance were coming up in B-suite, Anthony Murray added himself and his paraphernalia to the operating room team, and made lantern slides of the events for Dr. Kelly's records. When distinguished visitors came to the clinic, Anthony Murray was there to photograph them, sitting blank-faced beside Dr. Kelly in a staff group. When unusual tumors were removed Anthony Murray pursued them to the gynecological laboratory and there, with the help of Max Broedel and Tom Cullen, took their pictures.

And when there was an occasion to celebrate in his chosen department, Anthony Murray provided the celebration, inviting the whole staff, both doctors and nurses, to dinner and lantern slides in his home.

Tom Cullen remembers one such occasion when the first lantern slide after dinner was a picture of him, the senior resident, sitting in a bath tub reading the Baltimore Sun. It was one of Anthony Murray's early experiments in unposed photography, made during a heat wave.

Coming early to take operation pictures he had found the assistant surgeon cooling off for the operation in B-suite bath. It was a completely proper picture. Mr. Murray, though given to mild waggery, was the soul of propriety. But it made everybody laugh when it showed up on the screen, and embarrassed the subject a little.

Memory's other associations with B-suite bath tub are more soothing. It was there Dr. Kelly's resident took the cat-naps that kept him going through the longest day's work. With a warm blanket from the pile on the radiator outside the operating room door for mattress he would climb into B-suite tub in any lull, go to sleep and sleep until he was wanted:

As soon as they were ready for me in the operating room a nurse would usually come into the hall and ask where Dr. Cullen was. Being a light sleeper, I would hear my name, casually appear and go to work again. The bath tub was my secret restorer; that and the late train to Waynesboro.

When we had had exceptionally heavy work and I was tired, I would take a train out of Baltimore on Friday night, if everything was going well, leaving a sealed envelope on my desk in the hospital. On the envelope I had written "Enclosed is my address. Open in case of emergency," and inside, "I am at Dr. Barr Snively's in Waynesboro, Pa."

Barr was my friend. We had been friends since our first meeting, when he was an intern in the old Church Home, farther down Broadway. After he finished his internship in Baltimore he had gone back to Waynesboro to practise with his father and live on the old family place. His brother Robley, also a doctor, practised in Philadelphia. The family was one of the kindest I have ever known. Dr. and Mrs. Snively treated me as a son and I came and went like one of their own sons, arriving when I could and leaving when I had to. Without such friends I could not have got through all I tackled that year. Once on the train for Waynesboro I never stayed tired long. I was on holiday.

In Waynesboro on holiday Tom Cullen could even tackle extras like Henry Bailey's adhesions:

Henry was a tall lank old man who came in from the mountain one day to see Barr's father, Dr. I. N. Snively. He had been feeling bad for a long time, Henry said, and he wanted something done about it. Dr. Snively looked Henry over and then called me in. I had been showing him some new instruments Dr. Kelly had worked out and he thought they might be useful in diagnosing Henry's case. They were designed for making rectal examinations and with their help we discovered that part at least of Henry's trouble was a narrowing of the bowel high up. We told Henry how to use a dilator, giving him explicit instructions, and he went home to the mountain.

Three days later he was back. The dilator was no good to him he said. He'd been reading up his case in Dr. Chase's book on family medicine and he had decided that if we didn't do something for him he was going to die. Dr. Snively senior, who knew Henry, said if that was the way he felt, the only thing was to operate. Otherwise Henry would die; he was a very determined character. So I wired to Johns Hopkins and the next morning the instruments and dressings needed came by the fast mail and the operating party went on up the mountain by horse and buggy. Henry had walked home the night before and when we got to his place he was waiting for us. If there were any nerves on the scene of operation, they weren't Henry's.

It was to be my first major operation outside a hospital. My first assistant, Dr. Barr Snively, had never helped at an abdominal operation. My anaesthetizer, Dr. Robley Snively, had never given ether for an abdominal operation. Instead of a nurse to pass the instruments we had Max Broedel, a medical illustrator. But we had plenty of medical advisers. Barr's father and Dr. Percy Hoover had come along with the party as general superintendent and handyman. We prepared the room among us and then Henry brought the kitchen table in. When we had prepared that, he climbed up on it and lay down and we started.

It was very easy, as it happened. Henry had had an old peritonitis that had left some adhesions. All that was

142

necessary was to loosen them and the bowel straightened out. We sewed Henry up and put him to bed and were just starting to pack our things when Mrs. Bailey came in and said, "Doctor, can I have the table? I want it to set dinner."

Such a dinner as we had in Mrs. Bailey's kitchen off Henry's operating table — home cured bacon, eggs fresh from the barn, hot biscuits, coffee and wild raspberry preserves! I've never enjoyed a meal more. Henry lived fifteen or sixteen years longer and every Christmas, as long as he lived, he sent me a box of fruit as a reminder of his operation.

Not that I needed reminders. Apart altogether from Mrs. Bailey's dinner, I owed Henry too much to forget him. That first experience of operating under primitive conditions was invaluable; showed me I could go through with what must be done without letting the handicaps worry me too much. Naturally, every surgeon would choose to do all his work in a perfectly equipped operating room under ideal conditions. But even in the best-equipped operating room unexpected things can happen, and the surgical improvising I had to learn to do, starting with Henry's adhesions, has helped me more than once to meet emergencies. Of which there are many varieties.

One of the funniest I ever had to meet was in Waynesboro again, and with Barr Snively. He had asked me to operate for him in a very serious abdominal case. There was no hospital in the town then, and the operation could not be delayed. So there was nothing for it but operating in the patient's home. We prepared a small hall room, just wide enough for the table with Barr on one side and me on the other; we were both thin in those days. We were ready to begin when a stout lady who was a friend of the family turned up. She announced that she had promised the patient she would stay with her and she was going to stay with her. It didn't matter what we doctors said, she was going to stay with her right through the operation.

We doctors didn't say anything; it was evident that the lady's mind was made up. So we stationed her at the head of the table where she could get a perfect view of what we were doing and went ahead with the operation.

It wasn't long until the stout lady began to feel sick, and soon she said she thought she would go out. But we were well into the operation then, working together, and neither of us could safely quit his place to stand clear for the lady. So I told her to crawl under the table and get to the door that way but not on her life to jar the table.

She was well under when she stuck. Her shoulders had gone between the table legs but she broadened further down and there she stuck and could not budge. We warned her again not to jar the table and left her where she was for a quarter of an hour or so, until we reached a point in the operation where it was safe to delay for a minute. Then we rescued her. Or rather we told her she could back up now, and Barr stood aside to let her out the door.

She went fast, without a word about all she had promised the patient. I have always felt that Barr and I deserved great credit for our conduct in that emergency. Neither of us laughed.

When Tom Cullen's year as resident was three-quarters past he had a long unsatisfactory talk with his chief. Dr. Kelly had written Dr. Welch some time before a request that "if you will be so kind as to agree" Dr. Cullen might once more take full charge of gynecological pathology when he left the operating room in October. The postscript asked more: "I will be very glad if some suitable title can be given him to give him a distinctive position."

But, even if assured, a suitable title and a distinctive position added to an instructor in gynecology's salary of $200 a year were hardly prospect enough now. Tom Cullen would be twenty-nine in November. His family was his responsibility. His mother was entitled to more ease. If there was to be a future for him at Hopkins it was time to know it, and his talk with Dr. Kelly had given him no assurance. When his chief left for camp in Canada that summer of '97 Tom Cullen felt, for almost the first time in his life, uncertain.

144

The parting in Baltimore Union Station was not a happy one. Admonitions to practise the more passive Christian virtues fell upon stony ground that evening. But in a day or two Tom Cullen felt better and wrote a letter north. He has forgotten now what was in it, but he still has the answer posted at Magnetawan, Ontario, July 28, 1897:

"Dear Cullen: Just a line to tell you I am more pleased with your letter rec'd than with any piece of good work you have done. We Xians *must* be different from the world and its standards. We *must* show the fruits of the spirit if our profession is real — viz *'love,* joy, *peace, long-suffering,* gentleness, *kindness* etc.'

"I am glad all goes well. I will be back by Aug. 8-10.
"Faithfully Yrs
"Howard A. Kelly."

Dr. Kelly came back from camp. Tom Cullen's last weeks in charge of B operating room went by. September ended. Still the distinctive position had not been created or the suitable title coined by Hopkins Medical Board. Dr. Kelly's retiring senior resident made ready to leave the hospital that had been his life for six years. He was without assurance of a future at Hopkins but he had reached a decision; he was going to make a future in Baltimore and in surgery. He finished packing in the room next the bulge, telephoned for an express waggon, said his goodbyes. The big year's work in B had been good, but it was finished.

The postscript to the year was added with a restrained flourish, still to be admired, in the long second line on an envelope addressed in his chief's handwriting:

"To Dr. Thos S. Cullen
    Associate in Gynecology
        of the
            Johns Hopk. Univ.
            Balto."

Across one corner the envelope is endorsed, in the script of a new-made associate:

"Rec'd Oct 3/97
    Appointment made Oct 2/97
      T.S.C."

An invitation to oysters topped happiness:

                    "1 West Franklin St
                     "Tuesday

"Dear Cullen
"Beer, backy, oysters &c — with Camac at 9:30 at Pabst's Biddle St. tomorrow — join us if you can
           "Yours
               "Wm Osler.
"Very glad to vote for you
   as Associate in Gynecology."

PART III

CONTINUING IN BALTIMORE

I

A BOOK AND A BRASS PLATE

A DECISION to practise in Baltimore as a consultant and surgeon having been made, Dr. Thomas S. Cullen leased for that purpose a house and office at Number 3 West Preston Street. The lease was signed and sealed before his year as resident was up or his appointment as associate in gynecology assured:

I'd discovered by then that when it looks as if you had come to a dead end, with nothing but a stone fence in front of you, the thing to do is to keep on going ahead. You generally can find a path around when you get up to the fence.

Three West Preston was a big house just around the corner from fashionable Charles Street. The rent was high — $55 a month — the twelve rooms all unfurnished. The new tenant was a single young man without a bank balance, a stick of furniture or a patient to his name. He paid one month's rent in advance, signed a lease and ordered a brass plate for the front door. Then he went to a furniture warehouse, hired enough furniture for three rooms and was ready to practice.

The beginning was hard. Early patients were richer in gratitude than in cash. Lettered "CULLEN" in red and black on white, a memento of the less tangible riches sits, as it has sat for fifty years now, where Tom Cullen can see it each time he comes home:

149

One of my first patients was the wife of a man who worked in the marble-cutting works. I charged $25 for the operation — it was all they could afford — but he wanted to do something more for me, something nice. So he made me a marble doorstop with my name inlaid. It has been beside my front door ever since. You like to remember people who have done things they needn't do for you, especially when you were beginning.

At that, beginning was easier for me than for a lot of young fellows. I knew all the time that if I was right up against it Dr. Kelly would always lend me a little. But that was just what I didn't want to ask. Borrowing money for the book was one thing. For the rent it was something else. So I held out and time and again it happened that the same mail that brought my rent bill would bring a check large enough to pay it.

One great advantage the tenant of 3 West Preston Street had; waiting for patients he did not have to wait in idleness. His book ensured him all the specialized research he could do, his appointment as associate in gynecology an abundance of practical experience:

I had general supervision of all materials coming to the gynecological laboratory at the Pathological once more; but now with an intern doing his laboratory year in gynecology as assistant. I had the classes in gynecological pathology to take and the course to prepare for them, and I had Saturdays in B.

Saturday was my operating day; the day I had the teaching clinic in operative gynecology; and darn their hides they kept all the junk for Saturdays. Old and tedious cases, cases that had already been operated on unsuccessfully, cases in which the chance that surgery could do much good seemed small, were all put on the list for Saturdays when most of my seniors were away. So I got them and it was the best thing that ever happened to me. I not only operated on these difficult clinic cases, but I learned a lot by following them up personally. It was fascinating to watch the recoveries in cases that had been chronic and to see with your own eyes the evidence that some new approach, worked out in your department under your chief, was curing patients whose troubles had baffled previous operative procedures.

It was that first year, while I had time to give to organizing them, that we began the "Fridays at four-thirty." They were weekly conferences of the department staff and we held them Fridays at that hour without a break for more than forty years. Then the time was changed to Saturday morning, when they are still held.

The purpose of the Friday meetings was to review the week's work in B. Tom Cullen always presided. Dr. Kelly was there when he could be. Every operation done during the week in B. was reviewed in detail and, where other methods might have given better results, the alternatives were discussed. Operations done by senior staff men were given precisely the same survey as those done by the house staff, so the seniors concerned were generally on hand too. Those meetings had a fine effect on the whole department, Tom Cullen remembers.

So the first year was well-filled and by its end the results of work began to show. A new green carpet and a desk, not hired, were installed in the office at 3 West Preston. The appointment book beside the telephone began to show appointments written ahead. Early in December of '98 her boy Tom wrote Mary Cullen that he would not be able to come home for Christmas; he had agreed to go down to Cambridge on the eastern shore of Maryland in Christmas week, to operate at the new hospital there. It was the first of a series of weekly visits to Cambridge hospital that was to continue for ten years:

In the long run, of course, I lost a great deal more money on those trips to Cambridge than they ever brought me, by being out of Baltimore so much. But I can tell you they were very welcome in the beginning, and I got ten years' experience of general surgery there that saved me from the danger of over-specialization and helped me keep a sense of proportion. I can never be thankful enough that Brice Goldsborough asked me to do the surgery at Cambridge hospital when they opened it in '98.

The invitation to Cambridge was one of the products of a friendship that was to be lifelong and to produce other good things. An intern new to Hopkins had first seen Brice Goldsborough among other observers in B operating room. He had noticed this one particularly as a cheery young man who called Dr. Kelly by his first name; a thing few people did. Dr. Goldsborough was then already established in practise in Cambridge, where as their friendship ripened, Tom Cullen was asked to come for his first holiday on the Eastern Shore:

That first visit was a delight. After breakfast I would wander down through Brice's garden to the creek where there were a few oyster houses and many sailboats. Or I would slip down to the wharf with a big market basket to do a little crab-fishing and in half an hour have the basket full of crabs. Or I would go swimming, or watch the men tonging for oysters a little way from the wharf. The Cambridge oyster beds made a lot of employment for the townspeople in those days. I watched it die out as the water got dirtier and dirtier and it gave me some ideas about sewage and oysters and Chesapeake Bay that I am still working on. Cambridge when I first knew it was one of the most delightful and picturesque little towns I have ever seen and I was very happy there.

The Goldsboroughs, Brice and his wife and, later, his brother, were all my friends and you couldn't ask better. So naturally I was glad to be included in Brice's plans for starting a hospital in Cambridge. We had a lot of fun getting it started. The first building was two old houses knocked together and the operating room was a converted kitchen resting on six piles of bricks. In summer we had fine ventilation, but that first winter it was a little hard to heat. I remember they tried a small stove and the first time we used chloroform free chlorine developed and gassed us all. So we gave up the stove. Fortunately winters are not long on the Eastern Shore.

But they can be cold. Some of those winter mornings, getting off the night boat from Baltimore in the dark, I was colder than I had ever been in Canada.

The night boat was the one I always took to Cambridge. I would leave Baltimore after dinner, get to Cambridge about five in the morning, have breakfast and start operating. When I was through at the hospital I would have dinner with Brice and Mrs. Goldsborough and come back to Baltimore on the night boat again. Except when there was a load of calves on board and you had a cabin up front, it was a fine restful trip. Working with Brice Goldsborough was always a delight and grew to be more and more so as time went on. But in the beginning the very important thing about those trips to Cambridge was that they paid the rent. I did not have to worry about that after they started, so I could plan ahead for the family.

So began, for younger Cullens, a life that had a fairytale quality; a fairytale in which the reward of virtue was to stay with Tom in Baltimore. Tom in Baltimore, like God in heaven, was good and the source of good. He was, again like God, astonishing in his power and not to be questioned in his commands. Unlike God, he laughed a great deal and was full of ploys, and he could be counted on for instant understanding of the importance of a schoolboy's problems or a small girl's confidences.

At home in a Toronto suburb one lived in a house, not large for six, where none missed the luxuries all went without. One did a just measure of household tasks and shared in the clear certainty of Mary Cullen's affection and in the jokes and companionship of a large and friendly family. One went to school and studied honourably since that was what Mary Cullen expected of her children, since a Cullen who scamped on education could not expect to grow up a credit to Tom, and since every Cullen must of course prepare to earn a living. Life at home in school months was pleasant, healthy and not unduly exciting. But with holidays would come a special letter from Tom and a fortunate young Cullen, or two, would take a train at the Union Station and waken next morning to a new world.

Its centre was Tom's big half-empty house with just you and Tom in it. There was the telephone to answer for Tom when he was out. There the messages came to be written down carefully for Tom. There, if you were one of the girls, you played at housekeeping for Tom, going to market and ordering dinner and having a servant to do the things you did yourself or helped to do at home. From there, if you were one of the older ones, you went calling and out to dinner with Tom. If you were young you were called for by Tom's friends and taken driving or to tea in strange houses. There, beyond the door with Tom's name on it, lay the strange city to be explored with Tom when he had time; the clutter of old streets near the docks, the harbour with its ships, the trim squares and gardens running up and down hill, the miles of white doorsteps and green doors all alike. There, on Sunday mornings, you wakened to the rhythmic sound of Maryland biscuits being beaten in kitchens all up and down Charles Street. There excursions started. They would begin after Tom was through at his office, with a streetcar ride to the hospital, and have a long wait in the middle while Tom was busy there. Then they would start again, with Tom free and both of you happy, away and away, alone or in a party, for a steamboat ride on the bay, or by streetcar again to Druid Hill Park or the Fort, or even further. . . . Too soon your turn was over and you were back home, remembering it all for the others. It would be somebody else's turn next time. Or perhaps Tom would come home for a surprise visit first.

That was almost best of all, the youngest of the Cullens used to think; when Tom would walk in at home and surprise them all. For then the light she loved; the light that was specially for Tom; would shine suddenly in her mother's eyes and stay shining all the time Tom stayed.

By the end of the second year in West Preston Street more than half the rooms had furniture, none of it was hired and the tenant could afford a modest establishment. When young Dr. Cullen came home to Toronto for the Christmas of '99, a plan he and his mother had talked over before was broached to his eldest sister. It would not be right, Mary Cullen had decided, to move the family from Canada. The three still at school could be well educated in Toronto at less cost than in an American university; best keep the home there until it was done. Yet it was not fair that Tom should go on living alone, camping almost, in that big house. Would Minnie go to live in Baltimore and keep house for her brother?

Minnie would.

2

MARY CULLEN'S YEAR

HOME IN TORONTO AGAIN after seeing the new household established, Mary Cullen waited for the new year to bring good to her boy Tom. She had not long to wait. Tom was invited to come to Yale as its professor of gynecological surgery. Tom was made associate professor of gynecology at Hopkins. Tom was chosen to represent Johns Hopkins Hospital at the great international medical congress in Paris at which Dr. Osler represented Johns Hopkins University. Tom's first book was published. And, before the year ended, Tom brought all the Cullens together in West Preston Street for Minnie's wedding. In 1900 Mary Cullen was to know the fulfilment of faith and to accept it without astonishment.

"My dear son," she wrote as the year began, "you have no idea what a comfort you have been to your mother and I know the Lord will continue to bless you and open your way before you. I hope you will not work too hard on your book after your brief vacation. I wish you every success in it. Do not stay at home more than necessary as going out a little among your friends will make it pleasant for you . . . I was thinking just now that Tom would have returned from Cambridge by this time and none too soon if you have it stormy as we have it . . ."

Thus the home letters resumed — the letters which week by week reported, as from one partner to another, the progress of a joint undertaking. Things to be told were set down as they occurred; news of friends and words of encouragement and loving pride mingling with such essential items as flannelette nightgowns — "good quality at 49 cts. each, I bought five, the number we required" — new shoes for Rose who was walking the four miles to college every morning — "she says she feels better for it" — and steak and baked potatoes for the children's supper.

Good news from Baltimore the senior partner noted calmly, as welcome but not surprising. A new rug in the sitting room in West Preston Street — "it will soon be quite cozy looking with all the pretty things." A first dinner with Minnie as hostess and Dr. Welch as the guest of honour — "I am sure you both enjoyed having Professor Welch to dinner." An evening party given for Miss Cullen by Dr. and Mrs. Hurd — "Minnie, you were very kindly treated at Dr. Hurd's. On these occasions I often think of the old adage 'If you wish to have friends you must show yourself friendly.'" A concert at the Music Hall — "Minnie certainly had a treat in hearing Paderewski." An unusually big week of operations — "not much danger of Tom eating idle bread." A bouquet of violets with a cord and tassel for Miss Cullen from a new admirer named Mr. Ramsay — "it must have looked very stylish on your lovely crepon, Minnie, and your brown hat with fresh roses would be almost like new."

Above all news of the book, Tom's book, was waited and welcomed. No home letter was without its inquiry for the fortune of the work to which four years of tireless care had gone. "Are we to understand by Tom taking all the manuscript to New York that the work is ready for the press? I scarcely thought it possible that it could be ready yet, though I knew Tom was pretty smart . . . How little we know, Tom, what it means to write a book. I really do not think I will try it. Minnie, do you still

157

continue to brush Tom's hair well and rub in the tar water? I think it helps the hair . . . You must feel wonderfully relieved, Tom, to have the book at the publishers' . . . We are glad that everything in connection with the book is so satisfactory . . . The slight rest from your book work will not hurt you . . . How about the book? Have they gotten things in running order yet? . . . "

Before he left to spend the Christmas of '99 at home, Tom Cullen had all but completed his first book. The cases selected as typical were fully described. The relevant material culled by long research was assembled and digested. Operations performed were reported in detail and the post-operative history of each case brought up to date. Max Broedel and his associate artist, Hermann Becker, had made gross and microscopic drawings in black-and-white and colour to illustrate the text. Early in the new year, last revisions made, the author put the outline of his manuscript in his pocket and took train for New York. His appointment was with Willie Appleton, head of the publishing firm of D. Appleton and Co. It proved satisfactory:

I left New York that same afternoon, reached Baltimore in the evening, assembled my manuscript and pictures in two dress suit cases, took the midnight train back to New York and at eight the next morning was at Appleton's printing plant in Brooklyn. Just sixteen weeks later I had the first copy of my book.

It was among the earliest of the medical works to have coloured as well as black-and-white illustrations and one of the printers' big difficulties was with the colour. We finally solved it with a microscope after wasting hours trying to get the right shades. I took a train to Baltimore, brought some of the original slides and a microscope with me from the laboratory, had the men who were doing the colour work examine the slides through the microscope and in twenty minutes they had their colours exactly. Prang, the expert who developed the colour scale for printers, made the full-page colour plates and did a magnificent job and the reproduction Appleton's gave us was the best possible. I had determined that the book should be the last word in medical printing up to 1900, and it was.

It's this way. When you start to write on medical subjects you have to choose one of two courses. Either you are going to write a medical text book and spend half your time for the rest of your life trying to keep it up to date — and that's too much worry, I couldn't be bothered — or you are going to publish and lose money. I chose to publish and lose money.

Take that first book of mine. Once it was clear in my mind that such a book was needed and I had the assurance of Dr. Kelly's backing, I went to work on it. To be of the most use it had to be illustrated as well. So we gave it the best possible illustrations by the very best medical illustrators with costly colour plates. Then we fixed the price so that it would be within reach of the fellows on the firing line; practitioners without large incomes working in places where that sort of material would never be available to them at first hand. Then we published and I took the loss.

Altogether I have lost between fifty and sixty thousand dollars on my medical publications; but it's been worth it. With each major book I wrote, I took the same course. Insofar as I could, I assembled all the knowledge on that subject available at that date, presented it in as complete a manner as possible and published. That was definitive and I was through. The next man could take on from there.

As it turned out, Tom Cullen's first book was to be definitive in another sense for, even before it was published, it had decided its author's future. Late in February of 1900 the invitation from New Haven had come to Hopkins' associate in gynecology. Yale wanted Dr. Thomas Cullen to head its department of gynecology as a full professor. The opportunity was tempting. If a move was to be made the time for it was now, while personal commitments in Baltimore were still small. The Yale offer promised great usefulness and came as a welcome recognition of achievement. All the obvious considerations were in favour of acceptance. President Hadley of Yale himself brought the invitation and, at first, President Gilman of Hopkins himself advised accepting it. But Tom Cullen did not want to accept:

I went to see Dr. Gilman about it and he told me to go. Hopkins could not offer or promise me a comparable position, he said. I had been in Washington that morning checking references in my book against the originals in the Surgeon General's Library and I had the galley proofs of the first three hundred pages with me. I told President Gilman I did not want to leave Hopkins and I put the packet of proofs on his desk and said that was why. "It would take me twenty years at Yale to assemble the material I have here," I said. Gilman asked me to leave the proofs with him to look over that evening. The next day he sent for me and said "Cullen, stay."

I stayed. That was when they made me associate professor at Hopkins — and raised me two hundred dollars a year.

"So stay," Howard Kelly wrote affectionately, after the March meeting of Hopkins Medical Board. "We cannot let you go. There was not a dissenting voice at the Med. Bd. meet. as to your being associate professor. You have well deserved this title of our best American institution and your friends all prophesy great things of you for the future. Remember I will pay the 200 if the Bd. don't but they will. . . ."

Mary Cullen's letter of March 29 was serenely unastonished: "Tom you must never fear that you write too much personal matter for that is what we want, all you can tell us. It was indeed kind of Dr. Kelly to interest himself in getting you the appointment. I am sure he will never regret doing so. He has no doubt wished it before but could not appear too much interested in Dr. Cullen. The invitation to Yale was just the opportune time and I do feel so thankful that you have such a very honourable position. You have certainly earned it. Not many young men at your age have such a position. My dear boy you are beginning to reap what you have been sowing, may you have an abundant harvest. . . . "

Two weeks later serenity was ruffling a little under reticence: "Tom, when are you going to send us something concerning your recent appointment to put in the papers? Folks might as well know it." Another two weeks, and serenity was all restored: "My dear children, I have been fixing curtains and have stopped for a short time to converse with you . . . I think nearly all the papers, if not all, had the invitation to Yale and the appointment to J.H. University in them. We have been congratulated from all sides. If we cannot receive congratulations on our own account it is very pleasant to have such a distinguished member of the family for whom we can receive them. . . . Tom, we are glad you took a little trip to Waynesboro. It will do you good to have a change. Ernest was very much pleased with the cheque Tom sent for the new suit of clothes . . . Now my dear children you must take care of your health in the change of season. Tom, do not try to accomplish too much and overdo the thing . . . "

When the official delegate from Johns Hopkins Hospital sailed in July of 1900 for Paris and the international medical congress his book went with him — nine first-run copies in a telescoping valise. They were to give to Professors Orth and Pozzi, to George Nuttall, of course, to the great Treub of Amsterdam, and to friends in Vienna and Leipzig who had been good to a beginning pathologist:

I nearly lost the whole lot at Queenstown though. The customs officer there told me I couldn't take them into the country. Books couldn't be imported until they had been examined and if I wanted to import them I should have sent them earlier for examination. I explained that I didn't want to import them, just take them with me to Paris, and that I couldn't have sent them earlier because they had only been published in America the week before I sailed and only copyrighted in Great Britain yesterday. He still shook his head, so I pulled out a letter from the publishers to that effect, and unwrapped one of the books to show him the date of publication. As I opened it he spotted the dedication — to Kelly and Welch.

"Kelly?" he said. "That's my name. Leave me the letter and take yer books."

So the book was released for delivery, all nine copies were duly delivered, and the delegate from Johns Hopkins Hospital to the Paris congress had "a wonderful time." He found opportunities, before he turned home, to renew the friendships a boy had begun, to learn new things and to make new friends. In London his book had come before him and his welcome was prepared. It was September when he sailed from Liverpool for Canada, briefed for his homecoming by letters from his mother.

Minnie and his brother Ernest had returned safely from Baltimore, having closed Tom's house in West Preston Street. Ernest, starting medicine, was delighted with what he had learned in his visit to Johns Hopkins and "does not know how to pay Tom back for all he has done for him." Mr. Ramsay of Baltimore, donor of the violets with cord and tassel, had sent a very nice letter asking Mary Cullen's consent to his marriage with her eldest daughter, had followed the letter to Toronto and had stayed three weeks. They had chosen October for the wedding — "we are all delighted at the prospect of having Mr. Ramsay in the family . . . I said to Rose, what will Tom do? I thought you would have to do likewise."

"The children" had heard, before they left Baltimore, of the flattering things Dr. Kelly and Dr. Welch had said about the book, and Mary Cullen was sure her son must have been very gratified to find it ahead of him in London — "I should think just at this juncture to be able to see the author makes it doubly interesting. We are looking with great expectancy to see the noted Dr. Cullen ourselves . . . May the Lord keep you as within the hollow of his hand and continue to bless our Tom . . ."

The delegate from Johns Hopkins Hospital to the Paris medical convention returned to blessings after his own heart. The praises of his book received before he left Baltimore from Welch and Kelly, to whom it had been dedicated, were forerunners only. Professor Pozzi wrote from Paris, Professor Simpson from Edinburgh, August Martin from Berlin, Chrobak from Vienna, congratulating their young confrère on the importance of the work he had done for medical science. Congratulations as warm came from clinicians and scientists in Rome and London, Freiburg and Munich, Basle and Leipzig, Boston, Princeton and New Haven.

More welcome still to Tom Cullen was the measured approbation of his preceptor, Lesslie Sweetnam — "the work done would appear to be permanent, ensuring the value of the book for many years . . . " — and the generous admiration of his fellows. The men who had shared with him the forfeits, the pickles and the "shop" of the first eager years at Hopkins shared now in pride in his work. Lew Barker wrote, Simon Flexner, Franklin P. Mall, George Nuttall and a dozen others. And there was a characteristic note from a fellow-Canadian:

"Dear Cullen:
"1001 thanks for your magnum opus. What a labor it has been! But you will be repaid . . . nothing you can do hereafter can dim the superlative merits of such a study. 'Tis a credit to you, to the school and to our country!
"Sincerely yours
"Wm. Osler."

163

Minnie was married in October from West Preston Street. She was a lovely bride and Tom, in a new frock coat, gave her away. Gold chairs were hired for the big empty drawing room on the second floor, a caterer took command in the kitchen. The bride's family all came down from Canada. Counting up the cost to Tom; of wedding garments and railway tickets all around; of Minnie's trousseau and linens; of invitations and wedding breakfast; Mary Cullen trembled a little. "I only hope and pray," she wrote her son, "that your purse may be as big as your heart."

The year, her year and Tom's, was ending when she wrote again. She had stayed on in Baltimore after the wedding, taking a rare and happy holiday, playing visitor to Tom and Kate, the baby of the Cullens, released from lessons until January and promoted to temporary bliss as Tom's hostess. Writing from Toronto her thanks for "a lovely time" Mary Cullen gravely included the youngest with the eldest of her children. "It seems strange to be my own mistress again after being the guest of so distinguished a host and hostess for so long a time. Tom, we are certainly proud of you and our pride is enhanced if that be possible, when we see such criticisms as are published of your book. Just think, none adverse. How could there be? . . . Kate, when you come do not forget to bring my calling cards, also the French pickle recipe. And now my dear ones while we shall miss you very much at Christmas we won't complain seeing that it is not practical this year. The Lord bless and keep you . . . "

Mary Cullen had reason for pride in Tom's book. In medical and surgical journals of the United States and Canada the work was welcomed as supplying a grave lack in contemporary medical knowledge. In England, the Lancet gave it two and a half columns of judicious praise, the British Medical Journal a long notice, the British

[Photograph by ANTHONY MURRAY

" . . . entered with assurance into the human abdomen."   —page 101

Dr. Howard A. Kelly with his staff, Johns Hopkins Hospital, 1893. From left, back: Dr. W. W. Russell, Dr. Kelly, Dr. T. S. Cullen; front; Dr. John G. Clark, Dr. A. L. Stavely

Gynecological Journal a careful six-page review. Tom Cullen has them still:

"I'll tell you, when you're young and get reviews like that on your first book it makes you feel good. But what made me feel best of all was Councilman's praise. "Kn-n-new you were writing a b-b-b-book, Tommy," he said, "D-d-didn't think it'd b-b-be this g-g-good."

3

ROMAN TRIUMPH AND "THE MAG."

LESSLIE MATTHEW SWEETNAM died of a chance infection in December of 1901. His death bereaved Tom Cullen as even his father's had not. While his preceptor lived he had known the best reward of achievement; Dr. Sweetnam's pride in his apprentice was as discriminating as it was generous. A scientist twenty years ahead of his time in the application of theory to practice, Sweetnam never ceased learning. He followed with a sure eye for essentials the work being done at Hopkins and had won the affectionate respect of the heads there. Of the two seniors who shaped his career, Tom Cullen puts him first:

I learned more from Kelly as a surgeon but I learned more from Sweetnam as a man.

Before all, Sweetnam was a physician, selflessly devoted in the practice of his profession. His death at forty-six was one of the aimless tragedies of medicine; the destruction of a useful life in the preservation of a useless one. An operation on a tramp brought into hospital with a gangrenous leg; an infection developing from a prick under a fingernail:

I was operating at Cambridge one day in November of 1901 when a telegram reached me saying Dr. Sweetnam was ill and on his way to Baltimore. I met his train at Wayne Junction that evening and when we got into Baltimore station Dr. Kelly, Dr. Halsted and Dr. Osler were all there waiting. Dr. Halsted operated, removing the axillary glands. Dr. Sweetnam rallied swiftly and seemed to be making a good recovery. The last time I saw him he was shaving himself and counting the days till he could be back in Toronto at work. I started for Cambridge by train next morning and on the way received the telegram that said he had died.

It was a loss doubly bitter for its irony. With it, the book of Tom Cullen's youth was closed. He has his latchkey yet to the front door of the square-set house on Church Street in Toronto where he lived "in," in the old fashion, as Dr. Lesslie Sweetnam's student-apprentice. Though the house was torn down long ago to make way for a gas station, he keeps the key.

In August of 1901 young Dr. Cullen had done as his mother advised when his sister Minnie married — "likewise." His wife was Emma Jones Beckwith of Louisville, Kentucky, daughter, granddaughter and great-granddaughter of physicians, and a graduate of Hopkins training school for nurses. Miss Beckwith had been Dr. Kelly's head nurse in B operating room the year Dr. Cullen was resident in gynecology. Later she went from Dr. Kelly's service to Dr. Halsted's and at twenty-five, before she left Baltimore, was the hospital's night superintendent.

To all who knew her well, Tom Cullen's wife was "Rebecca." The nickname dated from her training years when a ward patient who found "Miss Beckwith" a hard set of syllables to handle eased them to "Miss Rebecca." The name, fitting better than her own on the tall vivid girl, persisted. "Rebecca" she became to her husband's family and friends when she returned to Baltimore as Mrs. Thomas Stephen Cullen.

They went to Europe in 1902. Dr. Cullen was a delegate and a speaker at an international congress of surgeons meeting in Rome. He was to give a talk, illustrated with

167

lantern slides, on adenomyoma of the uterus. The medical school amphitheatre of the University of Rome was crowded for it. His difference with von Recklinghausen on that subject was still a matter of lively interest among the Europeans:

The talk went very well, thanks to Max Broedel who wasn't there. I had prepared to speak in English of course, as the speaker who preceded me did. He was an American and he gave a fine address but since very few understood him he got very bad attention. During his talk, Professor Paul Zweifel of Leipzig, whom I knew well, was sitting in front of me. Halfway through he turned around and said "Cullen, you must talk German; there are not four people in this whole audience who understand English."

I told him I could not, but he said "You must." So when I was called on I tried, first explaining my predicament to the presiding officer who was Italian. I started to talk in German and kept it up for forty minutes and got good attention in spite of many mistakes. My pictures on the screen helped mightily of course.

Next year I received very pleasant proof that my attempt to speak in a language known to the majority of those present had been acceptable to our hosts in Rome. They made me an honorary member of the Italian society and I thanked Max who had kept on correcting my German every day since 1894.

They went to Ahmic in 1903. In the years before his marriage Tom Cullen had visited the lovely lake in the bush country of Magnetawan, as his chief's guest at the Kelly camp on Indian Point. To his mind Ahmic was the ideal place for a camping vacation:

Rebecca was as happy in the Canadian woods as I was, so we were both delighted when Dr. Kelly invited us to occupy Indian Point for a few weeks after he returned to Baltimore in September. In those early days we stayed in Baltimore all summer of necessity. Summer, when senior surgeons are on holiday, is the most remunerative time of year for the younger surgeons. They carry on for their chiefs in the clinics and in addition look after many patients who would go to the head of the department if he were there. It's profitable but it isn't comfortable. At the end of a long summer of it, a few weeks of cool September weather in the Magnetawan country with nothing to do but fish and loaf was something to look forward to.

As it turned out, the first night of our first September holiday at Indian Point was not as peaceful as we had hoped. I'll never forget it. As our small steamer ran down the river from Burk's Falls that morning, pivoting around the bends on one paddle-wheel and stearing clear of floating logs, it had been hard to remember that this time the day before we were sweltering in Baltimore. Here we needed sweaters, for we wanted to stay on deck. The scene was continually changing. A farmhouse or two would come in view in a clearing, rounding a bend a few wild ducks would be scared up, or a deer sent swimming for shore. A swing bridge would open for us, a crane would fly ahead lazily and, hanging over the banks, we would see bright clusters of beautiful berries. About half way to Magnetawan we stopped at the big woodpiles, tied up and loaded fuel. All the Magnetawan boats burned wood in those days and the woodpiles were a regular stop.

Beyond the woodpiles we came to Cecebe Lake, called at landings, left provisions and mail and went on down river again. A few more miles between wooded shores and we were at "the Mag" and the lock. Locked through, we called at the wharf, whistled for the swing bridge and, a little more than a mile farther down, the steamer pulled around to the right to land the Cullens, bag, baggage, and Tobie, the collie, at Dr. Kelly's wharf on Indian Point.

Rebecca and I went to sleep early that night in the big cabin. We were ready for a good long rest, but we didn't get one. About three I was wakened by a loud knocking at the door. Tobie was barking furiously. Still half asleep I called "Who's there? Come in and let me look at you."

It was Charlie Smith, a farmer from the other end of the lake. He told me there was a woman very ill on the farm next his, that Dr. Freeborn in the village was away and that he wanted me to come at once.

We got into a rowboat and started up river. It was so dark we couldn't see the banks until we ran into them, grounding in the marsh or bumping against stumps. By the time we got to Magnetawan I was thoroughly awake. I went to Dr. Freeborn's office above the drugstore, but the doors were locked. We got a ladder from somebody and I climbed in through a balcony door, gathered the instruments I needed, climbed down again and started off with a team and waggon, Charlie Smith driving. Up and down some very steep hills and over some very hard rocks, we came at last to a small log cabin across from Charlie's farm.

I found the patient in bad shape, told her I would have to operate at once, and was put right back to the days of my internship at Hopkins. She said I was too young and if she needed me she would send for me.

I explained to her that it wouldn't work just that way. I would either operate now, or I would not come back; if she would not do as I told her she must consult another physician and I advised calling the one from Dunchurch, fifteen miles away. She changed her mind, I operated then and there, and she made a fine recovery.

The night's struggle and its happy ending launched a fortunate succession of holidays. All the Cullens shared them, for the eldest gathered his family to him at Ahmic as often and for as long as he could. Autumn vacations in Dr. Kelly's camp continued five or six years, then Tom and Rebecca Cullen began to build for themselves on the hillside they had chosen, across the river mouth from Indian Point, looking westward over the changing waters of the lake. The main cabin of their camp, Ojibway, was built in 1909, its logs set among thick woods that rose to the hill top, its long gallery lifted above the water on a shoulder of bare rock. Thereafter Ojibway grew year after year; sleeping cabins, an ice house, a boat house, a wharf, more sleeping cabins. Long before it was completed Tom Cullen was earning and taking his full holiday — two months away from the summer heat of Baltimore:

170

A man can do more good work in ten months than in twelve if he spends the other two loafing and fishing. I could never have done my work year after year if it had not been for those months at Ahmic.

Loafing and fishing are occupations a companionable man likes to share. As summer followed summer at Ojibway there were always visitors coming and returning; fishing excursions to plan, trout streams to explore, new bass rocks to try and old ones to try again, berry-pickings and swimming parties and picnics to organize and, most important of all to Tom Cullen, friendships to renew. From that first broken night at Indian Point, Ahmic had been his lake, Magnetawan his village, its people his friends. Having adopted them, he joyously shared their life, doing those things required of a good villager with matter-of-course loyalty, repaying with generous interest the trust and affection of his fellow-villagers.

To see Tom Cullen, in patched and faded drills, his ragged red hat tipped to shade his sunburned nose, going to "the Mag" for groceries, is to see a happy man. Visiting outside the postoffice with friends of all ages, dropping in at the store for a talk, calling for the washing and the coal-oil and the paper, swapping stories on Raaflaub's wharf, putting back down river with the day's supply of news and provisions, Tom Cullen is more than happy; he knows it.

4

PARTNERSHIP DIVIDENDS

IN THE NEW CENTURY Cullens had been growing up fast.
Blanche was the second sister to marry and move away.
Ernest, having completed his medical course, came to
Baltimore to do postgraduate work under Dr. Welch at
the Pathological. "It will just put you in line for the
surgical work you wish to do later on," Tom wrote, congratulating his brother on the opportunity. Rose finished
university and went to teach in a girls' boarding school.
In 1906 Katherine, youngest of the family, graduated also,
prepared to teach. The task undertaken in partnership
by mother and son more than ten years before was done.
"The children" were equipped for life. The partners
made a new survey. . . .

From Chengtu, West China, a few months before she
died there in 1924, Rose Cullen Wallace mailed home a
record of memories. There was urgency in the writing,
as though she knew already that she had little time for
setting down the remembrance of happiness. When all
was written she added a page:.

"I sometimes wonder whether all families have as
strong a family feeling as ours. I doubt it. When we were
in Toronto Tom used to travel nearly a thousand miles
just to come home for Sunday dinner. . . . Mother, with
all her energy, unselfishness and will power could never
have given us the education we had unless Tom had been

back of her. Even when Tom was in Baltimore with only five cents in his pocket we looked upon him as the source of all our prosperity and the hope of the future. The greatest gift that any human being can give another is the chance to develop and grow and see life and understand it a little and this is what Tom has given each one of us."

. . . The partners made a new survey. Fares to England in a one-class boat were $42.50 each. Travel and an opportunity to study abroad would help the younger girls in their teaching careers. Both wanted to go. Tom said it could be managed. Mary Cullen gave up the house that had been home longer than any other in her children's memory, bought the tickets, stored her furniture. The month after Kate's graduation she was writing Tom from England.

Rose was writing too, describing for the brother who had made it possible their Cornish mother's return to her mother's home, St. Just-in-Roseland:

"We went to Falmouth where we took a small steamer for St. Maws. Here we were rowed ashore and then started along beautiful country lanes for St. Just. After about two miles we came to the churchyard, passing through a quaint lich-gate. The graveyard is on a hill which slopes down to the grey stone church. The sea comes right to the back step of the church. Here Grandmother Greene was baptized and confirmed and married and we saw in the rectory the marriage register, signed by Grandmother and Grandfather Greene. . . . Great-grandfather's farm came right down to the sea. On the shore they had a bathing house. Mother said Grandmother often told her of the good times they had bathing there. . . . Mother was strangely moved at St. Just, as if she were on holy ground."

Another month, the three were in Paris and the girls had begun taking lectures at the Sorbonne. Mary Cullen went with them to the public lectures. To one in particular she went eagerly and sat, a modest little lady with grey hair, listening to a modest little lady with dark hair lecture on *Les Ions Dans le Gaz;* the first lecture Marie Curie ever gave in the Sorbonne. Rose reported to Tom:

"Mme. Curie was short, quiet, almost bashful and looked far from being a public character. We knew nothing about ions in gas but were delighted."

They went to churches and galleries, to the Opera and to the Imperial Russian Ballet, though on that Mary Cullen had first to do a little heartsearching. "Mother," Tom learned, "thought perhaps she should not go to the ballet." Her daughters persuaded her; she could listen to the music and not look at the dancing. She went, decided demurely to look as well as listen and thought the dancing very beautiful.

Thus happily the senior partner began her sabbatical years. They were to be divided among her children and between America and Europe. Rose did not come home with her fellow-voyagers but stayed in Paris as secretary of the Student Hostel, returning after nearly five years only to marry and go with her husband to China. In the long college vacations her mother and her younger sister came again and again to holiday with her in the mountains or by the sea, or to live, while Kate brushed up her languages, in one old university city or another. Returning, Mary Cullen would find family reunions prepared for her at Magnetawan, and winter-long visits to Baltimore to stay with Tom and with Minnie. There were transatlantic meetings of Cullens too, contrived by Tom wherever and whenever he could stretch his own overseas visits to include one. He was going over now as often as he could, Rebecca with him:

So much that was new was coming out in Europe in those days you had to go over as often as you could. Seeing a man at work and getting to know him gives you the surest gauge of the value of his written work. I have read some very impressive papers by men with big reputations that I wouldn't give you two cents for, because I have talked with the man and know the way his mind slants, or else have seen him at work and know the kind of work he does. I learned things of the greatest value to me professionally each time we went to Europe but I sometimes think what was of greatest value was the chance I had there to measure the big men's reputations by the men.

That was why George Nuttall left Germany at last and went to England; he had got too many big men's measures and let them know it. One or two of the biggest had started claiming credit for work that wasn't theirs. Nuttall checked them up in their own scientific journals and gave the credit where it was due. He found after doing it that he could lead a more useful scientific life elsewhere. So he went to Cambridge as Quick Professor. He was wise. You could see the rot spreading among German scientists from visit to visit in the later years. The first time I went to Germany was in '93 and I came back feeling that if I could not live in America I would rather live in Germany than anyplace else. The last time I was there was 1913 and I came away feeling I would rather live anywhere than in Germany. That was the change in twenty years, but from first to last there was always plenty to learn.

The zeal with which Tom Cullen pursued learning is reflected in letters, written from Amsterdam, Berlin and Berne, from Paris, Lausanne and London to his brother at Hopkins. The pursuit would be taken up as a rule in Professor Treub's clinic in Amsterdam the day after the Cullens landed in Rotterdam. It was so in 1906:

We stayed three days, saw several excellent operations then came on to Berlin. . . . At the hospitals Leopold and Dowman, two of our old students have been of much help to us and have shown us many things. Professor Orth is away. . . . The operations at some of the clinics are fine, at others abominable. On the whole we have gained a great deal and have been greatly impressed by some of the gynecological pathological collections. The ladies are much pleased with seeing the emperor in the Tiergarten. . . . We hope to go to the surgical congress today. It is just around the corner. Already we have met several old friends and are anticipating seeing important things. Leave for Halle, Dresden and Leipzig Friday. . . .

We spent several days at Tübingen with Professor Döderlein and learned lots of new surgical stunts that made our eyes bulge. On Wednesday we went down to Freiberg and met Krönig. He is a bully fellow, has a fine clinic and is doing as good work as any man in Europe. They entertained us splendidly and we saw lots of work. . . . Next Wednesday we go to Lausanne to see Roux operate and later in the week come back to Berne to see Prof. Kocher. From here to Paris and London. . . . Must now hustle off to the hospital. . . .

In later visits the pattern was repeated with variations, the preposession with science slackening a little in Paris and London. In Paris there were dinners and long talks with Professor Pozzi and Professor Faure when the day's work at the clinics was done. In London Tom Cullen would relax, spend an evening with Cuthbert Lockyer, run down to Oxford to dine with Dr. Osler, journey to Leeds "to see Mr. Moynihan*," to Cornwall "to visit the land of Mother's birth," to Paris again for a few days' holiday with Rebecca or, with Rose, to Liverpool "to meet Mother and Kate arriving." Then the Baltimore party would turn homeward, heralded by a letter fixing the date for which "Miss Cora" could make engagements for patients to see Dr. Thomas Cullen in his office at 3 West Preston Street.

* The surgeon, afterwards (1929) Lord Moynihan, with whom at Toronto in 1930 Tom Cullen received an LL.D. from his university.

PART IV

ACHIEVEMENTS

I

THE CHURCH HOME, BALTIMORE

THE WEST WALL of the main operating room of the Church Home and Infirmary is of glass. Its outlook is across the valley where, under pavements and warehouses and railway tracks, Baltimore's forgotten river, Jones Falls, flows through a drain to the harbour. Climbing the far hill, the tall new city lifts itself from the place where the old one burned, above the docks and the ships and the freight sheds and the close-packed streets that should have burned. The main operating room at the Church Home commands a wide view.

It is the room where the chairman of the Church Home Medical Board does most of his surgical work. Its view has advantages. An onlooker unused to surgical work can turn to trace the intermittent progress of North American urban civilization through the west wall while, this side the glass, held to the tense present under its canopy of light, the work goes on. . . .

The stout little nurse-in-training paused momentarily in her task of wiping sweat from the brows and necks of the masked men and women at the narrow table, to give advice.

"Watch him," she said, jerking her head towards the shortest and roundest of the white figures about the table. "Watch what he's doing. That's Dr. Cullen giving the resident a break. He's the only one of the big men I've seen here that always does it."

"Always," she said, firmly and affectionately. "Always." Damping fresh gauze she wiped her own brow. "Ask any of the young surgeons," she said. "They'll tell you. Dr. Cullen always lets the assistant on an operation do his fair part of the work . . . "

"Wipe." The gowned figure at the surgeon's right spoke without turning. The nurse-in-training took more gauze and went back to wiping sweat. In the rhythmic silence of concentration and the heat of a Baltimore spring the work went on.

At intervals, the operator half turned from the table and bent his head to the right and the nurse beside him half turned from the table and lifted her left shoulder. A nose whose large curve rode untamed above its mask was drawn along the proffered shoulder and surgeon and nurse turned back together to the table, the timing of their work unbroken.

At intervals the rhythm was interrupted by a longer pause while the operator asked a question; always the same question.

"Satisfied?" the old surgeon said to his young assistant, hands quiet and head lifted. "Satisfied?" The young assistant nodded and the work went on, picking up the rhythm at the thing next to be done. Presently another pause and the same question, "Satisfied?"

Later, in her office in the operating suite, the owner of the shoulder explained the practised ease of its meeting with the nose:

"I don't know who first began it with Dr. Cullen, but it must have been a long time ago. Every operating room nurse who has ever worked with him knows the technique. It is standard hot-weather practice here, and at Hopkins too, I imagine. No mask made could keep that nose under for a whole operation and you can't have sweat dripping off the end of a surgeon's nose. It isn't aseptic. So we all do as you saw; turn a shoulder for him

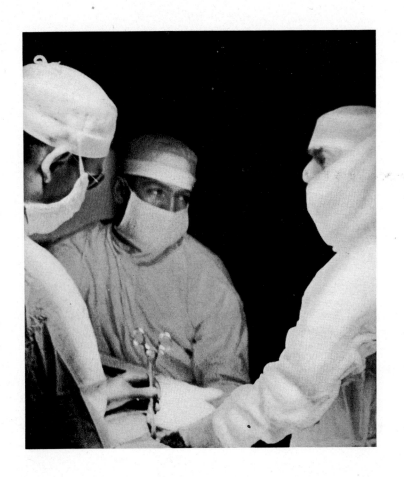

"Satisfied?"
—page 180

Tom Cullen operating

to mop his nose on when we see Dr. Cullen bend his head to the right. It's entirely automatic. I didn't know I had been doing it to-day until you told me."

Still later, in the cool dusk of his old house in Eager Street, Tom Cullen explained the repeated word:

I asked him if he was satisfied because I wanted to know. That's a fine boy and he had a lot of experience in the war and he knows his work. He gave me as good exposure today as I've ever been given in an operation of this sort. I wanted his suggestions. There is always something new to learn in this business. . . . It's like this; the important thing is not that I should have my way about an operation, but that the patient should get well. If there is a better way of doing something, I want to know it. So I ask the young fellows as we go along. . . . Understand me, I mean by better, better for the patient, not the surgeon. What's best for the patient is the only consideration always. That's one thing no physician and no surgeon can afford to forget as long as he practises. The other thing is to pass on the help he's had. Let me give you the picture . . .

In 1827 Washington Medical College was founded in Baltimore. In 1837 it was moved to more commodious quarters on Fairmount, the eastern hill overlooking the city and the bay. The new building on the hilltop was of Baltimore brick, with wide windows, white cupola, one long wing of wards and a high, cylindrical amphi-theatre, supported outside by four gothic-revival towers and surrounded inside by galleries. There Baltimore medical students of a century ago sat to watch operations and dissections. There, in 1849, in the tower room to the left of the amphitheatre entrance, Edgar Allan Poe died in the arms of the resident surgeon, Dr. Cullen.

No tie but the name can be traced between the earlier Cullen and the one who, more than half a century later, was to become the old medical school building's most

181

familiar friend. If the name was an attraction, the second Cullen did not know it. He was engrossed in his work; he went where it took him and did what it required of him. At the turn of the century the most pressing requirement was more space and equipment, plus more trained assistance, for the care of surgical patients. Tom Cullen and the Church Home and Infirmary came together on that.

Edgar Allan Poe being dead and Resident Surgeon Cullen and the medical college departed, the Episcopalian Church in Baltimore had taken over the college building in 1858. United and christened the Church Home and Infirmary, two diocesan charities were installed there. There, forty years later, still with their period title, they were still functioning. The amphitheatre had been divided horizontally to make a circular chapel and gallery above an entrance hall. A west wing had been added. As the need grew, a major piece of surgery was done in the new wing from time to time. But for the most part the inhabitants remained as they had been; invalids, convalescents and the old; the nursing staff was insufficient and the facilities for surgery rudimentary.

That was the Church Home in 1902, when young Dr. Cullen, starting practice for himself as a gynecological surgeon, was called to do an operation there. Dr. Louis McLane Tiffany called him:

Dr. Tiffany was one of the leading surgeons in the State, a graduate of Cambridge and the University of Maryland, and professor of surgery at the University of Maryland medical school. I was a Hopkins man just out of my residency. Yet he called me to do an abdominal operation he could have done as well himself, or better, and he stood and held the light for me until I finished it. He did it simply from kindness, to show his confidence in a young surgeon just starting his career. You don't forget things like that, or the men who do them.

Or their example, if you are Tom Cullen. The development of the Church Home in Baltimore as a modern surgical hospital and training school was not unique. At many such pressure points, small hospitals and private clinics were being equipped or established for surgery, by surgeons, to meet a situation that was fast growing intolerable. The special ingredient in the metamorphosis of the Church Home and Infirmary was something less tangible than equipment:

I've told you about Tiffany. Dr. Kelly had the same spirit. I remember asking him, years after I was through my training, why he did so much for his interns and assistants. He said that when he was resident in a Philadelphia hospital he had a chief who wanted to do everything himself; so much so that he once reported Kelly to the hospital trustees for overstepping his authority and amputating a finger. Kelly said he made up his mind right there and then that if ever he became head of a surgical department, his men would be given every opportunity. We all were, always. Naturally, a man who has profited by that sort of generosity wants to be generous when his chance comes. Mine came at the Church Home.

The notion that the Church Home and Infirmary should be developed as a modern hospital equipped for surgery struck young Dr. Cullen soon after he was first called there by Dr. Tiffany.*

A strong preference for being sick at home was then general among the prosperous, and surgeons were still required to do, and still did, major operations in private houses under conditions that any surgeon would now consider suicidal. But the careful were beginning to set limits

* Note by T.S.C.: "As I remember, I was doing another Church Home operation at the time, to the tune of 'Lead Kindly Light' on the chapel organ next door. But it takes more than a notion to make a hospital. Without the superb work of Miss Jane Nash as superintendent, the devotion of her associates and the unfailing backing of our board of trustees, the Church Home could never have become the fine hospital it is."

to what they would do to their patients at home. More
and more, first-class men were refusing the risks inseparable from extemporized operating rooms although, as
things were, a refusal was not always easy to justify. In
many cases it meant either that a needed operation would
not be done or that it would be done by a less fastidious
surgeon. All over the country surgical need had far out-
grown existing facilities for meeting it.

Each discovery in surgery, and discoveries were coming thick and fast, meant new demands on every surgical
clinic. Each patient restored to health by an operation
that, a year or two earlier, no operator would have
attempted meant a score of new patients eager for the
same relief. The situation in Baltimore when Tom Cullen started in private practice was acute. In every hospital
one group of senior surgeons and their assistants could,
and to a great extent did, monopolize the available operating rooms with their cases. However able, a rising young
surgeon outside the dominant group had small chance
to operate in Johns Hopkins or any other well-equipped
hospital. He must take the risk of operating in his
patient's home, or give up surgery.

The handicap did not affect young Dr. Cullen personally. As Dr. Kelly's associate in gynecology he had,
from the first, inalienable rights in B operating suite,
reserved for the work of the Hopkins gynecological staff.
But he saw the difficulties facing even the most brilliant
of the men following him, for most of whom hospital
staff positions were not available, and he set out to help
solve them in the way best for the patient.

The Church Home and Infirmary was the basic ingredient in Tom Cullen's solution. His purpose was to
turn the old Episcopalian nursing-home into a modern
hospital with a thoroughly equipped surgical side, and
without a controlling clique. Its trustees being convinced,
by degrees, that the transformation should and could be

made, the next thing was to begin making it. With the help of Dr. Frank D. Gavin, superintendent of the old infirmary, Dr. Cullen began. Men who worked with him in the enterprise say that no one will ever know how much of the work was done at his own expense. If a piece of special equipment was needed in the new operating room it was provided, and the bill did not always go to the Church Home trustees. If a costly instrument was required to ensure that surgeons operating at the Church Home should not be disadvantaged, Dr. Cullen bought the instrument and ordered it delivered more often than not prepaid. It is sometimes the easiest way to get things done, Tom Cullen has found, but you are not to suppose that he was thinking altogether of the other fellow in what he did to help make over the Church Home. There was a bit of insurance for himself in it, he recalls, and a time was to come when it was very comforting to have.

As the other fellow experienced it, the insurance, however comforting, and the instruments and equipment, however essential, were the least part of Tom Cullen's share in the Church Home's new usefulness. The great part was in one rule from which no departure has been permitted: that all the hospital's facilities must be open to all reputable physicians and surgeons. One of the many who benefited by that rule has written of Dr. Cullen and the Church Home:

"T.S. made the Church Home. By that I mean he made it into what it is generally acknowledged to be; one of the best hospitals, big or small, in this part of the country. Of course he didn't do it alone. No man does anything like that without a lot of help and Dr. Cullen had two inseparable partners in his enterprise; Dr. Guy Hunner and Dr. Griffith Davis. 'The Three Musketeers' we all called them and they made a perfect working team. In Dr. Davis the Church Home had the first full-time anaesthetist in Baltimore and, I believe, in the whole country. That was T. S's doing too and it is an example of the sort of leadership that makes a hospital's reputation. But still it wasn't the important thing. The important thing is the spirit T.S. put into the place, and keeps in it. He has been chairman of the Church Home medical board since it was formed in 1908 and all those years his constant care has been to keep the spirit inclusive. Graduates of all the Maryland schools work together on the board as they do on the hospital staff, and none of them, as far as I have ever seen, even thinks of trying to get a special advantage for his school or its graduates. If you know human nature, you will know what an achievement that is. It's all T. S.'s. Even now, at the first symptom of the cliquishness that can curse a hospital, T.S. is up and fighting from the drop of the hat. It wasn't a hundred per cent. smooth sailing to success with the Church Home, believe me. For one thing, T. S. was a Hopkins staff man and Hopkins was very unpopular for a long time with members of the profession in Baltimore who had trained in other schools. The fact was that Hopkins men really were better prepared in those early days. It was a new school with a new idea, it picked its men and it got the results that picked men can give, while older schools, bound by tradition and conservatism simply slept at the switch. But that did nothing to lessen prejudice.

"T. S. was one of the first to start breaking it down; in part by refusing to recognize it, in part by pitching in and fighting it where it could not be ignored, but mostly by just being a good physician and expecting other men to be the same. He never stopped to ask where they were trained before he called men into consultation. He never hesitated, when he got into a position to do so at the Church Home, to recommend good men for promotion or good work for commendation, because either was the product of another medical school. He never in any way, as far as any one of us can tell, has shown any preference for Johns Hopkins graduates over others with as good claim to recognition.

"We have now, in Maryland hospitals, as happy a blending of medical graduates as you will find any place in the country. T. S., I would say, has done as much as any single man to bring it about, and the Church Home has been his proving ground."

2

LIVER SURGERY

CHANCE LED TOM CULLEN to find, in 1904, the key to liver surgery. He was the first American surgeon to employ and report the value of blunt needles in suturing liver incisions, and it happened, he has explained, quite by accident. The difficulty of suturing incisions had been a major obstacle to the development of liver surgery. The liver, being in effect a mass of blood vessels, is certain to bleed wherever cut. It is almost equally certain to bleed wherever pierced with the point of a needle. The surgeon suturing a bleeding liver chanced causing more blood to flow in making the sutures. Resections of the liver had been done before 1904, but surgeons attempted them unwillingly.

The operating surgeon was no exception to the rule in the case with which Tom Cullen had to deal in June of that year.[1] The patient was one on whom he had operated more than a year earlier, removing a cancerous left kidney. When he was called to examine her again she had developed a large tumor occupying the region between the edge of the ribs and the right anterior superior spine. Her pulse was rapid, her temperature high and she was losing ground rapidly. An immediate operation was decided upon.

[1] Journal of the American Medical Association, 1905, Vol. XLIV, page 1239; Vol. II of T.S.C.'s collected reprints: *Large Carcinomatous Tumor of the Liver.*

On operation, the new growth was found to spring from the liver, to be larger than a child's head, almost globular, perfectly smooth and free from adhesions. It was attached on its inner side to the gall-bladder; the edge of the liver appeared as a crescent-shaped ridge above the centre of its forward surface. It was impossible to determine, examining it in position, whether it was a cystic new growth or an abscess formation. After careful examination had revealed no secondary growths in the liver and no evidence of metastases in other organs or thickening in the region from which the kidney had been removed, the surgeon made his decision; not to back out but to go ahead and remove the growth. To do so, it was necessary to remove with it a section of the liver.

The gall-bladder was exposed, the cystic duct clamped and cut and the proximal portion of the duct tied off. The lower half of the liver could then be drawn out through the incision, which extended from the free margin of the ribs downward almost to the anterior superior spine. The liver was everywhere walled off with gauze from the abdominal contents and a gauze rope was fastened firmly around it about an inch above the point at which the cut was to be made. Then the surgeon called for a cautery. Fortunately, as the subsequent history of liver surgery shows, the instrument would not work:

So I asked for a long needle and they unintentionally gave me one with a broken point. That solved the problem. No one wanting to knock down apples stands beneath the tree with a pitchfork and pushes it, prongs first, straight up. One would bark too many branches that way. The way to do it is to hold the prongs in the hands and push the handle up. That way the branches will be pushed to one side or the other and will not be injured. The same principle applied, I discovered, when I started using the blunt needle I had been given by accident to suture the liver.

The liver contains myriads of blood vessels, but the blunt needle did not bark any of them. It pushed them to one side or the other. Working with it, from left to right, I passed mattress sutures through the entire substance of the liver, placing them about one centimetre apart and each overlapping the next for about two millimetres. I used Pagenstecker thread for the greater number, making only the supplementary ones of catgut. After placing the first two or three sutures I commenced to cut, having the tumor held taut at the same time. The sutures were tied after I had cut a short distance. We continued the operation that way, placing two or three sutures, cutting, tieing and then repeating the procedure until the entire growth had been removed. The five or six large blood vessels we encountered spurted freely, but they were picked up at once with artery forceps and tied freehand with fine Pagenstecker thread. The whole operation was completed without the loss of two drams of blood. When the sutures had been tied there was absolutely no bleeding from the surface of the liver.

When the growth had been cut completely away a raw surface remained fully 16 centimetres long by 6 wide. Making traction on the sutures, I found that the raw surface could be rolled in on itself, so that the two halves formed flaps. These were brought together so that little or none of the raw area remained exposed. The tied ends of the sutures were used to bring the two edges together and iodoform gauze was used beneath the edge of the liver and also on its surface. Microscopic examination of the tumor showed it to be an adenocarcinoma.

The patient, who had been in a desperate state when the operation was started, stood it well and recovered from it rapidly, leaving the hospital in excellent condition in little more than four weeks. But cancer cells had been too deeply established for eradication. She died within a few months from a return of the growth where the kidney carcinoma had first been removed. But what her surgeon discovered while removing the liver tumor has since helped many to complete recovery. It was after this operation that Tom Cullen had his first liver needles made; some as long as four or five inches, some straight, some curved but all as blunt as his finger at the business end, so that they could not pierce or bark any structure they encountered.

Looking into the literature on the subject in the Surgeon General's Library, the Baltimore discoverer found that a Russian had been before him. The Russian, Kousnietzoff, had developed a blunt needle for liver surgery and had published a paper describing it, in Russia. Tom Cullen coming, by the chance of a broken-pointed needle, on the same discovery was the first to recognize its usefulness and apply it in American surgery.

Discovery of the uses of a blunt needle in liver surgery enlivened Tom Cullen's interest in that organ and its surgical treatment. Three years later he published in *Surgery Gynecology and Obstetrics* an article on surgery of the liver. His paper included a review of the comparatively few cases of resection of the liver recorded in America between 1899 and 1904, and a description of the techniques used in the increasing number of liver operations being performed with success since he had discovered and introduced to American surgery the use of the blunt liver needle.[2]

Twenty years, and the discoverer was still studying the liver and liver surgery. *The Archives of Surgery,* Vol. II, 1925, contains a 56-page paper by Dr. Thomas S. Cullen in which embryology and anatomy of the liver are thoroughly dealt with in the course of a study of the recorded cases of accessory lobes.[3] The immediate occasion of the paper was an operation performed by the writer to relieve a patient suffering from recurring and persistent attacks of jaundice. When he operated on this patient, in February of 1924, he found the stomach nor-

2 Surgery Gynecology and Obstetrics, 1907, Vol. IV, p. 573; Vol. II of T.S.C.'s collected reprints: *Surgery of the Liver.*

3 Archives of Surgery, 1925, Vol. XI, pp. 718-764; *Accessory Lobes of the Liver.*

mal and the gall-bladder entirely free of stones and, in its upper part, of adhesions. There were some adhesions, which he loosened, between the lower part of the gall-bladder and the duodenum. On the under-surface of the liver he found two or three small excrescent lobes of normal liver tissue. In all of this he could see nothing which seemed to him a sufficient cause of his patient's jaundice. But, on the under surface of the gall-bladder, three centimetres from the edge of the liver he discovered a small flat nodule hardly more than half an inch long by a quarter inch wide. It had sharp edges and the colour and consistency of liver and it was attached to the gall-bladder by a small piece of membrane:

We drew up this small mass, tied the pedicle with one catgut ligature and removed it. It was perfectly clear we were dealing with a small accessory liver, free from adhesions and well removed from the liver proper. I felt reasonably sure that we had located the cause of the trouble.

Max Broedel made me two drawings giving the relation of the accessory liver to the liver itself and also to the gall-bladder. Later he made a graphic reconstruction of the microscopic findings; it showed a miniature liver, perfect in every particular. The liver itself can be likened to a radiator. In its vessels and ducts, the accessory liver we had removed was identical in structure, but on a many times reduced scale. As I had thought, removing it we had got the cause of the trouble. The patient had no more jaundice, made a quick recovery and went home perfectly well.

Tom Cullen was still engaged preparing, for the *Archives of Surgery,* his paper on *Accessory Hepatic Lobes* when his knowledge of the liver and its possibilities was further increased in a way he would not have chosen. Early in 1924, a member of his immediate family was operated on at Johns Hopkins by Dr. J. M. T. Finney for the relief of a long-established condition characterized

by indigestion, severe headaches, and attacks of nausea
which recurred increasingly, most often in the form of
violent train- or car-sickness.

The operating surgeon found the liver thoroughly involved. The right lobe was abnormally long, stretching
down to within three-quarters of an inch of the right
anterior superior spine. To its lower end the hepatic flexure of the colon was firmly adherent for nearly an inch
and a quarter. This flexure was badly kinked. Freeing
the edge of the liver revealed that the colon was attached
to the under side of the right lobe from tip to base. The
lengthy adhesion was loosened, causing some bleeding
which was checked by suturing the liver, using a blunt
liver needle. Adhesions attaching the duodenum to the
liver also had to be shelled off. Their pressure on the
duodenum would have been sufficient to account for
some at least of the symptoms, for they attached its
median side to the under surface of the liver in such a
fashion as to be definitely constricting. The appendix was
six inches long and for two-thirds of its length embedded
in adhesions. The distal third was firm and stood up like
a finger. Greyish areas of scar tissue were noticeable on
the elongated lobe of the liver. This fact and the other
findings at operation, taken with the clinical history, led
Dr. Finney to feel that the abnormal length of the right
lobe of the liver might be traceable to an old appendicitis:

If that were so, the periappendial inflammation had
extended to the hepatic flexure of the colon, causing it
to adhere to the lower edge of the liver. With the continued traction of the frequently distended and partly
obstructed bowel this part of the liver would have been
drawn down and attenuated. This would account for the
greyish scar areas found in the substance of the right
lobe. The picture found at operation supported John
Finney's interpretation very strongly. Max Broedel sketched the liver condition as it was revealed at various stages

of the operation and from his series of sketches gave us the best picture of a Riedel's lobe that I have ever seen. The patient recovered promptly and was completely relieved of the distressing symptoms.

In Tom Cullen's experience it is best not to be hasty in blaming the liver for all the trouble in its region. He recalls an operation he did in 1905 when interest in liver surgery might have led him astray.[4] The patient for more than a year had had a smooth swelling under the ribs at the right side and latterly had suffered from pain in that area after eating. It was possible before operating to make out a large firm mass in the right upper quadrant of the abdomen, but impossible to tell whether it was a kidney tumor, a bowel growth or a pathological condition involving the liver and gall-bladder:

On opening the abdomen it appeared at first that the liver was the culprit. The front part of the mass proved to be a prolapsed and somewhat thickened right lobe of the liver. But looking farther we found that the back portion was formed by the prolapsed right kidney. We continued investigation and between the two found the real cause of the trouble: an appendix at least five centimetres long extending upward along the under surface of the liver, considerably thickened and adherent to the gall-bladder and cystic duct.

We removed the appendix and closed the abdomen, leaving the liver and the prolapsed kidney just as we had found them otherwise. The case is a striking example of how difficult it can be to determine the exact cause of abdominal trouble. The patient left hospital with the same smooth swelling under the ribs at the right side but with the pain and discomfort entirely relieved. It was not the prolapsus of liver and kidney but the tugging of the appendix adhesions which had caused the distress in her case.

4 Proceedings of Johns Hopkins Medical Society — Johns Hopkins Hospital Bulletin, 1906, Vol. XVII, pp. 150-155; Vol. II of T.S.C.'s collected reprints: Case VI, *An Obscure Abdominal Tumor in the Right Upper Quadrant etc.*

3

ADENOMYOMATA

TOM CULLEN'S SECOND BOOK *Adenomyoma of the Uterus* was not published until 1908, eight years after the publication of his first, *Cancer of the Uterus*. His third, *Myomata of the Uterus* published with Dr. Kelly as joint-author came within a year of the second. W. B. Saunders of Philadelphia published both and both had their genesis in 1894 and the backwater. The interval, filled with the making of a career as a surgeon and a reputation as a scientist, had not dulled or deflected the Cullen resolution to complete work undertaken. From B operating room and the gynecological laboratory at Hopkins, from the operating rooms at Cambridge and the Church Home hospitals, from his chief's private clinic and from the emergency hospital at Frederick, Tom Cullen had been gathering year after year material for the book he and Dr. Kelly had first planned to write together fourteen years before; a major clinical and pathological study of uterine tumors and their treatment. But when he came to digest the material assembled he discovered that he had not one book, but two:

We had the records of such a large number of cases of adenomyoma in the material we had gathered on the larger subject that it was perfectly clear a separate book should be made of them. If we merely mentioned the fact that, among the myoma cases we had studied, treated and recorded more than ninety were adenomyomata many readers might have doubted our veracity. On the other

194

hand, to give these ninety-odd cases the full consideration they merited would have made a general work unwieldy and unbalanced. Moreover the difference of opinion regarding the glandular structure of this type of tumor which von Recklinghausen and I had argued out in '96 had aroused an interest that lived after the argument died.

This was natural for, as pelvic surgery developed, more and more adenomyomata were being discovered and removed and the need for more knowledge of their clinical symptoms and histological appearances was increasingly recognized.

I remember well the first tumor of the type I saw, the one that started the argument. It was on an afternoon in October of '94 and I was making the routine examination of material from B operating room in our downstairs room at the Pathological. I came on a uniformly enlarged uterus about four times normal size. Opening it, I found that the increased size was caused by a diffuse thickening of the whole anterior wall.

This was a matter for reference to the second floor back. Tom Cullen took his discovery upstairs to Dr. Welch. Dr. Welch had not seen anything like it before either. He suggested that, for microscopic examination, Dr. Kelly's young pathologist should make sections from the entire thickness of the affected wall of the uterus. Tom Cullen made them and discovered that a diffuse glandular tumor occupying the inner side of the uterine wall caused the thickening and that the uterine mucosa flowed at many points into this diffuse myoma. Before the end of the year he found a second tumor of the same type among the material from B operating room. He embodied in a paper, published in the Johns Hopkins Hospital Reports of 1896, the conclusions he had reached after sectioning and examining the two specimens. It was this paper that brought him into collision with the great von Recklinghausen and the collision determined him to pursue every opportunity for research into the origins of adenomyomata.

195

Nothing he found in the course of his research caused him to doubt the accuracy of his first findings:

Microscopic examination of large sections of the first two specimens had clearly shown the origin of the glandular element in adenomyomata. It was perfectly apparent under the microscope that the glands originated in a flowing outward of the normal uterine mucosa. In all subsequent cases of tumors of this type, our examination was directed to checking the accuracy of this first conclusion.

Sometimes the mucous membrane origin was evident at once. In other instances a clear idea of the condition was only obtainable after examination of very large sections embracing the entire uterine wall. But in virtually every case in which diffuse adenomyoma existed we were able to trace the mucous membrane origin of the glands.

Ben McCleary was my great help in this part of the work. Ben came to the gynecological laboratory as an odd-job boy. He became interested in the work and stayed on, to develop into the finest kind of laboratory assistant. I was able to help him a bit and to advise him, and he went to night classes and matriculated while he was working with us, and went on to the University of Maryland medical school. He stayed with us as laboratory assistant until he graduated as Dr. Benjamin O. McCleary and he was always a tower of strength. Once I asked Ben to do a thing I could put it out of mind, knowing it would be done, and done well, whether it was making a frozen section or staging a practical joke.

The thoroughness with which Ben set to work each year to confuse the graduating class in gynecology always delighted me. When the students' practical test was due Ben would go to a butcher shop and buy sausage, bologna and other delicacies, bring them back to the laboratory, section, stain and mount them and mix the slides with those of the laboratory specimens the boys were to examine and identify. Then he would stand by with an absolutely straight face while the poor fellows puzzled over microscopes and struggled to find histological descriptions for the morbid processes revealed by a slice of liverwurst or a section of salami.

Ben was a great fellow and he came, before he died, to be one of the best, and best-loved, physicians in Baltimore. I was very proud of him as a medical man, and as a laboratory aide he was a jewel. It was always Ben who made the large and difficult sections for me when I was preparing the book on adenomyomata. He did them beautifully, and they did a lot for the book, for they made not only my work but the illustrators' far easier.

While I was on the subject there were two people I tried never to forget; the practicing physician and his patient. The clinical aspect of this type of tumor is of more immediate importance to them than its glandular origin. Studying each case, I watched for the symptoms by which an adenomyoma can be recognized clinically, with the idea of discovering any that might be peculiar to this type of growth. I cannot help feeling that anyone who reads the chapter on symptoms will agree that diffuse adenomyoma has a fairly definite clinical history of its own and that the majority of cases can be diagnosed with a relative degree of certainty.

This, at the time the book was published, was a definite gain in knowledge, and rewarded me for all the work entailed. Moreover, the value of studying the clinical with the histological aspects of a morbid process was clearly demonstrated and that is something which cannot be demonstrated too often. Those of us who do surgical work need to know all we can learn, both of the clinical symptoms and the histological appearances of the processes we are dealing with.

Dr. Joseph D. Bryant of New York set the seal of professional approval on Tom Cullen's second book. Bryant was already a noted surgeon when the younger man came to Hopkins as Kelly's intern. He was to become famous when the inside story of the panic of '93 was revealed. It was Bryant who, when Grover Cleveland became ill in the midst of the crisis, had been chosen to operate on the President. He had done the operation on a yacht at sea to ensure that no word of the illness should leak out and add to the general hysteria. The story of that dramatic surgery was still fresh when Tom Cullen met its hero in Appleton's printing plant in Brooklyn. Each was seeing a book through the press and their friendship was cemented over galley proofs and warmed by a common delight in the elder man's dry wit. The friendship and the delight endured and when Dr. Cullen's second book, *Adenomyoma of the Uterus* was published in 1908 one of the first presentation copies went to Dr. Bryant. The author treasured his note of acknowledgment:

"Dear Cullen: I want to thank you for sending me your new book. . . . I almost wish I had a womb of my own so that I could profit by your skill and experience . . ."

OF UPLIFT, TUMORS AND JOINT-AUTHORSHIP

JUST FIFTEEN YEARS AFTER they first planned it together, the 723-page volume bearing the names of Howard A. Kelly and Thomas S. Cullen as joint authors came off the press. Over the years, though the junior partner's interest remained constant, Dr. Kelly's enthusiasm for political purity and religious evangelism had somewhat outstripped his enthusiasm for tumors. There was even a point where it began to threaten the scientific work of his associate:

Naturally, I was prepared to do almost anything the chief might ask me to do for him, but there were one or two of his activities I would have been no good at. So I was a little disturbed when he called me into his office for a special talk one day and informed me that the variety of his interests was proving too much for his strength and he had therefore decided to hand over his missionary and uplift work to me.

I can hear him yet. "Brother Tom," he began, "I'm getting a little tired of this uplift work . . . " and went on, while my heart sank to my boots, to explain that he had chosen me as the man to take it over and carry it on. I had to think fast, and I did. I never thought faster in my life. I thanked the Chief for the confidence he had in me, but questioned whether I was capable of doing work of that sort as he would like it done. If I were to attempt it, I said, it must be at the expense of work I had already undertaken. I could, if he wished, give up my research for the myoma volume he and I had planned. It was about half completed, but I could give it up . . .

He thought it over for a bit, then he said, "Brother Tom, you had better go on with your research." I never heard any more of the missionary idea.

Doubt? I *knew* I couldn't do missionary work to Dr. Kelly's pattern. Every man must find his own way of doing his service. The Chief had found his and it suited him, but it would never have suited me. If he had insisted, I would have had to tell him so straight. But there is no sense in meeting an issue like that head on when you can save everybody's feelings by switching. I can tell you I was thankful to have found the right switch.

Of Kelly's highly individual combination of revivalism and surgery Henry L. Mencken has memories:

"Kelly wasn't, strictly speaking, a scientist. He was a magician, a conjurer. He could open a belly in thirty seconds and tie a suture with his third and fourth fingers but he got science and morality all mixed up. A terrible enthusiast, I've always felt. He had it all wrong what a doctor's for. A doctor's function is to make it possible for us to go on doing the pleasant things that are bad for us; smoking too much, eating too much, drinking too much and the rest of them; without killing ourselves off any sooner than is necessary. Kelly was one of those fellows that thought it was a doctor's duty to make life unbearable with rules for keeping alive. And he got enthusiasms — his missionary work was one of them, snakes were another, radium was another — and rode them out of bounds."

The Mencken estimate is an objective one of Howard Kelly in his later years. Few of those who worked with him, certainly not Tom Cullen who knew and loved him from youth, could ever be objective about "the chief." For them his enthusiasms were inseparable from himself; things to be humoured, admired, where possible shared and, when they got him into difficulties, defended. Again and again when Dr. Kelly had taken on more wickedness in high and low places; more saloons or snakes or sinners than his strength or his purse could handle alone,

Tom Cullen led a rescue party to his aid. The affectionate loyalty was repaid with boyish gratitude, occasionally intermitted by equally boyish self-absorption.

His chief's preoccupation did not trouble Kelly's senior associate. He was not only accustomed to it, but at times reckoned on it. The book for example; *Myomata of the Uterus, by Howard A. Kelly and Thomas S. Cullen:*

Kelly never saw it until it was published. I remember one day towards the first of nineteen-nine he said to me "Tom, I'm about ready to go to work on our myoma book."

"You're too late, Chief," I said, "it's in print." He asked to see the proofs and I said "Nothing doing" — I had thousands of references and cross-references and if he had ever started to annotate and rearrange them we'd have been sunk — "But I can tell you this," I said, "everything you have done is in it, and in the way you'd want it."

So he was satisfied and, when he started off for Mexico that year, I gave him a copy to take with him. As he read it, he would get off at stations and send me postcards to say how far he'd got in it and what he thought of it so far. I was delighted to find, when the last postcard came in, that he thought it was all right all the way through. But I wasn't really surprised. All his improved operations, and all the comments he had made throughout our years of work together I had jotted down on my case-cards, and they were all incorporated in the book.

That's what I had to point out to Dr. Welch. He told me the book shouldn't have Kelly's name on it; I'd written it. I told him I couldn't agree. It was Kelly's idea in the first place. He had worked out the techniques of the operations we described and perfected them, and more than half the material was his. When it was put to him that way Popsy admitted I was right; that the book should be published as a joint work.

As a matter of fact, Popsy himself had contributed an immense amount by placing all the records of the Pathological at our disposal and giving every possible co-operation in our laboratory studies. When the book was completed more than two tons of myomatous material was burned; material that he and Dr. Hurd had allowed us to keep for reference and re-examination.

To an outsider the saving for so long a time of all that vast material would have seemed unnecessary, and I don't know that it had ever been done before to such an extent. But it proved of the greatest value.

The book had been fifteen years in the making and they were years of great and dramatic change. Surgical treatment of womb tumors had developed during the period from the most insufficient and risky of experiments into carefully planned and simplified operative procedures, scientifically sound and technically adequate. The greatest contribution to that swift general expansion of knowledge and skill had come from Hopkins Department of Gynecology. It was Tom Cullen's purpose to document and present, for the use of physicians and surgeons and the benefit of their patients, the sum of the knowledge of uterine myomata and their treatment gained in the experimental years.

For that large part of his material which was drawn from cases treated by Dr. Kelly he could go back as far as 1889, the year Hopkins opened.

Beginning there he followed through, including in his survey not only Hopkins gynecological department but gynecological work done in the half-dozen hospitals where Dr. Kelly and he operated. In all, 1674 cases of myoma were reviewed, examined and classified in preparing the material for the book.

With each case the method was the same. A complete abstract of the case history was made. Each tumor removed was then re-examined, and anything of interest not noted in the original laboratory examination was added to the history sheet. The gross and histological appearance of each — how it looked to the eye and how it looked under the microscope — was described and likewise added.

Ernest Cullen, having completed his year of residency in Toronto, came to the Pathological in time to help with the clinical research. For more than a year he spent all his available time locating former patients, filling in missing data in incomplete histories and analyzing and comparing findings.

The material was assembled at last in a clueless mass. It remained to find a way through and write the book:

We started off with no plan except to analyze carefully the mass of material at our disposal. After we had spent several months doing that and getting nowhere I sent out and bought a bushel basket and several thousand cards. Then we started again.

Every history and pathological description was read over from the beginning and each point of importance was underscored. Then a card, marked with the case number and pathological number, was made for each point. That card went into the basket and another card was made for the next point and so on. For some cases as many as ten cards were needed, for some one card was enough. But when we had been through all the cases we had all the points of interest down, each on its own card in the bushel basket.

From there the way was comparatively clear. Sorted by points and cross-indexed by case and pathological numbers, the cards fell naturally under certain main headings that simplified our work immeasurably. When a given subject came up for discussion it was only necessary to pick out the cards of the relevant group and select from them the ten or twenty histories bearing on that subject, instead of each time wading through sixteen hundred histories with a strong likelihood of overlooking several important cases. I was extremely proud of our bushel-basket card index system; and I still am.

One thing Tom Cullen had decided long before he came to the writing of the book; that all the mistakes and mishaps that had occurred and all the deaths must be listed and described. The decision was not made on impulse:

Much more can be learned from failures than from successes. I felt that a frank statement of our mishaps would help other surgeons to avoid the unpleasant complications we had, from time to time, run into. And a report of all deaths, with the autopsy findings, was absolutely essential to the picture.

Our mortality — taking all myoma cases treated from the opening of Hopkins in 1889 to July 1, 1906 — was rather high; between five and six per cent. But the percentage was taken on a whole including all the early cases, many desperate cases, and also many cases of myoma associated with malignancy. Just before going to press I decided to bring the mortality figures up to date. So I went over the histories of our operations for the period between July 1, 1906, and January 1, 1909.

I found that, in 238 myoma operations, the death rate had been less than one per cent. In other words we had lost only two patients. As evidence of continuing improvement in our technique, I found that very encouraging.

Included in the later, encouraging, group of cases was the case of the record-breaking tumor.

Dr. Welch did not see the record-breaking tumor till it reached the Pathological:

He took one look at it and said, "Who did the autopsy?"

I said "It weighs eighty-nine pounds, Dr. Welch."

"Who did the autopsy?" he said.

"Nobody," I said, "she isn't dead." You should have seen Popsy's face.

The year was 1906, when tumors were big. Tumors remain usual and uterine tumors very usual. In their beginning they are not as large as peas; some stay small, some increase rapidly in size but none nowadays presents such major and serious surgical problems as faced Dr. Thomas Cullen when he undertook to remove an eighty-nine pound tumor from an eighty-five pound woman:

Understand me, every operation is serious to a good surgeon and to the patient any operation is a major one;

quite rightly. When I say there are no such serious operative problems in the removal of myomata now, I am speaking comparatively. It's a lot like fishing. When you start fishing remote lakes and streams in thinly settled country the fish are big and there are plenty of them. But as the fishermen increase in numbers the fish get fewer and smaller. The same thing has happened with tumors.

Fifty years ago, when each abdominal operation was considered the greatest sort of risk, most people preferred the risk of letting a tumor alone as long as they could endure it. When they gave up and consented to surgery they were apt to be in a pretty bad state. That is why we had so many large myomata to remove in the early years of the century. With the improvement in operative techniques and the increasingly good chance of complete recovery more patients each year chose to have necessary operations done in good time. So fewer tumors were left to grow to a large size. I doubt whether our claim to the record-breaking tumor will be challenged now. I would be willing to bet it won't be challenged on this continent.

In the case of the record-breaking tumor the patient was Mrs. McA. and she lived in West Baltimore. When she was admitted to the Church Home for surgical treatment, July 27, 1906, she weighed 174 pounds. The tumor, removed by Dr. Cullen July 30, weighed 89 pounds — four pounds more than the weight of the patient when she left the operating table. So far as the records show, it was the largest myoma of the uterus ever to be removed from a living patient who continued to live.

The patient was under ether for one hour and twenty minutes. From incision to complete closure the operation itself took five minutes less than an hour. For that speed the operator gives credit to necessity and his team. He had the B operating room staff from Hopkins as well as the Church Home surgical staff mobilized for duty in the Church Home operating room that day:

We had to be quick, and the operation would have taken much longer had it not been for the teamwork of the combined staffs. Everyone knew beforehand what he or she was there to do, we made every preparation we could before the anaesthetic was given and we had worked out in advance, as far as possible, procedures to meet the unusual requirements of the case. For example the sterilized footbath.

It was bound to be difficult to control a tumor of that size as we liberated it, and a slip could be fatal. So we had a large footbath sterilized and lined with a sterile sheet before the operation began. The assistant whose duty it was to hold the tumor as it was released and to guide it in the direction indicated by the operator used the footbath. It held about one third of the tumor and enabled him to control it without a slip, right through the operation.

We had to operate with the patient sitting up on the table because she could not breathe lying on her back. I made the incision over the most prominent part of the tumor and attempted to puncture it, for any fluid that could be drawn off would be so much less bulk to remove. No fluid escaped and the growth started to bleed. So I gave up that approach and continued the incision upward, going right to the breastbone for the reason that many large veins led into the tumor from above.

Some of these blood vessels were fully seven or eight millimetres in diameter and they were a problem; the rupture of one of the larger ones might have cost the patient's life before the hemorrhage could have been checked. So I had to do all the liberating under sight and to shell off the adhesions with the utmost care using only my hand. Since the tumor was densely adherent to both the back and side walls of the abdomen this necessitated a very large opening — before we had finished the operation our abdominal incision was almost four feet long.

In its lower part, the growth was extraperitoneal. I found accessory blood vessels running from the stomach and liver into it and tied them off, like the upper ones, as I found them. The stem of the growth, which sprang from the uterus, was not more than 1.5 centimetres in diameter and was located directly beneath the ribs, where the uterus lay, with the right tube and ovary, under the surface of the liver. As we worked, loosening the adhesions and tieing off the veins, the tumor supported in the footbath was moved as I directed, to minimize the danger of its partially released weight tearing tissues and organs still adherent.

When the footbath was finally drawn downward and outward and the tumor delivered from the abdomen I found that it had brought away a piece of liver tissue about three centimetres across. This was one possibility we had not prepared against. There were no blunt liver needles handy. So I used sharp Hagedorn needles, running the eye through first, instead of the point. This answered admirably, and the liver bleeding was checked by four catgut sutures. By this time the patient was beginning to show signs of collapse so I made no attempt to resect the abdominal wall, but closed the incision leaving only a small drain from the extraperitoneal pouch.

Mrs. McA. made a remarkably good recovery. She was, of course, a woman of unusual vitality. She was fifty-eight when I operated and she had then had the tumor more than twenty years and had born a healthy child after it was already so large that a gynecologist had advised its removal. The child was eighteen years old when the growth was at last removed. During all those years Mrs. McA. had done all the work of her household and, until three weeks before I first examined her, was still doing it. She had then started to run a temperature and to suffer from a good deal of watery swelling in the lower part of the abdomen and in the legs and buttocks. But up to that time her chief trouble was her inability to turn over in bed or to breathe while lying on her back. If she did get over on her back she would be "stalled" and her husband would have to turn her quickly before she suffocated.

The breathing difficulty was the cause of our only stubborn post-operative problem — a bedsore which developed at the base of the spine as a result of pressure from sitting, instead of lying, on the operating table. It was not large and it healed after she went home, but it did cause her some discomfort in the hospital. Otherwise she had very little. Kidneys and bladder were functioning normally by evening of the day of operation and a post-operative fever lasted only a few hours. There was no post-operative nausea.

The speed with which bones, muscles and tissues adjusted themselves to new contours is recorded as one of the remarkable features of Mrs. McA.'s case. At the first dressing after the operation her surgeon noted that the patient's ribs stuck out fully six inches from the abdomen and that the recti muscles lay on the bed on either side of her, while folds of loose and wrinkled skin covered the abdomen. But the tissues were already beginning to contract, for the gauze which had been placed to drain the extraperitoneal pocket just at the symphysis had been drawn up to the middle of the abdomen.

Two weeks later the recti muscles could be seen to have begun contracting and the arch of the ribs had flattened to some extent. Six weeks after the operation the operator was able to record that the recti muscles were well up in the abdomen and not more than ten centimetres apart, that the skin over the upper abdomen had contracted remarkably, that even the pendulous skin which had contained the lower, extra-peritoneal, part of the tumor was retracting and that the ribs were almost in normal position:

We did not have Mrs. McA. weighed for three weeks after the operation. By that time the watery swellings had entirely gone from her legs, stomach and back and her weight was 80½ pounds, just 93½ pounds less than when she was admitted to hospital. The tumor was weighed, as I told you, immediately after it was removed. It weighed 89 pounds net and almost filled a large washtub. Microscopic examination showed it to be a typical cystic myoma, unusual only in its size.

Tom Cullen saw Mrs. McA.'s tumor, or half of it, quite often after he removed it. It was in a case in the museum of the Surgeon General's Library at Washington for years. Mrs. McA. herself who lived to be nearly eighty he did not see again for fifteen years after her recovery. Then one evening when he was in West Baltimore he called on her with her physician, Dr. Marshall Smith:

I found a very slender, very active little woman of 73 who didn't know me at all, at first. When she recognized me she put her arm around me and I put mine around her, and there we were when Mr. McA. came into the room. He looked a little astonished, but I kept my arm around his wife until he recognized me too, and began to smile.

5

AS APPLIED TO MEDICINE;
MAX BROEDEL'S ART

Dr. Thomas Cullen sat in his high-backed armchair under Max Broedel's cartoon of *The Saint — Johns Hopkins;* a winged Osler in short draperies and a stiff collar riding a whirlwind above the Hopkins dome, toes out of shoes, eyes raised to heaven, germs, all terror-stricken but the defiant typhoid bacilli, scattering before him. As a Hopkins sinner he was looking back to 1910, his expression one of guilt remembered in tranquility:

Looking back, I suppose it wasn't just according to protocol. I started out to get the money without consulting anybody, because I had to get it fast to beat the Mayos. And when I'd got it I jumped the medical school entirely and took the offer straight to the university trustees and president; had their acceptance and their assurance that the department would be established before I said a word to anybody in the medical school. Since then they've made a rule that nobody connected with the university can ask for money for any university purpose unless the whole thing has first been approved by the president and trustees.

It's a good rule and necessary, on the whole, in a great institution such as this. But sometimes I wonder whether the rules necessary in a great institution such as this are so good for the purpose the institution was designed to serve. In the days when there were not quite so many rules we got a lot of things done at Johnny Hopkins . . . Let me give you the picture.

One above the other and lightly curved, the hands came together opposite the top waistcoat button. Craftsman's thumbs sloping backward from the top joint, thin fingers with the same sloped cushions, backs narrow and finely sinewed; they made a swift arc in the air and came to rest again. Their owner caught the eye that followed them and smiled:

Sometimes I have to laugh too, when I look at my hands. They're so little. I remember once I was a witness in a court case — it was straight blackmail but we won't go into that — and the complainant's counsel asked me how large an abdominal incision should be. I told him it depended on three things; what the surgeon was going in for, what he found he had to take out, and how big his hands were. Everybody laughed . . . We won that case. But let me give you the picture.

There was in Baltimore a kindly, curly-headed man, beloved of his friends and possessed of a passion for music. I can see him now as he arrived in Baltimore harbour on the Hamburg boat in January of '94. He was wearing a stiff black hat and the curly locks were welling out beneath the brim. He was a born artist and during his forty-eight years in Baltimore he revolutionized medical illustrating in the United States and Canada. No other man who ever lived has done as much to improve the beauty and accuracy of medical illustration . . . In after years, as he is now in many places, he will be recognized as the greatest medical illustrator who ever lived. That was Max Broedel, my friend.

If I hadn't got the money when I did, Max would have been lost to Hopkins and his usefulness to medicine would have been largely lost too. He would have done magnificent work for the Mayos and his example would have been of use but in Rochester he would have been working as an illustrator only. Here he was a teacher. You see the difference. At Hopkins he had already established, with Dr. Kelly's consent and at Kelly's expense, classes in medical illustrating. They had been started simply to help medical students with a gift that way, but year by year, though it was all unofficial, they were drawing talented young artists to Baltimore. Max was training a new generation in his methods and that was what we could not afford to lose. . . . So I lighted my corncob pipe, went down to my tent by the shore — it was at Ahmic — and dreamed up the new department, the Johns Hopkins Department of Art as Applied to Medicine, the first of its kind anywhere in the world.

That was in the summer of 1910 and Broedel's work for Dr. Kelly was to finish at latest the next spring. His answer to the Mayos' offer had to be given by mid-January and Hopkins, I knew well, had no funds to finance a new department. When we came down from camp in September I had four months to find a man of wealth who would endow the dream. . . .

The records of the search are filed in the Walters Art Gallery in Baltimore. Pencilled notes on scraps of paper, names, addresses, drafts of proposals, requests for introductions, queries about approaches, about second approaches, the first having failed, file copies of letters, replies, telegrams, memos of telephone conversations and interviews; they illustrate the unquenchable resolution of the seeker. But two months had gone before resolution turned up so much as one seed of hope.

Dated New York, November 7, 1910, a note from Henry Walters, the financier and amateur of the arts, acknowledged Dr. Cullen's favour of November 4 and promised an endeavour to make an appointment by telephone "next time I am in Baltimore." Six weeks later Henry Walters had not yet endeavoured to make an appointment by telephone. With less than a month to go and all other leads dead-ended, Tom Cullen wrote again, offering to come to New York for the appointment. The reply was forbidding enough; a suggestion that Dr. Cullen tell Mr. Walters in writing the nature of the subject he wished to discuss. The day after Christmas, 1910, Dr. Cullen did so; in a letter that had everything he could put in it:

The Saint Johns Hopkins Hospital

. . . a winged Osler in a stiff collar.
—page 210

"The Saint—Johns Hopkins Hospital," from the cartoon
by Max Broedel in Tom Cullen's possession

That letter was the result of meditation and prayer. I sweat blood over it; worked harder composing it than I ever did for myself; writing and rewriting to get everything put in the most effective way and the smallest space.

On January 7, 1911, Henry Walters telegraphed his answer; an appointment for "9:30 Monday morning, Belvedere Hotel, Baltimore."

Before noon Monday Tom Cullen, back from the Belvedere, was writing R. Brent Keyser, Chairman of Hopkins University Board, that a friend who wished to remain unknown and wanted no press notice of his generosity had offered the university $5,000 a year for three years to meet the expense of a chair of art as applied to medicine "in order that we might in the meantime raise the necessary $100,000 to endow a professorship." Chairman Keyser, President Remsen and a quorum of the Hopkins board met the same day to consider the offer. They decided to accept it.

So the beginning was assured. Tom Cullen took breath and set himself to find contributors to a permanent endowment. Max Broedel notified the Mayos that he would be staying at Hopkins for the present, and settled happily to his teaching, his art and his music. The Florestan Club was founded and Henry L. Mencken's memories of Max began:

"Max was a wonderful character. I didn't get to know him until 1910 or 1911. He and I were both charter members of a new music club we formed then, the Florestan. We'd both belonged to other music clubs but when we formed the new one we started playing four-hand instead of two. Max took first piano the first night and I fell back to second and that's the way we stayed. I was always second. Max was the best sight reader I have ever seen. He could play anything by sight and he never played anything but forte. There was nothing else as far as he was concerned. 'I play to be happy,' he would say, 'and this is the way it makes me happy to play.' So that was the way he played, with the rest of us filling in or following on.

"Once, I remember, we decided the club would play the Eight of Beethoven at a sitting. We started after lunch one Saturday at a little house one of us had — quite an isolated spot in the woods outside of town — and we stopped for dinner and we stopped for supper at midnight, and at three or four in the morning we stopped for another meal, and then Max started again. They say he got well into the Sixth, but I don't know. I don't think anyone knew; everybody who wasn't too drunk to know had gone home . . . What beer, and what music!

"Those were the days of home brew. Max was a specialist in home brew. One year when he came down from Canada he had half a dozen of Canadian beer on board for refreshment. Of course he had to empty them and throw the empties overboard before he got to the border. But after he'd passed customs he found one empty he'd missed, back of the seat cushion. There was a bit of beer left in it, and the suds. Max was German, he knew the yeast of beer was in the suds. He nursed that bottle all the way to Baltimore and rushed it to the Johns Hopkins laboratories as soon as he got here. They saved it for him and he worked it up and made beer for all his friends from it for a couple of years.

"All of them that is, but Tom Cullen. The only thing I know against Tom Cullen is that he doesn't drink. Tell him I said so. It was harder for me to get to know him than Max in the old days. He didn't drink, he wasn't musical and he worked so damn hard; butchering all morning, seeing patients all afternoon, writing about tumors all night. He did his playing in the summers when he went north. I imagine he and Max were closest there. They both liked fishing and camping. Some people do, you know. But I think what really drew Tom and Max together was their expansiveness. Complete extroverts both of them. Friendly as children. . . . "

Thus Henry Mencken. More memories crowd in. There are memories of morning lab at Hopkins, and Max there first, singing *The Mountaineers* at the top of

214

his voice to welcome the early worker. There is a memory of Max, absent-minded in the Mall, poking his stick into the middle of a shrub, running it out along the branches and trying with futile persistence to force it back the way it had come. Again and again he tried, to the delight of a loitering medical student, but the stick would not slide back through leaves and twigs to the stem. So presently Max gave it up and went on to his classes, absent-minded as ever, to all appearance. But what he had worked out, with the stick and the shrub and his abstracted pokings, was a new surgical idea; the kidney incision outward from the centre of the pelvis.

There are memories of summer afternoons in Broadway, the piano concerts that rolled from an open window in the top of Hopkins administration building, and the alfresco audiences that gathered to sit entranced on the grass of the Mall between the roadways, or drape the hospital gates. There are memories of winter evenings in Gill's boarding house, and an uncertain medical student playing Schubert on the flute while Max accompanied her at the piano in such volume as to make the flute inaudible. There are memories of spring mornings, and Professor Broedel arriving for his classes virtually invisible behind a bouquet cut in his garden as a surprise for Professor Cullen, "the godfather of our art department." . . .

Tom Cullen, still in his big chair, looking back across the years, remembered other things:

Max and I were young fellows together, both poor, both new to Baltimore, both deep in pathology. Max had come out from Ludwig's laboratory in Leipzig on Dr. Mall's recommendation. He had done work for Mall there and when Dr. Kelly wanted a medical illustrator for his first big book, *Operative Gynecology*, Mall suggested Max. That is why I was down at the dock to meet him. The Chief sent me, and almost at once Max and I were fast friends. He was not quite twenty-four then, I was just twenty-five and only a few months back from Germany. I had charge of the laboratory of gynecological pathology and that was where Max started to work, making sketches of tumors Dr. Kelly had removed.

It wasn't long before I was going to his little studio to read. We'd made a pact in the beginning; he was to talk only English to me and I was to attempt to answer him in German. It led to temporary misunderstandings but we kept at it and got along perfectly after a while. In my spare time, when he was at work on a drawing, I would read a German book aloud and Max would correct my pronunciation. We got through two large volumes on the Franco-Prussian War that way, besides several novels by Gustav Freytag. When it was warm we would walk out into the country in the evenings and sit on a fence and read; or we would take a trolley as far as Walbrook and walk along the millrace talking; Max English and I German. We stood by our original intention in writing, too. In forty-eight years of friendship I never wrote Max except in German, and all my letters from him were in English. All his life I don't think I spoke two hours of English to him, or wrote fifty words that were not German.

There was nobody like Max. He was a most lovable companion. I shall never forget our first hunting trip together, in New Hampshire in the autumn of '97. We went to Groveton and hired a one-armed guide who was a delightful character but didn't know his way through the bush. We got lost and had to sleep in the open and we didn't see a deer, but we had a peach of a time. It was the first of many, together in the woods.

We built our camps in the Magnetawan woods, just half a mile apart on Ahmic Lake and spent our summers together; fishing and swimming and loafing. Max did not loaf quite as thoroughly as I did. He sketched, and collected fungi and grew radishes; a new crop of them every week or so. When I went visiting around the lake I would always drop in to say hello if Max was fishing on his wharf. He would see me coming and leave his rod and slip behind his boathouse to the shore. By the time I was near, he would be back waiting for me with a red and green bouquet, a bunch of young radishes. That was typical of Max; his delight in sharing something of his own with his friends; a sketch he'd made, or his music or just a bunch of radishes.

Nobody ever had a better or a truer friend. And he was the best fisherman of us all. I can see him still, out in his small motor boat, fishing at the point at dusk. The sound of a motor boat across quiet water will always bring him back to me. . . . But about the department of art . . .

Less than a week after his morning interview with Henry Walters, Tom Cullen was on the trail again, looking for an endowment for the department he had dreamed up. During nearly ten years he was to go on looking. More than half of them were years in which his own future at Hopkins was in doubt, but he went on looking. The Hopkins Department of Art as Applied to Medicine must be endowed and he must find the endowment. He wrote, he telephoned, he talked. He travelled to Washington and Philadelphia and New York. He followed every clue and pursued any possibility. Keys to a character and an era are in the files of that unflagging search.

. . . A letter to Dr. William W. Polk, gynecologist of New York, asking an introduction to Dr. John W. Markoe, of the Society of the Lying-in Hospital, New York . . . A journey to New York to get the introduction . . . A letter to Dr. John N. Steele of New York asking "your brother Charley's" good word with J. P. Morgan . . . A note from Charles Steele advising Dr. Cullen to approach Mr. Morgan directly . . . A letter from C. P. Stokes, the Navy Department, Washington, promising to "corral my friend Spear" and enlist his influence with a Washington philanthropist named Thompson . . . A letter from Howard Kelly in Mexico, promising to help in the hunt when he returned and adding "there is no rebellion here at all"

. . . A letter from B. N. Baker introducing Dr. Cullen to E. J. Berwind and asking Mr. Berwind to "go with him to see Mr. Morgan." Mr. Berwind didn't go . . . A note from Hon. William A. Clarke, Exchange Place, New York, acknowledging an introduction from Granville Stewart of Butte, Montana, but expressing lack of interest in medical art . . . A letter from J. M. Glenn of the Russell Sage Foundation regretting that he could not give Dr. Cullen an introduction to Mr. Rockefeller . . . A letter from Dr. J. W. Markoe thanking Dr. Cullen for a present of books (illustrated by Max Broedel) and asking if Dr. Cullen could come to see him in New York next week. (Dr. Cullen could and returned home to file Dr. Markoe's promise to bring the matter of the endowment up with J. P. Morgan) . . .

A letter to Dr. Weir Mitchell of Philadelphia asking an introduction to Edward Robinson, director of the Metropolitan Museum . . . A letter to Mr. Robinson enclosing Dr. Mitchell's introduction . . . A memo on a journey to New York, to find Mr. Robinson "in no position to aid financially" . . . An envelope flap with a pencilled note; "try Mr. Eastman of Eastman Kodak Rochester Dr. Mulligan a friend of his." And so on.

There was a promise of $1,000 from Saunders, the Philadelphia publishers of Tom Cullen's medical books, contingent on the whole endowment being raised, and another promise, also contingent, of $5,000 from J. P. Morgan. Dr. Markoe's interest had got it, and Tom Cullen had hopes that Dr. Markoe's interest could get more. But a stray lunatic killed Dr. Markoe in church one Sunday as he was taking up the collection, closing that hopeful avenue abruptly. Tom Cullen tried others. He tried many others but, on January 17, 1914, when Henry Walters, in reply to his of the 15th, made an appointment to see him in New York January 24, none had led to the endowment.

The day before that of the appointment in New York, another note came from Henry Walters. It was written in pencil and dated January 21; a promise to continue the annual contributions for two more years "if found necessary." Keeping this support discreetly under cover Tom Cullen wrote on January 23 to Dr. J. Whitridge Williams, Dean of Medicine, of his hope that, the value of Broedel's department being now established, the medical faculty of Hopkins would be able to help ensure its continuance. Dr. Williams replied next day. The faculty had expressed great interest and referred the matter to the university board of trustees, hoping in turn that "suitable provision" might be made. It was not, and on February 15, 1914, "every effort having failed" Tom Cullen wrote to accept Henry Walters' promised help.

His two most recent efforts had been aimed to reach Henry Ford of Detroit and Edward Libby of Toledo, the first through a grateful patient, the second through a junior Libby. The patient was a sister-in-law of Alexander Dow, one of Ford's associates. She went home from Baltimore repaired by Tom Cullen's skill and determined to do her best for his Art Department. But presently Vina K. Dow wrote that her husband Alexander, "after a long quiet talk" advised against Dr. Cullen coming to Detroit to see Mr. Ford; "as far as we know, outside things do not tempt him."

The junior Libby lived in Baltimore. Tom Cullen enlisted her as an ally before she went to visit her wealthy cousin. When she remembered, she wrote home that "Cousin Ed" was awfully sorry but he could not afford to give "any more money for the proffessorship."

In 1915, having turned his efforts in a new direction and conscripted the Governor of Maryland's help, the lone hunter crossed the line of the Hopkins trustees. Very shortly after Governor Goldsborough undertook to

sound out Alfred duPont's interest in art for him, Tom
Cullen heard from the chairman of the Hopkins Board.
Dr. Cullen might not know that the University authorities were hoping to interest Mr. duPont in another matter; a chemical laboratory. Chairman Keyser felt that it
should be given priority. Dr. Cullen could not agree.
Three months later Governor Goldsborough was still trying to waken a latent duPont feeling for medical art. He
failed. The two years of grace were gone and the endowment was still to seek. Tom Cullen telegraphed Henry
Walters asking for another interview in New York and
Henry Walters wired back "Glad to see you."

Next entry in the file is a copy of a telegram, dated
New York February 21, 1916, signed by T. S. Cullen, and
addressed to President Goodnow of Hopkins to tell him
that the university's anonymous benefactor would continue to support the Department of Art as Applied to
Medicine for three years longer. Filed beside that message
is a letter from Henry Walters, thanking Dr. Cullen for
the fifth annual report of the department he supported,
and for the Broedel drawings — "as wonderful as ever" —
which accompanied it. "I am glad to say," Henry Walters
wrote, "that I hear (purely as an outsider) from a good
many quarters kind words in regard to the department
and of the real benefit that it is accomplishing."

After that Tom Cullen never again felt the same uncertainty for the future of his dream. Henry Walters'
interest was engaged. Nevertheless, he kept on searching
for other possible contributors; publishers of medical
textbooks among them. All agreed with Saunders and
Company of Philadelphia that the improvement in the
standard of medical illustrating could be "traced directly
to the work of Broedel." None except Saunders felt impelled to promise even conditional contributions towards
its continuance. Against this lack of cash recognition, war
provided an offset. Enclosing the department's sixth an-

nual report, Dr. Cullen wrote proudly on February 27, 1918, to tell Henry Walters of appointments of its graduates to American base hospitals overseas.

(They did it again this last war. Sent out medical art units manned by Max's pupils and the pupils of Max's pupils. Henry Walters would have liked to know that.)

Still the dream was not secure. In September of 1918 Henry Walters warned that, the future being uncertain, "I am unwilling to obligate myself beyond one more year." In September of 1919 he cut the obligation to six months. With only one of the six months to go, Tom Cullen wrote once again to ask an interview in New York. Two days later he had his answer. Mr. Walters "would of course be delighted" to see Dr. Cullen at any time, but he wished him to know at once that his, Henry Walters', Baltimore office had instructions to continue the contributions to the Department of Art as Applied to Medicine indefinitely "so that you see your financial resources do not cease on February 28."

Tom Cullen's answering letter was to thank Henry Walters "from the bottom of my heart." But, being Tom Cullen, he wrote another letter first. It was to President Goodnow of Hopkins, to try to get more salary for Max Broedel "now that the continuity of the Department is assured."

In December of 1921, still insisting on anonymity, Henry Walters gave Johns Hopkins University $110,000, as a permanent endowment for the department he had supported for ten years. The giver remained anonymous while he lived, but on each first of March for ten years more a complete report of what his department had accomplished in the year past, illustrated by Max Broedel and his pupils and accompanied by a letter from Tom Cullen, came to Henry Walters' New York office. Each year Henry Walters' letter of acknowledgment expressed increasing pride in the work done. The final sentence of the last of them is one Tom Cullen likes to remember:

"It is a great pleasure to me to know that you led me into establishing the Department of Art as Applied to Medicine, which has developed into so much real service to medicine and surgery."

After Henry Walters' death in 1931, the identity of the founder of the Hopkins Department of Art as Applied to Medicine was revealed, and the department he endowed was given his name, Mrs. Walters consenting. "I do not believe," she wrote, "there was anything that Mr. Walters did which gave him more satisfaction." As for Tom Cullen, he remembers as the peak of his satisfaction, the day when the years of uncertainty ended and he was able to tell his friend, Max Broedel, that his department had been endowed.

· · ·

When Professor Thomas Stephen Cullen was seventy years old and retiring from active clinical work to be Hopkins Professor Emeritus of Gynecology, his friends gave him a dinner. Nearly five hundred of them were there; men who had been his students and assistants and associates; men who had learned to know him unprofessionally as the one inexhaustible element in any undertaking designed to serve his city and state and his adopted country. Statesmen and politicians, judges and editors, bishops and party bosses came, with his peers in his own calling and men who were not eminent but were Tom Cullen's friends.

Many fine things were said of the guest of honour; of the distinctions he had earned, the work he had done, the value of his example, and his usefulness to his fellows. But the man who said and did the thing that was most right that night was Max Broedel. When it came Max's turn to speak he leaned down and kissed the top of Tom Cullen's bald head before he began. Then he said:

"The best of Tom Cullen is his warm and generous heart."

PART V

THE FIGHTING YEARS

I

FULL-TIME STORM AT HOPKINS; OSLER WRITES A LETTER

Tom Cullen sent the wire from Baltimore to his chief in Rochester:

"Osler's letter a peach. Fully delineates what you have done for Hopkins. Love from staff . . . "

The letter he celebrated was an open one addressed to President Ira Remsen of Johns Hopkins University. William Osler had written it from Oxford as his contribution to an argument that came close to breaking Johns Hopkins Medical School apart. So near was the break when the wire was sent in September of 1911 that Howard Kelly, recovering from an operation at the Mayos' clinic, was spending his convalescence shaping plans to meet it. They included his associate:

"If you can manage to work at the San and we can study out the cases together it will be a great help in the long run. It is going to be a difficult problem as we both have our fields as distinct as though we lived in different cities. I have a perfect equipment in every way — go look it all over carefully and study it out. We shall want some good business management and I believe you can furnish that . . . Osler writes me he is sending an open letter to Pres. Remsen and all the trustees about the proposed changes and F's report. Welch told a doctor he met in Alaska that it was 'Williams' plan' . . . "

The proposed changes were those required to staff
the main clinical departments at Johns Hopkins Medical
School with professors and associates working full-time.
Popsy Welch was perhaps over-generous in calling it
"Williams' plan."

The idea was not that new. Franklin P. Mall, Dr.
Welch's first postgraduate Fellow at the Pathological,
came back from Germany with it in the 'eighties. He had
got it in Ludwig's laboratory in Leipzig, where laboratory
scientists endlessly discussed means of raising clinical
medicine to scientific levels. Ludwig believed it could be
done by relieving medical school clinicians of the need
to practice outside their clinics. He convinced the young
American. Mall came home, took the chair of anatomy
at the University of Chicago, stayed there five years and,
in 1893, still with his idea, returned to Hopkins as the
new medical school's first professor of anatomy.

Lew Barker, Tom Cullen's fellow-graduate of Toronto,
became Mall's laboratory assistant and later his associate.
Barker and Simon Flexner, Welch's assistant at the Pathological — both, like Mall, laboratory men — were among
the first Hopkins converts to the "full-time" gospel.
J. Whitridge Williams' active interest came later. At the
time, he was fully employed on the clinical side shaping,
with Dr. Kelly, another revolution. Kelly's decision to
separate obstetrics from gynecology had been taken. He
was turning the new school's new department of obstetrics
over to Whitridge Williams.

In those early days William H. Welch merely listened
benevolently when full-time was preached. Some time the
system of fully-salaried professors and associates that had
proved itself best for medical science in his laboratory
would be applied in the Hopkins clinics. But a patient
innovator could wait his time, letting the less wary start
out-of-season hares.

"There was nobody like Max . . ."
—page 216

Max Broedel in Johns Hopkins anatomical department
laboratory, about 1900

Barker started the first when he went from Hopkins to Mall's old chair at Chicago. There, in 1902, in a speech to Hopkins alumni, he publicly advocated full-time clinical professorships. A year later, Frank S. Billings, Dean of Rush Medical School, also in Chicago, stirred another. In his inaugural speech as President of the American Medical Association, Billings plumped for full-time heads of the clinical departments of medicine, surgery and pediatrics in American medical schools. Cautiously he added that "to impart to students a better idea of medicine as a whole" departmental associates should be in private practice. Full-timers discounted the caution and counted a new ally.

For a few years yet Welch stood aside and let heat generate about the Billings proposals. Then in 1907 he went to Chicago and made a speech that was news in every medical journal; Welch of Hopkins had declared in favour of full-time heads of the clinical departments of medicine and surgery. He had done it although, only the year before, Johns Hopkins trustees had vetoed Lewellys Barker's wish to succeed Osler on a full-time basis. Barker, invited to accept Osler's vacated chair of medicine, had proposed that it be made a full-time fully-salaried professorship. The Hopkins board had rejected the proposal and Barker had returned to serve on the old terms, receiving a nominal salary for his work at the medical school and making his living in private practice.

The lull that followed Welch's Chicago speech was brittle. Bulletin Number Four broke it. Prepared by Abraham Flexner, the educator, for the Carnegie Foundation for the Advancement of Teaching, and published in 1910, Bulletin Number Four was a strong shock to American medicine. Even now, when many of the faults it uncovered have been corrected and most of the reforms it proposed effected, it holds interest. When it was issued it did more. Bulletin Number Four is down in medical history as the document that closed half the medical schools in North America.

As was natural, judgments set forth in the bulletin were influenced by the thinking of the foremost medical reformer of the period: William H. Welch of Hopkins. Abraham Flexner was a younger brother of Simon, Popsy Welch's disciple. As was inevitable, Hopkins Medical School was the standard by which less admirable institutions were measured in the Flexner report. As was hoped, its publication had far-reaching effects. Not the least of them were on Hopkins.

The Carnegie Foundation's fourth bulletin was fortunately timed to meet awakening Rockefeller interest. The year it was published Dr. Welch had made his first, unsuccessful, effort to tap Rockefeller funds for the endowment of a full-time professorship in pediatrics at Johns Hopkins. The next year Abraham Flexner was borrowed from the Carnegies by Frederick T. Gates, chairman of the Rockefeller-endowed General Education Board, to make a further medical survey. Flexner was to go to Baltimore, study the Hopkins and advise how best a million Rockefeller dollars might there be spent for the improvement of American medical education. Flexner went, stayed three weeks, talked long with William H. Welch and Franklin P. Mall and came back to New York to compose his report. It was a composition after Welch's own heart. Its result was a revolution; the introduction, backed by Rockefeller grants, of full-time professorships in all but one of the main clinical departments at the Hopkins medical school.

The end was not achieved at once, or without pain. Across a third of a century marks of the struggle still show. At its height it was fierce enough to threaten the happy associations of years and set one half of the Hopkins big four opposing the other. In its wake it left frictions that endured among lesser men.

The disagreement was, as is usual, on principle. Almost on theological principle. Whether salvation is by faith or works, in systems or in the spirit, is an argument at least as old as the Greek testaments. It came up anew in Baltimore. Promptly, the heads, faculty, students, associates and friends of Johns Hopkins University and Medical School chose sides. On the side of Osler, Kelly, Saint Paul and part time, Tom Cullen took his place. Loyalty, always the first of his motives, would have ranged him there even without conviction. For injustice had been done his chief, Howard Kelly, in his friend Abraham Flexner's report.

The same injustice had been noted in Oxford when the Regius Professor of Medicine in that University reached pages 14 and 15 in his study of the Flexner report. So William Osler wrote his letter to Ira Remsen. Privately printed in England it was privately circulated in Baltimore among Hopkins faculty members and trustees. It put with urbanely restrained feeling its author's doubts of the new course mapped for Hopkins Medical School and American medicine:

" . . . We are all for sale, dear Remsen. You and I have been in the market for years and have loved to buy and sell our wares in brains and books — it has been our life. It is always pleasant to be bought when the purchase price does not involve the sacrifice of an essential . . . but . . . we chance the sacrifice of something that is really vital, the existence of a great clinical school organically united with the profession and with the public . . .

"There is something very attractive in the parallel between the problems of the laboratory and those of the hospital . . . but only a very narrow view regards the director of a university clinic as chiefly an agent for research. He stands for other things of equal importance. In life, in word and in deed he is an exemplar to the young men about him, students and assistants. 'Cabined, cribbed, confined' within the four walls of a hospital, practicing the fugitive and cloistered virtues of a clinical monk, how shall he forsooth train men for a race of the dust and heat of which he knows nothing and — this is a possibility! — cares less? I cannot imagine anything more subversive to the highest ideals of a *clinical* school than to hand over young men who are to be our best practitioners to a group of teachers who are *ex officio* out of touch with the conditions under which these young men will live. . . . The danger would be the evolution throughout the country of a set of clinical prigs the boundary of whose horizon was the laboratory and whose only human interest was research . . . "

With feeling less restrained, William Osler went on to correct by the light of memory the errors and unfairnesses he found in the Flexner brief:

"Against the sin of prosperity which looms large in Mr. Flexner's report the clinical professor must battle hard. I was myself believed to be addicted to it. . . . The truth is there is much misunderstanding in the minds and not a little nonsense on the tongues of the people about the large fortunes made by members of the clinical staff. At any rate, let the University and Hospital always remember with gratitude the work of one 'prosperous' surgeon, whose department is so irritatingly misunderstood by Mr. Flexner. I do not believe the history of medicine presents a parallel to the munificence of our colleague Kelly to his clinic. Equal in bulk, in quality and in far-reaching practical value to the work from any department of the University, small wonder that his clinic became the Mecca for surgeons from all parts of the world, and that his laboratory methods, perfected by Drs. Cullen and Hurdon, have become general models, while through the inspiration of Mr. Max Brödel, a new school of artistic illustration in medical works has developed in the United States. And, shades of Marion Sims, Goodell and Gaillard Thomas! this is the department which the Angel of Bethesda, in the fullness of his ignorance, suggests should be, if not wiped out, at any rate merged with that of Obstetrics! . . .

"It is a pity the report was allowed to go out in its present form, as his remarks show a very feeble grasp of the clinical situation at the Johns Hopkins Hospital . . . To say, for example, that, as contrasted with the instructors on the laboratory side, the clinical staff has been on the whole less productive and less devoted is simply not true. I deny the statement *in toto* — they have been more productive and quite as devoted . . . To mention out of many, only five names, the most stable on the staff — Finney, Thayer, Bloodgood, Cushing and Cullen. It is not too much to say that these men have done scientific work of a standard equal to that of the highest of any laboratory men connected with the University; and in addition work which in practical import, in the translation of Science into Art, no pure laboratory men could have done. To speak as Mr. Flexner does of these men blocking the line and preventing the complete development of a race or school is perhaps pardonable ignorance but again is certainly not true. Take away the share of the reputation of the Johns Hopkins Medical School — particularly in Europe which knows chiefly the Hospital Bulletins and Reports — contributed from the clinical side and from the junior staff and you leave it, in comparison, poor indeed! 'By their fruits ye shall know them!' After showing the treasures of my library, it is my custom to take an intelligent bibliophile to a shelf on which stand twelve handsomely bound quarto volumes and to say — 'But this is my chief treasure — the five hundred contributions to scientific medicine from the graduates of the first eight years of our medical school.' It is a splendid record, but much more brilliant from the clinical than from the laboratory side; and a great part of the work has been directly inspired by this younger group of men . . . It is hard to say which is more prevalent on pp. 14 and 15 of the report — unfairness or ignorance; but in either case gross injustice is done to the men who have made the Johns Hopkins Clinical School."

The letter was support as well as comfort to beleaguered clinicians, but Osler was in Oxford, not Baltimore, and Popsy Welch's determination remained unshaken. In 1912 Ira Remsen retired from the Hopkins presidency. The next President, Frank J. Goodnow, was not chosen for more than a year. In the interregnum the revolution was achieved. Dr. William H. Welch, as acting president, completed in October 1913 the arrangement between the Hopkins University Trustees and the Rockefeller General Education Board which established Medicine, Surgery and Pediatrics at Hopkins as the first fully-endowed whole-time clinical departments in any American medical school. Kelly, Cullen and their associates in the Gynecological were left outside the new arrangement. So, for the time being, were Whitridge Williams and Obstetrics.

First direct result of the new order was Barker's resignation of the chair of medicine. The years since he had asked that his be made a full-time appointment had involved him in heavy obligations and modified his early faith. He was no longer as sure as he had been as a young laboratory scientist that there was but one way to clinical salvation. When the majority of Hopkins trustees decided for full-time and the Rockefeller grant, reversing their decision of 1906, Lewellys Barker offered his resignation. It was accepted. Returning from the comparative peace of revolutionary China to take up his duties in Baltimore, the new President of Hopkins was met by the full storm that followed. Tom Cullen smiles now, recalling its fury:

I remember I wrote Goodnow when the Board accepted Lew's resignation. I told him what I thought of it and ended by saying that the resignation of three or four more men of Dr. Barker's calibre would spell the doom of the Hopkins Medical School. Then I telephoned Phil Goldsborough, who was Governor at the time, and told him what I had done. Phil asked how the letter would affect my standing at Hopkins. I said "My self-respect is worth a lot more to me than my standing at Hopkins." Phil said "Send it, then." I said "It's sent."

2

PEACE, QUIET AND W. S. HALSTED

THE YEAR OF THE STORM, working in London after submitting the report that precipitated it, Abraham Flexner had received an invitation to join the General Education Board as assistant to its Secretary, Wallace Buttrick. His acceptance strengthened a family association with Rockefeller philanthropies begun in 1902 when, on Dr. Welch's advice, his brother Simon had been made director of the newly-formed Rockefeller Institute for Medical Research. The move was important to Tom Cullen for it put Abraham Flexner in a position to reconsider at leisure some of the swift judgments of men and clinics which, embodied in his Hopkins report, had angered Osler. Moreover it brought Cullen, through his friendship with Flexner, into intimate association with Wallace Buttrick, a man of his own humane and pragmatic habit of mind. Dr. Buttrick was shortly to succeed Frederick Gates as chairman of the General Education Board and to be succeeded in the secretaryship by Abraham Flexner. A long struggle to save his work at Hopkins lay ahead for Tom Cullen, but his good fortune was to give the man who first jeopardized it the desire and the power to save it at last. In the deepest of the uncertainties to come: "I never made a move without the advice of my friends Abe Flexner and Wallace Buttrick."

Those moves were yet distant. The immediate need, as all concerned for Hopkins quickly recognized, was peace. Battered but still serviceable, the goodwill in which the Hopkins tradition had been built survived. It needed rest and nursing, the Osler specifics. It got them from the leaders on both sides of the full-time controversy, and from the larger-hearted of their followers. A note written in a characteristic angular and open hand, dated September 16, 1914, and addressed to Dr. T. S. Cullen, throws light on the spirit in which the work of restoration was begun:

"Will you take *one* man and put him on some definite piece of work which he will publish either alone or with you? I will do the same. I don't feel that I dare hold my position and drift along as I have done in the past. Such is the good result of competition and all-time service in the other departments.
"Affectionately Yrs.
"Howard A. Kelly."

This was William Osler's "Kensington colt" in his finest form. The man who, more than any other, as Osler declared and Welch later agreed, had made the name of Hopkins by tireless, brilliant and original work, was then at the height of his career, his personal fame and his fortune. He could, as he had been prepared to do, have withdrawn altogether from his association with the medical school when the full-time decision went against him, without suffering in income or in professional standing. Instead, he accepted the decision, and taking himself to task in half-humorous, wholly honest, humility, set himself again to departmental dog-work, directing and sharing the researches of a junior. "Do you wonder," Tom Cullen says, "that I loved him?"

On his side, Halsted moved to heal the rift in a spirit no less generous. His letters written to Tom Cullen in that time have a warmth and affectionate lightness oddly at variance with the accepted picture of a caustic and unapproachable eccentric. The correspondence between the two was casual and desultory, on small occasion or none; notes exchanged to clear up a diagnostic point, to give thanks for a gift or a kindness, to acknowledge or offer an invitation or a courtesy. Yet it warms with its humour and friendliness the record of years that were to prove the most solitary and the nearest defeat of Tom Cullen's life.

The personal sorrows of those years were many. In the deepest of them; his mother's death early in 1916; Mary Cullen's boy was, inevitably, alone. Frustrations multiplying in his professional path he was prepared to meet in loneliness hardly less complete. It was relieved by Halsted's friendship, never proffered, rarely spoken. In it Tom Cullen found at need the support for his cause that he would not have asked for himself. Whether it was the merit of the cause or of its champion that dragged the older man from his dear passivity none now can say. But reading the letters and studying the likeness of William Stewart Halsted in the light of lively and affectionate memories, it is possible to guess.

The likeness is of a man witty and humorous, eager and retiring, completely engrossed in his chosen work and completely indifferent to its symbols of success. Halsted's surgery was not his living. He was a surgeon for love. Henry L. Mencken, who has not found it necessary to admire many famous men much, learned from his friends to admire this one. Halsted was an original:

"He was one of the first surgeons to employ courtesy in surgery, to show any consideration for the insides of the man he was operating on. The old method was to slit a man from the chin down, take out his bowels and spread them on a towel while you sorted them. Halsted held that if you touched an intestine with your finger you injured it and the patient suffered the effects of the injury. That was new doctrine when he began. Halsted introduced rubber gloves. He invented the technique of shutting off the area of operation, blocking it with shots of cocaine in the surrounding nerves so there would be less general shock. He was gentle — and a little inhuman. He had to be because he was so sensitive.

"He married a Johns Hopkins nurse, the Confederate General Wade Hampton's daughter. They lived a strange sequestered life in a great big house where each had his own quarters and neither saw anybody. Halsted had an odd detached way always, even when he was operating. He would start an operation, go on for a bit, then seem to get tired and say to his assistant: 'You see what I want to do, you finish it,' and walk away. But Max Broedel, who worked with them all, always said Halsted was the pick of the Big Four. He knew things."

There was more to the story of the rubber gloves. Tom Cullen completed it. Dr. Halsted introduced their use, he said, in the 'nineties, but not originally for their aseptic qualities. He was thinking of Miss Hampton's hands. She was his operating room nurse at the time. She had beautiful hands, and the strong antiseptic used in Hopkins operating rooms burned her skin. So Dr. Halsted suggested that she try wearing the new rubber gloves he had seen advertised as hand-savers for ladies who had to do their own housework. She tried them, liked them and advised Dr. Halsted to try them too. Soon Hopkins surgeons were all taking to rubber gloves, and it was not long until Miss Hampton's hand-protectors became fashionable operating-room wear in other hospitals. Even surgeons who did not go in for Johns Hopkins' excessive asepsis were obliged to adopt the Hopkins style in gloves.

Tom Cullen recalls a meeting with one such in the trolley on a morning in the late 'nineties. The older surgeon was on his way to operate at another hospital and he was a little late, he said. He took a pair of rubber gloves out of the tail pocket of his coat and was busy fitting them on when his startled junior left the trolley at Monument and Broadway. But, so strong is professional loyalty, even after fifty years Tom Cullen will not reveal the name of that time-saver. He would rather talk about Halsted:

A lot of people were afraid of Halsted. They said he was sarcastic and difficult. Diffident, I think, though he did have a dry humour that sometimes could be cruel. I remember one young surgeon who came to the Hopkins to work under Halsted and tired us all a little by recalling too often how things were done in the hospital he had come from. One day Halsted, making his rounds as head of the department, examined an incision for the dressing of which his new assistant was responsible. He found it dirty and neglected but he didn't, as many top men would have done, raise the devil there and then. He just examined the dressing, replaced it and said softly, "Hmm. This is how we do it in the Massachusetts General."

I can hear him, too, at the end of one long and difficult operation saying to his assistant in his tired, courteous way, "Would you mind moving a little? You've been standing on my foot for the last half hour. Thank you."

That way he broke tension for everyone. But it would be hard to say whether that was his purpose, for his face would never show it. He had a withdrawn, impassive expression that hardly ever changed. I remember driving to the hospital one morning in a taxi and passing Dr. Halsted standing on a corner smoking and waiting for a trolley going the other way. I had the taxi swing back, stopped beside him and asked could I give him a lift home. He looked at me solemnly and didn't answer. "You can't smoke in a trolley," I said. He climbed in with me then, but almost grudgingly. As he was settling down he said "Cullen, this will cost you a dollar." I said, "Dr. Halsted, it's worth five." He smiled at that. He had to. He had a charming smile when he let down his guard.

But it was hard for him to let it down. He was shy. He was the only shy one of the Big Four. I hadn't been at Hopkins long before I discovered it. I overtook him in a corridor one morning and fell into step beside him. Our walk was interrupted. Dr. Halsted had continually to stop to answer good mornings, to return nods, to shake hands. At last he sighed heavily and said: "Cullen, it is a great deal less trouble to walk these corridors alone, with bowed head, lost in contemplation."

Thus early a newcomer to the Hopkins was given the key he never forgot to William Stewart Halsted's character:

He had an almost morbid dread of personal contacts. He avoided them wherever he could and avoided even more carefully personal controversy. But when an issue was raised and he thought it worth while, he could intervene, unobtrusively, but effectively, to prevent an injustice being done.

So, when the issue was raised, he intervened for Tom Cullen.

3

ONE MAN AGAINST CANCER

ASSOCIATIONS to spread knowledge of cancer are international now. Societies founded to fight cancer with publicity are listed in every city directory. Research into the
cause and treatment of cancer makes news in any newspaper. The mental fogs of thirty-five years ago are gone,
almost past recall. But they were thick and dangerous
enough when Dr. Thomas S. Cullen, the successful Baltimore surgeon, decided to risk his career among them, by
bringing the battle against cancer into the open.

The first public campaign to check the mounting
death-toll of cancer was launched in the United States by
Tom Cullen of Baltimore. The year was 1913. The place
was *The Ladies' Home Journal.*

The risk was not taken blindly, or on impulse. "Thomas S. Cullen, M.B., Chairman of the Cancer Campaign
Committee of the Congress of Surgeons of North America" knew exactly what he was doing when he permitted
his name to be thus printed in a woman's magazine as
giving professional endorsement to the first popular article on cancer by a layman. He had every reason to know.
It was his committee, his campaign, and he had promoted
the article. He was not astonished to find himself denounced as unethical among the conservatives of his own profession, or surprised when local critics threatened to have
him dropped from the roster of Maryland medical men
for unprofessional conduct.

He was not even, he recalls looking back, very much worried. At forty-four, he had long since fixed on the twin principles that were to guide his professional thinking and doing. "What's best for the public is best for the profession," Tom Cullen said: "What's best for the patient is best for the doctor." He went ahead with his cancer campaign.

It had begun on a night in October, 1912, with a discouraging stocktaking; one of the periodical stocktakings he had made his habit. This one covered the results of two decades of swiftly improving surgical techniques as they showed in post-operative reports on one type of cancer treated at Johns Hopkins gynecological clinic; cancer of the neck of the womb. In T. S. Cullen's opinion, the results that showed were not good enough. After thought, he sat down to write a letter.

Twenty-one years before, a boy starting pathology in the Hopkins laboratory, he had made his first microscopic examination of operative tissue under the direction of Popsy Welch. Already, at that time, all tissue from Howard Kelly's operating-room at Hopkins went to the gynecological section of Dr. Welch's laboratory to be described and examined microscopically for the information of the operating surgeon. It was new practice and, like so much begun at Hopkins when the hospital opened in '89, widely regarded as needless; but from the first it justified itself in early discoveries of unsuspected cancer. As time passed the accumulating laboratory material and records proved more and more valuable to Dr. Kelly and his assistant-innovators in the gynecological clinic.

During his own three laboratory years in charge of gynecological pathology Tom Cullen had systematized the material and completed clinical records, as far as he was able, with a subsequent history of each case treated. He had measured the ground gained from death, as his chief's surgical experiments proved themselves, and had been heartened as the percentage of recoveries grew even in cases of cancer which, when he came to Hopkins, would have been classed as hopeless. Among such cases, in 1891, had been cancer of the neck of the womb.

Through the 'nineties, operative procedures permitting complete removal of a cancerous womb had been perfected and the Kelly clinic at Hopkins had led in devising new techniques which made the operation not only possible but relatively hopeful. Too many cancer cases were still coming too late to permit any complete operation, yet when he ended his Hopkins residence and began practice for himself in 1897 young Dr. Cullen had shared enough achievement and recorded enough recoveries to justify hope. One day not too far distant, he believed, a good surgeon operating on cancer might count at least on an even chance of defeating his toughest enemy.

The hope had persisted, to spur effort. Lecturing in the medical school, preaching and practicing pathology, taking the weight of the gynecological clinic as Howard Kelly's senior associate, building on skill, knowledge and tireless work his own name as surgeon, scientist and medical writer, Tom Cullen had never forgotten it. Neither had he failed to do his share towards making hope reality. His three published volumes: Cancer of the Uterus (1900) *Adenomyoma of the Uterus* (1908) and — with Dr. Kelly as co-author — *Myomata of the Uterus* (1909) had been directed to that end. Together they presented, superbly illustrated for the guidance of working members of the profession, an effective and complete picture of the new knowledge of uterine growths gained in twenty years of clinical and laboratory research. Their publication had cost their author forty thousand dollars, spent cheerfully with no idea of return:

It was only fair. I'd learned so much from books and from men. It was only fair I should spend a little to pass it on. I'd had the good luck, through no special merit of my own, to be in the place where new things were being done and to have a part in them. I owed it to the general practitioners, the men in the firing line, to give them all I could of all I'd learned.

But spending money earned and replaceable is one thing. Risking a reputation earned and irreplaceable is another. On that October night of the stocktaking Cullen of Baltimore was already internationally known for his published works on cancer and myoma. Nationally, he was recognized in his profession as one of the most brilliant of the group of brilliant surgeons who, being Hopkins originals, products of the new order of Welch and Halsted, Mall and Osler and Kelly, were under observation and knew it. Moreover he was a married man and a financial success; a fashionable consultant with a growing practice, many obligations and a necessarily costly way of life. The stocktaking went forward.

Its purpose was to measure gains in the combat against cancer by the results of radical operation in one type of case, making "five-year recoveries" the yardstick of success. The stock-taker, leafing through the record cards from 1889, eliminated the cases where radical operation had been found impossible. Then he classified the remaining cards and studied them, reducing cures to percentages, dividing hope by accomplishment. He found it depressing. The cards, when all were sorted, showed five-year recoveries to be only twenty-six per cent. even in the most recent group of cases under survey; cases in which a complete removal of the womb had been done by the best surgical methods of 1907:

That was of course a great advance. In the early days all died. Still . . .

Considering the alarming general increase in cancer, considering surgery's magnificent gains in other fields, considering the hope he had held so long, Tom Cullen remained depressed:

It was clear to me that our percentage of five-year recoveries was not large enough and the reason for it was equally clear. We were getting our cancer cases too late just about three times out of four.

So much being clear, the pattern of succeeding thoughts was, for Tom Cullen, inevitable:

Something will have to be done about it.
What can I do?

That night the letter was written and sent to Dr. Franklin H. Martin, secretary of the Clinical Congress of Surgeons of North America. A month later, at Dr. Martin's invitation, Dr. Cullen of Baltimore was in Brooklyn placing before a meeting of fellow-members of the Clinical Congress his reasons for believing surgery must make more cures in cancer cases and that, to get more cures, it was "absolutely necessary" to educate women as to the early symptoms of cancer:

If the women of the country are made aware of what can be done if cancer patients apply early for treatment, it is unnecessary to pay much attention to the men. The woman is the health guardian of the household.

Having made his case the speaker presented a plan of action and, taking the opposition unprepared, won approval for it the same night. If easy hopes sprouted from that first success they were cut back next morning in Baltimore station:

Coming from the meeting, I remember, a surgeon I knew well and respected came up to me in the station and said: "Cullen, if you go ahead with that cancer publicity you've planned, I'll bring you before the state medi-

245

cal board and have your licence to practise cancelled." I said "Go ahead. Go as far as you like." He didn't go quite that far, but for some years we didn't see much of one another. Then there was an AMA meeting in St. Louis and we came home in the same train. The first good chance I had, I stopped beside his seat and put my arm across his shoulder and said: "You're a hard man to convince, but I've always been very fond of you," and it was all over. We were friends until the day he died.

But reconciliations were far in the future the morning Dr. Thomas Cullen came home from Brooklyn. He had a fight on his hands. Yet he wrote cheerfully enough that night to his friend and younger brother Ernest, then starting practice in Detroit:

"We had a splendid time in New York and last evening I spoke at the meeting in Brooklyn. They appointed a committee for publicity in the cancer campaign. . . . Howard Taylor of New York, Jeff Miller of New Orleans, Frank Simpson of Pittsburgh, E. C. Dudley of Chicago, and your humble servant as chairman. The committee is to write articles for the daily press, weekly journals or magazines, as may be deemed wise. There is a pretty full report on the subject on the back page of the New York World this morning. The other papers hesitated to publish it."

The next letter on the subject that made New York news editors hesitate went to the editor of *The Ladies' Home Journal* in Philadelphia. Dr. Cullen wanted Mr. Harriman's advice on how best to bring before American women the life-saving knowledge of cancer and its early symptoms that should be theirs. Mr. Harriman did not advise immediately. Instead he took the train for Baltimore to get some advice for himself. Arrived, he went not to Dr. Cullen but to his chief, Dr. Kelly. He wanted to know more about cancer and about Cullen.

"Go and see Cullen," Howard Kelly said.

The editor of *The Ladies' Home Journal* took the advice. Only a few days later, Dr. Cullen returned the visit. The resolute campaigner arrived in the Journal office in Philadelphia with a short article on the early symptoms of cancer written by himself. Tom Cullen still chuckles, remembering that afternoon:

I can see Harriman yet, reading my article. He was smoking a long black cigar and the further he read the faster he puffed and the more he scowled. Finally, I asked him if it was not clear enough. "Too damn clear!" he said, "Our women readers would all grab their hats half way through and run to the nearest doctor." Then he took me in to see his publisher, Mr. Bok.

Bok was interested at once. He told me one of his dearest relatives had died of cancer and he wanted to do whatever was possible to help combat the disease. But he still was not convinced that a publicity campaign such as our committee proposed was the best means to use. He felt we should move cautiously: "You know I'm a Dutchman," he said. I said, at a venture, "Do you know Treub of Amsterdam?" Bok nearly jumped out of his chair. "Treub was the surgeon who operated on my mother!" he said.

So we talked about Treub who was a friend of mine and one of the greatest cancer specialists of his day and, before I left, the publisher of *The Ladies' Home Journal* had offered to do everything he could to help along the cancer campaign.

That was how Samuel Hopkins Adams came into it. He had lately finished the work that made his name; an exposure of patent medicine racketeering for which he was, next year, to be given honorary membership in the American Medical Association. His book on the subject, *The Great American Fraud,* was newly published and being read all over the country. The chairman of the campaign cheerfully agreed with the editor of the *Journal* that a layman might present to lay readers the necessary facts concerning cancer in a manner less startling than his own. Samuel Hopkins Adams was proposed and accepted as the ideal layman for the job. Mr. Harriman got in touch with Mr. Adams.

Early in the new year of 1913, Mr. Adams came to Baltimore to eat terrapin at the Maryland Club with Dr. Cullen and a few others. The list of his fellow-guests began with Dr. Welch, first of the Hopkins Big Four, and Dr. Joseph Bloodgood, associate in general surgery. It included six or eight more; pathologists, surgeons and physicians all specially qualified by knowledge and interest to discuss the subject in which Mr. Adams must be briefed:

We filled Sam Adams so full of it that he had to go to New Orleans to the Mardi Gras to forget about cancer. But he came around again, went to Chicago to learn more and to Rochester, where he spent some time with the Mayos. Then he wrote his article for *The Ladies' Home Journal* and sent it on to me. All I did was cut down the percentages of recoveries here and there. They were a little too high for most of the clinics.

Samuel Hopkins Adams' article "What Can We Do About Cancer?" was published in the May, 1913, issue of the *Journal* with "An Authoritative Endorsement" over the signature of Thomas S. Cullen, M.B., at its head. Two other articles on cancer by Adams were published within the month; one in Collier's and the other in McClure's Magazine. At the same time Harper's Weekly published one by another hand. The campaign's first barrage had shattered professional reticence beyond repair.

It was estimated at the time that more than eight million people read and talked about the three Adams articles. Dailies across the country suddenly discovered the cancer campaign as news. New York editors no longer hesitated to print the word on a back page. Extracts from "What Can We Do" were published by newspapers and periodicals all over the continent.

Public interest was high; so was professional argument. That signature in *The Ladies' Home Journal* was too much for Tom Cullen's critics; and for some of his friends. Bloodgood, whose work in surgical pathology at Hopkins was as outstanding as Cullen's in gynecological pathology, publicly associated himself with the campaign and defended both article and endorsement. Men with less knowledge had less courage and the critics were vocal. Recalling the storm, a Baltimore surgeon who was a Hopkins intern while it raged, remembers most vividly its personal bitterness:

"Cullen and Bloodgood were the chief targets. They had to face the criticism of their own profession to put the thing through and, believe me, it took nerve. It's hard now to go back and get the atmosphere of a time like that, but I can tell you there was very serious and severe criticism of Cullen as doing something entirely unethical when he allowed his name to go on that first cancer story in *The Ladies' Home Journal*. What he signed was simply an appeal to American women not to wait until too late before consulting a doctor in pre-cancer periods, but that was regarded as a grave offence against propriety by a good many professional bigwigs back in 1913. Their criticism didn't move T.S. though. I have never seen Tom Cullen swerved from a course of action he believed to be right by anybody's criticism. And I have never known him to take a course of action open to criticism except because he believed it to be right."

As a buttress to belief, Tom Cullen was soon to have proof that the publicity he had planned and risked was not only right but effective. From one centre after another physicians and surgeons wrote to report beginning cancers discovered and removed as a direct result of the published articles.

"What is best for the public. . . ." Ignoring the critics, the Chairman of the Cancer Campaign Committee set to work on his 1913 report to the Clinical Congress of

Surgeons. Public interest roused by the cancer campaign was still lively, he reported. Editors were willing to print articles approved by the committee. Cancer victims, having read the published articles, were profiting by their warnings and, some at least, coming for treatment in time. The value of educating the layman was established by the first year's work, and the chairman was pleased to report it. But the education was not finished. It was just begun. Authoritative articles in the press could do much, but not enough. "The symptoms of every form of cancer must be indelibly impressed upon every individual." That could best be done by personal contact with small groups. A speakers' campaign should be the next move and the place to begin was in women's clubs:

"Whether the etiology of cancer will soon be discovered is problematical, but in any event the people of the country should be made thoroughly cognizant of the early symptoms of cancer and of the fact that many may be cured by early operation."

Tom Cullen not only advised that first speakers' campaign, but took a leading part in it. His new fall from propriety roused his professional critics to new denunciations. But not such loud ones, or so long. From all over the country the reports of lives saved by the knowledge the cancer campaign had spread among ordinary people came and kept coming until presently criticism fell silent. The following year when the American Medical Association, meeting in Philadelphia, officially adopted the Clinical Congress of Surgeons' cancer committee and its campaign of public education, no voice of protest was raised. Nor did volunteers lack when the A.M.A. decided to celebrate the adoption by putting a speaker on cancer into every big Philadelphia church.

The lonely part of the fight was over. Dr. Thomas S. Cullen of Baltimore, Chairman of the A. M. A.'s new cancer campaign committee, was the speaker at the Sunday evening service in the biggest Methodist church in town.

4

TWENTY EAST EAGER STREET

THE WHITE MARBLE DOORSTOP with "Cullen" inlaid in black and red was removed from the front step of 3 West Preston Street to the vestibule of 20 East Eager in September of 1914. Tom Cullen's last letter home to Canada from the house that for seventeen years had been the centre of affection, adventure and delight for the Cullen family, described the back room they all knew "with everything packed up." Next week he was writing from his desk in his new consulting room. His books were in fine new cases. The painting was done. The paperhanging would be finished tomorrow and the plumbing and electrical work soon. Rebecca was making rapid progress with getting things settled, and by the end of the week everything should be shipshape.

The change defined and declared achievement. The household newly established in East Eager Street ran with generous ease. For the big rooms with their tall windows and marble chimney pieces, their cornices and lustred chandeliers, Rebecca had chosen decorations of soft green, ivory and muted gold. Against them, rubbed mahogany and polished silver and the colours of old Persian rugs glowed pleasantly under shaded lights.

Distinguished guests came to sleep in the south bedroom. There were dinners and coffee parties for them and for the Cullens' friends, and much coming and going, professional and social, in the new establishment.

The rewards of achievement being enjoyable, Tom Cullen was enjoying them. He had kept the child's ability to be both auditor and actor of his own play; the gift that can double happiness and halve disaster for the fortunate who carry it from childhood through life. He found success interesting.

The Governor of Maryland was taken ill and Dr. Cullen was called in consultation. He diagnosed acute appendicitis and operated in the governor's mansion at Annapolis, his friend and the Governor's brother, Dr. Brice Goldsborough of Cambridge, standing by . . . The Secretary of the Navy, Josephus Daniels, came down from Washington to speak and Tom Cullen, as chairman of the meeting was host to Secretary and Mrs. Daniels in his new house. William Jennings Bryan came to town that day, and Tom Cullen's gusto enlisted Secretary Daniels to arrange the surprise appearance of Secretary Bryan at the same banquet. . . . The twenty-fifth anniversary of Johns Hopkins Hospital was celebrated and Tom Cullen was in the celebrations to his eyebrows; preparing programs, organizing entertainment, planning publicity, welcoming returners, befriending the press.

A consultation in New York, a conference and operation in Ohio, a dinner with Dr. Halsted "to meet Dr. Dean Lewis of Chicago," a luncheon "with a couple of business men," a professional engagement at Asheville, N.C., a journey to Washington to dine with Chief Justice and Mrs. White; the weeks could hardly be stretched to fit the number and variety of their engagements. But among them time was always free to set all down for Mary Cullen, with the homely detail that kept her boy Tom near:

"John wanted me to go to the baseball yesterday, but I had a committee meeting . . . plans for the Hopkins celebration. Unfortunately Dr. Osler will not be able to

be with us. . . . I know that the news of last week must
have cheered everybody in Toronto. It certainly does
look as if France were to be spared. I do not think there
is the slightest doubt of the outcome . . . I have been busy
at the hospital. Ernest says it is impossible for him to get
away . . .

" . . . The arrangements are rapidly culminating and
we start in with a splurge Monday. I feel sure everything
will turn out all right. . . . I hope, after next week, to get
back to bookwork once more. That is, as you know, very
conducive to pleasure . . .

" . . . We had very lengthy opening exercises. They
reminded me of a missionary meeting where every speaker
spoke too long. Our program is now finished. The other
sections come on tomorrow . . . a dinner last night and
another this evening. Friday school work starts in earnest.

" . . . I know you will not be in the least worried at
not hearing from Rose. I feel sure that as a result of the
war, letters will be delayed quite frequently. Governor
Goldsborough is doing splendidly. Dr. Kelly and Dr.
Gorter were with me when I operated . . . I hope in the
course of a day or two to get down to book work again.

" . . . I am hoping to have Ernest with me in Dayton
a week from tomorrow, where I have to operate. . . . I
was very busy Saturday, was talking to Minnie on the
phone. . . . I think the foreigners in West China will be
perfectly safe. Warships would do them very little good
because they are two thousand miles away. Dangers in all
parts of Europe are infinitely greater. It is fortunate Rose
is not in Paris. . . . Things are moving along as usual, a
great deal of operating and no chance for any book work.
. . . You have not told me anything of being out driving
for the past week or two. . . .

"We had a first-rate time in Dayton. Ernest is looking
remarkably well. There is not a bit of doubt he is gain-
ing a strong foothold in Detroit. . . . Instead of giving my
talk in the morning, I gave it in the afternoon when
there was a much larger assemblage. . . . I would love to
get up to see you but am tied up at present. I will come
just as soon as possible, depend upon it. . . . You will be
glad to know Governor Goldsborough is in splendid
condition. . . . Be sure to get out all you can.

"Sunday night I was in Washington and again Monday afternoon and evening. Tuesday night we had a medical meeting. . . . I think I will visit home for a little while and get acquainted with the surroundings.

"Mother Dear: I was so pleased with your sweet birthday letter. . . . Time certainly does fly and ere long I will be an old man. . . . Sometimes I feel that you all greatly overestimate my good qualities. Never mind, it is a great comfort. . . . The morning is clear and sunshiny. I must start for J. H. H. to operate at nine. Again so many thanks Mother dear, for your lovely letter. Ever your boy . . .

"Yesterday Rebecca and I ran up to Newark. I had to go to New York to see a patient. We had a little dinner and I caught the train. . . . Rebecca joined me at the football game in Philadelphia Saturday. It was most interesting to see forty or fifty thousand people congregated in one vast field. . . . John and Mary are having a great time with their new dog. . . .

" . . . This week has been rather interesting, a moderate amount of operating and quite a bit of book work. . . . Secretary and Mrs. Daniels stayed overnight with us. Rebecca gave a little dinner for Mrs. Daniels. . . . Miss Cora sent you clippings telling about the meeting. We had addresses by two cabinet ministers. . . . Nobody had any idea of what was going on until I walked into the room with Secretary Bryan. Then they all cheered. . . . I wish you could see John with his new puppy. . . . Now for a little piece of news that I know won't hurt you. All being well Rebecca and I leave here sometime Dec. 23. . . . Tell Kate she will have to limber up that Christmas table."

Tom's letters of that year were tied neatly with others his mother cherished. Notes from her eldest daughter told of her children, her husband and her friends; of dinners and comings-out and symphonies and sermons, and an afternoon tea with Tom and Rebecca in their new home — "it is very beautiful." One reported the arrival, on Tom's birthday, of "John's cunning puppy":

"He is a Scotch terrier like Killie was. Tom gave him to John, was it not *dear* of him? The children went down

255

to Tom's to dinner Friday evening. Rebecca invited them; it was a birthday surprise to Tom. I went down later. Their home is lovely . . . "

There was a letter, too, from Ernest in Detroit, describing his day in Dayton with Tom; and concluding with affectionate pride:

"Tom did himself proud. I wish you could have heard the introduction given him by the toast master who is one of America's foremost surgeons. Tom has come into his own, and at an early age too. . . . Tomorrow night I send greetings to Thomas on his forty-sixth birthday."

When Christmas was past and Tom and his wife had gone back to Baltimore, Mary Cullen put the packet away beside those of years less prodigally fortunate, and sat down to write the first letter of another year. "My dear son," she began, as always, and, as always, ended with her prayer, "May the Lord ever bless and keep you.

"Your loving mother."

5

OBSTETRICS VERSUS GYNECOLOGY

THE WOMAN'S CLINIC of Johns Hopkins Hospital stands in Wolfe Street. Its back joins, by block-long corridors, the back of the old hospital on Broadway. Its entrance faces the columned porch of the School of Hygiene and Public Health across the way. It is a prim brick building topped with meagre copings. Architecturally, neither vice nor virtue marks it, seen from its own side of the street. But cross to the doorway of Popsy Welch's School of Hygiene and look back. From that vantage point the nondescript shows unexpected character, an aspect of settled surprise. Above its flat concluding cornice, unnoticeable from directly below, rises a many-windowed, solidly planted addendum. It is Dr. Thomas Stephen Cullen's other storey. He regards it with contentment:

If I had never done anything else, that would be enough. It is the principle that matters, and that has established the principle. I earned a lot of criticism in that fight, but it was from men who didn't understand what I was after. They thought I was fighting only for my own hand. What they couldn't see was that the principle had to be established. If I had quit then, or been beaten, it would have been a long time before another signpost could have been set up to show the right road. As it is —

As it is, in most of the medical schools in America, in virtually all in Europe except Oxford, obstetrics and gynecology, the incompatibles, remain linked in uneasy

257

union; senior and junior divisions of a single department under a single head; usually an aging obstetrician turned gynecologist. The fact, recalled to the victor more than twenty years after his victory was crowned in Wolfe Street, troubles him little. He takes the long view:

It will change, it is bound to change when the public demands it. Doctors are conservative and that is not a bad thing. The profession, as a whole, tends to resist change, but the thing that is best for the patient is accepted in the end. All we need to do is get the facts to the public and wait. The facts will do the rest. No body of men whose profession it is to serve the public can stand forever against the weight of public opinion that has the facts. I'm not worrying. The principle was established when the other storey went on, and they will come to it. Perhaps not in my time, but in the end they will all have to come to it. It is best for the patient.

The first, and the last, Professor of Obstetrics and Gynecology at Johns Hopkins was Howard Atwood Kelly. In 1891 when, fresh from his intern's service in the Burnside lying-in hospital at Toronto, young Tom Cullen came to Baltimore, obstetrical work was not being done at the new hospital. No provision had yet been made for it and Dr. Kelly's whole obstetrical practice was an occasional private case cared for at home. It was a state of things that could not last. After Hopkins Medical School opened in '93 it did not. An obstetrical clinic was established under Dr. Kelly's direction in the teaching hospital and a young and promising junior, J. Whitridge Williams, was chosen by Kelly as resident in obstetrics. Encouraged by his chief, Whitridge Williams went to Europe to study and came back to Hopkins to be appointed associate in obstetrics. Kelly had already made up his mind and set his revolutionary course. On his advice, his department was split a year or two after Williams' return and his young associate became a full professor and head of the new department of obstetrics. In Kelly's department of gynecology Tom Cullen remained an associate, specializing in gynecological pathology.

In those days few would have doubted that Whitridge Williams had chosen the better part. As head of his own department he had a free hand and used it wisely, finding time to do original work in obstetrical pathology that swiftly made his name known far beyond Baltimore. Cullen, meanwhile, was doing task-work for his chief; examining gynecological material from Kelly's operating room, writing up departmental cases for the Hopkins bulletins, assembling and collating clinical and laboratory data that would not see print for years; "having the time of my life." Perhaps more than any other who trained under Kelly he had caught, from the first, Kelly's vision of the future of gynecological surgery.

Those who failed to catch it were hardly to blame. Twenty-five years later Dr. Cullen himself described, for the enlightenment of the American Medical Association, gynecology as he was taught it in the 'eighties and as too many still regarded it during the 'nineties, and after:

In my student days the pupils learned that there were anteversions and anteflexions, retroversions and retroflexions, and that some of the displacements might be relieved by appropriate pessaries. We were told of erosions of the cervix and had the value of zinc chloride or Churchill's tincture of iodine as the proper agents in the treatment for such conditions drilled into us day after day. Much stress was laid on lacerations of the cervix, and many repairs were done. Now and again a torn perineum was also treated surgically.

Abdominal gynecological operations were limited almost entirely to the removal of large ovarian cysts. An occasional myomatous tumor was removed but the fatality in this class of case was so high that the operation was rarely attempted. We occasionally heard of cancer of the cervix or of carcinoma of the body of the uterus, but the only operative procedures we were familiar with for this dread disease were curettage and cauterization of the carcinomatous cervix. To entirely remove the uterus for this condition was not thought of.

Into the gynecological darkness thus pictured, young Howard Kelly had adventured, a surgical prodigy doing the impossible with incredible speed. His one-man hospital in an old house in the mill suburb of Kensington, Philadelphia, saw more original work done in gynecology in the years between 1885 and 1889 than all the other hospitals in the country. In those years Osler was in Philadelphia as Professor of Medicine in the University of Pennsylvania. He sought out the younger man, studied him and his work, made up his mind about both and never found occasion to change it.

Osler went to the Hopkins when the new hospital opened in '89. The same year, on Osler's recommendation, Kelly followed. He was thirty-one and looked and acted younger. His unorthodox professional manner irritated some in Baltimore and alarmed others. But Osler never wavered from his early judgment. He had "put his money on the Kensington colt." He backed his choice in every sort of going. Howard Kelly got the freedom he needed to build a clinical department after his own pattern in the field he had made his own. He was the man for such an opportunity, for he had insatiable interest, skill, daring, superb self-confidence and a gift for inspiring confidence in others. His mind was as inventive as it was practical, his impulses were generous as a boy's and he had a wide streak of natural showmanship that came in handy.

In that, though in little else, he was like Welch. In personal relationship he was always closest to Osler, and he shared Osler's gift for evoking and holding the almost-protective loyalty of the younger men who worked with him. Thus Whitridge Williams waited until 1919, when Howard Kelly retired from the Hopkins Department of Gynecology, to try out a long-maturing plan for restoring the departmental balance which, he had come to believe, Kelly unwisely destroyed by dividing obstetrics and gynecology.

Studied in perspective, history hardly supports Whitridge Williams' belief. The imbalance which had deprived obstetrics of its weight in the clinical scale was not peculiar to Hopkins. It was an effect of the astounding progress in surgery and medicine which marked the era. The high excitement of discovery in other branches left obstetrics as a specialty increasingly becalmed. Naturally, though mistakenly, the Hopkins professor of obstetrics thought he saw, as time passed and with it the relative importance of his department, the root of neglect in Kelly's original decision to divide obstetrics from gynecology. Naturally, he convinced himself that the cure was to be found in joining the two again in the old order. The echo of this conviction had been detected by Osler in 1912, in Abraham Flexner's suggestions for Kelly's clinic. "And — shades of Marion Sims, Goodell and Gaillard Thomas — " Osler had then protested, "this (gynecology) is the department which the Angel of Bethesda, in the fullness of his ignorance, suggests should be, if not wiped out, at any rate merged with that of obstetrics." Two years later Whitridge Williams made his position plain in a signed article in *The Journal of the American Medical Association.** There he charged gynecology with having usurped the place in professional interest that rightly belonged to obstetrics, and laid at the door of gynecologists responsibility for the lack of progressive obstetrical teaching in American medical schools.

* "Has the American Gynecological Society Done Its Part in the Advancement of Obstetrical Knowledge?" — J. Whitridge Williams, A.M.A. Journal, June 6, 1914.

The following year, 1915, Dr. Thomas S. Cullen, chairman of the section on obstetrics, gynecology and abdominal surgery, prepared an address for delivery at the American Medical Association Convention in San Francisco. In it he set forth and discussed the charge made by Whitridge Williams and the relevant evidence. His conclusions differed from Dr. Williams'. Not indifference but incompatability he held chiefly responsible for the comparative backwardness of obstetrical teaching. He traced its neglect to the custom, still followed in most medical schools, of associating obstetrics and gynecology as two branches of a single clinical department:

From what Dr. Williams has told us, the obstetrical training in America is not what it should be. Is it going to be improved if the head of the Department, naturally and gradually, drifts over into surgery leaving the obstetrical teaching, both practical and theoretical, largely in the hands of his associates? . . . In years past some of the prominent members of the profession tried to combine their labours in obstetrics and gynecology. A few succeeded but as their practices increased the majority either became obstetricians or confined their work almost entirely to gynecology. This was natural as these two branches cannot be well handled together.

Supposing the surgeon who practices these two specialties arranges for four abdominal operations tomorrow morning and that, just as he is leaving for the hospital to operate, he receives an urgent call to one of his primiparas who is on labour. If this confinement lasts several hours, these four operations have to be postponed, the postponement causing much added anxiety not only to the four patients but also to the various relatives. A few such delays as this and the friends of a patient will naturally look for surgeons that can be relied on to fill their engagements promptly. In a way this is very unfair to the obstetrician, inasmuch as the delay has been in no way his fault; and yet the fact remains that it has been due entirely to an attempt on his part to combine two specialties that are not compatible.

Again, let our surgeon arrange for a Wertheim operation on a cancer patient for tomorrow morning. This is without doubt one of the hardest abdominal procedures. The surgeon should be in the pink of condition and it should be his first operation of the day. During the night he is called out to an obstetric case and is detained several hours. If he operates on the cancer case on schedule time, is he doing justice to himself or to his patient?

Is it any wonder that many physicians have given up this combination of obstetric and gynecologic practice? Your young medical men will often say that they are at present paying particular attention to obstetrics, hoping later to enter the surgical ranks; older men who have good obstetrical practices are relegating that work to associates as their surgical practice increases. Do you blame them? Few there are who would not do likewise. When we look at the subject squarely it is clearly obvious that the obstetrical specialist is the true missionary of the medical profession and the most unselfish member of its ranks. Even though he be the head of his department, his time is not his own and there is no hour of the day or night when he may not be called . . . The obstetrician has the right to demand that every possible facility be afforded him. Not until this fact is so thoroughly realized that it is acted on by the profession will the best men be content to remain in this important but arduous field . . .

From that point the chairman of the section went on to complete his public statement of a thesis he had made his own; that gynecology and abdominal surgery, not obstetrics and gynecology, are the specialties which logically belong together.

His text was basic: "Any surgeon opening the abdomen should be capable of doing everything necessary in that abdomen." His illustration was homely: "When you and I take a watch to the jeweller we expect him to overhaul it thoroughly. If he returns it saying the mainspring which was broken has been repaired but the watch still will not go, we are naturally dissatisfied, and will try a more competent man."

The argument developed from Tom Cullen's one unchanging question: What is best for the patient? —

If the gynecologist confines his work entirely to the pelvis, he will not infrequently overlook lesions in the upper abdomen, and the surgeon in like manner can miss serious pelvic trouble. . . . Suppose I have done some pelvic operation and have overlooked gall-stones or a duodenal ulcer. The patient will usually be far from well and will, in a few weeks or months, decide to call in a man capable of treating the upper abdominal lesion. What does this lack of preparedness on my part entail for the patient? Twice the length of time in the hospital, twice the amount of pain, twice the amount of hospital expenses and two operation fees, not to speak of the added risk of a second operation. . . . It will not be long before the laity will demand that anyone who enters an abdomen must be capable of doing everything necessary in that abdomen, and in those cases in which, on account of the lesion present, a second operation is required, it will be necessary for us to explain carefully just why the abdomen must be opened again. . . .

In recent years business men have been much aided by economy or efficiency experts. . . . If we called in such an expert what would he say? In the first place he would point out that it is not necessary for two classes of surgeons to work in one abdomen — a space, the confines of which nature has so well defined. In the second place he would say to both the surgeon of the upper abdomen and the surgeon of the lower abdomen: "You have spent long years in preparing yourselves for doing abdominal surgery, you have mastered the fundamentals of medicine, you have a good knowledge of bacteriology and pathology and have perfected yourselves in the methods of operation; and yet, because one pelvis happens to contain a small round muscular body with two smaller bodies on the sides, one of you confines your work in large measure to men, the other to women. You are only running at half capacity. There is absolutely no reason why you should not both do abdominal surgery in the two sexes." . . . In other words gynecology and abdominal surgery logically belong together. This realignment is absolutely necessary if we are to accomplish the maximum amount of good for the patient.

The address was read at San Francisco, but not by its author. When the day came for delivering his challenge the champion of unified abdominal surgery was three thousand miles away, recovering in the Hopkins from a gall-bladder operation performed by a surgeon of the upper abdomen, his friend John Finney. His enforced absence was the pretext for an attempt to limit the spread of his doctrine. Objection was made to the inclusion of the Cullen address in the official report of the San Francisco proceedings, on the ground that only papers delivered in person were eligible for publication in A.M.A. convention reports. Notice of the objection reached Tom Cullen when he was himself again. From past A.M.A. proceedings he supplied the editor of the reports with precedent for the publication of a chairman's paper, read in the absence of its author. He added that, if objections to the inclusion of this one were insuperable, he would be happy to have it published and circulated to fellow-members of the A.M.A. with a note explaining the reason for its non-appearance among the official reports.

Dr. Cullen's paper appeared among the official reports. Its argument was widely accepted as valid by leading gynecologists and surgeons.

Among those who accepted was William S. Halsted, Chief of Hopkins Department of Surgery. In the struggle for the life of the Hopkins gynecological department the fact was to mean much. But Tom Cullen could not know, in 1915, how complete the acceptance was. Early in the year he had received warning that, if it came to a tug, he must make it without his own chief. Dr. Kelly, more and more immersed in his missionary journeys, his radium work and his "san" in Eutaw Place — to be incorporated the following year as the Kelly Clinic — was growing less and less concerned with the conduct of affairs at the Hopkins. In April from Eutaw Place he wrote his associate of his plans to retire:

"I am thinking seriously of dropping the work at the Hopkins next year. There is so much constructive work here which is pressing and which I cannot do carrying the double burden. I do not want to take any step, however, without talking the matter over with you first . . . "

6

PARTNERS' FAREWELL

A FIGHT WAS BREWING and Tom Cullen knew now it must be a lone one. He was Irish enough to wait the event without gloom, wise enough to ignore it, while he could, in the happiness of unclouded affection. His letters of that year — the last of her life — to Mary Cullen are mirrors of that clear mood. He wrote only of things to interest and content her: A medical meeting at his house "to decide what we should all do in case the United States came into the war"; excursions into the country; preparations for the journey to camp; the progress of the new book; a cheerful running commentary on the doings of his sisters and brother, all well established now; reports on old friends. Of her son's illness that summer his mother knew nothing until he was himself able to pencil a note, signed with his unvarying salutation, to tell her the operation was successfully past.

Followed a succession of long, reassuring letters, dictated from bed, to tell of his progress, his flowers, his visitors, news of the Baltimore grandchildren, of the good things he could eat again, of Ernest who had come from Detroit to be with him:

"You now see why Ernest came to spend a few days with me. It was a great comfort to have him here . . . You can readily understand that I am not going to San Francisco. My paper was written a long time ago and is already in print but it would hardly do to take such a long trip. As soon as I get through here I am going direct to

267

camp . . . Drop Rebecca a line. She had a pretty anxious time of it for a few days . . . Tell Blanche they used the alcohol on the adhesive. In fact I insisted on it and it helped matters greatly . . . It certainly is a great satisfaction to have everything over. I can now go to camp feeling comfortable.

" . . . All being well we leave Friday morning next. I can hardly realize I have gotten along so fast. . . . Miss Cora answered practically all the telegrams and cards and left me on easy street . . . I am so glad, Mother, that you are feeling well and enjoying the drives. Blanche is to let me know when the account needs replenishing. . . . "

That summer Mary Cullen spent in New Brunswick with her daughter Blanche. She was not again to see the northern lake she had grown to love, to enjoy the easy comings and goings of fellow-campers, the smooth-running pleasant life of her son's long, sunny-galleried cabin lifted on its rock to command the sweep of Ahmic lake and river narrows, islands and wooded shores. As if knowing an urgent need to share its untroubled beauty with her again, Mary Cullen's boy wrote, in the weeks at Ojibway Cabin, letter after letter, recalling for her happiness the familiar things, the accustomed places, the joyous expeditions she knew:

"The strawberries are ripe and on Tuesday last we caught twelve nice trout in Bell's Creek . . . Thanks for Rose's letter. It will go to Kate right away. Have heard from Ernest and Minnie so all the family are accounted for. . . . I have the wicker writing desk drawn up against the door near the fireplace and the sun is pouring in on my back to make me as warm as toast. Rebecca is sitting by the fire. . . . Now, Mother dear, many, many happy returns of your birthday. I hope next year it will be here . . . With a heart brimming over for you — Ever your boy . . .

"Today Roger and Florence and I picked wild strawberries and in a little over an hour got five quarts . . . For the last few days I have done little writing — so many picnics . . . Dr. Kelly and Olga were over here a short time ago . . . Our blueberries are ripe now. Not as many as last year but very sweet. On Thursday we had the team take the boat over to Clear Lake and caught twelve fine bass. We got nearly all of them in twenty minutes and then they stopped biting . . . Since writing you we have been very busy doing nothing. You know how it is. One day we went after huckleberries. We usually get more right here on the hill. Yesterday Rebecca picked strawberries and I picked raspberries. We are never in want of berries for breakfast . . . I am feeling stronger every day . . . Ever your boy . . .

"While we are at camp the book is being printed and Dr. Frank Smith in Balto is correcting the English. In September my work of correcting begins . . . Ernest wired me on Tuesday that he had been delayed by an operation and I at once sent him my congratulations on having one to do. I expect him on the morning boat . . . This morning it has been raining and now it is hesitating. The sun will win out . . . In a few minutes we are going over the hill into Old Man's Lake where the fishing is good. I am feeling splendid . . . Things here have been rather lively. We are continually going off on picnics. On Friday we had a barge party on the lake and made $60 for the Magnetawan Red Cross. Everything looked very pretty . . . If all is well, we leave in about two weeks . . . will stop over in Toronto to get a peep at you. I have had a man clearing up the brush in the woods back of the main cabin. It looks like a park. Rebecca, Dr. Kelly and Olga went to Deer Lake yesterday. They will be back Monday . . . Ever your boy . . .

"Hello Mother Dear . . . I am so pleased to know you and Blanche are having such pleasant little jaunts . . . Let me know when you need more money for drives, etc. I want you to go out as often as you can . . . As my new book is all in type and will require months of correction, a good start before school begins will help immensely. Accordingly I hope to leave here about Sept. 7 and if you are still determined to be in Toronto I shall have the chance to see you. It will be a great treat . . . We have had frost but now it is lovely, warm and sunny. Ever your boy . . ."

269

Early in May of 1916 Mary Greene Cullen died.

"Tom's new book," the book whose progress she had followed from week to week with proud and confident affection, was finished. Final corrections made, the printed sheets had gone to the bindery. Only the index page proofs had still to be corrected and the title page and dedication to be set when Mary Cullen's elder son received the last of all the messages that brought him to her side. It came too late to let him leave Baltimore that day.

Tom Cullen called Philadelphia and, though it was Sunday, got through to R. W. Greene, a partner in W. B. Saunders Company, his publishers. He asked help. If it could be done, he had to have a copy of the new book before the express left Baltimore for Toronto Monday afternoon.

He had it. Early next morning, in Saunders' Philadelphia plant, a printer and a binder were at work on it. Title page and dedication were hand set and run off on a proof press. The printed sheets and illustrations for a single volume were assembled with blank outer sheets, trimmed and bound in their covers. Then index, title page and dedication were pasted to the empty end pages. Saunders' vice-president himself brought the completed volume to Baltimore. Mary Cullen's last gift from her boy Tom was ready in time.

She was still conscious when he reached her bedside Tuesday morning and she smiled when, his hand holding the book in hers, he opened it for her at the dedication: "To My Mother."

7

UMBILICAL INTERLUDE

ACCUSED OF writing a book of 700 pages concerning an area not more than two centimetres in diameter Tom Cullen's defence is sufficient. There were only 680 pages and he never enjoyed himself more in his life.

The book was the by-product of an abdominal operation performed in 1904. It was the fourth and last of Cullen's major works of scientific research and he was nine years completing it. During three of them he spent three afternoons each week in the Surgeon General's Library in Washington assembling and digesting source material. When all was finished and the book in proof he made fifty more trips to Washington to check his references against the originals. The work was published in May of 1916 under the title *Embryology, Anatomy and Diseases of the Umbilicus Together with Diseases of the Urachus.*

The operation from which it all started was for the removal of a malignant tumor of the umbilicus; the first Tom Cullen had seen. The patient did well for a time but died later when large tumors developed in the abdomen. The surgeon was then in Europe and no autopsy was obtained, but microscopic examination had shown the umbilical growth to be a cancer of the gland type:

I was at a loss to explain the presence of glands in that locality. The textbooks had nothing enlightening to say on it, and my curiosity was aroused. Having two books on my hands at the time and other pressing problems, I was obliged to leave it unsatisfied for some years, but as soon as I could find time I set out to discover, if possible, just how an adenocarcinoma could develop in the umbilicus.

I was amazed when I began to go into the subject in the Surgeon General's Library to find the records of many cases of cancer of the navel. In the great majority of them the umbilical growth was secondary to a cancer of the stomach, gall-bladder, intestine or ovary, and of the same type. But I also found recorded a few cases of primary adenocarcinoma as well as of squamous-cell carcinoma of the navel; evidence that the primary growth does occur in that region, though rarely.

How it occurs, the records did not show as completely as a scientific mind might wish. Their testimony was inconclusive. The inquirer did not therefore foresake his new field of study. On the contrary, he enlarged it happily for he found himself exploring uncharted territory. First product of his exploration was a short article on surgical diseases of the umbilicus[1] published in the *Journal of the American Medical Association* in February of 1911. It was followed by an article on adenomyoma of the umbilicus[2] which appeared in *Surgery, Gynecology and Obstetrics* in May of 1912:

I had found among the many reported cases of umbilical tumors one group in which I was particularly interested. These tumors were small, they always occurred in women, they tended to swell at the menstrual period and some of them discharged a little blood. Some had been diagnosed as adenocarcinoma, some as carcinoma developing in a sarcoma; in diagnosing others the doctors had disagreed. Those examined histologically showed a stroma of fibrous tissue and muscle with typical uterine glands

1 *Surgical Diseases of the Umbilicus* — Journal of the American Medical Association, 1911, Vol. LVI, pp. 391-396. Reprinted in T.S.C.'s Collected Reprints. Vol. II.

2 *Umbilical Tumors Containing Uterine Mucosa etc.* — Surgery Gynecology and Obstetrics, 1912, Vol. XIV, pp. 479-491. T.S.C.'s Collected Reprints. Vol. II.

scattered throughout. The glands were in some cases surrounded by the characteristic stroma of the mucosa. These growths I identified, by their type of symptom-complex, as adenomyomata.

So true to type did the recorded symptoms run that in one instance I wrote to England and secured the section of a tumor which had been diagnosed a dozen years before as a possible remnant of the omphalomesenteric duct. The case had been reported before the London Pathological Society and published in 1899, but I was able to get the section and found the growth to be a typical adenomyoma, as I had thought.

To be able to identify as adenomyomata this group of umbilical tumors not before identified correctly gave Tom Cullen satisfaction. It crowned for him the successful research begun nearly twenty years before when, a junior pathologist in Dr. Welch's laboratory, he had differed with von Recklinghausen of Strasbourg concerning the origin of a certain type of diffuse uterine myoma.

Before he had finished recording the results of his work on umbilical adenomyomata his mind was made up; he was going to go on, do a thorough piece of work on the umbilicus, its lesions and diseases, and publish. Material for such research was not lacking. It existed in quantity, but all unorganized. The researcher's first task was to discover and assemble the scattered knowledge of diseases of the umbilicus. His second was to classify and analyze the various lesions to be found in that area in so clear a manner that they might easily be recognized with their clinical implications.

The field was his own. No more than four major treatises on umbilical lesions and infections had been written, and the latest of the four; Runge's on umbilical infections; was dated 1893. There was no single book which attempted to cover the whole subject. The medical textbooks discussed thoroughly umbilical lesions of only one type; hernias; those they discussed very thoroughly. That being so, Tom Cullen spent no time on them. But he devoted much time to both the anatomy and the embryology of the umbilical region; he had observed how many of the umbilical lesions occurring in adults develop from anatomical defects existent at birth.

The special anatomical equipment of an embryo should disappear before the child is born. As a rule it does. Of the various tubes running through the navel, the gateway between mother and embryonic child, most are absorbed or sealed off before birth, leaving only the umbilical cord with its blood vessels. But sometimes one or two tubes still run through the umbilical cord at birth and make trouble later. Partial or complete lack of closure of the omphalo-mesenteric duct, or of the urachus, in a newborn child can produce grave conditions in maturity:

For example, the remnant of an omphalo-mesenteric duct, remaining between the navel and the mesentery at birth may, as Meckel's diverticulum, produce in an adult serious intestinal trouble.

We had long been familiar with Meckel's diverticulum and the ills it could cause when I began my study of the umbilicus. But two facts; that the omphalo-mesenteric duct may be patent throughout its entire extent at birth, and that remnants of its outer end may give rise to the small polyps sometimes noted on the umbilicus when the cord drops off; had not been sufficiently appreciated. The polyps are important as indications of the possible persistence of other portions of the duct inside the navel — a possibility not to be overlooked.

When a patent omphalo-mesenteric duct is detected after the cord has come away immediate operation for the removal of the duct is indicated. Only thus can the child be saved all risk of the alarming and fatal complications which might develop. But where only a small polyp is evident on the outer surface of the navel it may be hard to make the decision for surgery. Yet the probability that the polyp indicates the existence of Meckel's diverticulum, or of a cord from the mesentery to the umbilicus, and the possibility of an intestinal obstruction developing later must, in such a case, not only be borne in mind but carefully explained to the child's parents.

As with his earlier works, the assembling of material for the umbilical volume presented no problem to Tom Cullen except that of finding time for it. The problems were in the classification and presentation of the mass assembled. One great part he was happy to class as of historic interest only: the records, as old as history, of devastating umbilical infections rampant among newborn infants before the era of asepsis. Another part; that concerned with the escape of peritoneal accumulations from the umbilicus in children, and with the occasional passage of gallstones from the umbilicus in adults; he set down as soon to be in the historic class. Early surgical treatment could eliminate both these possibilities. The task that remained was large enough; the interpretation, in the light of modern pathological knowledge, of hundreds of records and case histories, many made before pathology had become a science; and the scientific classification of all:

Fitting each case into its proper place was not easy. It is always hard to interpret the findings of others and I have no doubt I made some mistakes. But I found this part of the work simply fascinating. No puzzle could have been better fun.

Max Broedel, who illustrated the book, enjoyed himself, too. It was he who started the search for a normal navel and pursued it through the wards of Johns Hopkins until satisfied that no standard pattern exists. Four plates, depicting sixty normal navels, all different and all drawn from life by Johns Hopkins' Professor of Art as Applied to Medicine make that point clear to students of *Cullen on the Umbilicus*. The same enthusiastic thoroughness went

275

to the making of a series of studies of the embryology of the navel. For these Franklin Mall's unique collection of embryos in Hopkins department of anatomy was the artist's research ground. There he found the material he needed and used it with brilliant effect:

I only wrote the chapter on the embryology of the navel. Max did all the original research for the development of the drawings that make that part of the work. Between us, I think we produced a useful volume and I know that nothing I did in the nine years I was working on it gave me more pleasure.

One of the first copies of the completed work went to Dr. Halsted. It was acknowledged with the guileful promptness of the indolent:

"1201 Eutaw Place
"May 13, 1916
"Dear Cullen:
"Thank you most heartily for the precious volume on The Bull's Eye of the Human Mechanism.
"Having read every syllable of the fascinating book, from cover to cover, before breakfast this morning, I am reminded of the lines of Milton:
"'Within the navel of this hideous wood
Immured in modest shade a sorcerer dwells. . . .'
"God bless you Cullen for your many courtesies (curtsies) to your fellow man.
"Sincerely yours,
"W. S. Halsted."

The note of laughter is characteristic. Halsted the introspective and dilatory, withdrawn to the point of eccentricity; Cullen the punctual and gregarious; each had discovered the other's integrity and put his trust in it. The growth of understanding can be traced in Halsted's notes to his junior. Always witty and courteous, the earlier stiffen with embarrassment where a request is to be made or a favour acknowledged — "It mortifies me to appeal

. . . the happiness of unclouded affection.
—page 267

Tom Cullen, from a photograph taken at Hopkins about
1912

Mary Greene Cullen photographed during her last summer
in Magnetawan

to you . . . It is a shame to have troubled you . . . You were so generous before . . . " The later are easy with the unguarded ease of a man writing to a friend of whose response he is sure and in whose unquelled ardours he delights.

The umbilical lines from Milton varied a series of notes concerning an impecunious patient Dr. Halsted had referred to Dr. Cullen some months earlier. They ceased in early summer with the patient's return to her home in another city. Halsted wrote:

"You have been wonderfully kind to Mrs. M. I regret so much that I have never seen her. I have been dreadfully remiss and now it is too late to make amends — I mean to her, not to you. . . . It pains me to read that you have not yet decided to pour out your heart's blood in Mexico this pleasant weather. Oh, these hyphenated Canadians!"

A few weeks, and he was writing from High Hampton, in the North Carolina hills, urging a visit to him there and interpolating an irrelevant and irreverent "How marvellous, I might say amateurish, are the ways of Providence. For instance, I am the obstetrician of our valley . . ."

With autumn and the return to Baltimore and work, the affectionate bantering resumed:

"Thank you very much for the forceps and the kind thought. I shall try to learn to use them and to have occasion to bless you frequently." . . . "It was wonderfully thoughtful of you to request Dr. Dennis to send the particular brand of cigarette which I have adopted. If you will tell me the name of your favourite brand of cigars I will tell Dr. Dennis & try to remember each year to remind him of the services rendered by you and Dr. Burnam. It might be well to have engraved little reminder cards with blanks for itemized services, dates, etc. — perhaps credits for presents received or for expressions of appreciation.

These could be sent out annually" . . . "Thank you very much for the overwhelming bunch of reprints just received. You are so prolific I have little time for anything but to review your books and papers" . . . "You seem to have reprints of most of my papers. I am pleased to find that my affection for you runs back to ancient times. Yours ever . . ."

278

8

A LONELY CITIZEN PREPARES FOR BATTLE

Dr. Howard Kelly did not retire officially as chief of Hopkins Department of Gynecology until he had completed thirty years of service to the hospital, but early in 1917 he took indefinite leave. His senior associate was left in charge as acting Gynecologist-in-Chief.

That year, his twenty-sixth in Baltimore, Tom Cullen took out his first papers as a United States citizen. Their date was April 7, 1917, the day after the United States government declared war on Germany:

Why not sooner? Well, I might not have been staying. I was a Canadian, all my people were Canadians and though I loved Baltimore from the first, I didn't feel a fixture here for a long time. After the war started in 1914 I certainly was not going to give up my British allegiance for a neutral one. But when the United States declared war on Germany I applied for American citizenship at once. It seemed the right thing to do.

It was to be a year of deepening loneliness. Ernest Cullen went overseas. John Finney was sent to France in charge of a Hopkins hospital unit — *they wouldn't have me, darn them* — Popsy Welch, with whom through all doctrinal differences the bond of early association held, deserted the Hopkins for the army's health service. Dr. Kelly spent most of the year away from Baltimore recovering from an illness. Max Broedel, bereft of the Germany he had loved, needed more support than he could lend. In that year, too, Emma Beckwith Cullen —

Rebecca — began to suffer increasingly from racking head-aches, precursors of the brain tumor of which she was to die in 1918. And there were no letters any more for her boy Tom to write to Mary Cullen.

A small thing accented loneliness. Tom Cullen was notified that, Johns Hopkins Medical School funds being low, payment of his $300 a year honorarium as a part-time associate professor would not be made. Associate Professor Cullen replied that he would be happy to serve without payment but he would have to ask that $300 be added to his estimate of the gynecological department expenses for the year to replace his honorarium, which it was his custom to make over to his department for laboratory work. He heard no more of the proposed economy but recognized the meaning in that small move. He worked while he waited another sign.

Professionally, he was doing three men's work. War cuts in staff laid heavy duty on the Hopkins seniors remaining. His department demanded his presence a good half of every working day. His practice as a consultant was calling him to other cities more and more often and his fame as a surgeon was bringing him patients from half across the continent. In the Church Home, where he was now doing much of his operative work, the Chairman of the Medical Board found responsibilities accumulating, and shouldered them cheerfully:

You don't know how thankful I was in that time for the years I had put in, helping build the Church Home into a modern hospital with a finely-equipped surgical side. It halved my worries. If it had come to the worst at Hopkins I would have been able to get along perfectly well, professionally.

But Tom Cullen could never find it in his heart to believe that the worst might come for him at Hopkins. When an invitation came from Philadelphia that spring to the chair of gynecology in Jefferson Medical College he declined, though his chief, convalescing in Florida, wrote advising thought:

" . . . What an honour to have such an offer! Whether it will be better to accept must depend on the advancement of your own interests and needs careful consideration. Large as your returns now are, they would be doubled at least in a field like Philadelphia . . . "

Doubled returns did not interest Tom Cullen that much. His decision was made. He was staying at Hopkins to see the thing through. Meantime he continued to write and to publish:

In the long run it's what you can publish that counts. I found that out early, so I wrote up everything I could. The record is there and it stands and if the other fellow has the job in the end, what difference does that make? What you've learned is in print where it can help other men.

Cullen's fourth major volume of research, *"Embryology, Anatomy and Diseases of the Umbilicus"* had been published in 1916. In 1920 he published an intimate and affectionate biographical study of Dr. Henry Mills Hurd, the first superintendent of Johns Hopkins Hospital. In the years between he contributed a dozen original papers to medical journals and prepared his first volume as editor of the gynecological section of Dean Lewis's *Archives of Surgery.**

Extramural employment was added. While the war lasted Tom Cullen did protective duty; not light in a war port with a large floating population; putting his knowledge of German to use in collaboration with the U.S. intelligence service. He gave time and interest without stint to the work of the Enoch Pratt Library Board, to

* Vol. I, published 1920.

which he had been appointed in 1915. And with all he lost no chance to go to a ball game with his nephew and fellow-fan, young John Ramsay.

The illness Rebecca had long dreaded developed in the spring of 1918. Diagnosis was obscure at first and after she had spent some time in hospital, her husband was advised to take her to their camp in Canada. At Magnetawan she rallied for a little, then the symptoms worsened. She was taken home to Baltimore and a brain operation was performed. The growth was found to be, as she had feared, inoperable. Emma Beckwith Cullen died in Johns Hopkins Hospital, September 14, 1918.

That autumn, solitary in his big house, Tom Cullen worked and waited. He recalls the time as the loneliest of his life, and the most anxious. But he schooled himself to share neither his loneliness nor his anxieties. His letters of that year and the next are full of references to the pleasanter doings of every day, or to happy memories. Of one such, written a short time after his wife's death, Howard Kelly wrote him:

"Thank you so much for the cheering letter about our early work. It reminds me of 'cast your bread upon the waters and it will return again after many days.' How many years have we walked the path of service linked arm in arm? . . . "

Oblivious, apparently, to the direction the path threatened to take for his companion when their arms should be no longer linked, Dr. Kelly wrote on of other things and ended — "affectionately" as always. The anxiety for his department which was giving its acting head sleepless nights had left the founder of Hopkins gynecological clinic untroubled. Howard Kelly's Hopkins period was already put behind him. He had decided to retire next year and his mind had turned to fresh enthusiasms. Characteristically, his chief no longer felt Tom Cullen's deep concern for the future of their joint work and, characteristically, Tom Cullen would not burden with his trouble friends less intimately interested.

But, with a few departmental associates dropping in to his library in Eager Street to talk things over, he began in the months of waiting to discuss strategy. It was the beginning of the meetings of the "gynecological cabinet," the weekly councils at the round table in the bow-window that were to shape a plan of defence.

In that time, since he was not sleeping much anyway, Tom Cullen formed a habit of doing his heavy operations at an hour that strained his staff's affection. In Hopkins gynecological clinic, memories still persist of operating room teams, heavy-eyed but dutiful, scrubbed, gowned, gloved and ready to begin work on one of "T.S.'s ringtail snorters" before seven in the morning:

"When T. S. said he would start operating at seven he meant he would start operating at seven; not that he would get to the hospital at seven, or start scrubbing up at seven, or that the patient should be brought up at seven. At seven, if seven was the hour set, the team had to be in place around the table and the knife had to be in T.S.'s hand ready to make the incision. If it wasn't, somebody was in for a bad time explaining why it wasn't. It grew to be quite a game with his staff, trying to beat T.S. to the start, but I can only remember coming near it once.

"It was one of his seven o'clocks and we all stumbled up before six-thirty to prepare for it. At two minutes of seven every last thing was ready. The patient was on the table and prepared. The team was in position. No operator. At a minute of seven somebody said, too loudly, 'I wonder where old T.S. is now?' He hadn't finished saying it before that nose appeared at the glass of the scrubbing-up room door and we had the answer through the crack, 'Old T.S. is right here.' That morning, as usual, T.S. started operating at seven. 'Play ba-all!' he said, and began."

In that same time, the reversible table became the main operating room storm signal farther down Broadway at the Church Home. The table was one Dr. Cullen had himself purchased and presented to the operating room when the hospital was being equipped for surgery. It was in all ways an admirable table except for one gadget. By pressing a lever it was possible to turn the top, end for end, on its pedestal.

There was, according to one who remembers those reversals with horror, no actual advantage in them for the operator, whatever mental relief they may have given him. The disadvantage to the operating room team was drastic. All the carefully placed instrument trays, the sponges and basins, the clamps and sutures, to say nothing of the anaesthetist and his paraphernalia, were, by an eleventh hour switch, put wrong way to. It then became the task of the head operating room nurse and her assistants to soothe the anaesthetist, improvise order out of chaos and let no hitch develop in the supply of essentials to the operator and his assistant; and to do all, as it were, lefthanded:

"You can imagine what a despairing shiver would go around the suite with the word that Dr. Cullen had ordered the table turned. The actual turning wasn't the worst, either. We all knew what it meant; that something had upset him badly. Unless he is thoroughly upset, Dr. Cullen does not forget his operating room team. It was a bad morning that started with a table-turning. You might look for instruments to be thrown before it was through.

"Surgeons do throw them from time to time, as every operating-room nurse can tell you. If an operator is handed the instrument he hadn't asked for in the middle of a tense operation, he is quite likely to throw it on the floor hard. Some, of course, throw more than others. Dr. Cullen, even when he was working under the greatest pressure, rarely let go that way. But the mornings he ordered the operating table turned you could expect anything, and when he once started he was one of the best little instrument-throwers I have ever worked with. I can still see him, blazing with anger, throwing a pair of forceps clean across the floor and then turning to blast the bewildered young nurse who had handed it to him: 'I said *my* forceps! Those aren't *my* forceps!'

"The unlucky child's trouble was that she hadn't worked directly with Dr. Cullen before and hadn't realized that the Cullen elevator, an instrument designed for use at a certain point in certain operations, is literally his forceps — he invented it. She knew it perfectly well as a cullen, and would have handed it automatically to any operator who had asked for a cullen. But being asked for 'my forceps' threw her completely — and very nearly threw the rest of us too, that morning . . . "

A third story of Tom Cullen belongs in that time of waiting. It is of another sort, worth telling since it illustrates a habit he has kept through life. It concerns a Hopkins intern, newly appointed to the gynecological department and still holding the head of the department in more awe than affection. The boy got a message after midnight one night calling him home to his mother who was ill. The train he must catch left at three in the morning and he was scheduled to be on duty in B operating room at eight, for one of Dr. Cullen's operations.

Resolute to go to his mother, whatever his chief might say, the boy called Dr. Cullen at his home, got him out of bed and told him abruptly that other arrangements must be made for the morning, he was going home, his mother was sick. At that point Dr. Cullen took charge. Naturally, the boy must go home. No need to worry about the morning, that could be arranged. When did the next train leave? . . . Three? That gave them plenty of time. His car would be at the residence to take his intern to the station at half past two.

At half past two Dr. Cullen's car was waiting outside the hospital residence, and Dr. Cullen was in it. He had got up and dressed, driven to the station and bought a return ticket home for the boy. He had it sealed in an envelope with enough money to see the young fellow there and back, and a bit over for unforseeable expenses. He rode with him to the station and gave him the envelope there and wished him a happy end to his journey. Then he went home himself:

"Old T.S. has probably forgotten the whole incident long ago. He has done so many things of that sort for so many young fellows who needed a hand, and this was nearly thirty years back. But it gives you an idea of him; you won't wonder that his students and interns were devoted to him."

PART VI

"WHAT'S BEST FOR THE PATIENT . . ."

I

A SCHOOL AND OTHER HOPEFUL MATTERS

AT THE WORST OF TIMES, cheerfulness would break through. With peace regained, with his brother Ernest back from France and writing weekly of successes in his Detroit practice, with the young fellows in his department shaping well and working effectively, Tom Cullen was presently discovering reason to be cheerful. In the autumn of 1919 his inextinguishable delight in getting things done found something solid to take hold on and his spirit was restored.

Dr. Wallace Buttrick, Chairman of the General Education Board, was staying with him in Eager Street at the time, figuring, as usual, how best to make two Rockefeller millions do the work of ten in medical education. A need which Dr. Buttrick and Abraham Flexner, the secretary of the board, had long foreseen was becoming urgent; there was no adequate modern medical school serving the southern States. To choose the right place for such a school and the right man to watch over its beginnings was the task they had set themselves. They were both in Baltimore the autumn of 1919.

Smoking many cigars in the library at Eager Street, Wallace Buttrick talked to Tom Cullen about the general problem. Tom Cullen talked to Wallace Buttrick about a particular man. He had a lot of good stories about the man, Dr. James Kirkland, Chancellor of Vanderbilt University at Nashville, who had a camp near the Cullen and Flexner camps in Canada. Fishing stories from the summers at Ahmic, stories of pretensions gently deflated and pride given an easy fall, of salty sayings and casual doings, human and humane, they gave the picture of a man Tom Cullen loved. When he thought he had told enough stories, he suggested asking Dr. Kirkland to come up from Nashville for a talk. His listener said, "Let me speak to Abraham Flexner."

In his autobiography "I Remember," Dr. Flexner takes up the story:

"I had been brooding over the South, where there was not a really respectable medical school south of the Ohio River.

" 'Where could we even start?' asked Dr. Buttrick.

" 'At Nashville,' I replied, 'where there is little money but a great man — Chancellor Kirkland.'

" 'How can we educate him?' asked Dr. Buttrick.

" 'By getting Cullen, his summer neighbour in Canada, to invite him here for a week.' "

Tom Cullen goes on:

That evening after dinner Dr. Buttrick said "Cullen, that was a capital idea." I handed him a pad and pencil and asked him to write a telegram to Dr. Kirkland. He said "Do it yourself," so I wrote "Come to Baltimore at once" and sent the message off.

Dr. Kirkland, who had not been feeling well, wired back "Is it about my health?" I replied "No, it is about your medical school." He left Nashville by the next train and came to stay with Dr. Buttrick and me, here in Eager Street.

The education in medical education of the chancellor of an impoverished Southern university started at once. Abraham Flexner tells that before Dr. Kirkland had been a week in Baltimore "visiting laboratories and clinics, talking with Welch, Halsted, Cullen, Mall, Howell, Abel . . . he was so thoroughly disgusted with his own medical school that he wanted to go home and abolish it."

Meantime Wallace Buttrick — his host in Eager Street saw to it — had opportunity for the unguarded talks, the rambling exchanges of anecdotes and ideas, which were his assay methods with men. Taking his own time, he came to his own conclusions about his fellow-guest. Then Tom Cullen gave a dinner at the Maryland Club. The guests were carefully chosen; heads of departments in Johns Hopkins medical school, President Goodnow of the university, Wallace Buttrick, Abraham Flexner, Wickliffe Rose — the professor of philosophy from Tennessee who, with Buttrick's backing and Rockefeller funds, had organized the campaign that eradicated hookworm in the southern states — and the chancellor of Vanderbilt:

After dinner there was a brilliant discussion of the needs of medicine in the South, and of the claims of the various Southern cities and institutions that might be considered suitable for a large modern medical school. It soon became evident that all present were agreed on Nashville and on Vanderbilt University as offering the best opportunities for usefulness to such a school. Dr. Kirkland sat and listened, saying little, like the educational statesman he was, and the whole plan of the regeneration of medical education in the South that was to be begun at Vanderbilt with the help of the General Education Board had been mapped before we broke up.

A couple of days later, when I was seeing Dr. Buttrick and Flexner off for New York, Dr. Buttrick turned to me as he got on the train and said "Tom, the General Education Board will pay for that dinner." I said "Not on your life! That dinner made history." Not long after, the first Education Board grant to Vanderbilt; four millions for medical education; was announced. My share, of course, had been simply to help bring matters to a head. Dr. Buttrick and Abe Flexner undoubtedly had an eye on Vanderbilt Medical School for a long time. But I would not give up, for the price of a great many dinners, the happiness it is to remember that I did have a share in beginning the work Vanderbilt has done for medicine in the South.

A note of thanks in William S. Halsted's fine, unhurried hand is commentary, not only on the dinner that made history, but on the host's renewed zest for life:

"It was a delightful little (?) dinner you gave us at the club. I have thought of it many times — am not referring to the terrapin and canvasbacks . . .
"P.S. I shall expect to see you, escorting some good looking woman, at Newman's next lecture."

A letter preserved to mark a more personal event is in Tom Cullen's file for the following year. It is from Dr. Howard Kelly in Florida to Miss Mary Bartlett Dixon of Baltimore. The date is Palm Sunday, 1920:

"My dear Miss Bartie:
"It is a long time since my heart has been so stirred as by the news my dearest friend Tom Cullen has sent me . . . I am looking forward to years of great happiness for both of you and pray that He who alone can confer lasting blessings may bring all possible joy into your lives . . . I shall not be on hand for the great event, but my blessing will be there . . . "

Three weeks after his Palm Sunday letter, Dr. Kelly wrote again from Florida:

"Dear Tom:
"Just a line of affectionate welcome to you and the dear wife on your return to your home and new duties and relations . . . Tell Mrs. Cullen our hearts are up in the Canadian woods and she must learn to love the country there as much as we all do. I suggest a trip to Deer Lake in August. . . . "

Mary Bartlett Dixon and Thomas Stephen Cullen, both of Baltimore, had been married in Princeton, N.J., April 6, 1920.

Their acquaintance was not new. It had begun in 1900 shortly after Bartie Dixon, a daughter of the then chairman of Johns Hopkins hospital board, entered the

. . . emerged from contemplation.

—page 295

Dr. William Stewart Halsted, Chief of the Department of
General Surgery, Johns Hopkins Hospital, 1889-1922

training school for nurses as a probationer. At a staff dance she met Dr. Kelly's Canadian associate and found him quite handsome and very attentive:

"But he talked about the most embarrassing things, or so I thought then, being as silly as most girls of my age. I remember he began, when we were sitting out a dance, about an interesting tumor operation he had done that morning. It seemed to me a little queer and I imagine my lack of professional interest must have seemed as queer to him. Soon after that he went abroad."

In due time Dr. Kelly's Canadian associate came back from abroad with two fine travelling rugs he had bought in London. One he took home to his mother. The other he sent to Miss Dixon who, as a Hopkins nurse-in-training, promptly and properly sent it back. So Tom Cullen kept the rug for himself and after a time fell in love with another Hopkins nurse and was married.

He was fifty-one, an eminent surgeon and a widower when he sent Miss Dixon the travelling rug again. This time she kept it. It lies, as a rule, across the foot of the long chair that is Mrs. Cullen's in the porch overlooking the water at Morling's Chance, her summer home on the Eastern Shore of Maryland.

2

CHALLENGE ACCEPTED, BATTLE JOINED

By the close of 1918 the waiting time had passed for the defenders of gynecology. It was known then that Dr. Kelly's leave would end the next year in retirement. It was known that Dr. J. Whitridge Williams had been offered a professorship in New York. Hopkins medical board and trustees were soon to learn from Dr. Williams the terms on which he would stay in Baltimore. He would stay as a full-time professor heading a fully-endowed department but he would require a radical re-division of clinical material between the obstetrical and gynecological departments as a condition. The greater part of the material allotted Dr. Kelly's department when the division was made more than twenty years before would have to be turned over to obstetrics if Dean Williams was to remain.

In February of 1919 a joint meeting of Hopkins medical board and the advisory board of the medical faculty had considered Whitridge Williams' terms and voted, over the protest of the gynecological department, to accept them. The one modification was a time clause; the transfer of material was not to be made until a woman's clinic was built and ready for use. So Whitridge Williams stayed in Baltimore and obstetrics was added to the number of full-time clinical departments at Hopkins. The General Education Board provided a grant for its support.

That spring, accepting Howard A. Kelly's resignation, the President of Johns Hopkins accepted also his recommendation of a successor. Cullen was appointed to follow Kelly as head of the Department of Gynecology with the title of Professor of Clinical Gynecology. The official acceptance of the Williams conditions had made the succession one of meagre promise. Recognizing the fact, the newly appointed professor still welcomed the appointment. He had determined to make a fight for the future of gynecology and to make it at Hopkins.

Dr. Halsted, intervening, had made the fight hopeful. Aging, beginning to be ill, more than ever disinclined to personal encounters, the chief of the department of general surgery had emerged from contemplation to attend the May meeting of the medical board and offer marriage with his department to the threatened gynecological clinic. His motion was that the teaching and practice of gynecology be divorced altogether from obstetrics and added to general surgery as a major branch; the change Tom Cullen had advocated four years earlier in his San Francisco paper. The motion was approved. Hopkins medical board voted to record its agreement with the general consensus that the future advance of gynecology should be in the line of abdominal surgery. Then it adjourned and William Stewart Halsted went in search of Tom Cullen.

They met in a hospital corridor and the tall drooping senior spoke, abstractedly as always, to the younger man. He wanted to tell Cullen of the change the board had voted and to assure him there was no need to worry in the least; he would not be interfered with in any way. That was all. Lost comfortably once more in contemplation, the saviour went on down the corridor.

For the time being the flanking attack on the gynecological department had been outflanked. It was soon to be renewed. Funds for a woman's clinic building were given the hospital by a patient of Lewellys Barker's. A building site was chosen in Wolfe street. A building "to house the departments of obstetrics and gynecology" was planned, without reference to the head of the department of gynecology.

On the January day in 1920 when Tom Cullen first learned that plans for the new building were to be considered they were already complete. The quarters he and his staff were to work in having been designed he was invited by the hospital superintendent, Dr. Winford H. Smith, to come to his office and see the finished design. It had been drawn, Superintendent Smith explained, after advising with Dr. Whitridge Williams. Dr. Cullen might have the plans for a short time to study and to show to one or two of his associates, but only for a short time. Work was to begin on the new building without delay.

Dr. Cullen took the plans to study and invited his three senior associates, Dr. Guy L. Hunner, Dr. Edward H. Richardson and Dr. DeWitt B. Casler, to study them too. Study led all four to one conclusion; if the plans were carried through in the form shown, the gynecological staff would have no choice but to resign. The new woman's clinic building, as planned in 1920, provided less space by a fifth for the gynecological operating suite than it had been occupying since 1896. For clinical research in gynecology the new plans provided no room. Apart from the curtailed operating room area, the gynecological clinic was allotted for all its activities a small section of one floor. Tom Cullen showed the design to Dr. Halsted before returning it to Superintendent Smith. He recalls that the old man saw the picture at once and said it would not do. But Dr. Welch, back from the wars, was inclined to humour Whitridge Williams. The Dean of Medicine could be a useful ally.

William H. Welch could always dominate Hopkins medical board when he wanted to. After unhappy days of pressure and counter-pressure Tom Cullen wrote refusing responsibility for accepting the building plans as drawn, and asking that a full meeting of the medical board be called to consider and decide on them:

"I feel that the whole future of the Gynecological Department depends on this move and that this decision should not be left to me or to any small body of men . . . the Gynecological Clinic at Hopkins, with Dr. Kelly at its head, has long been recognized as the best in this country and it is but right that the full Medical Board should assume its part of the responsibility for the important changes contemplated."

The letter went on file, the medical board's decision went to Winford Smith. The building for the new woman's clinic in Wolfe street was begun with the plans unchanged except in minor detail.

Long before the work was completed William S. Halsted was dead. He wrote the last of his light and affectionate notes to Tom Cullen at the end of winter in 1922. "Was there ever such a prompt, punctilious and pervading friend" it began, and ended "ever yours." There was to be one more, dated at Johns Hopkins Hospital, August 31, 1922, and signed by a secretary:

"Dr. Halsted wishes me to tell you how much he appreciates your telegram and the messages from Mrs. Cullen and Dr. Kelly and to express to all of you his thanks. . . ."

It reached Tom Cullen at his Magnetawan camp just before the wire bringing the news from Baltimore that Dr. Halsted had died. There would be no more absent-minded emergences from contemplation to redress the balance of justice. But Halsted's motion that gynecology be made a separate department on the general surgery side still stood, with Hopkins medical board's vote approving it, one solid hope of the imperilled gynecologists.

A second hope dawned slowly as the day appointed for fulfilment of Dean Whitridge Williams' conditions approached. Under Cullen, the department of gynecology was doing notably well in surgery and in research, bringing credit to Hopkins among other medical schools, turning out surgeons and pathologists thoroughly instructed in their chosen work. It could hardly be submerged unnoticed and it clearly could not be dismembered piecemeal. Unpleasantness would not here be masked, in the traditional academic manner, by acceptance of a professor's resignation and promotion of one of his associates to his place. Professor Cullen's three senior associates, Drs. Guy Hunner, DeWitt B. Casler and Edward Richardson, were his advisers and supporters — "no man ever had squarer." Their concern was his and that of every member of his staff; to save their department and its work.

The more nearly the building in Wolfe street approached completion the more clearly it appeared that Whitridge Williams' terms could not be fulfilled without embarrassment.

3

TWO LETTERS AND A VICTORY

IN MAY OF 1923, the year after Ernest Cullen died, his elder brother wrote a last long letter to him. Tom Cullen was on the Eastern Shore all that spring, staying at his wife's old home, Bloomfield, on the Tred Avon. He was slowly recovering from a second grave abdominal operation, performed in February; the removal of a gangrenous gall-bladder. May 14 came; Ernest's birthday, a day he had not in thirty years let pass without its letter of affectionate remembrance. He wrote once more:

"Today a year ago my greetings and love went to you and I expressed my pride in you and in your work. A few weeks later you and I had a delightful day together in St. Louis. I can picture you now, exactly as you were as we rode to the station. A few moments together walking up and down the platform, a goodbye kiss, and you disappeared in the steam of my departing train. It was the last time I ever saw you . . . "

Tom Cullen's only brother had died early in July of 1922. Taken ill without warning on the eve of a holiday they were to spend together in Magnetawan, he was dead before the elder Cullen could reach Detroit from Baltimore. The shock passed and the first heavy grief, but the loss remained irreparable, for the two had been friends. Understanding more deep than affection had united them, the younger giving as the years passed an increasing share. He had been a laughing boy with an outrageous delight in joking, a delight the elder's had rivalled until their father's death weighted him with responsibility. Then for a time his enjoyment of Ernest was diluted by duty. The second of the Cullen brothers was not a born perfectionist and he grew up under an easier discipline than the first had known. His senior, noting with misgiving a youthful tendency to get by, set himself to eradicate it.

By the time Ernest had graduated in medicine at Toronto and spent several holidays and five postgraduate years at Hopkins, the aim was achieved. It is the measure of their affection that no residue of resentment was left in the younger man, for the elder was not an easy taskmaster. His resolve was that his brother should have every opportunity and no advantage; his fear, that fondness might betray him into showing the boy special favour. It made life hard for both in working hours. Ernest Cullen's contemporaries at Hopkins recall a time when feeling ran high among junior staff men in the gynecological clinic over what seemed to them the senior Cullen's injustice to his kin. They recall also that among all the resentment one person remained quite unresentful. The victim only smiled. He had, as all who knew him remember, a merry and expressive smile. It left no doubt of his ability to take what Tom might think necessary to administer in the line of duty. The handling was rough enough at times:

I remember coming into the laboratory one day when Ernest was doing an autopsy with a group of students, and asking what was the cause of death. He named a particularly virulent infection. So I let him have it. "You damn fool," I said, "what do you think I paid for your food and clothes and education for? So you could do this sort of work with your bare hands? What are rubber gloves for and why haven't you got them on?"
I laid him out flat in front of them all and it was as much for the students' sake as his. I don't think any of them would forget their rubber gloves again, when they were starting an autopsy.

Away from duty, that sort of thing was as if it had never been. Ernest's humorous devotion to Tom was unshakeable and none was so happy as Tom when good work earned Ernest praise or promotion. He has remembered always, as one of the proud days of his years at Hopkins, the day when Dr. Kelly, without consulting him, appointed his brother resident in gynecology.

It deepened the elder's pride that the younger, following his course, chose not to follow in his wake. When Ernest Cullen's year of residence was done he did not stay to be carried on his brother's reputation. He went to Detroit, as unknown as Tom had come to Baltimore, to make his own. When he died, eleven years later, he had already made it. At forty-four the younger Cullen was a surgeon widely known and well-regarded in his profession, professor of gynecology in Detroit medical school and gynecologist-in-chief to its new receiving hospital.

The Detroit years had been a time of reward for Tom too. "I want you," he had written while the boy was still an intern in Toronto, "to bend every energy to be one of the best surgeons in the land. You have the proper stuff in your makeup. Do not be satisfied until you are in the front rank." He had trained Ernest. His happiness in the result was deep. They met seldom; a few hours together at a medical meeting, a day or two at Christmas with their mother, while she lived; summer weeks at Magnetawan. It was enough: their understanding, deepening as the younger man matured, was self-renewing. It illumines the letters of that time; the elder's full of news and affectionate advice, the younger's, witty and humorously considerate notes to "dear Sir Thomas." Its loss was darkness, falling across Tom Cullen's life . . . The pen moved down the last page of the last letter he would write to the brother he had loved.

" . . . both you and I were proud to be sons of such a father and such a mother. Your life, like theirs, has left the world better. Whether you just now know what I am writing matters little. You have often heard the whole story from me before. What a comfort to remember 'a thousand years are but as yesterday.' With this measure of time as our guide, it won't be long until our whole clan are united again.

"Brother Tom."

Ernest's death and his own long illness had, in a sense, released the elder Cullen. No personal victory would again be quite worth striving for. Even the values that endure could not possess him with the same immediacy. Grief piled on grief in the years of struggle had set him free at last from hope and fear. The fight was still worth making for a principle, but defeat could not crush him if it came; he had known too many sorrows more crushing than defeat. His last birthday letter to Ernest, dead now ten months, was written. He locked it away with the others.

In Wolfe Street in Baltimore the building that was to house Johns Hopkins' woman's clinic was nearly built. The issue on which he had chosen to stand came closer to inevitable decision with every brick laid. Tom Cullen sat on the porch overlooking the water at Bloomfield and thought of other things. Through the lovely riot of flowering that is spring on the Eastern Shore of Maryland, into the crowding ripeness that is summer he stayed on; to remember and to set down old memories of springs more bashful and summers less bold — the springs and summers of his youth in Canada.

When autumn came, he returned to life, but with a new detachment. The fact gave him what must have seemed to his adversary an entirely unfair advantage in the hour of trial. It was a Tom Cullen aloof from circumstance who, at the request of Hopkins medical board, sat in committee of two with Dean Whitridge Williams that November to discuss problems outstanding between the departments of obstetrics and gynecology. The problems, as he saw them, did not face him.

Whitridge Williams was the one who, when the building in Wolfe Street was all but ready for occupancy, had been impelled to ask a parley. Hopkins medical board met, in November of 1923, to re-open at the Dean of Medicine's request the issue decided four years earlier to suit the Dean of Medicine. Dr. Williams had found himself ill-prepared for the event he had himself invited. If his 1919 conditions were fulfilled, the gynecological staff would resign. If the gynecological staff were to resign his department must risk collapse under a weight of surgical and laboratory work, of teaching and clinical duties, it had not strength to carry. For his own sake it was necessary to revise the four-year-old decision by the light of reason. By that light it was revised, Tom Cullen acting as lightkeeper.

It was Dean Williams' plan, not his, that was up for revision. Under its terms, as they stood, the greater part of the work of the gynecological department must be turned over to the department of obstetrics on completion of the new woman's clinic building. The new building was near completion. How the obstetrical staff could handle the mass of gynecological material and the number of gynecological cases that would soon be all theirs was undoubtedly a problem. But it was not his. He and his associates and the senior staff men in his department had long since faced their problem and agreed on a solution. They were united in conviction that, if the Williams plan were carried through, resignation was the solution for them. Their resignations were ready and none wished to withdraw.

Therefore, Tom Cullen had no problem. As a member of the committee of two he could wait in dispassionate

calm while Whitridge Williams strove with his. He did
so, merely turning the light of reason on evidently insufficient solutions as they were advanced. The method of
elimination proved effective. Convinced at last that he
had not departmental means to support the obstetrical
imperialism of his dream, Whitridge Williams folded it
away. The committee of two reported unanimously, advising that the department of gynecology should continue
as it had begun, including in its province virtually all
the clinical material allotted it under Kelly. The report
was adopted by Hopkins medical board as defining present and future boundaries of the two departments.

Its adoption was vindication, as complete as could be
wished, for the department of gynecology and its chief.
The claims Whitridge Williams had made in 1919 he
himself, in 1923, acknowledged to be untenable. His staff
rejoiced for Tom Cullen more, he was interested to find,
than he rejoiced for himself. He was happy that the principle had been established.

The flaw in the peace terms was the new building in
Wolfe Street. It had been planned and constructed on the
assumption that gynecology could and would be reduced
to a subdivision of the department of obstetrics. It was
ready for occupancy. Its solid red brick encased a problem
for the gynecological chief and his associates. Should they
content themselves with a moral victory and begin their
new lease of departmental life in the inadequate new
quarters they were invited to occupy? Or should they stay
out, standing disagreeably on principle?

Tom Cullen left the decision to his gynecological cabinet and his staff. It was unanimous against moving into
the new building. Drs. Hunner, Casler and Richardson,
having inspected it, reported the errors in planning for
their department to be so fundamental and the space
allotted it so inadequate "that we cannot think of carrying on our present volume of work in the new quarters;

much less can we think of future expansion." They advised that the gynecological clinic should stay where it was until such time as a new surgical building was built and then, as Dr. Halsted had proposed, join the other major branches of surgery:

"We are assured by the general surgical department that they would welcome our work in close association with theirs. . . . "

The head of the gynecological department sent his associates' report to Superintendent Winford Smith. Then, for the first time in the long struggle, he appealed to Caesar. The decision to stand out against all attempts to inveigle or railroad gynecology into the insufficient quarters prepared for it having been made by others, he could champion it with more force; by-passing lesser authority to plead the point of principle with the chairman of Hopkins hospital trustees. The letter he addressed to Judge Henry Harlan was mild and objective. It presented the facts and reviewed the steps that had led to the present impasse, detailed the advantages of moving gynecology to a place with the other surgical activities of the hospital, recalled that such a move was overdue, the medical board having voted in favour of it five years earlier, and came to the point.

"Respectfully" Tom Cullen requested "that we be allowed to continue in our present operative suite until space of similar size or larger be allotted to gynecology in the new building to be erected for general surgery." There indignation was permitted to spring the cork a little. He wished, Hopkins gynecologist-in-chief wrote, "to emphasize the fact that, had it not been for Dr. Williams' request and the medical board's acquiescence thereto in 1919, this contingency would never have arisen."

The letter, dated January 2, 1924, was the pattern-piece of a new year. Considered as a chief protagonist's review of a struggle five years long and deeply entangled in personalities it is, save for the one flash, a model of flatly factual presentation. Its writer had come through to the place where good fighters are apt to win; all vain dread of losing being past.

Early that month Hopkins' department of obstetrics moved into the new woman's clinic building in Wolfe Street. The department of gynecology remained in B operating suite.

4

THE OTHER STOREY GOES ON

ABRAHAM FLEXNER wrote from New York that he would be coming down in a few weeks to see Dr. Buttrick. His letter was to Mrs. Cullen. "I want Tom," he wrote, "to have peace and quiet for his work and not to be required to spend his time fighting."

As the years passed, the General Education Board's increasing gifts to medical education had brought its chairman and secretary more and more often to Baltimore for counsel. As always, when honest men grow better acquainted with complex situations, judgments had been readjusted. Flexner no longer adhered in 1924 to the snap opinion which had irritated Osler in 1912 that Hopkins gynecological department should be, if not abolished, then merged in the obstetrical. Wallace Buttrick, his chief, had come with acquaintance to hold in high regard the Hopkins Professor of Clinical Gynecology, his work and the principle on which he worked — "What's best for the patient. . . ."

The two, Buttrick and Cullen, had early been drawn to each other by a deep conviction shared; that most of life's collisions can be headed off with the right funny story told to the right man at the right moment. Thus firmly based, their friendship stood. During the planning of the Vanderbilt Medical School endowment it deepened to affection. The Chairman of the General Education Board came to see, as fully as Dr. Halsted had seen, the importance to medicine of the Cullen approach.

So, in the beginning of 1924, when it became evident that the victory won in principle was likely to be lost in hospital politics, the two on whom Tom Cullen had depended for disinterested advice in his long defence decided to offer something more concrete. The claims to obstetrical hegemony, lately abated in the light of reason, were taking new shape in schemes for a unified woman's clinic. The reprieve which had left the gynecological clinic in B-suite was clearly only temporary. Work on the new surgical building, long planned, would soon start. If Tom Cullen was ever to get the principle fixed that would ensure the future development of gynecology at Hopkins on lines best for the patient, it must be now.

Abraham Flexner came from New York to Baltimore, talked with Wallace Buttrick, who was in Hopkins for treatment, talked with Tom Cullen. The most direct way through the tangle was chosen; a proposal to raise money for a "Howard A. Kelly floor," to be devoted to gynecological surgery, in the new surgical building. With its chairman's approval, the secretary of the General Education Board accepted Tom Cullen's invitation to lunch with him at the Maryland Club and there put the proposal to the men who must decide on it. The list of those invited to lunch with Dr. Flexner was short; Judge Henry Harlan, chairman of Hopkins hospital trustees; Dr. Frank Goodnow, president of the university; the gynecological cabinet and Dr. William H. Welch — "Popsy," whose weight was always decisive with the advisory board of the medical faculty, the policy-making body in all that concerned the medical school.

Dr. Welch owed much to the chairman and secretary of the General Education Board. Obligation required that, if he accepted the invitation to lunch, he must come with an open mind prepared to give generous consideration to any proposal for Hopkins presented by Abraham Flexner

"We established the principle . . ."
—page 310

The Gynecological Cabinet meets again. From left: Dr. DeWitt B. Casler, Dr. Edward H. Richardson, Dr. T. S. Cullen and Dr. Guy Hunner, photographed in the library at Eager Street, fifteen years after on Wallace Buttrick's advice. But Popsy was suffering from a recurring and very human complication; prior personal commitments.

Thus the unforeseen happened. After Dr. Cullen's invitation to lunch was accepted by Dr. Welch but before the day set, the advisory board of Hopkins medical faculty was called, with the medical board of the hospital, to shape policy for the woman's clinic. The boards met and decided that in the interest of the medical school the department of gynecology should be moved into the new woman's clinic building, if suitable operating room facilities could be made available.

In the shadow of that decision Tom Cullen welcomed his luncheon guests. One extra came uninvited. Breaking out of hospital Wallace Buttrick arrived, late for lunch but in time to change the fortune of the day. As his host recalls it:

After lunch I explained the reason we had had for meeting but added that, the advisory medical board having already decided against it, the subject naturally was not up for discussion. Dr. Buttrick said at once, "Flexner, there is only one thing to do isn't there; put an extra floor on for Cullen?" Flexner said "Yes." Nobody else said anything.

Dr. Buttrick got up and said "Flexner, come out into the hall. I want to talk to you." They went out and in a short time Flexner came to the door again and called Judge Harlan out. In two or three minutes they all came back and Dr. Buttrick said, "although not speaking officially," he and Dr. Flexner felt sure the General Education Board would give $100,000 for the addition of a floor to the new Woman's Clinic building, for the use of the Hopkins gynecological department.

It was all settled in twenty minutes from the time luncheon ended, and in twenty-five minutes Abe Flexner was on his way back to New York and Dr. Buttrick on his way back to hospital. He told me afterwards that nothing would have kept him away from that luncheon and that he had made up his mind what must be done before he left the hospital for the club. Without two such friends I don't know where we would have landed.

Even yet, all was not plain sailing in Wolfe Street. Months passed and the other storey was not begun. Delays multiplied until rising construction costs made the General Education Board gift insufficient for the work. Then the project was laid aside "for lack of funds" and uncertainty descended once more to cloud the future of gynecology at Hopkins. The final clearing came far from Baltimore on a late summer day in 1925. Tom Cullen, recovering slowly from an acute bronchitis, was sitting in the sun outside his cabin on the shore of Ahmic Lake:

I spied a familiar figure in khaki trousers, weather-beaten coat, old hat and disreputable shoes, coming down the path. As he came he waved a piece of yellow paper and called, "This will cure your bronchitis, Tom!" It was Abraham Flexner, and the paper he waved was a telegram telling us that the General Education Board had voted fifty thousand more towards the cost of adding our top storey, to ensure its early completion. Abe was right. It cured my bronchitis.

The new floor of the Woman's Clinic building at Hopkins, dedicated to the teaching and practice of gynecology, was opened January 24, 1927; eight years after Tom Cullen's struggle to save the department began:

It was a long fight, but worth making. Good came of it all around. Dr. Williams, whose clinic had for years had totally inadequate quarters, obtained a fine extra operating room and even more space than he had planned for his work. The gynecological department obtained a clear division of fields, with what belongs to gynecology and what to obstetrics decisively defined. It also got, with the addition of the extra floor to the Woman's Clinic building, adequate space, and an operative suite that cannot be excelled. Most important, it got its independence recognized; we established the principle. . . .

310

So each side won something; the best way for such a fight to end. There need be no bitterness left then, and I like to think there was none in this case. . . . Whitridge Williams used always to walk to his work in the mornings, but in bad weather, when I overtook him on the way to the Woman's Clinic, I would stop and pick him up. I remember the last time well. It was not a bad morning, but on impulse I stopped the car and called "J.W., get in." He did, and we finished the journey together. It was the last morning he ever went to his classes at Johnny Hopkins.

5

TEACHER OF MEN

About teaching I have only one important thing to say;
never start a lecture at half past two. Everybody goes to
sleep on you.
— *T. S. Cullen.*

THE YEARS THAT FOLLOWED the opening of the other
storey in Wolfe Street were as full of a number of things
as any Tom Cullen had known. The long uncertainty
concerning the future of his department at Hopkins was
put behind. Gynecology was established in independence
in its own place. Its champion could rest content or turn
released energies elsewhere. He turned them in so many
directions that the record becomes hard to sort.

President of the Medical and Chirurgical Faculty of
Maryland; a director of the transportation company that
linked the eastern and western shores of Maryland with
Chesapeake Bay ferries; trustee, chosen by the episcopal
bishop of Maryland, of the Hannah More Academy for
girls; deacon in the Presbyterian church of his own
choice; thirty-third degree Mason; writer still — four
papers by Thomas S. Cullen were published in American
medical journals in 1927, two in 1928, two in 1929 —
speaker by special invitation at the 1929 meeting of the
British Medical Association in Manchester; elected by the
House of Delegates of the American Medical Association
to be one of its nine trustees; all these Tom Cullen was or
became in the half-dozen years after the other storey was
built. All these he added to the spare-time recreations of

312

a famous surgeon and teacher, department head in Johns Hopkins Hospital, professor in Johns Hopkins University, member of the Maryland State Board of Health and vice-president of Baltimore's public library system; all these and an LL.D. too.

When Johns Hopkins' Professor Emeritus of Gynecology turns out in style for an occasion of academic state he wears, not without pride, the scarlet robe and pink-lined scarlet hood of a doctor of civil and canon laws of the University of Toronto, his old school. He received the degree in 1930 at the convocation called to celebrate the opening of Toronto's new research centre; the Banting Institute.

He was very happy at that convocation in Toronto; especially happy for two things. First of the two was the companion of his honour. One other distinguished surgeon was among those who came to Toronto to receive an LL.D. (honoris causa) in the special convocation. He was Lord Moynihan, King George's surgeon, the same Mr. Moynihan Tom Cullen used to travel from London to Leeds to see, when both were young men at the beginning of their work. The second cause of happiness was slighter, but no less real; the presence in a front faculty seat on the platform in Convocation Hall of an ancient oppressor:

It was old A. B. Macallum who plucked me in physiology in '87, my first year. I caught his eye with the tail of mine as I went up to get my hood, and we both smiled.

The early 'thirties were to be embellished with another title of honour; the title belonging to the post Tom Cullen had filled since 1919. Johns Hopkins' professor of clinical gynecology became professor of gynecology in 1932. The change marked a change of administration and of academic heart, a belated local recognition of an eminence in his chosen field long since recognized in Europe and elsewhere in America. The recipient was pleased but not puffed up. His attachment was to something more enduring than academic titles. It rooted in grateful remembrance of all that Hopkins had meant to his youth. As he saw his duty to the university and medical school, it was the same with or without icing. His task, and his delight, were to impart to the youth he was privileged to serve the excitement of discovery he had first known here; to open to it such opportunities as had been his for the experience and the emulation that enlighten learning.*

The picture of Tom Cullen as a teacher has long perspectives. He has taught every class that has graduated from Johns Hopkins medical school; and fifty-one classes have graduated. Some of the first graduating classmen were as old as, some older than, their instructor in gynecology. In 1895, when his appointment to serve as instructor was approved, Howard Kelly's gynecological pathologist was twenty-six.

The things that his contemporaries note in an instructor of twenty-six are not apt to be the things their grandsons discover in a professor-emeritus of seventy-nine. Yet in this case, wherever the stuff of memory is tried, one strand holds. That which impresses Professor Cullen's youngest student about his latest lecture is the thing Dr. Kelly's new pathologist applied in his first demonstration; the conviction that you cannot teach men, you can only show them what there is to learn.

* Replying to a query on the long delay in giving him the customary title of a department head Tom Cullen wrote from Baltimore March 15, 1948:

"In 1919 Dr. Kelly resigned and I took over full charge of his work for the next 20 years. The title doesn't amount to much. I had full charge of the department. It was when there was a change of administration that I was made professor of gynecology in 1932. I think I have told you the story of the dealer's horse which, let loose, ran into the side of a barn. The prospective purchaser said 'The horse is blind.' The dealer said 'No, he's not blind; he just doesn't give a damn.' This horse had all the honour, all the work and all the headaches that Dr. Kelly relinquished."

The youngest student put it differently. Old T.S., he said, lectured as though he were letting you in on something. The lecturer, being questioned, developed the idea:

I've never wanted to teach my men anything. I've just tried to show them how to find things out. . . . The point is don't teach 'em. Let 'em learn. Get men thinking and they will teach themselves . . . And never talk down. Any man who thinks he is the whole thing is no good, and that is twice true of a teacher. . . . Detective work. It's all detective work. Once you've learned that you never stop learning. . . .

Of the many hundred Hopkins men Tom Cullen has shown how to find things out, the men in his service found out most about the teacher, as distinct from his subject. In the close partnership of departmental work few quirks go unnoted and the partnership in the gynecological department at Johns Hopkins was very close. The designer of the five-year post-graduate apprenticeship system established under Kelly took a designer's pride in seeing that the product was good. So he worked with it, making sure that the men who came up under him should have every chance to teach themselves. It is easy to find among them memories of his method. Recollections of Tom Cullen in his classes, his clinics, his laboratory and departmental work and in more personal aspects are not hard to come by. But the best of them come with a condition that their owners shall remain nameless. One made the matter clear for all. "T.S.," he said, "knows what I think of him, but it would embarrass us both if he were to see it in print with my name to it."

So the picture must be reproduced as a portrait by unknown hands:

"His students have always called him 'T.S.' among themselves, those that did not call him Uncle Tom. They have all had an affection for him, inherited by each new class. He is pre-eminently a teacher of men. The secret of his hold on his classes is his own; a personal mixture of enthusiasm and optimism and intelligence and understanding that could never be duplicated. Lecturing in the same subject week after week and year after year, he never lost interest in it or failed to interest his classes. He would be so sure that every new class must be interested that he could command interest without trying.

"He used to make me think of an enthusiastic schoolboy sharing a hobby. If he found an unusual tumor, or worked out a new technique in operating he would tell his class about it as though they would certainly be as keen as he was. So most of us were. In my experience, and you will find many who agree with me, the best lectures given on the surgical side in Hopkins school of medicine in my time were those given by Cullen in gynecology and gynecological pathology. Especially gynecological pathology. He was Popsy Welch's disciple as well as Kelly's, remember, and he has not only taught but preached pathology to every student who has come under him. Pathology — the importance of laboratory work — I can hear him yet."

It was in their laboratory work that the men in the gynecological service came to know their chief best. The assistant who, after his year in general pathology, was moved on to have charge of the gynecological laboratory found the department head waiting to take his measure. The laboratory was Tom Cullen's child and gynecological pathology his unfading passion. He was never too busy to help a lab. man with advice or to work through a problem with him. "Old T.S.'s" interest in a young fellow on his way to the departmental residency was in precise ratio to the young fellow's interest in gynecological pathology.

When he discovered one who shared his ardour Tom Cullen was a happy man, and so was the young fellow. They worked common ground and anything the young fellow needed to help him work better was apt to be found; if necessary at his chief's expense. There is one

who remembers that he wanted a slide-file cabinet; a piece
of equipment far out of reach of the gynecological laboratory's modest budget. Though augmented with Professor
Cullen's full professorial wage — at the end of forty years
of service it had reached $633.33 per annum — still the
sixth floor laboratory's income did not run to luxuries
like slide-file cabinets. But the young fellow wanted one.
He was a good and an ardent pathologist and he wanted
a cabinet for the laboratory slide files. So he wrote a letter
to the head of the department explaining how great was
his need. In due time he got the answer he had hoped
for, signed T. S. Cullen:

"Dear H----------
"Your letter would bring tears of blood from a beet.
Go ahead and buy the cabinet and tell them to send the
bill to me."

As long as John Shaw Billings was there, Hopkins'
Professor of Clinical Gynecology used to take a Pennsylvania Railroad carload of his fourth year students over
to Washington one Saturday afternoon each year. They
would go to the Surgeon General's Library and its
librarian would give the afternoon to showing them the
treasures he had there. It was Tom Cullen's method of
induction. John Shaw Billings, described by Welch as
"about the wisest of all the men I have ever known," had
had a great part in shaping Hopkins medical school before the beginning. He had made the Surgeon General's
Library at Washington from a mixed bag of medical works
into the greatest of medical libraries. He had the gift of
communication and the sense of history.

So Tom Cullen made it his business to convoy graduating class after graduating class from Baltimore to Washington in a Pennsylvania railroad car, in order that their
youth might be exposed to John Shaw Billings, their raw
assurance mitigated by his mellow wisdom and their

imaginations fired by the books he loved; books the masters of their mystery had written in other times and places for the enlightenment of such as they. His boys had reason to believe that T.S. was interested in them.

Junior men in the gynecological service found the interest a little embarrassing at times. Their chief's ability to keep track of their extramural activities was for them a matter of mingled amusement and terror. One can remember a long unprofitable night spent trying to raise $17.45 to bail a friend out of a Baltimore police station, where he had been locked after argument with a traffic officer:

"I might have saved myself a lot of time and trouble by going straight to Uncle Tom and asking him to lend me the money. For next morning at the eight o'clock surgery he already knew all the angles. How he got them I never knew; the variety of his contacts and sources of information was uncanny and he was as pleased as a kid to be able to mystify us. I shan't forget the time he caught up on my car licences. I had bought an old car I couldn't afford and was trying to stretch the life-cycle of a set of plates as an economy measure. It was a stock joke around the residence. Any time one of the other staff men wanted a little fun he would get me on the phone and say he was the State Police and what about those licence plates? Then one call was the State Police. I had gotten quite gay with the caller, joshing him along, when something in his voice convinced me suddenly that I was making a bad mistake. So I explained and apologized and promised to reform, all in a great hurry.

"That was about eight at night. Before eight next morning Uncle Tom was in the surgery telling us all about it, including what I had said to the police officer. For days he kept me guessing how he got to know about it but at last he relented and said he had been out to dinner that night with the state commissioner of police. I never did find out for sure whether he had planted the whole thing, but I bought the new plates."

Stories come down from class to class. One is of the assistant resident who went out from Hopkins to help Dr. Cullen in an emergency operation at a little place near Hagerstown in the Maryland hills. They left by train at six in the morning, carrying their equipment with them. The operation was done before noon in the sick woman's home. Then they cleaned up, packed, had dinner in the late operating room, climbed a few hills, at the senior surgeon's suggestion, to stretch their legs and caught the evening train for Baltimore.

Half way back the engine ran off the track and the train sat there most of the night. Finally, the wrecking train arrived to clear things, the travellers started again and reached Baltimore some time after four in the morning. Dr. Cullen's assistant got back to Hopkins by five, dead for sleep and hardly able to drag himself to bed: "Dr. Cullen, who had spent the night talking to everybody on the stranded train and knew the personal histories of the conductor, the brakeman, the candy-butcher and all the passengers, came into the hospital before eight as fresh as he left and ready to operate. He had gone home, bathed, changed, had his breakfast, read his paper, telephoned long distance to ask after yesterday's patient and was all set for another day's work."

Though he lived to tell the tale, the assistant could not, even after thirty years, tell it without feeling tired. He said that sort of thing was always a little hard to forgive in T.S. . . . Yet it had compensations. You had to be his resident before you really knew how to appreciate them.

"T.S. gave his residents a tremendous amount of responsibility and demanded a lot of them. But he was always there in reserve and he always had time to see you. And when he was wanted, no matter what the time of day or night, he would come. I have called him in the small hours of the morning, shaking in my boots for fear he would be angry, and found him as cheerful and interested as if it were working hours. If the problem seemed too big for the phone, he would offer to come right over and the offer was no empty gesture. Whether the patient you were worried about was a private or a ward patient made no difference. He was needed, and he came. But unless he was needed he left his resident alone, and that is a rarer virtue than you might think."

Of Tom Cullen under stress Hopkins men have many memories, all vivid. But again it was his residents who really knew T.S.'s temper:

"I attribute it to his early training in the parsonage, but if ever there was a man who could raise particular hell without cussing, it is T.S. And when the heat is off nobody can forget a blow-up faster, and make you forget it too. I have seen him when his nose was as red as a turkey gobbler's head, practically raising the roof of the operating room over something that went wrong when he thought it shouldn't have. The next minute it would be all over and forgotten, except that, if T.S. thought he had been unfair to anyone in anger, he would always say so. When things had gone wrong through nobody's fault he was at his best, improvising, making decisions, taking the chance that had to be taken without hesitation, never looking for an out for himself, but accepting all the responsibility while he pulled everyone's spirits up to meet the emergency.

"He can do that as few men can. He has the most remarkable effect on people. I have seen him come into a meeting that was dead, where everybody had his chin on his breastbone, and fire up the crowd in no time. And I have seen him join a group that had just about come to blows and change the atmosphere in two minutes, with a grin and a couple of stories. . . . I hope he lives to be a hundred. He's a human dynamo and he can put a charge in anything. But remember the big thing is that he's a teacher, a very great teacher of men . . . "

The medical profession has its own variant of the Harvard man story: "You can always tell a Hopkins man, if he doesn't tell you first." Ask Tom Cullen about it; he smiles but shakes his head. It is one story he has tried to kill:

I have done what I could to impress our graduates with the wisdom of not telling where they come from as if it gave them some special importance. The irritation that sort of thing can create is natural, and justified too as a rule. It is true that here at Hopkins we did make the start in many new things but that was because we had, at the time, special advantages and opportunities. Now there are plenty of medical schools on the same level. I tell my boys never to volunteer information about the school they have come from, but if anyone asks admit it with modesty. Myself, if anyone asks where I come from I just say Baltimore.

6

"PUBLISH, PUBLISH, PUBLISH . . . "

"A GREAT GYNECOLOGIST, an inspiring and generous leader and a man whose genius is excelled only by his humanity . . ."

The definition of Tom Cullen of Baltimore is from the British Medical Journal of October 7, 1939. In that issue, the organ of the British Medical Association reviewed the fourth and fifth volumes of the collected papers of members of the gynecological department of Johns Hopkins Hospital.

When, in 1919, he was made professor of clinical gynecology and appointed to succeed Dr. Kelly, Tom Cullen had already been acting head of his department for two years and virtual head for more than five. No great change in the conduct of departmental affairs marked his formal assumption of office. But one innovation he made at once; the practice of binding and distributing reprints of the fugitive papers written by his staff. He had long been doing it with his own, for his own satisfaction. From the time he became head of the department officially it was a departmental rule. Each member of the gynecological staff was required to supply his chief with reprints, one hundred at least, of any article he had published. When enough reprints had been assembled to make a volume they were bound and distributed. In the twenty years during which Cullen was chief of gynecology five volumes of the original papers of members of his staff went from Hopkins to the leading medical libraries of the world.

The two last volumes were published on the fiftieth anniversary of the opening of Johns Hopkins Hospital (May 7, 1889). They included 122 reprints, the published work of Hopkins gynecological staff for the years 1927 to 1938. The British Medical Journal reviewer found them worthy of the great gynecologist and generous leader who had inspired them:

"Many in this country will remember with great appreciation the address on *The Training of the Gynecologist* read by Dr. Cullen to the section of obstetrics and gynecology at the annual meeting of the British Medical Association held at Manchester in 1929. They will recall that in his opinion 'the finished product is (1) a man who has a good knowledge of general pathology and an intensive knowledge of gynecological pathology, (2) a man with a comprehensive knowledge of gynecological and abdominal diseases, (3) an expert gynecological and *abdominal* surgeon, (4) a surgeon who has formed the habit of looking at his cases from every viewpoint.'

"The collected papers of men who are the products of such a system of training are a glowing tribute to the way in which Dr. Cullen's ideals are achieved in practice . . . No exaggerated pride is revealed by Professor Cullen in the simple preface to these volumes when he writes: 'My affectionate regards and sincere thanks go to all members of the gynecological staff for their admirable co-operation, their unflagging energy and for all that in these volumes they have added to our knowledge of gynecology and abdominal surgery.' The contributions that have been made by this department in the last ten years are very considerable and for that reason the record made by the collected reprints is a valuable one. . . ."

323

The address from which the British Medical Journal quoted was that read by Tom Cullen ten years earlier when he came by invitation to speak at the British Medical Association's annual meeting in Manchester. Into its twenty-minute compass he had packed convictions ripened by years of experience, dwelling on two that had become central to all his work at Hopkins: that every surgeon must be a pathologist and that every gynecologist must be an abdominal surgeon.

In his first decade as chief of his department Tom Cullen had experienced the good effects of the pathological departure he had persuaded Dr. Kelly to make twenty years earlier. Virtually all his departmental associates and assistants, all the junior members of his staff, were products of the departure; trained pathologists who had done their laboratory year in gynecological pathology before coming on to the residency in surgical gynecology. He had seen the lead followed in other branches of surgery at Hopkins, and in other teaching hospitals. In his own department the principle was broadened and systematized. A graduate must spend five postgraduate years, two of them devoted altogether to pathology, working up to and through the gynecological residency.

It was of this system of training — his own — that Tom Cullen spoke in Manchester. Having defined the reason for it and listed the four essential qualifications of its finished product, he described its progress in methodical detail:

"At the Johns Hopkins Hospital each year, five of the graduating class are assigned to the gynecological department. During the year these men have charge of the patients in private and public wards, take all the histories, assist at operations and work in the gynecological and cystoscopic dispensaries. At the end of the year, after conference with the house staff and visiting staff, one of the five men is selected for promotion . . . The man who has

. . . in time to change the fortune of the day.
—page 309

Dr. Wallace Buttrick, chairman, and Dr. Abraham Flexner, secretary — 1913-28 — of the General Education
Board. Picture of Dr. Buttrick taken at Hopkins, 1924.

been selected drops out of the gynecological department for a year and becomes an assistant of the professor of pathology. During his intern year this man has obtained a very good idea of the difficulties encountered in the various abdominal and pelvic operations, and consequently is better able to appreciate the opportunities offered him in the pathological department. . . . He is now permitted to make numerous necropsies and gains a clear idea of the gross pathological lesions. While making the necropsies he has the opportunity of dissecting out the ureters and of learning the relations of the pelvic structures. He dissects out the bile ducts . . . and has ample opportunity to observe the lymphatic ducts carefully. He also gains a lasting knowledge of the relations of the abdominal organs and of the blood supply. After a year in such work he should never again get lost in the abdomen. In addition to all this he gains an insight into the lesions in all parts of the body and has the opportunity of studying the various histological pictures presented at necropsy . . . and of participating in the invaluable pathological conferences held each week.

"At the end of the year our assistant in pathology returns to the gynecological department; he examines and describes all material coming from the gynecological operating room, supervises the cutting and staining of sections and gives a detailed and careful description of the histological findings. Ample time is afforded him to work on special gynecological problems and he is within easy distance of the Surgeon General's Library, where practically every medical book and periodical that is worth reading can be obtained. He also has an opportunity to see all the interesting cases treated in the department.

"During the following year he is first assistant, assists at operations, has general supervision of the wards and when the resident is away is in charge. During his final and fifth year he is the resident gynecologist and has full charge of the department and, in addition to assisting the visiting surgeons, performs many major and minor operations himself. . . . A man with such a training will not only do justice to his patients but should also prove an admirable teacher. He is bound to add to the sum total of our knowledge of gynecology and abdominal surgery.

Few men who have become real investigators will ever be satisfied to relinquish this fascinating field during their active period of surgical life."

There the speaker turned to his second basic conviction and his own case books. He described half-a-dozen gynecological operations complicated by major lesions demanding the most skilled and radical abdominal surgery and went on to make his point:

"I have cited these cases to show the extensive and alarming conditions with which the gynecologist is sometimes confronted . . . We are in duty bound to so train our young gynecologists that they will be capable of handling any abdominal emergency that may arise, if that be surgically possible . . .

"One surgeon may prefer to do stomach and gallbladder surgery and another pelvic surgery in the female, but when either has an abdomen open it is only fair to the patient that every lesion found in that abdomen be treated at the time . . . It is no excuse for the surgeon to say that the lesion is out of his line, or that he is not capable of doing the operation. . . . I confidently predict that in the very near future no surgeon, except in the rarest emergency, will be accorded the right to open an abdomen unless he has been trained to handle any and all complications he may find."

A time-lag longer than he had hoped has intervened between Tom Cullen's confident prediction and fulfilment, but he is still confident. In abnormal times developments do not take normal courses, and these are abnormal times. War conditions forced enormous strides in unexpected directions in both surgery and medicine. In other directions, this among them, they deflected or retarded expected progress. But it will come, the prophet in him says. It is bound to come. It is best for the patient.

The five volumes of original papers written by members of his staff and distributed in the years between 1919 and 1939 were testimony to the strength of the third of Tom Cullen's central convictions — that findings are made to be published:

It was what I always told my boys, and still tell them: publish, publish, publish. Write up your interesting cases and publish. Nobody can take what you have published away from you. You are bound to have disappointments as you go along. The chances are that from time to time other men will get the opportunities or the rewards you think you have earned. But what you have published, if you are any good at all, will put things straight in the long run because the record stands. If you're sure of your findings don't hesitate. Publish. You've got to be up and doing or somebody's going to run off with your preserves. Some German tried to steal my blue umbilicus on me. Wrote a monograph and claimed to have been the first to discover its symptomatic meaning. I had published six months before, so he couldn't get away with it.

But beyond that there is a principle involved. A man has no right not to publish if he has found something that can be of use. We have all made use of other men's published work. Other men are entitled to the chance to use ours if we have anything worth using.

It was the Hurd tradition Tom Cullen passed on in the volumes from his department. Johns Hopkins teaching, as he had taken it in youth from Henry M. Hurd, was all against withholding knowledge from the general fund, and all against presenting good material ill-prepared:

The Hopkins idea is to publish and to publish adequately; to do so thorough a job when you undertake to deal with a subject that it won't be worth anyone's time to touch it again for twenty or thirty years. When we started, and for quite a time after, it was not generally accepted and it did not make us too popular; but it has proved itself.

I remember going in the summer of 1909 to a meeting of the British Medical Association in Belfast. At the final banquet they put me next a fellow who opened the conversation by saying he didn't like Kelly. Now Kelly was my chief, but I didn't blow up right away. I said "Do you know Kelly?" and this fellow said "Never met him."

I let him have it then, told him he had no right to form an opinion, let alone pass judgment on a man he didn't know but, since he had chosen to do so, what was there about Dr. Kelly he thought he didn't like?

He said "All you Hopkins people are too lavish, spend too much on your publications." So I told him we spent what we thought was necessary to present our material adequately and make it of the most use to the profession. We didn't have a great deal to say to each other for the rest of the evening.

By jove, it wasn't until months later, when I was home again, that it suddenly struck me who the man was. He brought out a book on cancer of the uterus the same year I published. But we beat him to publication by about six months and, with our illustrations, his work when it came simply couldn't compete. He was naturally a little irritated and without knowing it I had hit him right between the eyes.

The blue umbilicus the German tried to steal is in the textbooks as "Cullen's sign." It got there by chance; one of those chances that, according to M. Louis Pasteur, "only favour those who are prepared." Tom Cullen still smiles to remember how it happened:

I have more than once worked on a subject for years and in the end produced a paper I thought had real merit, only to find it given relatively little attention. Then one day I have a hunch, dictate a few lines, enlarge the note to a page and a half and lo and behold, "Cullen's sign" is the result. My name is safe in the annals of medicine attached to a blue navel.

Tom Cullen had his hunch in the spring of 1918, two years after his fourth major work, *Diseases of the Umbilicus*, was published. A patient admitted to the Church Home for treatment was its immediate cause.

She was a woman in her late thirties, thin, prematurely aged and the mother of seven children. She had been suffering for three weeks from pain in the right lower abdomen with intermittent abdominal swelling. A week after the trouble started the skin about the navel became bluish black, although there was no injury in that region. The abdominal swelling was too marked at the time the patient was admitted to hospital to permit a satisfactory pelvic examination. Dr. Cullen decided to operate.

A pre-operative examination, made with the patient under anaesthesia, revealed, in addition to the dark blue navel, a slightly enlarged womb and, to its right, a freely moveable mass about eight centimetres in length. Tom Cullen remembered something on page 307 of his book on the umbilicus and felt a hunch coming on.

Page 307 contained reference to a case reported from Cincinnati by Dr. Joseph Ransohoff. The case was that of a man suffering from an obscure abdominal condition of which the most startlingly evident symptom was an Isabella-coloured umbilicus. On operation, Dr. Ransohoff had discovered that his patient had a ruptured bile duct and that the jaundiced appearance of the umbilical region was caused by the quantity of free bile in the abdomen and its absorption at this, the thinnest, part of the abdominal wall. Tom Cullen's hunch developed strongly. Before beginning to operate he dictated a note:

"The bluish-black appearance of the navel, unassociated with any history of injury, together with the mass to the right of the uterus, makes the diagnosis of extrauterine pregnancy relatively certain, although the patient has not missed any period and although there has not been any uterine bleeding."

Then he went ahead with the operation:

Opening the abdomen I found it filled with dark blood. Attached to the fringed end of the right tube was an extra-uterine pregnancy. It was possible to remove this without sacrificing the tube. The patient made a good recovery and was discharged from hospital in less than three weeks. I expanded my note and recorded the case in order that the sign might be watched for in cases where a ruptured extrauterine pregnancy was a possibility. Whether it would prove to be a relatively common symptom of the condition or a very rare one I had no idea at the time. I merely set it down as a definite sign of free blood in the abdomen and one more likely to be found in thin individuals than in fat ones.

At Johns Hopkins that year, 1918, the men who had worked with and under him were preparing for Sir William Osler's seventieth birthday a gift after his own heart; a volume of original papers presenting the results of recent research. Tom Cullen wrote up his notes on the case of the blue navel and had the paper illustrated in colour by Max Broedel for inclusion in the gift volume. It was published there, among the other *Contributions to Medical and Biological Research, Dedicated to Sir William Osler, in Honor of his Seventieth Birthday, July 12, 1919, by his Pupils and Co-workers.*

From Osler's birthday volume "Cullen's sign" went directly into the literature of abdominal surgery, and into the clinical teaching of gynecologists. The swift and general recognition it gained amused its discoverer and continues to amuse him. "Cullen's signs" turning up at odd times and in odd places, are still being reported back to their namesake. One was reported in November of 1944 from the Sixtieth Field Hospital of the U.S. Army on the Western Front in a letter from Captain J. Mason Knox:

" . . . One of the boys was shot in the abdomen and there was considerable discussion as to whether there was internal bleeding. I insisted he was bleeding because he had a positive 'Cullen sign' and, sure enough, when I explored I found he was bleeding from the liver and stomach. . . . "

330

PART VII

GETTING THINGS DONE

I

PUBLIC HEALTH AND PRACTICAL POLITICS

WHEN DR. ARTHUR B. KINSOLVING, long rector of the
mother parish of Baltimore, St. Paul's, began to talk of
his friend Tom Cullen he quoted Terence.

"Homo sum; humani nihil a me alienum puto," he
said. "It could have been written for Tom. I have known
him forty years and I have yet to find anything human
that does not interest him. Doctors, you will find, divide
into two classes. There are those who become immersed
in their craft, and there are those who overflow the chan-
nel of their craft to become great human beings. Tom
is one of the greatest of the latter. He has the talent for
growth. Some men have it and some have not. Tom has
it. In all the years I have known him he has never ceased
growing. In the apostolic succession of great physicians
and surgeons who have also been great human beings
he succeeds Welch. His influence on the young fellows
who have been his students has been immeasurable, but
it goes beyond them to his patients and to the community.
Tom is a villager at heart and Baltimore is his village."

When Howard W. Jackson, for sixteen years mayor
of Baltimore, began to talk of his friend Tom Cullen he
smiled, a faintly rueful smile, and put the idea differently.
Mr. Jackson does not think any man in Baltimore ever
asked more various things and got more of the things
he asked for from a city government than Tom Cullen
from his. Mr. Jackson remembers clearly how it was done:

333

"Tom never asked for anything for himself. He never asked for anything he didn't want. He never asked for anything unreasonable. And when he once started asking he never stopped. Never."

In the things that are the stuff of politics Tom Cullen's early interest was small. He sat out the battle for civic righteousness that enlivened Baltimore in the 'nineties. As a voteless Canadian he was excused from partaking, though his chief was deeply engaged. The exemption suited the beginning pathologist; compared with his laboratory Baltimore politics lacked appeal. Moreover, he was heir to a slower-going political tradition. At his youngest, he was never quite as sure as were the young American reformers of the period that every evil can be erased by a suitable legislative enactment.

Observation confirmed hereditary doubts. Baltimore's old and corrupt Democratic party machine was smashed at last in 1895 and a militant coalition of Republicans and reforming Democrats emerged triumphant with a new city charter. Yet bosses and boss-rule did not therefore disappear from town. The onlooker from Canada noted presently that two machines and two sets of machine politicians were contesting for control of the government established under the new charter. He noted further that, in accordance with the rules of the game as played then in every American city, each time the machine in control was voted out all its major and many of its minor appointees, from the health commissioner to the dog-catcher, went out with it. The waste entailed bothered Tom Cullen and, as time went on and his affection for his chosen city deepened, it bothered him increasingly.

Educating politicians and political office-holders in the civic values of cleanliness and sanitation was slow business at best. It was dishearteningly slow when the task had to be started all over, with a new set of public officials as well as a new set of politicians, each time the balance of civic power was upset. Yet, led by Welch and Osler, Hopkins had committed itself to the improvement of Baltimore's health. A man who was loyal to Hopkins and to Baltimore could not shirk the share of the task that came his way. Evidence that it needed doing was too much with him:

You would have known Monday morning in Baltimore then if you had come back from the dead, by the bluing-water running in the gutters. They were wide-open gutters on each side of every street, with stepping stones at the crossings to take you from the sidewalk to the cobbled roadway; and bluing-water was by no means all they accommodated. Furthermore, a great deal of raw sewage went right into the harbour and the smell from it on warm summer nights was abominable.

The city drinking water came from Roland Lake. The district around was already building up and the water was impure. People got typhoid from it, but typhoid was generally regarded as inevitable. As it was — given those conditions. Most of the smaller houses in the city had privies in the back yard and soil carts made regular nightly rounds. Flies were the regular thing in daytime. They swarmed around the open market stalls and followed the street vendors and met the milk waggons at every stop. Milk was delivered at the curb in big cans that stood on the floor of the waggon. The milkman dipped it out with his tin dipper into the customer's pitcher and neither of them minded a fly or two. There were no precautions taken to keep milk clean and it was often very dirty.

Tom Cullen recalls such things without censure. People didn't know, that was all. The germ theory of disease was still so new in the 'nineties that even doctors, like the surgeon he met in London, could call it poppycock. So you would hardly blame a poor woman for not demanding clean milk, or a practical politician who jibbed at spending the millions impractical scientists said he should on sewage disposal plants and pure water. They were both ignorant and they both needed to have things explained to them.

Dr. Osler, patiently enlightening the general darkness concerning tuberculosis and its causes; Dr. Welch, taking the cholera scare of '92 as his cue for a campaign against typhoid, had shouldered their share of explaining from the first. Between them, they had done much to insert public health into the public consciousness. By 1910 most people knew that flies carried disease germs, that dirty milk killed babies, that consumption was infectious, that sewage and drinking water produced typhoid epidemics when mixed.

For the medical profession the principles of public health were clearly laid down. The plan for a Hopkins school of hygiene where they might be studied in their widest application was already shaped in Dr. Welch's mind. But certain immediate problems remained unsolved: How was a workable public health policy for Baltimore to be established and maintained in the middle of a cut-throat party war? So long as health department jobs were included among the spoils of party victory, how could any nucleus of responsible officials be formed to carry through a public health programme?

When Osler went from Hopkins to Oxford; when Welch moved to wider policy-making on Baltimore's new charter commission; the problems were left, still unsolved, on the most promising doorstep: Tom Cullen's. Nearby, Popsy had dropped one of his pawkier bits of advice: "Under our existing political conditions, experience seems to show that more can be accomplished by the quiet, intelligent and well-directed efforts . . . which do not directly antagonize those who wield political power than by spasmodic movements for reform."

Tom Cullen took the advice and applied it to the problems, in a fashion peculiarly his own.

He was by then well established in the practice of his profession and the life of the city. He knew half the town and liked something about everyone he knew. A natural taste for humanity had made Tommy Cullen the friendliest of little boys. It persisted in Dr. Thomas Cullen the successful surgeon and gynecologist. He found the unregenerate as easy to get along with as the righteous, the appendixes and tumors of the socially unacceptable as interesting as those of the socially elect. As his practice widened, the number of his friends grew even faster than the number of his patients. For every patient had a family.

Among the families of his patients Tom Cullen found, before he had been many years in practice, several friends who could be useful. In a good cause he had no hesitation at all in using them, and he had grown to count public health among the best of good causes. It was his desire to hasten the day when a man doing useful work for public health in the service of his city could be sure of continuing to work undisturbed, no matter who lost or won a civic election.

A modest enough desire, looking back on it. But when its owner began to work towards its fulfilment every key position in every department of civic as of state government was a temporary job in the gift of the temporarily dominant party. A public payroll existed to provide a winning party boss with suitable rewards for loyal partisans; that was the commonest political sense of the time and place. Tom Cullen's modest desire challenged its first premise.

In those less shamefaced days three bosses were recognized as ruling Maryland for the Democratic party; Frank Kelly, Daniel Loden and John Mahon. "The Royal Family of Baltimore" they were called and the last of the line was "Sonny" Mahon . . .

The matter being political and therefore delicate, Tom Cullen has thought best to tell the rest of this himself:

337

While Cullen was no politician, if he wanted to get support for something he did not hesitate to go to those men who were friends of his. Looking into the matter, we find that he came into contact with two men well able to get things done, through operating on members of the family of each. The two were Frank Kelly and John Mahon, both powerful in the Democratic party of Baltimore and Maryland. Looking still further, we find that it was chance which gave Cullen his first opportunity to lay the case for taking the city health department out of politics before the one best able to help with it.

It happened one day when he had to go to Elkton, Maryland, to operate. He caught an early train and sat down in a vacant seat beside John Mahon who was going to the races at Havre de Grace. Cullen did not at first notice who he was sitting beside. When he saw who it was he said "Mr. Mahon, there is something we doctors want you to do for us."

Hampson Jones, who had been assistant health commissioner for Baltimore, had lost the position when the Democrats won at the polls. Later, Jones who had done an excellent job was made commissioner but on a very precarious footing. Since both posts had until then been political, with incumbents changing with every change of the party in power, his future and that of the good work he was doing were both uncertain and there was strong likelihood that he would go with the next change.

Cullen gave John Mahon the facts. Then he said "Mr. Mahon, when I operated on your daughter you didn't care whether I was a Democrat or a Republican as long as I could produce the goods. I am a Democrat and Dr. Jones is a Republican but we want Hampson Jones left where he is because he can produce the goods."

Without a moment's hesitation Mahon said "He won't be touched." And he wasn't. When Sonny Mahon promised a thing it was as good as done.

The understanding established on the race train to Havre de Grace continued for some years to benefit the public health of Baltimore. Civic governments came and went and office-holders in other departments came and went with them in traditional fashion. But, however Democratic the victory, Sonny Mahon's promise held. The Republican commissioner remained untouched in the city health department and continued to produce the goods. Inevitably, health policy ran foul of party politics from time to time. Then, if the issue were serious, Dr. Cullen would be called into consultation and, if it were serious enough, would take it to John Mahon; putting the case and getting a decision that, once given, was never questioned.

Purists among the local reformers looked on these unorthodox parleys with disapproval. Tom Cullen knew it and lost no sleep. The parleys worked. The promises held good. Bit by bit citizens and politicians alike were coming to take it for granted that the party spoils system did not apply in Baltimore's department of health. At last a day came; and with it one of the purists:

She was a lady I knew well, one of those who had always deeply regretted Sonny Mahon's influence in city and state politics and disapproved of my friendship with Mr. Mahon. She was, as I knew, very eager to see certain remedial laws passed by the state legislature and, in particular, one medical bill which was being blocked at the time by powerful interests. She told me the whole story and I sympathized with her. Then I waited. She seemed a little embarrassed but she didn't say anything more. So at last I said it for her.

"What do you want me to do?" I said. "See Sonny Mahon?"

She had to swallow hard first, but she answered "Yes." So I went and saw John Mahon and told him the story of the medical bill, just as it had been told me. When I'd finished, he said "Who's bucking it?" I gave him the name of the man; a very respectable state senator.

"He's a fish" Sonny said, "I'll fix it." And he did. The bill went through at Annapolis with no more trouble at all. I was delighted to be able to tell the lady that John Mahon had fixed it for her.

339

In 1923, judging the time to be ripe and the occasion sufficient, John Mahon's backstage health adviser decided to reinforce the quiet efforts which do not antagonize with a public health campaign. Being Tom Cullen, he campaigned with a difference, undertaking to prove to practical politicians the practical political wisdom of foregoing party patronage in health department jobs. The event justified his unusual approach. The Democratic candidate for the mayoralty of Baltimore ran that year on a promise to "take the health department out of politics" and establish the Republican Hampson Jones in office as full-time health commissioner. He was elected. He kept his promise.

The non-partisan administration of Baltimore's health services has never since been seriously threatened. But Tom Cullen believes in good fences, and the health commissioner's board of consultants remains in being. The board of consultants is his idea of a good fence. It was, in fact, one of the first of the things he asked for after Howard Jackson was elected mayor. A politician in office, so benevolent observation told him, quite often only wants an excuse for doing the right thing. When party pressure is on, the politician needs a strong excuse and a departmental official cannot always make it strong enough; but an independent board of consultants very often can. A health commissioner who has a group of well-known and politically disinterested physicians as his advisers on policy can usually get a good policy accepted, even if it costs money. For he can provide the reigning politician with the best possible excuse for doing the right thing and the strongest possible shelter against pressure to do the wrong one.

"Osler and Welch got the typhoid out of Baltimore's drinking water and Welch got the dirt out of its milk. Cullen got politics out of the health department and I'm not sure it wasn't the hardest job of the three. We've gone on since, and added education and public welfare to the non-political list, but it started with Cullen and health." The witness is Huntington Williams, health commissioner of Baltimore.

. . .

Charles Street in certain lights can revert. The sky clears after storm, the day thins and recedes. Along Charles Street, Baltimore is again the Baltimore Tom Cullen knew in youth; the town whose portrait is engraved in old prints; withdrawing in mannerly perspective before the eye of the beholder, accepting with the happy serenity of the well-proportioned the homage of regard. It was so, coming to Eager Street on a remembered evening.

New snow on sills and cornices laid soft-edged accents below and above the ordered rows of lighted windows. The west was blue-green over the gas lamps of the climbing cross streets, the east pale with reflected brightness. Against it on the far hilltop a dome showed — small and dark beyond the balustrade of Mount Vernon Place and the lines of lights falling away and lifting again — the lanterned dome of Johns Hopkins. Tom Cullen broke a silence that was long for him.

"I love this old town," he said.

341

APPLIED IDEALISM, MARYLAND STYLE

PEOPLE, politicians and the medical profession are all fundamentally decent. Thomas Stephen Cullen believes it. But he does not believe in socialized medicine. They are not all that decent.

Knowing more than he chooses to remember about human nature, Tom Cullen is opposed in principle to socialized medicine. In principle he could not oppose it more. Yet from the record a timid capitalist might judge him a dangerous socialist. The facts are there; in his years in Maryland he has promoted, launched and defended more health measures and health services which, by dictionary definition, are socialist or socialistic than has any other except William H. Welch.

Accuse him of it, and his eyebrows gather. Then he smiles, half-pitying, half-forgiving. Since you do not understand he will explain. From time to time certain things have had to be done to give the best possible medical services to the people of Maryland. If they could not be done one way they had to be done another. That's all.

That is all but the story of how they came to be done. It goes back a long way; to remembered summer evenings at Cambridge on the eastern shore of Maryland and to two young men, tired from a big day's work, sitting talking in a garden by the water. The two were at the beginning of their careers. One was to become an eminent surgeon and teacher. One was to live and die a country doctor. Neither was ever for a moment to fail the other, or his own vocation of healing. Each was clear-sighted enough to recognize the magnitude of the task of healing that faced his generation and profession and to understand that it could not be accomplished without allies. Being practical idealists with a lot to do, both were quite prepared to use the aid of the state, or to demand it, if that seemed the best way to get necessary things done.

Many things needed for the protection of health and the healing of sickness were still to be done in 1899. The two talked of them, sitting in Brice Goldsborough's garden after their day's work in the new Cambridge hospital, waiting for the whistle of the steamboat Joppa that would presently take Tom Cullen back to Baltimore. . . .

The years passed and, one by one, the things most needed were done in Maryland. Each in his own fashion, the two young men had a hand in most of them:

We made a pretty good team, working together, but I remember once in Annapolis I nearly scared Brice to death. We had come down as a delegation of two to ask for a bigger state grant for the hospital at Cambridge; the one Brice started in '98. Brice had given the committee the whole picture; the needs of the district the hospital served, the growing demand for its services, the insufficiency of its resources and the inadequacy of the sum the legislature was proposing to vote towards its support.

He did a fine job, but an economy wave had hit Annapolis and I could tell by the tone of the questions we weren't getting anywhere. So when my turn came to talk I told them I was only there for one thing; to advise the committee that the hospital at Cambridge should be closed if it could not be adequately supported.

I could hear Brice gasp behind me — he said afterwards he almost fainted — but I stuck to my guns and sat down without saying another word. We got the grant we had asked for; every cent of it.

Brice thought I had taken a terrible risk, but I hadn't. I knew they couldn't afford to let the Cambridge hospital close. It meant too much to the community, and politicians have to get elected.

Brice Goldsborough's knowledge of conditions and Tom Cullen's knowledge of men were to combine many times more. With the rest of the little group who shared their conviction that disease is a public enemy, they were in for a long campaign. It was to win for rural Maryland at last a state health service leading every other in the union.

The better to direct the campaigners, Dr. William H. Welch had accepted, in 1900, the chairmanship of the Maryland state board of health. But for some years after Popsy took it in hand, the state board of health remained an imperfect instrument of direction. It had been formed to function in such crises as smallpox epidemics. Between crises it was expected not to interfere. The health affairs of Maryland, like the health affairs of Baltimore, were party business. Partisans who happened to be doctors directed them and were paid for party services with appointments to sinecure posts as medical officers. The duties attached need not be taken seriously and the perquisites were enjoyable; actual and presumptive beneficiaries, however opposed in politics, were agreed on that. None saw any reason for changing existing arrangements or embarking on the sort of root-and-branch revolution in health services that Dr. Welch seemed to want. And they also were physicians.

Once more it was the slow business of education. Tom Cullen and Brice Goldsborough, with the other apostles of public health, set about it. Presently fortune gave them an ally where one could be most useful. Phillips Lee Goldsborough, Brice's brother, was persuaded to run for the governorship of Maryland.

The family belonged in Cambridge and shared the sense of obligation which inherited association can give. Phillips Goldsborough was deeply proud of his brother's service to the community and as deeply conscious of the handicaps that frustrated much of it. Knowing rural Maryland, he did not have to be convinced that its health care could be better. He was a sympathetic listener when his brother and Tom Cullen discussed means to that end; and he was elected.

Credit for the public health law which was added to the state code in the first year of the Goldsborough governorship has been claimed for more than one campaigner. There is credit to go around among all who had a part in the long labour of education that made it possible. But for the bill itself, its design and the time and method of its presentation, the man who knew most about it knew where credit belonged. In framing and introducing the law that first lifted Maryland's public health services out of partisan politics, Hon. Phillips Lee Goldsborough depended on the judgment of two advisers.

"It was done," the retired governor would explain courteously to any inquirer "in the year 1912, on the advice of my brother, a country physician practising in Cambridge, Maryland, and of Dr. Cullen. I took my brother's advice in these things, and Dr. Cullen's."

Governor Goldsborough's health legislation was more revolutionary in its implications than in its wording. It read innocently enough as a bill to empower the state board of health to appoint a medical officer for each of the 23 counties of Maryland, such officer to give his whole time to the medical service of the county and to be permanently employed under the direction of the board of health. Its effect was three-fold. It ended party sinecures in health administration. It provided the state with a corps of working medical officers. It gave an independence they had never before enjoyed to the state board of health, setting them free to plan long-range programmes, in the certainty that the execution would be in the hands of trained men permanently and wholly employed on the work and protected from political interference by the authority of the board.

The opening Dr. Welch had been waiting for was made by the Goldsborough bill. Having got his foot in the door, he never looked back. With all a fuller-brushman's aplomb and more than twice his guile he made one thing lead to another. A corps of permanent sanitation experts was added to the corps of permanent medical officers, and sewerage systems and local sanitation came under the board's jurisdiction. A bureau of bacteriology, a bureau of chemistry and a bureau of child hygiene were established and the principle of Governor Goldsborough's legislation was applied to each in turn. When appointments in all the state's health services were made by the state board of health under the merit system inaugurated in 1912, the dean of public health campaigners counted one conquest consolidated, and went on to others.

Popsy Welch was in his eightieth year when he decided to retire from the Maryland board of health. He named Tom Cullen his successor:

The first I knew of it was when I picked up the Sun at breakfast one morning, saw my picture on the back page and wondered whether I had died again. Ten years before I had found my own obituary in a medical journal; only four lines long, too. That was what made me tired. This time there were more lines and I was relieved to find I had not died; just been appointed to succeed Dr. Welch on the state board of health. Popsy had fixed the whole thing without saying a word to me.

The year was 1929. There may have been in Popsy's fixing some bashfulness; an unspoken acknowledgment, long owing, of qualities too like his own for earlier recognition. It is hard in the ordinary way for a senior diplomat to estimate at their true worth a junior's gifts in his own line. Until an occasion demands their use he may even be tempted to discount them. But not longer, if he is a diplomat as wise and a servant of humanity as great as was William Henry Welch.

Maryland's state board of health had been developed, slowly and with caution, into an effective instrument for the service of democracy. In its functional design, its safeguards and its possibilities of growth and usefulness it was a pattern piece among state health authorities. But it could be, as such things can always be, crippled as easily by ineptitude as by enmity. Popsy Welch, deciding to retire, named Tom Cullen his successor.

At the time, certain difficulties were looming. The city of Baltimore had its own health commission, equal in authority to and in no way dependent upon the state organization. In a number of places, as the state health services extended, friction threatened to develop between city and state health officials. Other friction spots were showing where state health programmes touched fields which private practitioners of medicine had regarded as their own.

Being in private practice himself and immediate past president of the Medical and Chirurgical Faculty of Maryland, Popsy's successor could meet on their own ground the medical men who feared state encroachment, and calm their fears. It was simply, he found, a matter of putting things in their proper perspective before his fellow-physicians. Every doctor wanted to see diphtheria immunization, for example, made available to every child in Maryland, but everyone had not then seen that the one way to make sure no child should be missed was to lay the responsibility on the state board of health; and so on. Most of the problems of that sort solved themselves once all the facts were set out plainly, and in proper perspective. As for differences between the state board and the city health commission, in nineteen years none has developed. The two bodies are co-equal and co-operative;

Tom Cullen providing the unofficial link, Baltimore's health commissioner the official one, between them.

The old partisan eruptions into the administration of Maryland's health services belong to history too. It has become an accepted axiom among the senior politicians of the senior parties in the state that, if you want to stay in politics, you keep politics out of public health. But it could change. It could slip back even yet. Tom Cullen has seen many gains lost through thinking them sure. He considers it best never to be too sure of any gain:

Assume that everybody wants to do the right thing, but make it as hard as you know how for anybody, including yourself, to do the wrong one.

In June of 1945 the latest of the revolutionary changes promoted in the health services of Maryland by its board of health became law. It is written in Section 44A of Article 43 and provides the legal foundation for a seventh bureau, added to the six already functioning under the board. The seventh, a medical services bureau, is empowered to establish and administer a state-wide and state-supported system of medical and hospital care, free at need to citizens of Maryland. But it will not socialize medicine. On the contrary:

It will provide a reasonable solution of a difficult problem which, left unsolved, might lay us open to the socializers at some later time. I'm proud it was a Cullen, Dr. Victor Cullen of Baltimore, who chaired the committee that put it over.

One of the provisions of Section 44A is for state payment of the cost of medical services to "indigent or medically indigent" citizens. That is to say, the state contracts to pay an adequate fee to doctors, nurses and dentists authorized by the bureau to attend or treat citizens who are not themselves able to pay an adequate fee. "Medically indigent" is the key phrase. It ensures the sick of

Maryland against having to sink to pauperism before they can receive, as a right, treatment for their sickness at public expense.

The bureau of medical services is required to interpret and apply that new definition, together with the rest of Section 44A's wide innovations, with the help of a council of medical services. Of the council's fourteen members, two are chosen by the state board of health. The rest are appointed by and representative of the medical schools and hospitals of the state, the medical, dental, nursing and pharmaceutical associations and the state department of welfare. That, as Tom Cullen sees it, is Section 44A's safeguard against the perils of state medicine. It leaves practitioners of the art of healing free from bureaucratic dictation while ensuring to every citizen who needs it prompt and personal care in sickness, regardless of his ability to pay. It guarantees the conscientious practitioner of medicine against losing money by having a conscience, while guarding public funds and services from exploitation by the conscienceless. And it puts responsibility for the direction of the medical bureau's activities where it should be in a free country; not with a state employee but with an independent council of men and women representative of the interests and organizations affected by the bureau's work.

Tom Cullen went down from Baltimore to Annapolis to see the Governor's signature and seal put on Section 44A of Article 43. It was a fine thing done at the right time and he was all for it. He would not want to see the state board of health or the medical profession in Maryland let things drift along until the state-medicine men had an argument:

Where there is a real problem, responsible leaders of the profession concerned need to supply a reasonable solution. If they don't, people will go for an unreasonable one. That's human nature.

349

Though the phrase is new, and a little fancy, the problem of the medically indigent is both real and old. It was old fifty years ago, when Tom Cullen started practising. But there were so many problems more pressing that it had to wait. Sick people who were poor but not destitute went without the care they needed. Or the charity of their community was called on. Or all the members of a poor family mortgaged their futures to pay the cost of the sickness of one. Or, most often, the problem was solved at the expense of a doctor with a conscience. Knowing they would receive no payment and expecting none, good physicians would travel miles to answer the calls, or treat over long periods the ills, of patients hardly more impoverished than themselves. The effect on the good physician can be read too often in the mortality records. He was apt to die universally beloved at the age of forty-six or thereabouts, leaving his wife and family no estate except a lot of accounts marked "uncollectable."

Tom Cullen has known it happen again and again to good men, especially in country districts where a doctor's life is hardest. That is why he was particularly happy to see the provision in Section 44A which ensures some payment from public funds to physicians attending poor people . . .

Me? That's different. I have been fortunate in having a specialty that is well paid when it is paid. So I could always afford to do a certain amount for nothing. But many men have done it who could not afford it and cannot.

Of fifty years' work as a gynecologist and surgeon, what part the certain amount done for nothing would be Tom Cullen has no idea. But one may be gathered. One may be gathered virtually any place he is known. Since he is known intimately and thoroughly on the Eastern

Shore of Maryland, take the evidence of an Eastern Shore-
man as it was given on a spring morning crossing in the
ferry to Sandy Point:

"There was a poor man in the town where I live. He
was pretty sick and the neighbours came around to me
and said you know Dr. Cullen, maybe you could ask him
to stop and see him next time he comes by.

"And I said if the man's sick I wouldn't have to ask
him to stop in, he'd stop for anybody's asking. But anyway I called Dr. Cullen that afternoon and asked him
when he was expecting to be down our way again. And
he said not for a couple of weeks was there anything special? And I said no, nothing special except some of the
people in town had been around to ask me if I'd get him
to stop and see a sick man next time he came by because
he was pretty sick and needed attention.

"And he said if he needs attention he needs it now,
not two weeks from now, I'll be down this afternoon.

"And I said I must tell you he's just a poor man living in a little shack on the edge of town, just him and
his wife and I don't suppose he knows what a dollar bill
looks like, 'Tisn't likely you'll ever get paid.

"And he said who said anything about pay? I'll be
down this afternoon.

"So he came down that afternoon all the way from
Baltimore and saw the man and sent for an ambulance
and had him taken in to Baltimore to the hospital and
operated himself.

"It was too late, the man had cancer and he died of it.
But his wife never got a bill for anything and Dr. Cullen
wouldn't even let anybody pay his way down and back.
I know because I tried. That's just one of about a million
cases you could find if you asked around."

But Tom Cullen says that was different. That was an
Eastern Shore emergency and in the family.

"In the family" is the unvarying phrase when Dr. T.
S. Cullen is refusing a fee. Those included in the family
receive no bill for professional services from their surgeon,
no matter how great and how exacting the services may

351

have been, and the family is expansive. Relatives of relatives of connections, eager to avail themselves of his skill at any fee they can pay, find when the work is done that they can pay no fee. They are "in the family." Employees of businesses in which he has invested, members of the staffs of organizations with which he is associated, friends and the friends of friends, the friends of servants and the servants of friends; all are "in the family" if they are sick and their sickness can be healed with his help. Dr. Abraham Flexner recalls that, when he was its secretary, the whole staff of the Rockefeller General Education Board was added, for purposes of abdominal surgery, to Tom Cullen's family. After he became a director of the Claiborne-Annapolis ferry line, one of the first to be included in Tom Cullen's family was a Negro stewardess employed on the ferries. She was not known to him except as an old and obliging servant of the company, but he had come to look for her when he was making the crossing to the Eastern Shore and he missed her when she became ill. So he enquired for her and learned from Frank Sherman, manager of the line, that she was very ill. Then, as Mr. Sherman remembers, things moved swiftly:

"Dr. Cullen had her brought to hospital at once, operated himself, a major operation, and saw that she had a nurse night and day for several weeks. No bill for anything was ever rendered. He being a director of the company and Eliza Burke an employee, he explained, it was all in the family. I think that will illustrate to anybody the goodness in the man."

But Tom Cullen still says that's different.

· · ·

About bills, when he does send them, Dr. T. S. Cullen has clearcut ideas. They have not always been considered orthodox.

The time to send your bill, he says, is the day the incision heals. Its size should bear some relation to the size of the patient's bank account:

If the fee is asked at once it is promptly settled as a rule. The patient still remembers how much more his life is worth to him. If it is allowed to lag, other expenses creep in and he thinks the surgeon may as well wait; he can afford to. I have watched it happen time and again, and have had to deal with it occasionally.

If a man comes and puts his cards on the table I'll meet him. I'll cut a bill in two and cut it in two again, or cancel it altogether if he can't pay. But if a man who can pay tries to do me out of ten dollars he owes I'll spend a hundred to get it; and I'll get it. Partly for my own satisfaction, partly for the sake of the profession. A man, or a woman, who tries to get out of paying a specialist who has done a definite piece of work will, if he or she is let get away with it, certainly try to get away with forgetting to pay the general practitioner. So I don't let 'em get away with it. When I am tempted to, I remember the meanest woman in Ontario.

The meanest woman in Ontario lived near Magnetawan. The village physician, his friend, Dr. Freeborn, told Tom Cullen about her. Dr. Freeborn had for years attended her husband, who was an invalid, without having a bill paid and had supplied from his own dispensary, also without pay, the invalid's medicines.

When death delivered him at last, Dr. Freeborn was called in to sign the death certificate. That formality completed, the grieving widow beckoned to the woodshed behind the summer kitchen. There, packed in rows of baskets, were all the invalid's medicine bottles.

"How much will you give me for the lot?" she said.

Getting back to bills that can be collected, Tom Cullen was never of the school that favours rigid schedules of charges. The circumstances of the case, and of the patient, must be considerations, he holds. He has been

heard to defend a certain rich surgeon of Hopkins against
the accusation that he had no ceiling on his charges:

Sure he had a ceiling on them. Only there were a lot
of holes in the ceiling. . . .

He has himself been more often accused of holes in
the floor; a fault frowned on even more severely in certain professional quarters. His equanimity has outlived
the frowns:

I haven't always run with the crowd on this bill business and I have had enmity over it in my time, but it
works out in the end. The majority of the men I have
trained look at it the way I do. What is best for the most
people is the thing that lasts.

3

THE CHESAPEAKE BAY AUTHORITY

A MAN WHO HAS SLEPT four nights a month for ten years
on the bosom of Chesapeake Bay retains a feeling for that
body of water. A boy whose first taste of exotic delight
came out of a tin of Baltimore oysters keeps through life
a warm place in his heart for their native bottoms. An
adopted son of the Eastern Shore who can wake on summer mornings, in the grey stillness before dawn, to the
putter of the crab-fisher's outboard and the drone of song
that the crab-fisher sings, lifting crablines along the
branch, has his happiness firmly rooted in Chesapeake
Bay mud.

Naturally, if he is Tom Cullen, he wants the mud to
be unspotted and the water to be pure and the oyster
beds to be healthy. And, as naturally, having found that
they are not he has to do something about it. For this is
a man of action.

This is altogether a man of action where Chesapeake
Bay needs a champion. Diplomacy be hanged. The man
of action bought himself a half-page of advertising space
in the Chestertown, Kent County, Enterprise, and there-
in published an open letter to the citizens of Chestertown
on the subject of their sewerage.

The letter was written on May 24, 1930, less than a
year after Dr. Welch had fixed it for Dr. Cullen to succeed him as the Maryland state board of health's diplomat. It was written as a member of that body, though not
evidently as its diplomat. The date may have had some-

355

thing to do with it. There were always fireworks on the twenty-fourth of May when Tom Cullen was a boy in Canada. The twenty-fourth of May was the Queen's birthday; fireworks were essential.

Fireworks, to satisfy the liveliest vestigial memory, were what the letter in the Chestertown Enterprise set off. Reading it again after eighteen years Tom Cullen philosophizes calmly enough:

I put it in the other two Chestertown papers too, the same size. . . . In my early days on the state board of health I sometimes overstepped the traces, not realizing that state matters cannot always be handled with the expedition that surgical cases can. I learned in due time that, with a little judicious delay, the desired results can be obtained. . . .

But there could have been small calm by the Chester River on the May morning when, in twelve-point boldface italics, on the other side of a peaceable advertisement of secondhand cars — Model A 1929 Ford Coupé. Not a year old. $315.00 — citizens of Chestertown read the open letter addressed to them with warm personal regards by theirs faithfully Thomas S. Cullen. In the century and a half of Chestertown's history as a centre of Maryland culture no townsman had received a letter like it, no town paper had printed one so unrefined.

Sewerage was its subject. "You have a lovely town, a wonderful river, a fine college and, best of all, a charming group of people but — " thus with brief preliminaries it was reached — "but you have no sewage disposal plant and dump your sewerage into your best asset — your river. How do you think a yachtsman who anchors in your river is impressed?"

No sooner asked than answered, with accuracy and without reserve: "Sometimes he sees raw sewerage emptied into the river near the main dock and also coming out under the main bridge, and observes fecal masses lazily floating on the river or clinging to the shore in front of pretty lawns. Next morning he lifts his anchor rope and finds that fouled with sewerage and, worst of all, he sees small boys catching crabs and fish near the sewer.

"This condition is bound to make a bad impression" — a flick for Southern pride here — "on people coming from the North and West and" — salt in the cut — "if not corrected public opinion will soon force the state board of health to take action as the law requires."

The rest was gentler: a light but humiliating comparison between the Eastern Shore's elder seat of learning and a small boy in his Sunday clothes "who has forgotten his pocket handkerchief and uses his coat sleeve as a substitute"; an assurance of high regard for friends in Chestertown; an avowal of unique responsibility for anything in the letter which might possibly offend; "no other member of the state board of health has the slightest idea that I have written it." The concluding prayer had its infinitive split for greater emphasis; Tom Cullen's own mark:

"I beg of you to at once take action towards the establishment of an adequate sewage disposal plant. You will then have a safe place for your children to swim in and the river will be a joy instead of a menace."

When the open letter was read in Chestertown its author was back at work in Baltimore. But echoes of indignation from across the water were heard in the Charles Street offices of the state board of health. The new board member, duly regretting all the feelings hurt by his brash letter-writing, remained impenitent at heart. Contamination was spreading in Chesapeake Bay. Board records, to which as a member Tom Cullen had access, mapped its spread. Oyster bottoms, crabbing grounds, fishing waters, muskrat pastures and bathing beaches were showing increasing infection. Of the sources of pollution mapped, Chestertown's sewage outfalls were most flagrant. Long persuasion had not interested Chestertown's local government in other methods of sewage disposal.

Moreover, but for the letter, Tom Cullen might not have become chairman of the Chesapeake Bay Authority, a federal body vested with power to promote and subsidize plans for cleaning up Chesapeake Bay and its tributary waters; all 5,000 square miles of them; from the Elk River to Hampton Roads and from Chestertown Md. to Washington D.C. And that was a lot of fun.

When Franklin Roosevelt was elected President of the United States, in November 1932, the country was deep in depression and Tom Cullen rather deeper in efforts to get raw sewerage out of Chesapeake Bay. His Chestertown opening had been improved by the less arresting educational methods of state board of health experts. On both shores of the tidewater public education had progressed. But contamination of the bay had progressed faster. Surveys made three years after he joined the board showed sewage pollution still spreading. Tidewater towns, endangering life and destroying sources of income by discharging raw sewerage into their harbors and rivers, knew what they did and did not know what else they could do. A time of general bankruptcy was not a time for floating municipal bonds to pay for costly sewage disposal plants.

Tom Cullen recognized the fact and cocked an ear towards Washington. His friend George Radcliffe of Cambridge, had told him something of the presidential plan to fight depression with public works. Supposing the bay towns were to forget resentments and agree together on a board of health clean-up programme covering all, but ensuring that cleaning jobs most needed should be first done. Supposing such an agreement could be reached in good time; ready for any Washington decision to spend federal money on public works projects. Supposing someone were to start early, with the idea in mind:

Personally, I did not altogether like the President's plan for spending great sums on work-making schemes. I was not so sure that federal pump-priming would end the depression. But if the money was going to be spent anyway, I saw no reason why some of it should not be usefully spent, cleaning up Chesapeake Bay. . . .

Though a talented conniver at stratagems, the most talented Jeff Peters ever saw, the late Andy Tucker might have learned a good deal that spring of 1933 following Tom Cullen around. Early in June the stratagems culminated in a private dinner for sixty at the Maryland Club in Baltimore. Dr. Cullen was the host. The guests included the mayors of tidewater towns and cities and villages. Key men from the state board of health staff and Washington's public health service were there, with independent authorities on public hygiene, federal and state government representatives and newspaper editors vowed to secrecy. Fireworks were not desired on this occasion:

We did not want the public unduly exercised by reports of the extensive sewage pollution in the bay. Surgeon General Hugh Cumming, who was one of those who came from Washington for the dinner, agreed with us that it would be wise to improve conditions without saying much about them until the danger was eliminated.

Three sentences and a concluding comment from the notes Tom Cullen made when the dinner was over, tell the rest of the story: "Frederic Lee, Governor Ritchie's financial adviser in Washington, gave us a very clear idea of what might be gotten from the government for civic enterprises . . . The dinner was delightful, a vast amount of good has been done and the greatest harmony exists. . . .

Before we left, the mayor of Chestertown had his arm around me and mine around him . . . Comment: If the government advances the money, the Chesapeake Bay will be better than ever and our revenue therefrom will steadily increase instead of diminish."

George Radcliffe, who came from the Eastern Shore and knew the President well, sat at Tom Cullen's right the night of the clean-up dinner at the Maryland Club, Three weeks later the two friends lunched together to talk of PWA. The Federal Emergency Public Works Administration was being organized under Mr. Ickes, with presidential direction, to lead a nation-wide attack on unemployment. Divided into PWA districts, each with its own regional director, the country was to be set to public works. Regional boards of dollar-a-year men were to allocate grants and oversee PWA projects, endeavouring as far as possible to ensure that each should be of value to the country as a whole, as well as to local interests. George Radcliffe had been sounded; if the President wanted him .to take the direction of District 10, would he serve? Included with much else in the eight-state compass of District 10 was the Chesapeake basin. Yet, as Tom Cullen remembers now, he advised his friend against acceptance: "Don't touch it George. You have your hands full already."

A few weeks later the adviser, holidaying at his camp in Canada, received by telegram the news that his advice had been ignored. George Radcliffe wired that he had not only taken District 10 but had appointed Tom Cullen to its board. The apostle of Chesapeake Bay purity returned to Baltimore in September one of F.D.R.'s dollar-a-year men. With the other members of District 10's board he shared the responsibility of choosing from among work-making projects locally acceptable those most desirable from a national view.

What could be more desirable from a national view than the purification of Chesapeake Bay, from which 41 million pounds, shucked, of the nation's oysters, and seventy per cent. of all its crabs, to say nothing of terrapin, clams and fishes, were each year drawn? Tom Cullen had the answer.

The administrative pattern of District 10 swiftly developed as one of geographical areas over-riding state boundaries. In each area authorities were set up under the central board to plan, direct and correlate workmaking projects. Tom Cullen was not surprised to find the Chesapeake basin designated as one area; but he was surprised and happy when he was made chairman of the Chesapeake Bay Authority. The federal organization of PWA was ideal, as he saw it. State boundaries were not permitted to cut problems in two.

Tides and currents, crabs and fishes, erosions and pollutions had always ignored the Maryland-Virginia line across the middle of the bay. It could now be ignored with the same completeness by the authority responsible for financing improvement projects over the whole area. There was no need for any of its members to clear decisions with state legislatures where rival partisans might make capital of interstate jealousies:

We had a common problem and we didn't have to ask each other more than once to help out. We began with an all-day conference. Everybody concerned was there and every aspect of our problem was discussed. When the meeting was over it was perfectly clear that the immediate work for the Chesapeake Bay Authority was to clean up the bay as far as possible by eliminating the sewage. It was also clear that Maryland and Virginia must act together if the clean-up was to be successful. We went to work on that basis.

Before the Chesapeake Bay Authority had been a month in existence its first PWA-subsidized sewage disposal plant was under way. Annapolis, with plans already prepared, got the preference. Chestertown came late to the clean-up. Cambridge was before it, Easton after Cambridge:

Within a few years we in Maryland began to see daylight. Moreover PWA projects had got the last of the raw sewerage from Washington out of the Potomac; but in Virginia, things moved less satisfactorily. We cleaned up minor sources of pollution but with the main one, Hampton Roads, into which untreated sewerage from a half-dozen big towns at the bay mouth ran, we could not get a start.

There was no agreement among the municipal governments concerned; there was no common approach to the problem; there was no over-all plan large enough to meet the requirements of the whole area and on any attempt at a partial solution millions must have been spent to no purpose. What was needed was a fresh grip and a new survey, but the powers of the board of District 10, PWA, did not include the power to spend PWA funds on anything so nebulous as an unrequested survey. Taking his committeemen from Virginia with him, the Chairman of the Chesapeake Bay Authority went to Washington to see Secretary Ickes. . . .

He came home happy with a couple of Mr. Ickes' best stories and Mr. Ickes' decision to allot PWA money for a complete new survey of the Hampton Roads pollution area. The U. S. public health service made it, under the direction of Surgeon General Hugh Cumming. It covered all aspects of the problem to the satisfaction of the Chairman of the Chesapeake Bay Authority:

But we had still to get the co-operation of all the municipalities concerned. At first there was very little enthusiasm, but a committee was formed and went to work and it was a joy to see how, as a result, public opin-

ion changed and came to favour a clean-up. I helped
where I could, meeting the Virginia group in conference,
giving statements when they wanted them given, going
down to Norfolk to talk to the medical men there and
enlist their interest, travelling to Washington with depu-
tations to interview PWA officials on ways and means.
With George Radcliffe backing us all the way, we won
out at last.

Disagreements were dissolved and the last of the
Chesapeake Bay Authority's major jobs of cleaning was
under way when PWA was wound up.

Federal loans of $5,000,000 had been advanced and
the preliminary work was well ahead at Hampton Roads
when Pearl Harbour and a more universal threat of pollution stopped it. But the project was on far enough to
be easily resumed. In the spring of 1946 work began again.
When it is finished a single system of sewage disposal will
serve the whole Norfolk port area and the last big source
of pollution in Chesapeake Bay will be gone.

Latest reports on the purity of Chesapeake Bay find
the senior member of the state board of health of Maryland not ill-satisfied with the results of the Chesapeake
Bay Authority's expenditure of federal funds. Only a little
more than one-half of one per cent. of Maryland's quarter-
million acres of oyster bottoms have now to be restricted
because of sewerage pollution.

4

PRESIDENT OF THE PRATT

IN THE Baltimore civic election of May, 1947, taxpayers were invited to vote on a money bylaw authorizing a library loan of a million and a half dollars. The loan was opposed by the new civic efficiency commission, and by the most influential Baltimore newspapers. It was approved on election day by a majority of 23,000 votes.

The majority pleased Dr. Thomas S. Cullen, president of the board of Baltimore's public library system. In the seventy-ninth year of his age and the tenth of his library presidency, against the civic efficiency commission, and against his old friends the Sun papers, he had led the campaign for the loan, and he had won. It had not been hard either:

> I wrote a short personal note to all our library staff members explaining the importance of getting the facts in proper perspective before library patrons. The staff members are the people who know best how badly the loan was needed, and the library patrons are the people it will benefit most. If you can give the right picture to a hundred and fifty thousand book borrowers all of whom stand to gain by it, you do a good deal to ensure the right vote.
>
> We naturally got all the other help we could from interested groups like teachers and parents and study clubs and so on, and I did what I could, personally, to give the picture to the public. But I feel sure it was the staff work, especially in the branches, that turned the trick. . . . No, I am not a politician.

364

Denying the unjust charge, the president of the board of the Enoch Pratt Free Library of Baltimore City spoke severely. Then a reminiscent glimmer far back under his brows widened to match a smile that emerged; a smile that was childlike and bland. Tom Cullen was about to confess:

I am not a politician — but I sometimes think I might have made one.

Enoch Pratt, a wholesale hardware merchant who came from Titicut Township, Mass., gave Baltimore its public library. Before his friend Andrew Carnegie annexed the idea, Enoch had it. With a million and fifty-eight thousand of his own dollars he built and endowed the Enoch Pratt Free Library of Baltimore City. The year was 1882. He struck a Yankee bargain with the city fathers. He would give outright a library building and $833,333.33; what was left of the million-and-more after the big library in Mulberry street was built, stocked and fitted with a staircase newel worthy of his gift's magnificence; "a solid block of dove-coloured marble from which rises an elegant bronze gas fixture." In return Baltimore must guarantee to his free library in perpetuity an annual income of $50,000.

The annuity part of the bargain was, Enoch Pratt said, "about the only thing I ask credit for." Looking back, the modesty seems excessive. The budget provided from taxes to keep Enoch Pratt's library system serving the citizens of Baltimore is now more than $1,400,000 a year. The sum includes carrying and amortization charges on $4,500,000 borrowed, on Baltimore's credit, to pay the cost of new buildings, extensions and improvements. It does not include the perpetual annuity. Moreover, trader Pratt gets a good return on his money in other ways. The library system that bears his name is of good repute far beyond Baltimore. Among American public libraries, the Pratt rates high, Pratt-trained librarians command recognition and Pratt innovations are followed with interest.

Tom Cullen was chosen president of the board of the Enoch Pratt library for the first time in 1938. He accepted the post on one condition; that he be relieved of it the following January. He has been elected president every January since. That pleases him, too; affection for Baltimore's free library and pride in its service have long roots, for him. He has been a Pratt trustee for a third of a century. His first year was 1915.

Charles Joseph Bonaparte, last of the original board of nine selected by Enoch Pratt to administer his gift, was its president then. Grandson of that irresolute younger Bonaparte, Jerome, who loved and married a Baltimore beauty and deserted her at his brother's imperial order; son of Jerome Napoleon, chiefly famed as the founder of the Maryland Club; Charles Joseph had become, in a long life not without diversions, almost as much a civic institution as the Pratt. The new board member had his approval. He gave it as an observer of men.

An early exchange on library business illustrates the observer's point of view. It concerns a book and two flags. President Bonaparte had mentioned the book, Trustee Cullen had proposed the flags at the June, 1917, meeting of the Pratt board. In Tom Cullen's opinion, the free library of a free city in a free country now at war with Germany should have ready, against the day of victory, a new stars-and-stripes and a new flag of Baltimore. Fellow-trustees approved the sentiment but made no cash provision for the purchase. So Trustee Cullen wrote President Bonaparte a letter next day, enclosing a contribution towards the cost of the flags. He added a postscript asking the full title of a book the president had praised during the board meeting. The answer, written ten days later from the office of Charles J. Bonaparte, Attorney at Law, reflects the quiet enjoyment with which an old and easygoing Baltimorean watched Tom Cullen getting things done:

"My dear Cullen:
"The cost of the two flags was $23.70. Distributed among nine trustees, this represents an impost of $2.63 levied on each one of us. I have just paid the bills and enclose you therefore my cheque for $22.37, being the amount of your contribution of $25.00 less $2.63 which you ought to contribute.
"The book to which I referred at the time of the last meeting is Moxon's Mechanic Exercises, and if you still have a laudable desire to present it to the library, that institution will receive it with appropriate sentiments. I feel bound to add, however, that I do not think you ought to consider yourself under any obligation to get it.
"Believe me as ever
"Yours most truly
"Charles J. Bonaparte."

Tom Cullen got the book and, as time went on, got other things for the Pratt library, its patrons and its staff. When things were difficult to get, especially at the city hall, it became usual for him to try to get them. On the library accounts committee, he found his duties included those of liaison with civic governments. Year after year his was the task of softening hard-boiled budget officials when library estimates were coming up, of persuading justly skeptical politicians that they risked no votes by promoting literacy among their constituents, of steering salary increases through economy waves and generally justifying, in the eyes of unbookish guardians of the tax-rate, the expense of attaining Enoch Pratt's "great object — the free circulation of the books of a large and ever-growing library among the people of the whole city."

Of his method a fragment remains, treasured by one of many who, from time to time, have accompanied Trustee Cullen on pilgrimage to the city hall. This time they went to make a special request from the Pratt board for an increase in the chief librarian's salary, and it was known in advance that the mayor was against it. As the accompanist remembers, the mayor tried to sidetrack the delegation and its request with a joke. Dr. Cullen capped it. The mayor tried another. Dr. Cullen capped that: "then he settled right down to swapping jokes until the mayor gave in at last and agreed to the increase."

Tom Cullen is not a politician. But the makings being there and accustomed to employment in the Pratt's service, their owner was not surprised when, early on a February morning in 1927, he got an emergency call from the Pratt for help in political straits. He knew about Hazazer's Hall.

Hazazer's Hall had been sold to real estate speculators six months before. Baltimore's oldest dancehall, it stood in west Franklin street back to back with the main Pratt library in Mulberry street. In 1890 the building, already aged, could have been bought for little, but Enoch Pratt, then president of his own library board, saw no reason for buying it. The library he had built was plenty big enough. For 1890's needs it was, but long before 1927 it had grown too small. Pratt trustees had considered and rejected plans for enlarging it; it was not only too small but too unhandy; its day was past. All recognized that the real need was for a new central library building. All agreed that the original location was still the best. All saw the difficulty; money. Neither purchase of land nor erection of a building was possible until Baltimore taxpayers had voted approval of a money by-law authorizing an issue of bonds.

Thus far the Pratt board had reasoned when the sale of Hazazer's Hall in Franklin Street enforced a conclusion. Hope of getting the land needed for a bigger and better library at the old site would be gone if, as was reported to be their intention, the new owners of Hazazer's Hall replaced it with a costly block of offices. The library board decided on an immediate campaign for a new central library building. Its purpose was to rouse and inform public opinion to the point where civic politicians would feel the pressure and authorize the necessary vote on a library bond issue. The Pratt librarian, Dr. J. L. Wheeler, was entrusted with its direction. He found the point difficult to reach. On the February morning when Tom Cullen, sitting at seven o'clock breakfast in his library, was disturbed by a telephone call, public opinion in favour of a new Pratt library building had not risen enough to be worth any politician's notice. The telephone rang again and Tom Cullen answered it:

Dr. Wheeler was on the telephone. "I want to see you," he said. I told him I had a class from nine to ten and was operating from ten to eleven at Hopkins. "But I must see you," he said. I said "All right. Hopkins at five minutes before ten." He was there and told me the story. They were right up against it. This was the last day in which an enabling act, permitting a library loan bylaw to go to the vote in the next civic election, could be introduced into the State Legislature. The Mayor of Baltimore was the only person who could sponsor the act at Annapolis — "and he is against the loan," Dr. Wheeler finished.

I rang up the Mayor's office and asked him if he were going down to Annapolis that afternoon. He said he was, driving down; would I like to come with him? "Nothing would please me better," I said.* So we drove down together after lunch and on the way had a very earnest conversation. Finally Mayor Jackson said, "Well, it might be wise to allow the people to decide for themselves; I'll introduce the act."

He did it that afternoon. The people voted on the bylaw in May. They gave a majority of fifty thousand for

* Hon. Howard W. Jackson, the Mayor with whom Trustee Cullen rode to Annapolis would emend the narrative here. As Mr. Jackson remembers, he did not ask Dr. Cullen to ride to Annapolis with him. Dr. Cullen told him he was going to.

TOM CULLEN OF BALTIMORE

a three million dollar library loan. So we went ahead and bought the land we needed in Cathedral and Franklin and Mulberry streets, and made our plans and we have the new building. It was a near thing, for the slump of 1929 came before another civic election. If we hadn't got our enabling act that day, so we could put the bylaw to the people, we might have had to wait a good many years for our library.

It was at the June quarterly meeting of 1927, the first after the civic vote made the new building sure, that Tom Cullen was elected vice-president of the board of the Enoch Pratt Free Library of Baltimore City.

The Enoch Pratt Free Library stretches through from Mulberry to Franklin now, a block long on Cathedral street. The Roman arch of its entrance faces the lovely Ionic porch of Baltimore cathedral across the way. Like the cathedral, it wears its classicism with a difference. The casual and engaging raffishness of byzantine cupolas topping Greek severity in Benjamin Latrobe's masterpiece on this side of Cathedral street is matched on the other by the twelve bayfronted show windows which sit unabashed between the stately pilasters of the Pratt library front. Pratt show windows are for show, and no bones about it. They are dressed in bright colours. They are changed with the regularity of department store displays. They are designed to interest and entertain and they are Tom Cullen's particular pride. The Pratt was the first major public library in America to be built with show windows. Its president gives credit for them to Dr. J. L. Wheeler, then Pratt librarian, and has no doubt that the descent from dignity has been good.

Take the library records. Pratt records show that in 1947 library users borrowed 2,889,717 books. The figure, divided by population, works out at 3.4 books per Baltimorean per year. It is better than Boston's annual average, a third greater than New York's, more than twice that of

Philadelphia and almost twice that of Baltimore itself in years before the show windows. President Cullen does not suppose for a moment that show windows make the difference; Pratt library services have been improving steadily and in many ways; but he is convinced that they have helped to make it. Show windows keep Baltimoreans interested in their library:

If they have something good, you let people know about it. That is just horse sense.

Horse sense is President Cullen's specific for all the Pratt's non-literary problems. He found it helped even in a problem that was only settled when he and the Pratt were taken to court.

The Supreme Court of the United States decided the Enoch Pratt Free Library case in September of 1945. The decision was for the appellants. Though Thomas S. Cullen was the first-named of the appellees, the outcome did not disturb him greatly. He had lost the case and got what he wanted; a decision, made irrevocable by the highest constitutional authority.

While the suit was pending he, as president of the Pratt, had been denounced a good deal in certain quarters. He thought, on the whole, the denunciations were unmerited. The case was a test case. The issue once raised had to be settled constitutionally and finally. The only sensible thing to do was to take it to the Supreme Court and have it settled there, once and for all. From that point it would be possible to go on:

For you can't, if you are administering a public service dependent on public support, go faster in any direction than public opinion will come with you. And in things that can rouse race prejudices you have to be more careful how you go at the Mason and Dixon Line than you need to be either above or below it. That is some-

thing neither Northerners nor Southerners can understand, but you learn it after you have been long enough
in Baltimore.

The case the Supreme Court settled, by denying the
appellees' request for a writ of certiorari, was the case of
T. Henderson Kerr and Louise Kerr against the Enoch
Pratt Free Library of Baltimore City, its president and
trustees. The complainants charged that the trustees' decision not to accept Louise Kerr's application for admission
to a library training class was a violation of the Fourteenth Amendment. The defendants claimed that the
Pratt Library, having been founded as a private corpora-
tion was not, as were agencies of government, ruled in
administrative actions by the Fourteenth Amendment.
The defence was accepted in a Maryland court and rejected by a federal appeal court. The appeal court's judgment was upheld by the Supreme Court.

Enoch Pratt, making his gift, had provided against
political interference in library affairs by incorporating
it with a self-perpetuating board of trustees. He had provided as carefully against colour barriers among the
patrons of his library; "my library shall be for all, rich
and poor without discrimination of race or colour who,
when properly accredited, can take out the books if they
will handle them properly." That provision was and is
faithfully fulfilled. The acceptance or training of Negroes
for librarians' posts was another question, and a new one.
It had not arisen in the first fifty years of the library's
existence, for the reason that can be learned by living
long enough in Baltimore. Local public opinion had not
come very fast or far in that direction since the Fourteenth Amendment was added to the Constitution of the
reunited states of the Republic.

Pratt training classes were a development of the
library's growth, limited in size by its needs. No more

. . . but he sometimes thinks he might have made one.

—page 374

Dr. Thomas S. Cullen, President of the Board of the Enoch Pratt Free Library of Baltimore City applicants were accepted for training than could, in the ordinary course of events, be employed in the library or one of its branches after training. The policy began with the first organized class in 1928 and still continues. Refusal to consider the application, for admittance to a training class, of a young well-educated daughter of a Negro tax-payer was defended on that ground: In the ordinary course of events she could not be employed after training since the only two library assistants' positions open to Negroes were filled. It would be unfair to waste her time and the library's training facilities on a course of studies that must prove unprofitable to both.

This part of the defence, like the first, was ruled out. The appeal judge found racial discrimination in the refusal to consider the application and declared that, the library being supported out of public funds, its trustees were "representatives of the state to such an extent and in such a sense that the great restraints of the Constitution set limits to their action." He therefore ruled the Fourteenth Amendment's guarantee of civil rights without discrimination applicable in the case. His ruling was upheld by the Supreme Court.

When the Pratt trustees next met the opinion of the appeal court judge was read into their minutes, with a resolution "that all further action of this board . . . be had in accordance with the language and spirit of that opinion." The postscript was written by Tom Cullen in the spring of 1948: "We have now six coloured librarians and assistant librarians on the Pratt staff and they fit in beautifully."

Opportunity for further action in the spirit approved by the Supreme Court came from a new direction in the autumn of 1946. Tom Cullen took it.

Timorous taxpayers had complained to members of Baltimore City Council that a library branch had been misused for the purposes of subversive propaganda. There were demands that the employee responsible be dismissed and that the civic grants supporting the library be withdrawn; for a CIO meeting had been held in Branch 17.

The chief librarian of the Pratt was required to go before the civic budget committee to defend, if such a thing were possible, the desecration. President Cullen went with him to the interview with the committee. His purpose, as on so many other occasions, was to put the facts in proper perspective. Two facts were first; that Enoch Pratt had provided in the terms of his gift that his library should be for the use of all citizens, and that current administrators of the gift were still bound by its provisions. An eyewitness has reported his presentation:

"Dr. Cullen told the committee the meeting in Branch 17 had been called to discuss the cost of living, a matter of interest to most citizens. It had been conducted in conformity with library rules. Its conveners had been warned by the librarian that partisan politics must not be introduced. An observer present for the library reported that they had not been. It was true he said that those who organized the meeting were members of the political action committee of the CIO but the fact did not invalidate their rights as citizens. Then he stuck out his chin-whisker a bit and said:

" 'I have no more fondness than have most of you gentlemen for the CIO. But I have discussed this matter with our chief librarian and have concluded that he could not have done anything but what he did. We are a public body, appointed to serve the people. We must let library buildings be used for any lawful purpose. It's only fair.'

"After that he told them a couple of Kelly stories — the committee chairman's name was Kelly — and got everybody laughing, and that was the end of it."

Tom Cullen is not a politician but he sometimes thinks he might have made a good one.

374

5

TOMORROW TO FRESH WOODS

SEVENTY IS THE RETIREMENT AGE for professors of Johns Hopkins medical school. In November of 1938, Hopkins' professor of gynecology was seventy.

There was a banquet in his honour on the night before his birthday. The senior U.S. senator from Maryland, the governor of the state, the mayor of the city, the president of his university and his old chief, Dr. Kelly, were among the speakers on that happy evening, and four hundred and seventy-five other friends of his were there. The orchestra played "The Maple Leaf Forever." President Bowman accepted, for the university, a portrait of Johns Hopkins' second professor of gynecology "to be hung in the green room of the Woman's Clinic at Johns Hopkins Hospital, so that students and house officers may look up to Dr. Cullen in the future as we older men have looked up to him in the past."

Tom Cullen continued his clinics and classes until the following June, then he retired from the direction of the department where his work had centred for nearly fifty years.

From departmental control he retired with thoroughness. It is by invitation only — the invitation of his successor and pupil, Dr. Richard W. TeLinde — that the professor emeritus comes, once or twice each year, to the sixth floor in Wolfe Street to conduct an operative clinic in the gynecological operating room he planned and take a lecture hour in the green room with the graduating class. From nothing else did Tom Cullen retire in the least. He changed pace and went on; giving the new leisure at his command to interests already in hand, the energies released from harness to fresh employs.

Ranking next the Church Home and Infirmary, the Pratt Library and the State Board of Health among interests in hand are the Surgeon General's Library in Washington, the American Medical Association and Chesapeake Bay oysters.

Tom Cullen's interest in the Surgeon General's Library is deep; his aim is to do something about it. The greatest of the world's medical libraries should, he holds, be fitly housed, adequately safeguarded and easily accessible as near as possible to the centre of the nation's capital. He goes to Washington from time to time to explain to congressional committees why it should be.

A proposal made not long after the first great war was to move the library to one of Washington's outer suburbs. Dr. Welch was among its supporters. At the time, the U.S. Army's big medical centre, the Walter Reed, was being built on the northern edge of the District of Columbia. Army medical chiefs favoured building an annex of the new hospital to house the Surgeon General's Library. Dr. Cullen led the opposition:

We had it out one night at dinner at the club. The army men came over from Washington and Popsy was there and the idea seemed to be that we should all agree on the move that evening. It was a very warm evening before it was over, but the decision went against the move.

I think it was a fortunate thing for American medicine that it did. The Walter Reed is more than six miles from the centre of Washington. It is a fine healthy site for an army hospital. But it is no place for a great medical research library.

The arguments for the army medical chiefs' proposal had been largely of expediency. In the old building housing it the library was overcrowded, awkward for research, ill-protected from fire. It would have been comparatively easy, while the Walter Reed centre was building, to get the authorization and the money needed for a library annex. It might be a long hard task to convince Congress of the need for a worthy building on a suitable site in the middle of Washington.

It has proved to be so. Twenty years later the Surgeon General's Library is in its old inadequate quarters. The worthy building on a suitable site is yet to be built and Tom Cullen is still appearing before congressional committees to explain why it should be. Nevertheless he remains convinced that to move the library into a hospital annex in an outlying suburb would have been a grave mistake. Quite as grave, he believes, as it would be to move the National Art Gallery or the Science Museum from the centre of the capital. The Surgeon General's Library belongs at the centre with other unique treasures of the nation.

On another point he argues, as on the warm evening at the club, from an experience Dr. Welch, against whom he argued then, did not share. Popsy was already established and able to afford cab fare when he came to use the Surgeon General's Library regularly for his research. He could not feel personally the importance of easy access. Tom Cullen could. He began his big work on cancer of the uterus, his greatest piece of original research, as a junior laboratory scientist, earning two hundred dollars a year and working on borrowed money. Before he completed the work he had made the trip to Washington for a day in the Surgeon General's Library, hundreds of times, at a cost of less than $3.50 a time. He could do it, wasting no money and no minute of his day, because the library was where it was. So he has striven to ensure that it shall stay thereabouts. He believes that the research of zealous youth can still contribute to the science of medicine. He

377

assumes that young scientists are still not rich enough to waste time and money on six-mile taxi rides. He wants to see America's greatest medical research library not only fittingly housed and protected but as easily and cheaply accessible to penniless young medical men in the future as it was to Tom Cullen when he was young and penniless.

Half the battle was won in the late thirties, when a central site, close to the Library of Congress, was approved. The other half he stays with, as a matter of course — see note dated Baltimore, April 7, 1948:

" . . . I am leaving for Washington in half an hour to appear before the appropriations committee of the Senate. Object; the new Army Medical Library Building."

.   .   .

For nine years before his retirement from Hopkins, Dr. T. S. Cullen had been a member of the American Medical Association's nine-man board of trustees. For a quarter century before that, beginning in 1903, he had been an A.M.A. delegate from Maryland, off and on. He continued as a trustee three years longer, retiring in 1941, and served as senior Maryland representative in the house of delegates for six years after that. His devotion to A.M.A. service transfers from a friend who did much to shape the association to its present usefulness. To his mind, the spirit of George Simmons of Grizzly Gulch is still the moving spirit of the A.M.A.

Dr. George H. Simmons practised medicine and kept a drugstore in Grizzly Gulch, up Chalk Creek in Colorado, before the railway went through to the coast. Howard Kelly found him there in '79 when he was sent to Colorado for his health. The young medical student from Philadelphia became the volunteer apprentice of the frontier physician and their friendship endured. Simmons was a personality. He grew with the West, leaving Grizzly Gulch and the drug store to become editor of the Western Medical Review. Later he moved to Chicago as secretary of the American Medical Association and editor of its Journal. He put his imprint on both.

Memories of George Simmons go back a long way for Tom Cullen. They date from a day in the 'nineties when the Westerner appeared in Hopkins gynecological clinic to see what his old Grizzly Gulch apprentice was doing there. Simmons had the quality that makes and holds friends, not only for a man but for his ideas; and he was full of ideas. It was natural that, after his death, the affectionate loyalty he had inspired should be given to Olin West who succeeded to the secretaryship of the A.M.A. and to Morris Fishbein who followed Simmons as editor of A.M.A. publications. Both men were chosen and trained for their work by George Simmons; recommendation enough in itself, to Tom Cullen's mind. He is convinced that, as the years pass, the figure of the drugstore proprietor of Grizzly Gulch will bulk large in the history of American medicine.

An A.M.A. legend popularly regarded as historical illustrates Tom Cullen's care to rescue, from among doctrinal differences, the spirit George Simmons instilled into the counsels of the A.M.A. It comes from Chicago and concerns a reference committee meeting that broke up in laughter and the light of day instead of in the general bitterness feared. Since it showed the temper of his mind, Tom Cullen was asked about the legend. He remembered it:

The fight was over a piece of legislation which, if adopted, would have far-reaching effects. I supported it because it seemed to me best in the long run for the profession. But a lot of good men were opposed. The association was divided over it; so were the house of delegates and the reference committee and the arguments were hot.

379

The committee sat all night hearing representations for and against and discussing them, and once or twice we pretty nearly came to blows.

At daybreak we voted on the main motion and our side won. After that, in very bad temper, we shaped the bill to be presented to the House of Delegates that day. There was a good deal of argument over the phrasing, but we got to the last clause by breakfast time, thoroughly angry and tired. Mitchell, the chairman, who had been my chief ally through the night, was on the point of declaring it approved when I said, "Wait a minute, I want to move an amendment."

Even the men on our side glared and the chairman looked as though he could kill me, but I went right ahead. "I wish to move," I said, "that this committee meet annually on this date to commemorate this happy occasion." Everybody howled, Mitchell most of all, and all the bad feeling of the night was forgotten.

Best of all A.M.A. stories for Tom Cullen is the one on himself. It comes from St. Louis and 1909:

The A.M.A. met in St. Louis the year Saunders published *Myomata of the Uterus,* the work Dr. Kelly and I brought out together. Naturally, the publishers advertised at the convention, and they did a fine job. In the coliseum where the scientific section met they had big display cards hung in the commercial exhibits with the title of the book and the authors; "Kelly and Cullen."

On a building right across from the entrance to the coliseum was a really big display. It read, "Welcome to the American Medical Association. Cullen and Kelly, Undertakers."

It wasn't a practical joker's trick. Cullen and Kelly are still in the undertaking business in St. Louis. They sent me a box of match-books only last year to prove it. But I've never had a funnier joke played on me.

.   .   .

Concerning oysters and the Chesapeake Bay Tom Cullen has a five-year plan.

About the time young Tommy Cullen, at home in the parsonage on the Fourth Concession of Sydney, Ontario, tasted his first oyster out of a tin stamped "Baltimore" Maryland statesmen started worrying over the disappearing oyster.

First production of their statesmanlike anxiety was a report, made by Professor W. K. Brooks of Johns Hopkins University after long study of Chesapeake Bay oysters in their beds. The report was dated 1884. Seven years later oysters were still diminishing and oyster beds still overdredged. Maryland was in danger of an oyster famine and indifferent to its danger. To rouse its citizens, *The Oyster*, a popular summary of the Brooks report was published. Daniel Coit Gilman, first president of Johns Hopkins University, himself wrote *The Oyster*'s introduction, a solemn warning of the approaching "decline and fall of the oyster empire of the Chesapeake."

The Oyster made his meaning clear: oyster beds were being stripped, oysters were yearly becoming fewer and farther between, yet the ten million bushels of oysters taken each year from Chesapeake Bay were less than a fifth the number that could safely be taken with proper cultivation. Professor Brooks advised farming the oyster grounds and ending free tonging. Fourteen years later, hope triumphing over experience, *The Oyster* was reissued. The oyster empire of the Chesapeake was still declining and falling, and sewage contamination had been added to the perils of the oyster. Little had been done to promote private cultivation. Oystermen opposed it. They feared monopolies and exploitation if their freedom to tong were restricted.

Twenty years more and towns like Cambridge on the Eastern Shore, where oyster tonging, shucking and packing had once been a main employment, had not an oyster shucker left. Grounds that had supported dozens of oyster boats were infected and condemned and sewage contamination was spreading. The Chesapeake oyster's future looked black when Mr. Roosevelt launched his emergency relief works programme and Tom Cullen became chairman of the Chesapeake Bay Authority under PWA. The next ten years changed the picture. Sewage contamination no longer threatens Maryland's oyster beds. In purity, the upper end of Chesapeake Bay is nearly where it was in 1884; in purity, but not in oysters. The oyster empire of the Chesapeake needs restoration. To achieve it is the purpose of Tom Cullen's five-year plan.

Before the war with Japan was over, talking one day with a scientist who had worked with the Japanese, he heard something that clinched his resolve to plan. His friend said Japanese scientists had told him before the war that if Chesapeake Bay were in Japan they would produce from it alone enough food each year to feed the sixty-five million people of their island. Tom Cullen allowed for a difference in approach; what can be done by scientific regimentation to feed a regimented populace cannot be done among the free and independent oystermen of Maryland; but remained determined. A way must be found to increase Chesapeake oyster crops without regimentation. He believes he has it in the five-year plan.

The five-year plan is one of education, and education is always slow. Its success must depend on willing co-operation between the free citizens and statesmen and oystermen of Maryland. It would begin by dividing Maryland oyster grounds into four educational districts. Oystermen of each district would be asked to choose from among their number one they knew to be a good oysterman and a good worker. To each of the four so chosen by their fellows the government of Maryland would entrust an experiment in oyster culture.

Each would be allotted ten acres of oyster bottom and the seed oysters to stock it. The help and scientific direction needed for planting and cultivating new oyster beds would be given by government experts. It would continue during the five years needed to bring the beds to maturity. During the same years each of the four chosen oystermen would be paid by the State enough to support his family in comfort. At the end of the time set, the four tracts of mature oyster beds would become the property of the four men who had developed them:

In other words the State of Maryland would stake these four oystermen for five years in this educational experiment and set them up at the end with an oyster farm apiece made by themselves. It might cost the State $100,000. It would be worth millions.

For it would be an experiment made by oystermen for oystermen. It would be watched by every one of them. By the time the five years were up they would all have had time to make up their minds for themselves on the value of oyster culture and to decide among themselves what should be the next step in the development of the oyster industry. The thing would grow out of local interest in what was being done locally. There would be healthy rivalry between district and district, and none of the resentment that develops when outsiders come in uninvited to tell a man how he should run his own occupation.

Tom Cullen is certain that with a five-year plan like that for a beginning it would not be many years before all the oyster bottoms in Maryland's end of Chesapeake Bay were fully cultivated:

The oystermen would see to it themselves, and that is the best way I know to get a thing done so it stays done in a free country. This oyster question must be taken right out of politics or we get nowhere.

He works to that end. He wants to see his five-year plan set going. He wants it for the evident reason of its public usefulness; and for a private reason of his own. A good story, he has always held, should not end; it should go on. And how could the good story that began for him in a Canadian parsonage, with a fat little boy eating an oyster out of a tin stamped "Baltimore," go on better than this?

6

THAT REMINDS HIM

HE HAS AND KEEPS a boy's engaging willingness to believe that everybody wants the right thing done. It is not the least ingredient in his ability to get it done. Friends, patients, patients' families, professional associates, political and business acquaintances — most of those who know him conspire to guard his faith from contact with a naughty world's realities.

That willingness to believe is not precisely equivalent to believing; that eyes as clear as his may, through the years, have discovered quite a few realities; these things seem seldom to occur in his company, even to cynical politicians. Friends, patients, patients' families, professional associates, political and business acquaintances — biographers, too — find themselves doing nobler deeds than they had planned, that Tom Cullen's illusions may remain unmarred. And if, occasionally and fleetingly, any suspects him of misleading into the paths of righteousness, it is only occasionally and fleetingly. The illusion that he has illusions is effectively established. Under its cover he approaches new exploits.

His approach has always been cheerfully pragmatic, whether to sewage in Chesapeake Bay or a stone in a gall-bladder, an adenomyoma or an evident injustice: Something wrong here? and, in inevitable sequence, What can I do about it?

If Tom Cullen finds something he can do about it, he begins doing it at once and goes on doing it, for years if necessary, until it is done. If he finds nothing he can do about it he dismisses the matter from mind with a swiftness startling to his acquaintances and irritating to his critics.

In conversation his method is the same. That is why the most consistently irritated of his critics are all conversationalists. For the thistle-tufts of talk, the humours and abstractions, the conversationalist delights to keep afloat with sidewise breaths, he has no time or taste. The airy nothings of discussion are not for him. Neither are they for anyone else if Tom Cullen is of the party. Airy nothings frustrate him and he does not like being frustrated. What can I do about it? he asks himself. An onlooker can see the question shaping an eyebrow and feel the relief with which an answer is found.

Once fixed, his course with a wandering conversation is swift. He takes it in hand, kindly but firmly. He changes the subject. He tells a story. He lifts it bodily from the swamps of speculation and sets it on the solid ground of narrative. What may happen to the conversation in transit is no concern of his. He has rescued it from quicksand suppositions. He has ended the purposeless pursuit of will-o'-the-wisps. He is happy again. He tells another story.

It may be apt, though apocryphal, like the one about the friend of his who was told to go to hell — "I'm on my way there," he said, "but I'm in no hurry" — or a test story like the one about the young fellow with a stutter:

He went from Baltimore to live in New York and the first friend from home who visited him thought his stutter seemed a good deal worse. So he asked about it; "Aren't you stuttering more since you came to New York?"

The young fellow nodded. "B-b-b-b-bigger t-t-t-t-town," he said.

Tom Cullen has found that, as a rule, the people who like that story like one another. He likes it very much, himself, and in another sort he likes the story of young Dr. Coffey.

Young Dr. Coffey was the son of a West Coast surgeon and he came east to intern in St. Agnes's Hospital in Baltimore. His father, meeting his confrère from Hopkins at a surgical conference not long after, asked him to look the boy up. Tom Cullen did better; he asked Mrs. Cullen to write young Coffey inviting him and his wife to Sunday dinner in Eager Street. The note was delivered to the newcomer at breakfast in the interns' dining room at Saint Agnes's:

He read it and tossed it across to a Baltimore intern. "Who the hell is Cullen?" he said. The story had gone the rounds of the hospital by night and I had it first thing next morning. A friend dropped in with it hoping, I suspect, to get a rise out of me.

I had been too long in the game for that. Sometimes, when you have succeeded in saving a patient whose chances seemed about nil, or when you have discovered something new in the laboratory, you are tempted to soar. But I discovered long ago that it is better to keep a foot on the ground. As sure as you don't, something will knock a wing off you. In this case young Dr. Coffey was perfectly right. A man has to know where he is taking his wife to dinner. After he had found out who the hell I was he accepted Mrs. Cullen's invitation and we had a delightful visit.

Tom Cullen is seldom or never in young Dr. Coffey's difficulty. In Baltimore, he knows who everybody is and receives and returns greetings in his walks abroad like a boy in his own block. Not once in fifty times does he fail to recognize any fellow-Baltimorean who salutes him. When he does there is always a reason.

The lady who tried to catch her surgeon's eye in the theatre one night and failed, knew why, for example, and explained the reason in tones clear enough to be heard in the next box, where friends of her surgeon received the explanation with joy.

"There's Dr. Cullen," she said, "and he doesn't recognize me. He'd know me well enough if I were in bed."

That sort of thing keeps a man from taking himself seriously and it is easier to get along with the world, Tom Cullen has found, if you don't take things too seriously. Most non-surgical troubles begin with taking something or somebody too seriously; he reached that conclusion early and has verified it often. So he keeps a stock of stories against seriousness, stories like the one about Theodore Roosevelt in Brooklyn. That one, tried out on an academic superior with whom he was arguing a point, proved very useful. The academic superior had decided to dismiss the argument. "I'm God around here," he said. Tom Cullen laughed:

By jove, I said, that reminds me of the one about Theodore Roosevelt in Brooklyn. Theodore was making a speech at a big meeting there and not getting the respectful attention he felt he deserved. So he broke off and asked a question.

"Does anybody here know Abraham Lincoln?" No answer.

"Does anybody here know George Washington?" No answer.

"Does anybody here know God?"

He got his answer then from the back of the hall: "Is his second name Damn?"

The argument, he remembers, was resumed on a more equal basis. Equality he holds essential as a basis of argument. But experience has taught him that equality is neither possible nor desirable in all human relations:

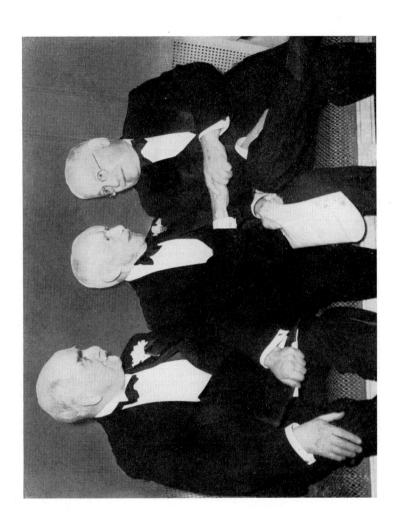

. . . and his old chief, Dr. Kelly.
—page 375

Tom Cullen, with Dr. Howard A. Kelly and Dr. J. M. T. Finney, at his seventieth birthday party

When you are dealing with people there is one thing you have to remember; that they must be treated differently according to their status. . . . Treat all men alike? You can't do it. If a person is well-off and feels secure you can be as direct or as rude as you find necessary. But with people who are poor or timid or uncertain you have to be gentle and go out of your way not to offend them or hurt them. So you can't treat everybody alike. You have to differentiate that way.

No one, Tom Cullen recalls, knew better how to differentiate that way than Fred Baetjer, first head of the first X-ray department at Hopkins. Stories of his devastating directness with professional equals and economic superiors have become Hopkins legends. One is of a brush with a patient who, in the early days of the department, was sent to Dr. Baetjer for X-ray examination. When the examination was complete the patient wanted to know what it showed. The examiner said he would send a report to the surgeon. The patient insisted on seeing the plates and having them explained to him. Dr. Baetjer said no and said it more firmly:

The patient was a little huffed. It didn't really matter, he said; "I don't know that there is anything in this X-ray fad." Baetjer came back like a flash; "I am not interested, sir, in the extent of your ignorance."
That the man he was talking to was the president of the trustees of Johns Hopkins University didn't interest him either.

Another story from the early days is of Fred Baetjer and a socially ambitious brain surgeon. The surgeon had a distinguished confrère from London lunching with him in the senior staff dining room at Hopkins. The talk came around to Dr. Baetjer's work:

Fred had done a great deal of experimental work in the beginning — he died at last from the effects of the X-ray burns he got then — and in talking of his experiments he spoke of his wife's interest in his work and explained that she had been a Hopkins nurse. The visitor asked more questions and found that several others among the senior men at table had married nurses. Finally he turned to his host and said "Did you marry a nurse too?"

"No," his host answered. "My wife is a lady." Fred Baetjer smiled. "Too bad she married out of her class," he said.

Better than the stories for one who listens are the asides and afterthoughts, distilled from experience and held in a characteristic phrase. Settling back in his armchair, half turned from his desk, swinging spectacles by the earpieces between finger and thumb Tom Cullen will talk. About surgery and a surgeon's training, for example:

Good horse sense, a sympathetic personality, an aptitude for cleancut operating, a thorough knowledge of aseptic technique and a scientific knowledge of surgical pathology are the foundation stones of surgery . . .

Thus far the surgeon and pathologist. Then Tom Cullen cocks an eyebrow and takes over:

If I have to choose between a scientific man and one with horse sense, I'll take the horse sense. But I'd rather have horse sense with a scientific training. Then you've got something.

Or about a surgeon's training and its general usefulness:

A surgeon's training is one of the best for preparing a man to make decisions and take responsibilities. He has to do it on a second's notice in the operating room and so he forms the habit. . . . You make mistakes — everybody does — but averaged out you'll make fewer that way than any other.

Or about being at large:

Four blocks below my house in Eager Street is the State penitentiary. I always drive around that way when I can. It's two blocks without a cross street and I'm so glad I am outside the wall. . . . Certainly I mean it. The side of the wall he is on is the big distinction between the best of us and the worst of us as far as I can see.

Or about money:

Don't despise money. Stocks and bonds are mudpies for grownups. If people could only remember that they would save themselves a lot of trouble. But money is a tool and a very useful tool. You can use it to get things done. . . . The fun is in getting things done. Let the other fellow have the credit — but get things done.

Memories Tom Cullen delights to recall are of coincidences. He has known many in his life, none more delightful than that on which he and retired Surgeon General Thomas Parran first came together. Hugh Cumming was Surgeon General at the time, and Dr. Parran his associate. He came from Washington to talk about a health problem in which all three were interested and, arriving ahead of time, waited in the library in Eager Street. When Dr. Cullen came in he found his guest ready to question him:

"Did you plant those two books on your desk?" Parran asked me. The two books were a fine old copy of Walton's Compleat Angler, a favourite of mine — and of Parran's, as it turned out — and an even older copy of William Cullen's *Practice of Physic*. I didn't know what Parran meant by "planting" them, and said so. Parran said "Open that book by Cullen."

I opened it and he showed me something I had not noticed before, written on the page next the fly-leaf in brown faded ink; "Thomas Parran his book, 1785." The volume William Cullen of Edinburgh wrote in 1774 was, to the physicians of his century, what Osler's *Principles and Practice* has become in this. The one I had, had

391

belonged to one of Tom Parran's ancestors. And there the two of us were, a century and a half later and an ocean away, a Parran and a Cullen, still pursuing the practice of medicine.

The book was mislaid after that and only towards the end of this last war my secretary found it again. I had her send it off at once with a note to Surgeon General Parran. From his letter of thanks, I gathered that a present of a million would hardly have pleased him more.

7

GOING ON WITH THE STORIES

As LITTLE AS POSSIBLE and as much as necessary . . . a
hundred stories to one prescription . . . anybody home?
. . .

They are Tom Cullen phrases, as characteristic of him
and as familiar to his patients as the eyebrows, the nose
and the unmistakable sound of his half-trot along a hospital corridor. Or as the bob-curtsey with which he cuts
short thanks.

"Anybody home?" Accompanied by a knock on a door
already open to him, it is his post-operative greeting. If
the victim, bed-bound by saline drip, nose tube or other
indignities, smiles at its absurdity Tom Cullen counts it
one towards recovery.

"A hundred stories" is his recovery programme, explained as a rule far on in convalescence, applied as a
rule from the moment the anaesthetic wears off. "By jove,
that reminds me . . . " and self-pity's deepest hiccup is
interrupted by the one about the Scotchman at sea.

"As little as possible" is the masterpiece of reassuring
accuracy, designed to meet a recurring need:

It is natural for a patient to ask the surgeon what he
is going to do. After all, no one can be more interested.
But it can be a hard question to answer. Often you do
not know definitely; sometimes you know too well; always
it is essential not to limit yourself in advance. No one
can tell what he may run into, even in the simplest opera-

tion. The surgeon's problem is to find an answer that will be honest, reassure the patient and at the same time leave his hand free. I found one long ago and it has served very well.

When a patient says to me "What are you going to do, Doctor?" I say "As little as possible and as much as necessary. That's what you want me to do, isn't it?" It always has been, so far.

His is a trustable evasion, grateful and comforting before surgery. Later, the normal desire for sympathy being then insatiate, convalescence can find it less soothing. As a clinical conversationalist, Tom Cullen has drawbacks. He is elusive. The one thing he quite evidently does not want to talk about with a patient returning to health is the current stage of the return. The fact has been known to exasperate. The lady who produces symptoms as the bird sings, the gentleman convinced that his sufferings are unique and must be told, both have found their surgeon unsatisfactory as a bedside visitor. Not that he cuts off convalescent confidences with blunt abruptness. Rather he is too quick for them. He can see one coming and escape it on a story a good thirty seconds before the baffled confider has completed a suitable opening.

But where trouble is ahead and the outcome doubtful Tom Cullen makes no effort to escape. He stays to tell another story, and another, and still another, till courage is rekindled.

What the story will be he seldom knows until it begins. The story comes with its occasion. If the occasion demands emphasis on the need for a calm spirit and confidence in the surgeon, it might be the one about Carrie. Carrie had both:

Carrie was cook in the family of a friend of mine. She wasn't well and my friend asked me to examine her. She proved to have a large abdominal tumor which required surgery and I arranged to operate. Before the operation a friend of the family called to see Carrie to wish her a good recovery. She found her quite untroubled.

"I done prayed the good Lord to get me well," Carrie said, "and Dr. Cullen, he's goin' to operate. If he cain't do nothin' I'se goin' to stop prayin'; 'tain't goin' to do no good."

Or it might be the one about the old gentlewoman on whom, after a serious accident, Dr. Cullen was called to operate in her home in a Maryland village. She was only semi-conscious when the surgeon arrived, and when he had done his work and was ready to say goodbye she was not yet completely out of the anaesthetic. But she spoke, though her eyes stayed shut, as a hostess and a woman of spirit:

"Goodbye," she said to me, "I am very happy to have met you. I trust we may know each other better under pleasanter circumstances. I am well worth knowing." We did, and she was.

Or it might be the one about the patient that nearly got away.

She came to Dr. Cullen for examination, sent from a neighbouring state by her physician, who had diagnosed the case as one that required surgery. Dr. Cullen confirmed the diagnosis, advised an early operation and, at the patient's request, arranged for her admission to hospital that day. He was leaving the same evening to operate in another city, but before he left he had everything in train for an eight o'clock operation the morning of his return.

That morning, Tom Cullen and his anaesthetist came straight from the station to the hospital and, at twenty-five to eight, were turning into Broadway. Half a block from the hospital gate the surgeon called to the driver to turn back to the last car-stop. Something about a woman they had passed standing there, with a suitcase on the pavement beside her, had caught his eye:

Though she had been across the road, and we had passed quickly, I suddenly had the crazy idea that that was my patient; the one I should be operating on in twenty-four and a half minutes. I'd only seen the patient once, two days before when she came to my office, but I decided to turn back anyway and make sure the idea was as crazy as it seemed. It wasn't; she was my patient all right. I got out and said goodmorning, put her suitcase in the car and said I would drive her where she was going. She said she was going to the station to take the train home; she couldn't go through with the operation. So we got in and started for the station, but after we had discussed things for a few blocks we turned around and headed back to the hospital.

The young lady at the entrance wicket called to me that they had cancelled my eight o'clock operation. "Your patient is gone," she said, "She paid her bill and left twenty minutes ago." "We'll cancel the cancellation," I told her. "My patient decided to come back with me."

We were a little late starting that morning; about five minutes, I think. But it was a very successful operation.

Or it might be any of ninety-seven others. Tom Cullen never knows. When it comes to stories, one thing leads to another. A Westminster chime sounding from the tall clock in his office can start a memory of the morning he went half-shaved from a barber's chair to ride in an ambulance with a woman nearly dead, stop a hemorrhage and get an appendix he had been wanting for months. It was quite a morning as he remembers it, and he can not forget it long. The chimes do not let him:

The patient was the wife of a doctor, a neighbour of mine. Her health had been bad for some time. I felt convinced the trouble was an appendix but another surgeon didn't agree and while we differed the appendix stayed in. This morning, I remember, I was in the barber chair

[*Photograph by* A. AUBREY BODINE

"Leaving Eager Street at noon . . ."
—page 402

Tom Cullen of Baltimore

only half clipped when my friend the doctor came in, very white, to ask me to come at once, his wife was hemorrhaging badly. I wiped off the lather and came.

It was an abdominal hemorrhage following a tubal pregnancy and very bad. We called an ambulance, telephoned ahead to prepare for an emergency operation and started for the hospital with the sick woman. Half way there she said she was dying, and very nearly did. But we pulled her out of it and got to the operating room and I operated. When we had dealt with the hemorrhage I said to the anaesthetist "Can you let me have five minutes?" He said he could manage it, so I went ahead, got that appendix, and proved my point. When my patient had recovered she felt better, and continued to feel better, than she had in years.

Naturally there was no fee. Between doctors I couldn't hear of it. But my friend and his wife got around me. I came home to lunch one day a month or two later and heard chimes sounding as I let myself in the door. They sounded very close for Christ Church or the cathedral and I was surprised. But I was more surprised when I climbed the stairs and discovered a grandfather clock striking two in my own office. It has been a great pleasure to have it all these years and to remember how I got the appendix. . . .

A present of turkey will recall the time Brice Goldsborough, carving Thanksgiving dinner, found birdshot, reproached his man Sam with having forgotten that this year the turkey was to be a tame one, and got Sam's answer:

"That turkey's tame sure enough like you said Doctor. Them shots was meant for me."

From there it is no distance to one of the classics of abdominal surgery; the story of the one birdshot that caused a stoppage of the large bowel:

Late on a Saturday evening in November of 1902 my friend Dr. Charles E. Simon of Baltimore went out for a walk. When he came in again he smelled camomile tea and started around the house to find who had a pain. It was the cook, a young woman who had prepared supper for Charlie that evening. He examined her, found marked rigidity over the appendix, had her taken to hospital at once. I operated at 1:30 in the morning.

There was an escape of thin, watery pus as soon as I opened the abdomen and the intestines were flaked here and there with fibrin. The appendix was tied down with adhesions. I removed it, sponged out the pelvis and, just as a precaution before closing up, carried a stalk sponge up into the right kidney pocket. To my surprise a dark fluid escaped, of a sort entirely different from that found in the pelvis. I lengthened the abdominal incision upward at once and we found a perforation four millimetres in diameter in the ascending colon. This was closed temporarily, to prevent more fluid escaping through it from the large bowel. Then I went ahead with the operation, taking out the lower third of the ascending colon, the cecum, a part of the small bowel and some enlarged lymph glands in the meso-colon.

Examining the specimen, we found a dense stricture of the ascending colon just beyond the perforation. This had so contracted the bowel that one small birdshot had completely blocked it at the point of greatest stricture. The perforation we found had really been a temporary safety valve. The lymph glands showed typical tuberculosis. The bowel stricture had been produced by an annular tuberculous ulcer gradually contracting until what had been a large lumen of the intestines was so reduced in size that a single birdshot the girl had swallowed eating a piece of wild turkey had completely closed it.

The precaution of sponging the right kidney pocket was what made the difference in this case. If it had not been taken, I probably would have been satisfied that the appendix was responsible for all the trouble and the patient would certainly have died. As it was she made a good recovery and Charlie Simon did not lose his cook. I heard from her a year and a half later when she was well and back at work.*

* Reported in the American Journal of Medical Sciences, March, 1904, Vol. CXXVII, p. 431, *Tuberculous Stricture of the Ascending Colon etc.*, Reprinted in Vol. II, T.S.C.'s collected reprints.

Large share of credit for this happy ending was allotted by its reporter to Dr. C. E. Simon's early, non-medical, training. If Charlie Simon had not grown up among the old-fashioned who hold, with Master Nicholas Culpeper, that a decoction made of camomile and drunk taketh away all pains and stitches in the sides and easeth torments of the belly, the chances are he would have gone to bed that Saturday night without looking for the trouble behind the smell of camomile tea brewing. He might even have not known the smell.

. . . .

That was one time I was scared. . . .

Tom Cullen was recalling his most famous patient: a stout white-haired woman with a humorous smile and an indomitable chin who came to him for treatment early in December of 1931. His reputation as a surgeon and diagnostician had spread far in the years since he and the hired furniture moved into three West Preston Street. Patients were coming to him from all parts of the country. This one came from Chicago where her work was, and her name a household word. After examination, Dr. Cullen advised an operation, and operated:

And that was one time I was scared. While I was operating the patient's pulse started to drop — to 80 — to 72 — to 64 — to 60. I could see the headlines in every newspaper across the country — "Jane Addams Dies On Operating Table" — but I kept on going. I had to.

We pulled her through all right. She was past seventy then, but she made a good recovery and went back to her work in Chicago. The trouble recurred later in an inoperable form, but we were able to give her the happiness of going back to her work. I wouldn't take a fee, of course, so she sent me a covered silver bowl of Chinese work for a keepsake. It is one I've been delighted to keep.

A patient so notable as Miss Addams entailed daily press conferences for her surgeon, but Tom Cullen found them no great hardship. He does not share the severe dread of reporters which afflicts many eminent medical men. Jane Addams of Hull House was a national figure; the public had a right to be interested in her progress and the press a duty to inform the public:

So I saw the press every day and gave the reporters a statement for publication. Then I gave them an explanation off the record of Miss Addams' condition and the trend of her symptoms. Nothing I told them off the record ever saw print. I have only once in my life been double-crossed by a reporter, though I have always made it a point to give them, in confidence, as much background information as I could on any story they were entitled to. Once in a lifetime is not a bad record.

Jane Addams' case was one of that class on which great argument is made by doctrinaires. When a surgeon operating finds a condition graver than he had hoped, and can only partially relieve it, is it his duty to tell the patient exactly what the condition is? Tom Cullen says not. The patient's family, Yes. The patient, No. The companion question, whether to tell a patient he or she is going to die, has seldom to be met head on. Or so he has found in his experience:

In the first place, who can tell for sure? The verdict may be most unfavourable and yet the patient may recover. I remember I operated on a patient and removed an advanced cancer not long after I started practising. I told the family the condition I had found but did not tell her; wisely I think. The operation was done in 1903; she died in her sleep at the age of 80 in 1944. I do not think she would have gone along in such comfort of body and mind if she had had the knowledge I withheld.

When a man or woman has business or professional interests that must be arranged for the sake of his family or associates, the case is different. Such a person, where the probability of recovery is small, should be told so as gently as possible, so that he or she may set urgent things in order. Or when people are old and tired, have borne the brunt of the day and are anxious to go, then it is kinder to tell them that the end of their world is near.

Very often when death is close it is not necessary to say so. The dying man or woman knows it as well as the surgeon. Each has clearly in his mind that the other is aware of the exact condition, but neither puts it in words. There is no need.

It was thus that Tom Cullen said goodbye to an old friend in the summer of 1946.

Their acquaintance went back to 1917. J. C. McReynolds was then a rising lawyer and a Southern Democrat not uninterested in politics. A favourite sister came to Hopkins for treatment and Dr. T. S. Cullen operated. When, seventeen years later, a second operation became necessary Dr. Cullen was again the surgeon. In the interval, the acquaintance had become a friendship which included the patient's family, and the patient's brother had moved to Washington, to be appointed by President Wilson a Justice of the Supreme Court. In Washington Tom Cullen was a welcome visitor in the McReynolds' home and there, over the years, Justice McReynolds formed the estimate he set down a year or two before he died: "Always I count him among the great whom I have known."

The measure of the trust between the two is in a pathetic and painfully pencilled note forwarded from Baltimore to the Eastern Shore where Tom Cullen was spending the summer of 1946. It was written by Justice McReynolds from a Washington hospital, to ask his old friend to come if he could and see him soon. The day the note reached Tom Cullen at Morling's Chance he telephoned, then drove, to Washington:

There was nothing I could do, but naturally I went at once. After I had examined him and talked with his physicians we had a talk. "Old man," I said, "there come times when the best thing is to play a waiting game. These X-rays have been giving you a lot of discomfort. So they have decided to stop them for the present. We'll play a waiting game."

I didn't need to say any more. We both knew we'd not see each other again.

There was nothing he could do. Tom Cullen drove back to Morling's Chance on the Eastern Shore. The Eastern Shore, having seen men come and go for a long time now, has developed a certain detachment.

Morling's Chance is Mrs. Cullen's. A few years after her marriage she bought the land, up the branch from Bloomfield, where she had picnicked as a child. Thirty acres of woods and meadow, lying along Raccoon Creek, the place had had its odd name when it was owned long before by a Quaker ancestor. She built a small white house there, close beside the water, and there Tom Cullen spends leisurely vacations and long weekends in the serenity of an ordered countryside well known to him, almost as well-loved as the bushland of Magnetawan, and a great deal handier. Leaving Eager Street at noon on Friday and crossing by the Sandy Point ferry he can be at Morling's Chance by mid-afternoon:

I put on old clothes at once and then Bartie shows me around and I get a clear idea of what has been happening since my last visit. The ducks may have come back or the young robins may have started flying or the dogs may have routed out a muskrat. In spring the ladies' slippers may be out in the woods. In fall the persimmons may have ripened. It is a toss-up every fall whether I or the small animals will get the persimmons from the two trees by the water.

After supper and possibly a bridge game, sleep with absolute quiet around. We are fully a mile and a half from a main road and there is no sound except for an occasional boat and the songs of the birds. Imagine waking after a fine night's sleep and hearing a bob-white calling just outside the door. Then an early breakfast and half an hour in the screened porch smoking and watching the cardinals and bluejays playing in the birdbath on the bank, or having their morning meal from the stone tray nearby, where Bartie puts sunflower seed for them.

A walk in the woods with the dogs — Lassie, Jamesie and the Babe — then we drive to Easton for supplies. The mail has come by the time we return and there are letters to read and the morning paper. Then dinner, a good long nap, an evening row on the river after supper and one day is over. A second goes as quietly and on Monday morning I start for Baltimore ready to work again, perfectly rested.

Outside the window as I write this is a moonflower vine. Last night it had five perfect blooms. Tonight we shall probably have just as many . . .

Operative Clinic Sixth Floor . . .

The sixth floor sits, as has been said, above the cornice of the Woman's Clinic in Wolfe Street. The sixth floor operating theatre is grey; grey tiled walls and floor, grey painted doors and ceiling, greyed glass in the windows, banks of grey seats slanting steeply behind a slanted glass screen, and a shadowless light like a giant grey mushroom head above.

All is as the Gynecological Cabinet planned it when the other storey was added; impersonal as an instrument tray, studied in detail as a stage set for drama.

Thirty or forty students wait, white-gowned, capped and masked, in the banked seats behind the screen. Alone on the floor, outside the empty light diffused from the mushroom-head in the ceiling, a nurse in gown, cap, mask and gloves arranges instruments on a thin, curved table. She drops one and the clatter of its fall is reflected from the tiled walls. A second nurse enters, ungloved, picks up the fallen forceps, carries them to the far corner, lays them in a tray, goes out. An orderly comes through a door, right, crosses left, pulls a set of foot benches to the middle of the pool of light, arranges them in twin lines at right angles to the glass screen, leaving a narrow space between under the metal mushroom. From against walls he pulls small wheeled tables, wheeled racks and cabinets and puts them, as in a pattern fixed by law, to frame the two rows of benches with their black-ribbed tops. One stool he pushes close under the glass screen, at the top of the lighted space, places a low stand beside it, steps back out of the light. The operating theatre is prepared.

One of the gowned students clambers down past the end of the screen, tiptoes along the right wall, comes back nodding. "He's there," he says, and settles back. "He's scrubbing up." The class grins knowingly, and hands first, Johns Hopkins' Professor Emeritus of Gynecology is in the theatre, walking lightly on battered old running shoes, a stout little champion ready for a contest. A dripping rubber apron covers the front curve of his drooping surgeon's suit, a gauze burnouse swathes his head and neck; eyebrows and nose, untamed and untameable, ride clear of gauze and mask. He stands while the apron front is wiped with a sterile towel, dries with another, holds out arms for the sleeves of his operating gown, hands to be fitted with rubber gloves. The ritual of asepsis accomplished, a third sterile towel is opened and hung muff-fashion over the gloved hands and bare arms. The operator is prepared.

But on the morning of December 4, 1946, a hitch developed there. The subject was not in the theatre at nine o'clock, the hour set for the Hopkins Medical School's professor emeritus of gynecology to begin his operative clinic before a fourth-year class.* This, though he did not know it yet, was unfortunate for the stout fourth-year classman in the front row right. Hands in towel, the professor perched on a stool under the big north light and swung to face the double-doors with the clock above. The clock said 9:02. From the midst of the gauze burnouse, one eyebrow lifted towards it. An interne hurried out through the double doors, and hurried in again, white coat-tails bobbing.

"Patient coming in a minute?"

"Not quite ready yet."

---

* Note from Hopkins' professor emeritus of gynecology: "No criticism should be inferred. Unavoidable delays can occur in the ward or in anaesthetizing. Some patients take three times as long as others to go under . . . T.S.C."

The eyebrow stayed up. Its owner turned to greet his students.

"Good morning! Is Mr. Brown here?"

The stout classman rose at the right of the front row. "You examined the patient, Mr. Brown. Give us the history . . . Pain? Where? . . . Right or left? . . . Don't know? . . . Why? It is important to know where, Mr. Brown."

Mr. Brown moved his feet uneasily and said again he didn't know. "Appendix, that's why." Lifting his regard to the class at large, the lecturer launched into description of the clinical symptoms of a case in his experience in which pain at the menstrual period did not involve the uterus, but only the appendix. The eyebrow lifted again to the clock. 9:07. "Patient ready yet?" The interne's coat-tails bobbed out, bobbed in. "Not quite yet." The round figure in its white wrappings settled back on the stool beneath the big window. "Now, Mr. Brown . . . " The question was one of post-operative treatment. The stout classman missed the answer. The questioner tried another, and another; two more misses. At 9:12, both eyebrows trained on the clock, the professor emeritus of gynecology was remembering prompter days.

"I can see Dr. Kelly coming in a little late one morning and hear him whistling coming down the hall. I remember it clearly because in all my years of association with him, he was so seldom late. If you know an operator is going to be a little late you don't get tired waiting. If you don't know, waiting tires you right out. It's exactly the same principle as in clothes. You don't care a hoot what sort of clothes you wear, as long as you've got a couple of good suits at home."

Past 9:15 by the clock over the double doors. "Now, Mr. Brown . . . " Mr. Brown, sweating heavily, had missed again. The doors swung at last to admit the operating table with its burden. Nurses and orderly waiting at the doors wheeled it into the space between the foot-benches. A nurse capped and masked like the rest came to sit on the low stool under the glass screen, a rack of tall glass flasks filled with coloured fluids at her right side, ruled charts on the stand at her left, a stethoscope hung from her ears, the end of the tube covered. Carefully she adjusted grey tubes between the flasks and a dark mask. When the head wearing the mask lay tilted back from the high table, level almost at the knee of the woman on the stool, she leaned over it, listening, making small delicate movements among levers and taps on the rack of coloured flasks, charting, listening, charting. Alone with each other the masked woman and the masked head appeared curiously unrelated to the business above them an arm's reach away. There, covering sheets withdrawn, the front of a naked body was being painted and painted over with iodine. The smell, sharply defined, cut like clean pain through the sickliness of ether. The body was covered again, all but an oblong of bright brown skin framed in thick folds of white. The patient was prepared.

Prompt and unhurried, the small alert figure on the high stool swung around, took hand from towel to make an arc in the air. "Now you can see from the contour," the professor emeritus said to the class, "there's a tumor." He stood up and handed the towel to the waiting nurse. The students in the banked seats leaned forward. The operating team waited, each in position. Quick and confident the operator walked around the still group to his place, the place that had been his so many hundred times, on the higher bench of the two at the right side of the narrow table under the light.

The stout classman sighed and began to ease into his seat: old T. S.'s back was to him now. The seat creaked. "Now, Mr. Brown," said T. S. without turning, "If you come down here and stand beside me you can tell the class what I'm doing." The stout classman lumbered down to stand under the light. Before he reached his place a thin scarlet line was drawn the length of the oblong of stretched skin and the knife in the small sure hand was moving down the line again. As it moved the operator talked: across the table to his assistant: "A nice knife. Some of them you could sit on, but this is sharp." To the nurse beside him: "Another knife, please." Silence for a stroke or two, then, to the boy behind his shoulder: "Mr. Brown, why did I ask for another knife?" Mr. Brown looked back to the benches for help, got none, mumbled unhappily, "Wasn't sharp?"

"Sure it was sharp," the operator was working as easily as he talked. "I wouldn't have complimented my assistant here if it wasn't sharp. I asked for a new knife because I'd gone through the skin and the fat with the first one, and I was starting into the abdominal cavity. There could be infection in the skin, and so I needed a new knife. Sponge, please. Now, let's see. What's the first thing you'd do, Mr. Brown? . . . No-o, I don't think we should try that first. There's a guy-rope here, what's it? . . . Right, a ligament. The round ligament. I'll cut it and we'll see something . . . tie, please . . . No-ow, let's see, that won't come. Remember the youngster at the circus? He hunts all around for a point of advantage where he can crawl under. That's what you do here . . . Mr. Brown, would you advise removing the ovaries in this case?" The stout classman shifted uneasily. From behind the screen his fellows signalled: shaking heads, shaping mouths to O's. He caught a signal: "No".

"Right," the operator still worked as he talked. "Right, they are not involved. Long ago, Mr. Brown, when we started to work out the most satisfactory operative prac-tice — now let me have the forceps — for cases of this kind, we followed up patients for years after an operation — sponge please — Some we followed — another sponge please — as far as India and China and we found — tie here — where there was no malignancy and the ovaries were not, or only slightly, involved, it was — tie again — better for the patient — now let me have an Ochsner here — to leave them in . . ."

Hands and voice paused together. Around the raw stretched split, steel clamp handles were clumped, bright empty eyeholes against white. In the mouth of the split the curve of a purple-pink globe rose, shining and patterned with dark veinings. "Satisfied?" The operator spoke across the table. His assistant nodded. The work and the talk resumed. "Now, Mr. Brown, I'll puncture just below here, where there are no blood-vessels . . . Now, let me have . . thanks! You didn't get the ovarian vessels there. Got them now? All right . . . There you are, catch this in the middle and leave both sides . . . long forceps please . . . now then, hold this over . . . an Ochsner again . . . fine . . . fine . . . now, chase me around to the left . . . a longer forceps here, you've got a longer reach than I have . . ." The stout classman, forgotten for a moment, eased off, only to find himself remembered. "What are we doing here, Mr. Brown? . . . No . . . No. But you have another guess . . . Bladder? You're away out. What is the abdominal policeman, Mr. Brown?"

Mute and miserable, the stout classman shook his head. His questioner's eyebrow lifted to the banked seats behind the glass "Anybody know? . . . The omentum? Right. Wherever there's trouble, the omentum goes . . . There, we've separated the omentum."

Gleaming slipperily, a magenta globe lay sideways on a towel, held by a last red tag.

"Now, give me a Kelly . . . Somebody hold that . . . See, not much blood . . . Careful now, the laboratory man won't want the mucosa injured."

A swift cut or two, a glance as swift, and the globe is dismissed. "Fibroid," the operator said, and was back at work.

"Now, we'll dilate the neck of the womb. Why, Mr. Brown? . . . That's it, infection. If there should be an infection it would drain away naturally this way." The talk paused while the talker waited with hand outstretched holding a needle. An assistant, pink browed and apologetic, took the needle and put another in its place. "That's all right, lady. I should have asked you for it. Why do we want a round needle when we stitch near the ureter, Mr. Brown? . . . Because with a sharp-edged one we'd run a risk of slitting or of puncturing . . . elevate the table please . . . There gentlemen, we've finished here. Light please."

The foot of the table came up. A spotlight turned on the clamp-bordered incision in its frame of white sheeting. The young men on the benches stood to look along the beam into a small tidy, bright-pink cavern; the empty place where the tumor had been.

"Table down," the professor emeritus said, and was at work once more. "Now then, we're back at the round ligament. Why do I take this piece off? . . . Because you never want too much tissue distal to the suture if you can help it . . . Now, watch this carefully. Taking out the appendix while the abdomen is open is standard practice now. I would feel very badly if anyone opened me for another purpose and left mine in. But I can remember . . . " The story was of a medical student of nearly sixty years ago watching doctors wait for an appendix to burst . . . "They didn't dare operate. All they knew to do was wait, and hope it would burst out. They waited a week and it burst in. So the patient died."

A length of pink bowel was in the opening now, held delicately in a brown-gloved left hand. Two clamps gripped the limp pink tag to be removed from it. A nurse wheeled a stand trailing a cord into the pool of light, took a metal rod from the stand, held the handle toward the surgeon. He half turned, slipped his gloved right hand into the white cotton mitt held waiting, closed it on the handle of the rod, turned back to the table momentarily. When he turned again the tag was loose. He dropped it in a basin. The nurse at his right elbow took rod and mitten, pushed stand and trailing cable back to the wall. Before the acrid smell of burning reached the watchers behind the glass screen, the surgeon was already back at work, turning in the seared stump of the tag, making all smooth. A matter of seconds more . . . "That's all, gentlemen. Close up, please. Thank you, Mr. Brown."

Restored to his fellows, the stout classman scrambled with them to the top bank of seats, rattled down the steps to the low corridor door. Dr. Cullen's operative clinic in fourth year gynecology adjourned to the green room.

APPENDIX

Books by Thomas Cullen with their dates of publication:

1. Cancer of the Uterus; its Pathology, Symptomatology, Diagnosis and Treatment; 693 pp., Appleton (1900).
2. Adenomyoma of the Uterus; 270 pp., Saunders (1908).
3. Myomata of the Uterus (with Howard A. Kelly); 723 pp., Saunders (1909).
4. Embryology, Anatomy, and Diseases of the Umbilicus; 680 pp., Saunders (1916).
5. Henry Mills Hurd, the First Superintendent of the Johns Hopkins Hospital. Small volume. The Johns Hopkins Press (1920).

The short papers of Thomas Cullen have been collected into four volumes. The titles of the articles are as follows:

VOLUME I

Abscess in the urethro-vaginal septum—*J. H. H. Bulletin*, April, 1894, Vol. V, p. 45.

Pyometra in a cat—*American Veterinary Review*, September, 1894, Vol. XVIII.

Papillo cystoma of the ovary—*J. H. H. Bulletin*, November, 1894, Vol. V, p. 103.

Angio-sarcoma of the ovary—*J. H. H. Bulletin*, December, 1894, Vol. V, p. 134.

Tumor developed from aberrant adrenal in the kidney—*J. H. H. Bulletin*, March, 1895, Vol. VI, p. 37.

A rapid method of making permanent specimens from frozen sections by the use of formalin.—*J. H. H. Bulletin*, 1895, Vol. VI, p. 67.

Hydrosalpinx.—*J. H. H. Reports*, 1895, Vol. IV, p. 351.

Post-operative septic peritonitis.—*J. H. H. Reports*, 1895, Vol. IV, p. 411.

Tuberculosis of the endometrium.—*J. H. H. Reports*, 1895, Vol. IV, p. 441.

Adeno-myoma of the round ligament.—*J. H. H. Bulletin*, 1896, Vol. VII, p. 112.

Further remarks on adeno-myoma of the round ligament.—*J. H. H. Bulletin*, 1898, Vol. IX, p. 142.

Fatal puerperal sepsis due to introduction of an elm tent.—*J. H. H. Reports*, 1896, Vol. VI, p. 109.

Pregnancy in a rudimentary uterine horn, rupture, death, probable migration of ovum and spermatozoa.—*J. H. H. Reports*, 1896, Vol. VI, p. 113.

Adeno-myoma uteri diffusum benignum.—*J. H. H. Reports*, 1896, Vol. VI, p. 133.

Multilocular adeno-papillo-cystoma of the ovary with sarcomatous nodules on the inner surface of one of the cysts.—Am. J. of Obstetrics, 1896, Vol. XXXIV, p. 358.

A rapid method of making permanent specimens from frozen sections by the use of formalin.—*J. H. H. Bulletin (second reprint)*, 1897, Vol. VIII, p. 108.

Silkworm gut as a subcutaneous suture in closure of abdominal incisions. —*Amer. J. of Obstetrics*, 1897, Vol. XXXVI, p. 171.

Demonstration of specimen myomata.—*J. H. H. Bulletin*, 1897, Vol. VIII, p. 216.

The early diagnosis of carcinoma of the uterus.—*Memphis Lancet*, Dec., 1898.

A rare variety of adeno-carcinoma of the uterus.—*Contributions to the Science of Medicine by his pupils to Wm. H. Welch on the twenty-fifth anniversary of his doctorate and J. H. H. Reports*, 1900, Vol. IX, p. 401.

A rare form of extra-uterine pregnancy. By Brice W. Goldsborough and T. S. Cullen.—*American Medicine*, 1901, Vol. I, p. 32.

The cause of cancer.—*American Medicine*, 1901, Vol. I, p. 298.

Tuberculosis of the pelvic organs in the female.—*Canada Lancet*, January, 1902.

Exhibition of cases.—*J. H. H. Bulletin*, 1902, Vol. XIII, p. 148.

Traitement operatoire du cancer de l'utérus.—*Revue de Gynécologie et de Chirurgie abdominale*, No. 5, Sept.-Oct., 1902.

Retrocaecal abscess.—*New York Medical Journal*, 1902, Vol. LXXVI, p. 1111.

Report of gynecological cases.—*J. H. H. Bulletin*, 1903, Vol. XIV, p. 89.

A simple electric female cystoscope.—*J. H. H. Bulletin*, 1903, Vol. XIV, p. 166.

Uterine myomata and their treatment.—*The Canada Lancet*, 1902-1903, Vol. XXXVI, pp., 778-796.

VOLUME II

Tuberculous stricture of the ascending colon, with sudden total obstruction of the bowel.—*American Journal of the Medical Sciences*, 1904, Vol. CXXVII, p. 431.

Uterine hemorrhages and their cause.—*Annals of Gynecology and Pediatry*, Boston, 1904, Vol. XVII, p. 413.

A series of Mistaken Gynecologic Diagnoses:

Case I—Diagnosis: Very large ovarian cyst. Actual condition: A partially parasitic uterine myoma, associated with 51 liters of ascitic fluid. Recovery.

Case II—Diagnosis: Myomatous uterus. Actual condition: Adenocarcinoma of the body of the uterus, with secondary subperitoneal nodules.

Case III—Diagnosis: Subperitoneal and intraligamentary myomata. Actual condition: Hydrosalpinx, adenocarcinoma of the right ovary, involvement of the small bowel and marked extension to the bladder.

Case IV—Diagnosis: Pelvic abscess, with retroverted myomatous uterus. Actual condition: Rectal diverticula, with rupture into the surrounding rectal fat, producing a definite tumor. Small abscess between the tumor and the pelvic floor.—*Jour. of the Amer. Med. Assoc.*, 1904, Vol. XLIII, p. 1511.

Vaginal cysts.—*Transactions of the American Gynec. Society*. Vol. XXIX, 1904, p. 459; *Johns Hopkins Hospital Bulletin*, Vol. XVI, 1905, p. 207.

APPENDIX

Cysts of Bartholin's glands.—*Jour. Amer. Med. Assoc.*, 1905, Vol. XLIV, p. 204.
I. Fibroma of the abdominal wall.
II. Primary Carcinoma of the right fallopian tube.
III. An accessory and twisted omentum.—*Johns Hopkins Hospital Bulletin*, 1905, Vol. XVI, p. 397.
Large carcinomatous tumor of the liver.—*Jour. Amer. Med. Assoc.*, 1905, Vol. XLIV, p. 1239.
Uterine elevator forceps.—*Jour. Amer. Med. Assoc.*, 1905, Vol. XLIV, p. 1369.
Johns Hopkins Medical Society, January 8, 1906:
  Case I.—Early tuberculosis of the kidney. Diagnosis of the tuberculous process made from thickening of the ureter detected on vaginal examination.
  Case II.—A very rapidly growing squamous-celled carcinoma of the inner side of the thigh.
  Case III.—Early tuberculosis of the appendix.
  Case IV.—Tuberculosis of the appendix, caecum, colon and small bowel.
  Case V.—The right ovary in the abdominal scar following an operation for appendix abscess.
  Case VI.—An obscure abdominal tumor in the right upper quadrant consisting of an elongated right hepatic lobe, a prolapsed right kidney and an appendix adherent to the gall-bladder.
  Case VII.—Abscess between the abdominal peritoneum and omentum four weeks after labor. Involvement of the lower edge of the liver. Opening of abscess; secondary exploration in region of liver with marked tearing of the friable organ. Hemorrhage controlled with blunt liver needles. Complete recovery.
  Case VIII.—The velvety feel of an unruptured tubal pregnancy.
  Case IX.—Pregnancy in one horn of a bicornate uterus, giving symptoms identical with those of tubal pregnancy.
  Case X.—Adenocarcinoma of the abdominal peritoneum complicating uterine myomata.
    Johns Hopkins Hospital Bulletin, 1906, Vol. XVII, pp., 150-155.
A series of intestinal anastomoses.—*Canadian Jour. of Medicine and Surgery*, Toronto, 1906, Vol. XX, pp., 1-34.
Immediate examination of uterine mucosa and myomatous nodules after hysteromyomectomy to exclude malignant disease.—*Jour. Amer. Med. Assoc.*, 1906, Vol. XLVI, pp., 695-697.
A series of interesting Gynecologic and Obstetric Cases:
  Case I.—An eighty-nine pound cystic myoma.
  Case II.—A large parasitic myoma.
  Case III.—Multiple perforation of the uterus due to a macerated fetus.
  Case IV.—Abdominal pregnancy of four years' duration.
  Case V.—Chorioepithelioma.
    —*Jour. of the Amer. Med. Assoc.*, 1907, Vol. XLVIII, pp., 1491-1497.
Surgery of the liver.—*Surgery, Gynecology and Obstetrics*, 1907, Vol. IV, pp., 573-584.
Parasitic uterine myomata.—*Jour. Amer. Med. Assoc.*, 1907, Vol. XLIX, pp., 1994-1998.
Adenomyoma of the uterus.—*Jour. Amer. Med. Assoc.*, 1908, Vol. L, pp., 107-115.
The condition of the uterine mucosa in myoma cases.—*Transactions of the American Gynecological Society*, 1908, Vol. XXXIII, p. 298.

The early diagnosis of cancer of the uterus; operative technic.—International clinics, 1909, Vol. IV, 19th series, p. 193. *Pennsylvania Medical Journal,* 1909-10, Vol. XIII, p. 110.

Some points in the operative technique of vaginal hysterectomy for prolapsus.—*Surgery, Gynecology and Obstetrics,* 1910, Vol. X, pp., 307-309.

A large cystic tumor developing from the iliopsoas bursa.—*Jour. Amer. Med. Assoc.,* 1910, Vol. LIV, pp., 1181-1184.

A right pelvic kidney; absence of the left kidney; absence of the uterus; both ovaries in the Inguinal canals.—*Surgery, Gynecology and Obstetrics,* 1910, Vol. XI, pp., 73-75.

Carcinoma of the right Fallopian tube readily palpable through the abdomen.—*Johns Hopkins Hospital Bulletin,* 1911, Vol. XXII, p. 20; *Surgery, Gynecology and Obstetrics,* 1910, Vol. XI, pp., 75-76.

Surgical diseases of the umbilicus.—*Jour. Amer. Med. Assoc.,* 1911, Vol. LVI, pp., 391-396.

A malignant intestinal growth requiring the removal of an unusual number of abdominal structures.—*Surgery, Gynecology and Obstetrics,* 1911, Vol. XII, pp., 76-78.

An extra-abdominal multilocular ovarian cyst.—*Jour. Amer. Med. Assoc.,* 1911, Vol. LVII, pp., 1251-1255.

A pseudohermaphrodite.—*Surgery, Gynecology and Obstetrics,* 1911, Vol. XIII, pp., 449-453.

Umbilical tumors containing uterine mucosa or remnants of Mueller's duct.—*Trans. Southern Surgical and Gynecological Assoc.,* 1911; *Surgery, Gynecology and Obstetrics,* 1912, Vol. XIV, pp., 479-491.

Address in Gynecology.—*Canadian Medical Assoc. Journal,* 1913, N.S. III, pp., 658-671.

The radical operation for cancer of the uterus.—*Surgery, Gynecology and Obstetrics,* 1913, Vol. XVI, pp., 265-272; *Trans. of the American Gynecological Society,* 1912, Vol. XXXVII, p. 329.

Operations on patients with a haemoglobin of forty per cent. or less.—*Surgery, Gynecology and Obstetrics,* 1913, Vol. XVII, pp., 276-294.

Report of cancer campaign committee.—*Surgery, Gynecology and Obstetrics,* November, 1913.

Adenomyoma of the rectovaginal septum.—*Jour. Amer. Med. Assoc.,* 1914, Vol. LXII, pp., 835-839; *Trans. of the Southern Surgical and Gynecological Assoc.,* 1913, Vol. XXVI, p. 106.

An historical sketch—The church home and infirmary.—Baltimore, Md., 1915.

Unusual cases illustrating points in diagnosis and treatment.—*Surgery, Gynecology and Obstetrics,* 1915, Vol. XX, pp., 260-268.

    I. A calcified lymph-gland producing symptoms somewhat suggestive of gall-stones.

    II. An old and infected abdominal pregnancy with extension of the long bones into the bladder and into the bowel.

    III. A further case of adenomyoma of the rectovaginal septum.

    IV. Operation for the radical cure of an umbilical hernia in a patient weighing 464 pounds.

    V. Removal of a large tuberculous cyst of the mesentery of the jejunum together with the corresponding segment of bowel; recovery: later, death, apparently from tuberculous meningitis.

The relation of obstetrics, gynecology and abdominal surgery to the public welfare.—*Jour. Amer. Med. Assoc.,* 1916, Vol. LXVI, pp., 239-243.

Early tuberculosis of the cervix.—*Surgery, Gynecology and Obstetrics,* 1916, XXII, p. 261.

APPENDIX

Adenomyoma of the round ligament and incarcerated Omentum in an inguinal hernia, together forming one tumor.—*Surgery, Gynecology and Obstetrics,* 1916, Vol. XXII, pp., 258-260.
Endometritis.—*Maryland Medical Journal,* 1898, Vol. XXXIX, p. 571.

VOLUME III

America's place in the surgery of the world.—*Transactions Southern Surgical Association,* 1916, Vol. XXIX, pp., 1-35.
The surgical methods of dealing with pelvic infections.—*Surgery, Gynecology and Obstetrics,* 1917, Vol. XXV, pp., 134-146.
Adenomyoma of the recto-vaginal septum.—*Johns Hopkins Hospital Bulletin,* 1917, Vol. XXVIII, pp., 343-349.
Bluish discoloration of the umbilicus as a diagnostic sign where ruptured extrauterine pregnancy exists.—Contributions to Medical and Biological Research, Dedicated to Sir William Osler, in Honor of his Seventieth Birthday, July 12, 1919.
Dr. Howard A. Kelly.—*Johns Hopkins Hospital Bulletin,* 1919, Vol. XXX, p. 287.
What animal experimentation has done for gynecology and abdominal surgery. A vindication of vivisection.—*Georgetown University School of Medicine,* Washington, D.C., 1920, pp., 32-41.
The distribution of adenomyomas containing uterine mucosa.—*Archives of Surgery,* 1920, Vol. I, pp., 215-283.
Three cases of subperitoneal, pedunculated adenomyoma.—*Archives of Surgery,* 1921, Vol. II, pp., 443-454.
The weak spot in American surgery.—*Surgery, Gynecology and Obstetrics,* 1921, Vol. XXXIII, pp., 67-72.
Early squamous-cell carcinoma of the cervix.—*Surgery, Gynecology and Obstetrics.* 1921, Vol. XXXIII, pp., 137-144.
Pregnancy following implantation of the outer end of the only remaining fallopian tube into the uterine cornu after resection of a cornual pregnancy (by Henry N. Shaw).—*Johns Hopkins Hospital Bulletin,* 1921, Vol. XXXII, pp., 305-306.
The abdominal surgeon of the future.—*Surgery, Gynecology and Obstetrics,* 1922, Vol. XXXIV, pp., 217-220.
Method of dealing with intestinal loops densely adherent to an umbilical hernia.—*Jour. Amer. Med. Assoc.,* 1922, Vol. LXXVIII, pp., 564-566.
Uterine hemorrhage.—*Jour. Amer. Med. Assoc.,* 1922, Vol. LXXVIII, pp., 1592-1596.
A normal pregnancy following insertion of the outer half of a fallopian tube into the uterine cornu.—*Johns Hopkins Hospital Bulletin,* 1922, Vol. XXXIII, p. 344.
Further remarks on diseases of the umbilicus.—*Surgery, Gynecology and Obstetrics,* 1922, Vol. XXXV, pp., 257-283.
The value of a local hospital to the people of smaller cities and towns.—*Address delivered at the opening of the Waynesboro Hospital,* Waynesboro, Pa., Oct. 2, 1922.
The use of sutures as tractors in the vaginal operation for prolapsus.—*Amer. Jour. of Obstetrics and Gynecology,* 1922, Vol. IV, pp., 544-551.
A pillow at the foot of the bed after abdominal operations.—*Jour. Amer. Med. Assoc.,* 1923, Vol. LXXX, p. 1521.
A few practical points in pelvic surgery.—*Atlantic Medical Journal,* 1924, Vol. XXVII, pp., 619-625.
The end-results in nearly three hundred cases in which the gall-bladder was drained—not removed. (By H. L. Darner).—*Surgery, Gynecology and Obstetrics,* 1923, Vol. XXXVII, pp., 579-598.

A progressively enlarging ulcer of the abdominal wall involving the skin and fat, following drainage of an abdominal abscess apparently of appendiceal origin.—*Surgery, Gynecology and Obstetrics*, 1924, Vol. XXXVIII, pp., 579-582.

The evolution of gynecology.—*Ohio State Medical Journal*, 1924, Vol. XX, pp., 484-495.

In Memoriam—Ernest Keys Cullen, M.D., 1878-1922.—*Transactions of the Southern Surgical Association*, 1922. Vol. XXXV, pp., 521-526.

VOLUME IV

Surgical pathology and the young surgeon.—*Surgery, Gynecology and Obstetrics*, 1925, Vol. XLI, pp., 689-690.

Accessory lobes of the liver.—*Arch. Surg.*, 1925, Vol. XI, pp., 718-764.

Pancreatic cysts. With Report of Seven Cases. (By Julius Friedenwald and Thomas S. Cullen.)—*Amer. Jour. of the Med. Sciences*, 1926, Vol. CLXXII, pp., 313-334.

Early medicine in Maryland.—*Address of the President of the Medical and Chirurgical Faculty of Maryland*, April 26, 1927.

Acute and chronic pancreatitis; clinical observations. (By Julius Friedenwald and Thomas S. Cullen.)—*Arch. Surg.*, 1927, Vol. XV, pp., 1-29.

A point in technique for supravaginal removal of myomatous uterus with foul uterine discharge.—*Surgery, Gynecology and Obstetrics*, 1927, Vol. XLV, pp., 80-81.

A fibrolipoma closely simulating in form and location a tumor of the right kidney; Subacute appendicitis.—*Trans. South. Surg. Assoc.*, 1926, Vol. XXXIX, pp., 326-330. Also: *Surgery, Gynecology and Obstetrics*, 1927, Vol. XLV, pp., 152-155.

Carcinoma of the pancreas. (By Julius Friedenwald and Thomas S. Cullen.)—*Amer. Jour. of the Med. Sciences*, 1928, Vol. CLXXVI, pp., 31-41.

Uterine hemorrhage and its treatment.—*Jour. Missouri State Med. Assoc.*, 1928, Vol. XXV, pp., 457-466.

Bleeding: A danger signal.—*Jour. Missouri State Med. Assoc.*, 1929, Vol. XXVI, pp., 103-05.

The training of the gynecologist (Read in the Section of Obstetrics and Gynecology at the Annual Meeting of the British Medical Association, Manchester, 1929.)—*British Medical Journal*, 1929, Vol. II, pp., 941-943.

An address on Dr. C. Hampson Jones on the occasion of the unveiling of his memorial portrait, May 27, 1933.—*Baltimore Health News* (Health Dept., Baltimore), July-Aug., 1933.

Research in Abdominal Surgery Broadcast for *American Medical Association* over a network of the National Broadcasting Company, Jan. 8, 1935.

Henry Mills Hurd. First Superintendent of the Johns Hopkins Hospital. —*J. H. Alumni Magazine*, Mar., 1928.

Testimonial Dinner to Dr. Howard A. Kelly.—*Bull. J. H. H.*, Aug., 1933.

Intestinal Obstruction Due to a Hole in the Mesentery of the Ascending Colon.—*Jour. American Medical Assoc.*, Mar. 14, 1936.

Dr. Brice Worthington Goldsborough. (Address at Dedication of Roentgenological Laboratory and the Unveiling of Portrait of Late Dr. Brice W. Goldsborough, Cambridge-Maryland Hospital, Nov. 24, 1936.)

Cullen and Broedel—Lesions of the Rectus Abdominis Muscle Simulating an Acute Intra-abdominal Condition.—*Bull. J. H. H.*, Nov., 1937.

APPENDIX

CULLEN DINNER, SEVENTIETH BIRTHDAY, NOVEMBER, 1938.

Discussions of papers by Dr. Cullen: Dr. C. R. Edwards' paper, "Acute Cholecystitis with Perforation into the Peritoneal Cavity."—*Transactions, Southern Surgical Association*, Vol. LIII, 1940, p. 186.

    Dr. J. Garland Sherrill's and Dr. D. P. Hall's paper, "The Management of Bilateral Renal Stones."—*Transactions, Southern Surgical Association*, Vol. LIII, 1940, p. 219.

Remarkable Advances in Medicine and Nursing. An address to the graduating class of nurses of Emergency Hospital, Easton, Md., May 9, 1942. Reprinted from *Easton Star-Democrat*, Easton, Md. (Printed in *Star-Democrat* at paper's request in summer of 1945.)

Howard Atwood Kelly: The Last of the Johns Hopkins Hospital "Big Four."—*Johns Hopkins Alumni Magazine*, Vol. 31, Nos. 3 and 4, March and June, 1943.

Jane Evans Nash. Address at unveiling of portrait, December 7, 1943.

Max Broedel: Director of the First Department of Art as Applied to Medicine in the World.—*Bull. Medical Library Assoc.*, January, 1945.

The Class of 1890. *Canada Lancet & Practitioner*, Toronto, June, 1934.

INDEX

ABEL, JOHN J., 290.
Actinolite, Ontario *see* Bridgewater.
Adams, Samuel Hopkins, 247, 248.
Addams, Jane, 399, 400.
Adenomyoma of the round ligament, 126.
Adenomyoma of the umbilicus, *see* tumors, umbilical.
Adenomyoma of the Uterus by Thomas S. Cullen, 194, 198, 243.
Adenomyomata, 124, 168, 194-97, 273, 385.
Adhesions, 142, 143, 191-93, 206, 207.
Ahmic Lake (*see also* Magnetawan), 67, 168, 170, 171, 212, 216, 268, 290, 310.
Aiken, Dr. Thomas, 57.
Allgemeine Krankenhaus, Vienna, 111.
American Gynecological Society, 261.
American Medical Association, 229, 246, 247, 250, 251, 259, 262, 265, 376, 378-80.
American Medical Association, Board of Trustees, 378.
American Medical Association, House of Delegates, 312, 378-80.
American Medical Association, Journal of The, 261, 272, 379.
American Journal of Medical Sciences, 398.
Amsterdam, 104, 105, 161, 175, 247.
Anglican Church, 17, 18, 21.
Annapolis, Maryland, 253, 339, 343, 349, 362, 369.
Appendix, 101, 192, 193, 396-98, 406, 410.
Appleton, D. & Co., 158, 159, 198.
Appleton, Willie, 158.
Archives of Surgery, 281.
Asepsis and antisepsis, early techniques, 66, 67.
Asepsis, 97, 238, 275, 405.
Asheville, N.C., 253.
Awde, Albert, 58.

BABE, the, 403.
Bacteriology, 112.
Baetjer, Frederick, 389, 390.
Bailey, Henry, 142, 143.
Bailey, Mrs. Henry, 143.
Baker, B. N., 218.
Ballet, Imperial Russian, 174.
Baltimore, 30, 70, 71, 73, 78, 106, 109, 111, 113, 115, 116, 119, 126, 128, 130, 132, 145, 149, 151, 153, 155, 158, 159, 162, 163, 167-70, 172, 174, 179-81, 184, 209, 211, 212, 214, 219, 221, 230, 231, 233, 241, 244-46, 248, 249, 256, 258-60, 267, 270, 277, 279, 282, 289, 290, 292, 294, 297, 299, 301, 307, 310, 314, 317, 319, 321, 333-36, 338, 340, 341, 343, 344, 347-49, 351, 355, 357, 360, 364-66, 368, 369, 371, 372, 378, 381, 384, 386, 387, 397, 401, 403.
Baltimore; Albion Hotel, 78; ball park, 118; Belvedere Hotel, 213; brick, 181; Broadway, 77, 78, 94, 103, 141, 215, 238, 284, 395; cathedral, 370, 397; Cathedral St., 78, 370; Charles St., 78, 149, 154, 341, 357; charter commission, 336; Christ Church, 397; city charter, 334; city council, 373; civic budget committee, 374; civic efficiency commission, 364; Druid Hill Park, 154; Eager St., 78, 140; East Eager Street, Twenty, 252, 283, 289, 290, 341, 387, 391, 402; East Fayette St., 1640, *see below* "Gills', the"; Episcopalian Church, 182; Eutaw Place, 265, 266, 276; Fairmount, 181; fire, 179; Fort McHenry, 154; Franklin St., 368, 370; Gills', the, 77, 79, 81, 86, 87, 215; Hanselman's saloon, "the church," 84; Hazazer's Hall, 368, 369; health commission, 347; health commissioner, 334, 338-41, 348; health commissioner's board of consultants, 340; health department,

421

licity against cancer, 241; his reasons and the risks, 242-46; publicity proves its value, 247-50; professional opposition overcome, 251; the move to Eager Street, 252.

A principle established in another storey, 257, 258; Kelly's early division of gynecology from obstetrics at Hopkins, 259; regretted by the obstetrical department head, 260; moves to restore the old order, 261; countered by Cullen with argument for "unified abdominal surgery," 262-64; his illness prevents personal presentation before American Medical Association, 265; paper read at San Francisco in his absence widely accepted, among others by Halsted of Hopkins, 265; Kelly's retirement and a struggle to save the gynecological department foreshadowed, 266; new research nears completion, 267-69; Mary Greene Cullen's death, 270.

Fourth major work, *Embryology, Anatomy and Diseases of the Umbilicus* published, 271; genesis and implications of the work, 272-74; Max Broedel's part, 275; W. S. Halsted quotes Milton on the achievement, 276; and discusses other topics, 277, 278; Kelly takes leave of absence, Cullen in charge as acting gynecologist-in-chief, 279; declines invitation from Jefferson Medical College, Philadelphia, to chair of gynecology; continuing at Hopkins, he continues research and publication, edits his first volume in Dean Lewis's *Archives of Surgery*, 281; Rebecca Cullen's death, 282; threats to the future of his work at Hopkins increase, 282; the "gynecological cabinet" begins to plan defences, 283; recollections of Tom Cullen under pressure, 284-86; Vanderbilt University medical school benefits by a visit in Eager Street, 289-90; and a dinner that made history, 291; second marriage, 292; plan to unite gynecology and obstetrics at Hopkins matures, 294; as Howard Kelly retires and Cul-

len succeeds with title of Professor of Clinical Gynecology, 295; Halsted moves to rescue gynecology and add it to general surgery, Hopkins medical board votes approval, 295; new building planned for obstetrical and gynecological clinics without reference to department of gynecology, 296; gynecological associates and staff agree to resign rather than carry on in insufficient quarters planned, 297, 298; Halsted's death, 297.

Hopkins Woman's Clinic building approaches completion, 302; a united gynecological department standing fast, 302; the head of the department of obstetrics retreats, 303; Hopkins medical board reverses a four-year-old policy and recognizes the independence of gynecology, 304; surveying the new building's inadequacies, Gynecological Cabinet advises against moving in, 305; Cullen takes their advice and writes a letter; his department continues in B-suite, 306; gynecology again in danger, 307, 308; Halsted's solution revived by Abraham Flexner of the Rockefeller General Education Board, 308; blocked by Welch, 309; Flexner's Chief, Wallace Buttrick takes a hand, making Rockefeller funds available to enlarge the Woman's Clinic building, providing independent accommodation for Hopkins' department of gynecology, 309; the other storey goes on, 310.

Recreations and rewards, 312-14; Hopkins Professor of Gynecology becomes Toronto LL.D., 313; the teacher, 315-21; his staff's collected papers, 322; win him high praise abroad, 322, 323; address to the B. M. A., "The Training of a Gynecologist," 324-26; the Hopkins idea, 327; Cullen's sign, 328-30; inherits public health problems from Osler and Welch, 334, 335; works out an unorthodox solution with the help of a party boss, 337-39; finds the solution

Cullen—*Continued*

good and safeguards it, 340; as disciple of Welch helps start state-aided health services, 343, 344; Goldsborough Health Bill, 345; succeeds Welch on Maryland state board of health, 346; developments of state health services, 347-50; Cullen on bills, 352-54; adopts Chesapeake Bay pollution as his problem, 355; and finds it a tough one, 356-59; Roosevelt to the rescue, 360; PWA and the Chesapeake Bay Authority, 361; Chairman Cullen of CBA recruits the help he needs to clean up the Chesapeake basin, 362, 363.

The President of the Pratt gets out the vote, 364; his long association with Baltimore's public library system, 365-67; the Pratt is provided with a new central library building, 368-70; a Supreme Court decision, 371-73; non-political library activities, 374; Professor Emeritus of Gynecology, Johns Hopkins University, 375; champions the Surgeon General's Library building plan, 376-78; serves the American Medical Association, 378-80; plans for the oysters of Chesapeake Bay, 381-84.

The pragmatic approach, 385; stories and their occasions, 386-88; life's inequalities and Fred Baetjer, 389; asides, afterthoughts and old books, 390-92; the healer, 392-98; the time he was scared, 399; friendships, partings and a moonflower vine, 400-03; operative clinic in the other storey, 404-10; adjourns to the green room, 411.

Cullen, Victor, 348.
Cullen, Washington Medical College resident surgeon, 1849; 181, 182.
Cullen, William, 23.
Cullen, William, of Edinburgh, 391.
"Cullen's sign," *see* umbilicus, blue.
Culpeper, Nicholas, 399.
Cumming, Hugh, U.S. Surgeon General, 359, 362, 391.
Curie, Marie, 173, 174.
Cushing, Harvey, 233.

DANIELS, JOSEPHUS, 253, 255.
Daniels, Mrs. Josephus, 255.
Davis, Griffith, 185.
Dayton, Ohio, 254, 256.
Democratic party, 334, 337, 338, 340.
Demorestville, Ontario, 20, 25.
Dennis, Frederic S., 277.
Detroit, 219, 246, 254, 256, 267, 289, 299, 301.
Detroit medical school, 301.
Devonport, Devon, 16.
Diverticulum, Meckel's, 274.
Dixon, Mary Bartlett, *see* Cullen, Mrs. Thomas S.
Döderlein, Albert, 176.
Dooflickers, *see* Leake, Mr.
Dordrecht, 104, 106.
Dow, Alexander, 219.
Dow, Mrs. Alexander, 219.
Dowman, Dr., 175.
Dresden, 110, 175.
duPont, Alfred, 220.

EASTERN SHORE, THE, 151, 152, 293, 299, 302, 312, 342, 350, 351, 355, 357, 360, 401, 402.
Eastman, George, 218.
Easton, Md., 362, 403.
Eberth, J. C., 82.
Ederny, County Fermanagh, 21.
Edinburgh, 163, 391.
Ehrlich, Paul, 127.
Elk River, Md., 358.
Elkton, Md., 338.
England, 17, 164, 173, 175, 231.
Erasmus, 104.

FALMOUTH, 173.
Family Medicine, Dr. Chase's, 142.
Fan, 24, 25.
Faure, Jean-Louis, 176.
Fernwald, Braun von, 111.
Finckle, Abe, 30.
Finlay, Carlos, 82.
Finn, Huckleberry, 92.
Finney, John M. T., 191, 192, 233, 265, 279.
Fishbein, Morris, 379.
Flesherton, Ont., 20, 22, 24.
Flexner, Abraham, 229-33, 235, 261, 289-91, 307-10, 352.
Flexner, Simon, 85, 90, 91, 103-05, 113, 163, 228, 230, 235.
Flint, Hon. Billa, 10, 32, 33.
Flinton, Ontario, 10.
Florence, 268.

428